David Andress is Professor of Modern History at the University of Portsmouth, where he has taught since 1994. He is the author of a number of acclaimed studies of the French Revolution and its international context, including *The French Revolution and the People* (2004), *The Terror* (2005), and *1789* (2008). As well as broadening his writing interests to embrace the British Isles, he recently edited the Oxford Handbook of the French Revolution.

'David Andress writes well, charts the British experience of the struggle against Napoleon in a manner that is as thorough as it is enthusiastic, approaches his subject from a refreshing perspective and fills a serious gap in the historiography . . . a book that . . . should be read by all those interested in Britain's role in the Revolutionary and Napoleonic Wars' Charles Esdaile, *Literary Review*

'Andress's vivid account of Britain's history during the war years . . . He writes movingly about the reality of war, the experience of the common soldier and especially of the sailor . . . He shows commendable skill in interweaving the two narratives, the military and the political, to offer a convincing overview of the age' Alan Forrest, *BBC History Magazine*

BEATING NAPOLEON

How Britain Faced Down her Greatest Challenge

DAVID ANDRESS

ABACUS

First published in Great Britain in 2012 by Little, Brown as *The Savage Storm*
This paperback edition published in 2015 by Abacus

1 3 5 7 9 10 8 6 4 2

Copyright © David Andress 2012

The moral right of the author has been asserted.

A CIP catalogue record for this book
is available from the British Library.

ISBN 978-0-349-14166-4

Typeset in Electra by M Rules
Printed and bound in Great Britain by
Clays Ltd, St Ives plc

Papers used by Abacus are from well-managed forests
and other responsible sources.

MIX
Paper from
responsible sources
FSC
www.fsc.org   FSC® C104740

Abacus
An imprint of
Little, Brown Book Group
Carmelite House
50 Victoria Embankment
London EC4Y 0DZ

An Hachette UK Company
www.hachette.co.uk

www.littlebrown.co.uk

For Norman

CONTENTS

ACKNOWLEDGEMENTS

My thanks go to Charlie, Tim, Iain and all those involved in the production of this book. I am grateful, as I have been for many years now, to all my colleagues at the University of Portsmouth, who help to maintain a friendly and productive environment in times of ever-growing difficulty. To my students, I am equally grateful for challenging me to express my ideas with all the clarity I can muster. To Jessica, Emily and Natalie, I owe everything that makes all this worthwhile.

I dedicate this book to the memory of Norman Hampson, who first introduced me to the study of eighteenth-century France from which all my subsequent career has flowed, and who was an outstanding example of a humane scholar, and an English gentleman in the very best sense.

PREFACE

This book chronicles the remarkably dogged, occasionally despairing, but at last overwhelmingly successful British fight against the continental power embodied in the 'Grand Empire' of Napoleon Bonaparte. It follows on from my previous work, 1789, in which I explored the global ramifications of that year, positioning Britain as a state almost as much in crisis at that point as were its American and French rivals. In the course of researching that book, it became clear to me that the British elite displayed a profound resilience in the face of potentially catastrophic circumstances. Such a trait, regardless of one's views about the justice or iniquity of the underlying social arrangements, is always a worthwhile object of study.

More personally, exploring the years of what was, until the twentieth century, Britain's 'Great War' offered the opportunity to bring together two aspects of historical study that have long appealed to me. Before I put away childish things I was, like many another studious boy, captivated by the panorama of military history. In particular, the sense of epic story available in the conflict that climaxed in 1815 has always stayed with me. I like to think that I figured out at a fairly early age that battle is a terrible thing, but Napoleonic battle in particular also has an undeniable grandeur –

perhaps never better captured for the modern eye than in Sergei Bondarchuk's superb 1970 film *Waterloo*.

For a long time, as a budding historian, I felt that this interest was something of a guilty secret. It coexisted with an engagement, both intellectual and to an extent sentimental, with the social history of the era of industrialisation. Immortalised by E.P. Thompson in the 1960s as *The Making of the English Working Class*, the radical and insurrectionary movements of this period were a key topic of my student education. Thanks to Thompson's work, groups such as the London Corresponding Society emerged from the background of a picturesque eighteenth century of boisterous but essentially harmless 'mob' activity, to take their place in a story of planned and determined resistance to tyrannical authority every bit as epic as the campaigns of Wellington. Historians no longer squabbled over the dry details of the 'standard of living question', but recovered the thoughts, activities and martyred suffering of flesh-and-blood workers and craftsmen, denied the freedom to influence national life in a country that claimed to be fighting for the liberty of Europe.

This, I felt, was what a critical history should be about. Yet approaching this period critically also raised uncomfortable questions about these very heroic struggles. Thompson's own trajectory as a historian suggests a consciousness of similar issues. Originally undertaking the *Making* as a prefatory study for what he regarded as a climactic working-class movement, the Chartism of the 1830s and 1840s, he moved on to delve deeper into the eighteenth-century past, evoking eras when 'class' as a concept could only be spoken about through exercises of mental gymnastics – ones he seemed less and less inclined to carry out (even while never giving up on his personal political radicalism).

Other historians following in his wake have broadened our understanding of the radical and oppositional cultures that were born in the 1790s and flourished through into the mid-nineteenth century, illuminating their depth and range of references, their symbolism, their rootedness in long histories of communal assertion and resistance. But all have also faced the brick wall of these movements' failure. Apart from a brief blip in the early 1830s, when the coincidence of middle-class demands for suffrage made the position of the political establishment quite seriously shaky, the radical campaigns in the years after Waterloo never came close to influence, let alone overthrow. Few social historians have tried to address why that should be, except to lament, as radicals since Marx himself have done, the hideous cunning of capital.

While social historians thus tend to treat the struggles of this era as objects of commemoration rather than reflection, other histories of the period, those that focus on the high politics of Cabinets, generals and diplomats, tend simply to ignore them. To read even up-to-date works on the diplomacy and campaigns of the period is to find only occasional reference to discontent at home, or the potential for political difficulty it might create. Yet in this almost quarter-century of conflict, Britain faced mass revolt in Ireland, concerted mutiny in its own fleet, movements for radical change that brought tens of thousands to open-air meetings (and sometimes hundreds of thousands to more raucous protest), alarmed reports of conspiratorial armed insurrectionary movements, near-famine conditions, and the most widespread period of violent and coordinated revolt in England since the Civil Wars of the 1640s, or perhaps ever since.

This book is thus an attempt to provide an intersection between these different ways of viewing such a turbulent time, rather than allowing them to pass each other in the historiographical night. Unashamedly, I have tried to focus on the remarkable, the intriguing, and dare I say it sometimes even the exciting elements of a long period of hard-fought war. One element that will emerge clearly for the reader is the Emperor Napoleon's own near-obsession with defeating the 'English', and how that itself helped bring him to his doom. But in chronicling the dramatic turning points of conflict, I have also tried to consider how they affected both high politics and social resistance; how international war was also ideological strife, and how a land of 'freeborn Englishmen' standing stoutly against invasion was also a bitterly divided society of hunger and grief, and an iron-fisted imperial power. I have avoided overt entanglement with scholarly debate – I say what seems to have happened, and what I think it meant – though I have given references both to direct sources and suggestions for wider reading for those interested.

How all this struggle and contradiction should be understood and remembered is a question with many different answers, most of which are for the reader's reflection. Underlying my narrative, though not strictly part of it, for the details come from a very different sort of history, is the economic history of the Industrial Revolution, and the global empire on which it was based. If there is an enduring lesson for the present to be drawn from this distant era, it must surely be that there cannot be a great national role on the world stage without the resources to back it up. Thanks to the swelling boundaries, and seemingly boundless resources, of empire, the absolute conviction of Britain's place as a global leader was firmly entrenched even before Napoleon's rise, and his fall cemented it unshakeably – perhaps so much so that the nation is yet to really come to terms with the concept that such eminence is already over, and even its shadow may yet pass away. I trust, however, that readers will not come to a book of this length seeking only a soundbite, so there is much more to reflect on along the way.

When I wrote about the turmoil of the French Revolution in *The Terror*, I was criticised in different places for being both too sympathetic, and not sympathetic enough, to actors on both sides of the great political divides of the era. Since I could not hope to convert everyone to my point of view, such an outcome seemed to me to be a good second-best. Writers, readers and critics all bring their own preconceptions and prejudices to a work. I do not like the Emperor Napoleon, for example, but I am prepared to forgive the Duke of Wellington for his outrageous snobbery in the light of his many other virtues. I feel that the terrible situation of visible, looming social catastrophe that drove Luddites to bloody and futile revolt should be understood by any student of this period, but what passed for 'radicalism' in the hands of many others was a fantasy of bar-room braggarts and self-promoting dilettantes.

When it comes to the grim realities of combat, I stand amazed at the steadfast conduct of soldiers and sailors, and appalled at how they were sometimes treated by their own country – but I also try to understand the reasons why such men themselves sometimes acted in ways that can only be described as appalling. In discussing the remarkably resilient ruling class of the nation, I respect the strategic acumen and personal labours of the men who took on the huge personal burden of leading the nation and its forces, while recog-nising that many of them were corrupt, almost all had a callous indifference to the human cost of war, and most shared an ingrained contempt for the political rights of the ordinary people of the age: my ancestors, and almost certainly yours.

This book is the product of many decisions and reflections that are entirely personal, but which to my mind are necessary to portray a rounded picture of the people bound up in this titanic conflict, to see them as products of their age without either dismissing or excus-ing their deeds and attitudes. These are my preconceptions and prejudices; if they clash with yours I can only hope that the debate is fruitful.

David Andress
Waterlooville, Hampshire
July 2012

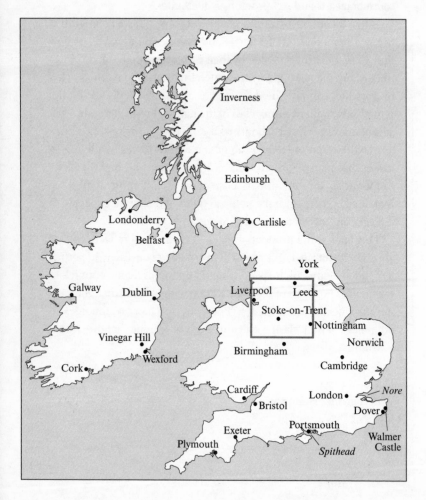

Inverness

Edinburgh

Londonderry

Belfast

Carlisle

York

Galway

Dublin

Liverpool

Leeds

Stoke-on-Trent

Nottingham

Vinegar Hill

Wexford

Birmingham

Norwich

Cork

Cambridge

Cardiff

London

Nore

Bristol

Dover

Exeter

Portsmouth

Plymouth

Walmer Castle

Spithead

REPORTED LUDDITE MOVEMENTS, 1811–12

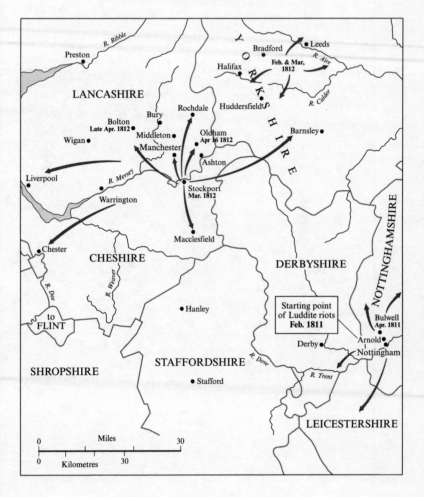

NAPOLEON'S EMPIRE AT ITS HEIGHT, 1811–12

	France in 1789
	Regions annexed to France
	Satellite kingdoms
	States allied with Napoleon
✂	Battles

FINLAND

ESTONIA

LIVONIA

Borodino (1812) ✂   Moscow ●

COURLAND

Smolensk (1812) ✂

Friedland (1807) ✂

GRAND DUCHY OF WARSAW

RUSSIA

GALICIA

UKRAINE

AUSTRIAN EMPIRE

HUNGARY

BESSARABIA

TRANSYLVANIA

O T T O M A N   E M P I R E

PERSIA

Acre (1799) ✂

PALESTINE

Aboukir Bay (1798) ✂

ARABIA

Alexandria (1801) ✂

Miles	
0	300
0	600
Kilometres	

Pyramids (1798) ✂

EGYPT

ENGAGEMENTS OF THE PENINSULAR WAR

PROLOGUE:
BATTLE IN EGYPT

On the morning of 1 August 1798, thirteen French line-of-battle ships lay at anchor in Aboukir Bay, a shallow crescent of water adjacent to one of the Nile's many mouths. Each vessel was a miniature social world, and the most complex product of human ingenuity yet created. Their hulls were delicately curved below the waterlines, the fruit of hundreds of years of practical experience, recently combined with scientific advances in hydrodynamics and streamlining copper coatings. They rose bluffly from the surface, however, broad beams and blunt bows creating the maximum possible space for wielding the great guns they carried. Approached, as they usually were, in a small open boat, such ships towered above an observer. The mighty barrels of the cannon, especially when run out to bristle through the regular lines of gunports on each side, gave clear testimony of their devastating potential. Above them rose the soaring masts, always three on a true 'ship', made of the greatest trees that old-growth forests could yield, and still needing to be segmented, stacked and locked together by complex assemblies of blocks and sockets in order to reach the great heights required to support the sails. Each ship was webbed by a complex mesh of 'standing rigging' that held up the masts against the strains of wind and wave, and a further set of 'running rigging' that controlled the long horizontal yards from which the sails actually hung, raising and turning them to steer with or across the wind.[1]

Here, between the great guns and the great masts, stood the paradox at the heart of these massive creations. Though huge seasoned timbers made up the 'scantlings' or side panels between the gunports, and offered some protection, almost every other part of these huge weapons of war was horrifically vulnerable. An assemblage of wood, hemp ropes, tar that caulked seams in the decks and coated the standing rigging, and expanses of sun-bleached sailcloth, there was hardly anything aboard that would not burn. Yet the job of such ships was to unleash upon the enemy their cannon-fire, driven by black powder, and in battle the cartridges of such explosive material were carried to every corner of the ship in a constant flow, vulnerable at every second to spillage, overturned lantern-flames, and even – if engaged at close range – the blast from enemy cannon. To the rear of each ship, the stern was an expanse of glass, often elegantly curved and ornamented, letting light into the officers' quarters. But in battle this was literally an open window for devastating cannon-fire to reach the heart of the vessel, if the enemy could manoeuvre to expose it.

So overwhelming was the concern to give the ships offensive force, that when in action all interior fittings on the gun-decks were cleared away, and the guns were packed in as close as it was possible to crew them. The whole design of the ship was a fine balance between the strength of the wooden materials that made up the hull, and the quest to place a great weight of artillery within it. Far larger than the cannon normally met with in land battles, and firing iron balls of twenty-four, thirty-two and sometimes thirty-six pounds' weight, the biggest guns weighed several tons apiece, and needed crews of over a dozen to keep them under control after firing, and haul them back to the gunports when reloaded. An average battleship in this age carried two main gun-decks, each with around fifteen guns per side, in a space less than 200 feet long.[2] Some forty to fifty feet wide at the waterline, ships narrowed substantially in a 'tumblehome' as the decks rose, to moderate the effect of the guns' weight on stability. The largest ships carried three main gun-decks within their hulls, and all such vessels also had additional guns mounted on the open decks above. French ships crammed in over 700 men to crew a two-decker, up to 1000 for the larger hundred-gun ships. The British managed with around 100 fewer, but still put around 200 men on each gun-deck in action. The concentration of firepower was immense, but the potential for carnage from enemy fire was similarly enormous.

Built over years, and at huge cost – the expense of competing with Britain's Royal Navy had helped bankrupt France in the 1780s and bring on its Revolution – a battle fleet could be destroyed in hours by a foolish commander. Enemy action was not the only threat, and throughout the age of sail more vessels were lost to storms and other shipwrecks than ever fought a major battle. Safeguarding their fleets from all the potential dangers of the sea could become an obsession for admirals. In Aboukir Bay, the French Admiral Brueys had carefully planned his defences. The battleships were anchored across the width of the bay, their line guarded at either end by shoals and rocks, on some of which hasty fortifications had been erected and manned. Smaller vessels formed outposts of their line, and it was held together, or so Brueys had ordered, by cables strung between the battleships, tying them into a continuous battery of artillery. In this way, other weaknesses of the situation could be mitigated, not least the need to send large parties ashore to gather food and fresh water, while protecting themselves from attacks by hostile local tribes.

A compromise, and a mistake, would prove crucial in what followed, however. The mistake was not to police effectively enough the individual ships' captains charged with linking their ships together, for some did not bother with that order. The French navy, slowly recovering from almost a decade of revolutionary upheaval, was still not immune to dissension and dereliction. The compromise was to keep the ships each held by only a single anchor, around which they could pivot on their cables with the winds and currents. Giving them more freedom to resist the weather, this also abandoned any effort to weld them into an impregnable defence. Setting out two anchors for each ship in opposite directions would have fixed them much more firmly in place, and allowed them to be drawn more tightly together, but risked exposing them to severe damage from any sudden squall. It was not the weather that was about to destroy Brueys' fleet and cost him his life, but rather the collision between two men marked out in their own minds for greatness, blindingly ambitious in its pursuit, almost bewitchingly charismatic, and capable of orchestrating the carnage of battle with ruthless dedication to victory.[3]

Napoleon Bonaparte, commander of the expedition to Egypt, had long had a romantic sense of his own greatness. Revolutionary upheavals in the early 1790s had given him the opportunity to abandon his heritage as a minor nobleman, and to parlay his talents as an artillery officer into high command amongst the armies that fought successfully against all the older powers of Europe. Dark and brooding in looks, he was similarly truculent in personality, sometimes to the point of petulance. He succeeded in taking command of a small army in Italy in 1796, and built a series of victories that formed the basis of a legend of true greatness, as well as helping to establish France as the dominant power in western Europe, only a few short years after it seemed that the nascent Republic would be crushed by a grand coalition of all its neighbours. Despite this, Bonaparte was a figure who made the civilian leadership of the Republic nervous.

Behind the rhetoric of republican heroism, and the sparkle of his youth – he was still only twenty-seven when his first conquests were secured – lay an appetite for glory and its trappings that no amount of bluff rhetoric about sharing the hardships of his troops could conceal. After Bonaparte's victories in northern Italy he had lived as a virtual viceroy for months, and showed no signs of being uncomfortable at the centre of what amounted to a monarchical court. Recalled to Paris, he had kicked his heels as a mere subordinate again, and rumours swirled of his behind-the-scenes machinations. In early 1798, he was given command of a projected invasion of England, something that offered the theoretical chance of a knock-out blow against the inveterate foe, but was also a poisoned chalice for such a troublesome hero. There was every likelihood of gallant failure removing his inconvenient presence permanently, while success would keep him at arm's length from a Republic that would then be able to consolidate itself at peace. The more Bonaparte considered it, the less the enterprise appealed.[4]

Deeply concerned with his own image, Bonaparte foresaw only ruin if he stayed in France: 'Everything here wears out; already I no longer have any glory. This little Europe does not supply enough. I must go to the East, all great glory comes from there.'[5] A two-week jaunt through the ports where the invasion was being planned proved to his satisfaction that it was a waste of time, and by the end of February 1798 he had bullied the Republic into supporting his new dream: he would go to Egypt. Once again, for his civilian overlords, this was a no-lose proposition. Conveniently distant, Bonaparte could reap all the glory he wanted, potentially establishing a permanent French colony to rival British India, a gateway to myriad possibilities for trade and enrichment in Africa and Asia. If he lost, he would already be out of the public gaze, and some new, more malleable hero could be raised up in his place. Thus Bonaparte was allowed to gather an expedition with remarkable speed: by late May 1798, 38,000 troops and 100 cannon were ready to sail from France's Mediterranean ports, in 400 transports escorted by a mere thirteen battleships and seven frigates.

Such a mediocre force seemed sufficient, because the Mediterranean was at the start of 1798 a French lake. Military success in Italy, coupled with a Spanish decision to leave the anti-French camp and switch sides, had forced the withdrawal of outnumbered British forces over a year before. However, almost as Bonaparte's armada sailed, a small advance party of British warships off the southern French coast was being reinforced to equal the expedition's strength, and its commander, Rear-Admiral Sir Horatio Nelson, was determined on a confrontation. Nelson, like Bonaparte, came from obscure provincial origins, though not so obscure as to prevent a steady rise up the ranks of the naval officer class after beginning his career at sea, as was customary, at twelve. He was now in his fortieth year, already a senior captain when war had broken out five years earlier, with a long tally of successful operations against the French and Spanish to his credit that made him the ideal candidate for this venture back into his old cruising-grounds.

Nelson was a man of high nervous energy, gifted with the ability to make inspirational emotional connections to his subordinates. Already a popular hero from his previous actions, he relished playing to crowd adulation on visits to London, and nurtured a vanity on such occasions that other distinguished figures found quite repellent.[6] He was rampantly ambitious for glory – saying before battle on more than one occasion that it would bring him 'a peerage or Westminster Abbey'. But as the latter reference to glorious commemoration implied, he never hesitated to put his own safety on the line, and unlike Bonaparte, he was a loyal and devoted servant of the system that had raised him. He had led from the front far too many times to be accused of merely using others' sacrifice for advancement, and paid a heavy price. He lost the sight in one eye – blasted by debris thrown up by an enemy cannonball – leading offensive operations in Corsica in 1794. Three years later, during a daring and ultimately unsuccessful raid on Spanish positions in Tenerife, his right arm was shattered by a musket shot leading to amputation and a long, painful convalescence, barely completed before new duties recalled him to action.[7]

On the morning of 1 August 1798, Nelson and his ships had

been hunting the French for almost eight weeks. With the five-year-old war at a low ebb for Britain, the fear that the French might open a decisive new front – perhaps in the Americas, perhaps even in Ireland – made the quest a desperately urgent one. Nelson's original scouting force had been unable to do anything about the French fleet's departure in late May, as they had been driven over 250 miles south by a two-day storm. Beating back to their station off Toulon, arranging to meet the promised reinforcements and heading south in pursuit consumed nearly two more weeks, until Nelson's full force reunited near Naples on 10 June. This was the day Bonaparte's forces began a three-day assault on the island of Malta – neutral territory under the control of the ancient order of the Knights of Malta – which after its surrender was systematically looted of a vast stock of wealth. As the assault concluded, Nelson learned from a passing ship that the French were somewhere south of Sicily. Having no choice but to make a fateful decision, and with this information suggesting that the enemy was not heading west for the Atlantic and British waters, he concluded that diplomatic rumours of an assault on Egypt were most likely justified, and set off in pursuit eastwards.

Ironically, Bonaparte's fleet did not sail from Malta until the 19th, and three days later the fleets came within a few miles of making contact south-east of Sicily. Nelson, consumed in a strategic conference with his senior captains, decided an initial sighting of four frigates was not worth following up, and his ships ploughed on, with highly favourable winds giving them a rapid passage, arriving off Egypt's main port of Alexandria on the evening of 28 June. The French were not there – their lumbering transports had slowed them – but Nelson worried that they might instead have been aimed at Turkish waters, and headed north. Little more than a day after the British departure, the French arrived, and launched a precipitate invasion. Even before most of the troops were offloaded, Bonaparte personally led an advance column of five thousand men, without horses, cannon or even food and water, to Alexandria, a full day's march distant from their landing beach. Arriving exhausted and thirst-ravaged, the French nonetheless smashed their way past the city's feeble defences in three hours. By 7 July, a week after their landing began, the French army was fully established. One column set out to secure the coastal delta, and Bonaparte himself led the strongest force south towards the capital, Cairo.[8]

Nelson's fleet, desperately short of scouting frigates, was reduced to floundering around the eastern Mediterranean in search of news. Abandoning a cruise off the Syrian coast at the start of July, they returned to Sicily to resupply on the 20th. Nelson wrote to his wife that while 'no person will say' that their lack of success 'has been for want of activity', he had to admit that 'I cannot find, or to this moment learn, beyond vague conjecture where the French Fleet are gone to.'[9] Heading back to sea, the fleet was off southern Greece on 29 July when they at last learned of the past month's events from a merchant vessel. Making all sail southwards, they arrived off Alexandria on 1 August to find the harbour occupied and defended by French batteries, but no sign of the French fleet.

One captain recorded that 'despondency nearly took possession of my mind', but a signal from a scouting ship early in the afternoon revealed the enemy's presence in Aboukir Bay, less than a dozen miles distant.[10] With light winds, closing that distance would involve the ships in a risky night action, but Nelson and his captains were fully prepared to take their chances. As he later famously wrote, 'I had the happiness to command a Band of Brothers', and the weeks of frantic searching, allied to his reputation and the qualities he himself dubbed 'the Nelson touch', had infused his command with his relentless quest for victory. All this enabled him to pitch them into the looming battle without hesitation.[11]

Major fleet actions had until very recently been cautious affairs. The professional navies of the eighteenth-century maritime powers had developed rigid line-of-battle tactics, sailing in single-file formations that confronted an enemy with a wall of gunfire. Opposing fleets thus tended to edge up against each other as the wind direction allowed, avoiding exposure of their vulnerable bows, and often broke off action without major casualties. Though such battles could secure both tactical and strategic success by blocking enemy plans and ambitions, they did little to negate the threat of the enemy fleet for the future. The Royal Navy pioneered efforts to break this deadlock. At the Battle of the Saintes in 1782, in the Caribbean theatre near the end of the American War of Independence, a fleet under Admiral Rodney managed to send several ships through the French line, from where they could bombard their opponents' vulnerable bow and stern, producing a victory and the capture of five of the thirty-five enemy vessels. At the 'Glorious First of June', a fleet engagement far from land in the Atlantic in 1794, the British fleet under Howe abandoned cautious manoeuvre when confronted by the poorly sailed ships of the revolutionary French navy, and attempted to penetrate their line in numerous places. The risks of the tactic were shown in a severe battering: although the British claimed the victory, and took or sank seven of the twenty-six French, only eleven of their own twenty-five vessels escaped heavy damage.

As the years of war went on, British blockades increasingly confined their enemies' main fleets to harbour for years on end (and the ravages of political upheaval took a further toll on the professionalism and competence of the French in particular). The rising disparity of organisation between the experienced British fleet and their enemies resulted in even more aggressive tactics: at Cape St Vincent in February 1797 the British (including Nelson) more or less charged directly at a Spanish fleet, while at Camperdown the following October Admiral Duncan was willing to hurl his fleet into action against the Dutch, noted fierce fighters, but who had been cooped up in harbour for many months, and were less than fanatical allies of the French. Even in this famous victory, however, more than half the enemy escaped, forcing the continuation of an arduous blockade, just as the ennobled Admiral Earl St Vincent remained condemned to patrol the waters where his eponymous victory had been achieved, keeping the Spanish confined to Cadiz.

Nelson's unhesitating commitment of his ships to the action in Aboukir Bay was in this aggressive tradition. It was not done without planning, however, and his aim was to concentrate his forces on the rearward two-thirds of the French line, anchoring his ships along-side them to join battle from the seaward side. He ordered specific preparations for this strategy, including the use of 'springs', addi-tional lines attached to anchor cables that would allow the ships to be swung around to bring their guns to bear on a series of targets (and to defend their own weak points). Like any good plan, it assumed a prepared enemy, but what followed was decisively shaped by the French fleet's compromises and mistakes.

The two fleets came in sight of each other around two in the afternoon, and for the next four hours a game of nerves was played out as the British strength was slowly revealed. Admiral Brueys con-sidered setting sail, but his shore parties could not be recovered in time. As the British ships were seen to slow down (to gather into closer formation), he decided that they might be preparing to wait for the following dawn, and stood firm. He did order men from his lighter ships into the battleships to man the guns, and after the British began to advance again, ordered springs to his own ships' cables, ready for action. It is not clear that this was achieved, how-ever, and as the British closed in, events took an unexpected and decisive turn.

The need of the French ships for room to swing at their single anchors was the fatal point in the arrangement, spotted by eagle-eyed officers on the first British ship – the *Goliath* – to sail up towards them head-on from the west. This ship, and eventually five more of the thirteen British vessels, cut into the channel of deeper water inshore of the French line that had necessarily been left for their movement. On this side of the enemy vessels they found the guns unmanned, and in some cases actually obstructed by piles of stores. Closing in pell-mell, sometimes swerving around each other, the British ships seized the initiative, assailing the front half of the French line and pouring ferocious fire into the hulls. Their approach to battle was captured in an anecdote from a young midshipman aboard *Goliath*:

> [the British ship *Theseus*] passing with ten yards gave us three most hearty cheers, which our men returned from their guns pretty well. The French were ordered by their officers to *cheer in return*, but they made such a lamentable mess of it that the laughter in our ships was distinctly heard ... I still distinctly recollect the stirring feelings of these men's cheers.[12]

In the heart of battle, the spirit shown here added its impact to the success in enveloping the French line, and together made the critical difference between merely besting the enemy and comprehensively beating him. Royal Navy ships were crewed by an astonishing assortment of men (and, occasionally, women). Individuals from every corner of the British Isles served alongside Americans, former slaves, Scandinavians, other Europeans (including sometimes nominal enemies), and even a scattering of Indians, Malays and Chinese picked up on the ships' global roaming. Few of the Britons and Irish were lifelong naval sailors, almost all were brought aboard ship either initially as boys with nowhere else to go, or much more commonly as press-ganged conscripts or nominal 'volunteers' (who earned a bounty by agreeing to serve willingly, even if initially pressed by force). At war's outbreak, such impressments swept merchant sailors into service by the tens of thousands. By the latter half of the 1790s, such was the need for men that recent drafts to the fleet had been quite literally the sweepings of the jails, bringing ill-health, and sometimes seditious sentiments, aboard, along with a monumental task of training to make useful hands.

The naval discipline that succeeded in imparting such training was mythically brutal, but such brutality only stands out in hindsight. Corporal punishment, for example, was commonly doled out by the ordinary courts, so naval flogging was not exceptional – and was strikingly accepted even by hardened offenders, who most often received lashes for drunkenness and fighting. The dangers of naval service, battle apart, were no worse than those of seafaring in general, and naval ships carried far larger crews to share the burdens of making sail. They also provided ample if monotonous rations, and at least a bare minimum of medical attention, which a merchant sailor might not get. There were sadistic, and simply bullying, officers and captains, but the performance of British ships in action time and again demonstrated that for most, something other than fearful obedience to hierarchy bound the crews together.

The aim of naval battle was brutally annihilating. The massive concentration of available firepower inflicted huge damage when unleashed. Continental navies traditionally gave more attention in action to bringing down rigging and masts, while the British stereotypically shot for the hull and the crew, but in a close action such as this one, the difference was marginal, and ships pounded one another almost muzzle-to-muzzle. To endure such an assault for more than a few minutes, as iron shot smashed lethal chunks from the very fabric of your ship, and your comrades' ghastly wounds sprayed the air with blood, seems impossible. Yet combat like this lasted for hours.

It plunged officers and men alike into a hell of fire, smoke, shot and splinters. The first discharge of guns was almost literally deafening in the confines of the gun-decks, and each successive salvo, with the timing growing more ragged as crews tired and men fell, only added to the cacophony. After a few discharges, the individual cannon themselves became dangerously hot, to the point of exploding prematurely if not swabbed out properly, or leaping from the decks as they recoiled. Loading and preparing them to fire was unrelenting and exhausting work, undertaken in a fury of battle, and by British crews traditionally in a roar of self-motivational cheering. They were fighting for their lives, of course, but despite their diverse origins, despite their unwilling service or dissident politics, despite the vast social gulf between them and their officers, despite the fact that their enemies fought for liberty and equality, they consistently fought better, faster and longer.

This horrific process was well under way on 1 August when Nelson's own ship arrived in time to lead the second half of the fleet down the enemy's seaward side. It took several hours for all the ships to join battle, by which time dusk was falling. By darkness at seven all the British were engaged, and within an hour had battered the first few French ships into devastated silence. They then proceeded to move further down the pinioned line, repeating the grim process at will. With the wind in their faces, the French had no choice but to await the onslaught (or cut their cables and run, which they gallantly declined to do).

At this point, around 8.30 p.m., Nelson continued his tradition of suffering physically for his triumphs. A piece of flying metal struck him on the forehead, leaving a gory flap of skin hanging down over his good eye, stunning and effectively blinding him. Carried below, he cried out 'I am killed', but demanded to take his turn behind the other wounded, in the stout naval tradition.[13] A portrait now in the National Maritime Museum, intended to represent this moment, highlights Nelson's romantic image: it shows him bloody and bandaged, and also improbably wearing the 'Nile Medal' not issued until months later, his hand across his breast in a gesture of sentimental self-absorption.[14]

By the time Nelson's wound had been cleaned and bound, it was clear that victory was in his hands. Admiral Brueys had already paid the ultimate price for his looming defeat, cut nearly in half by a cannonball. At around twenty to ten, his massive 120-gun, three-decked flagship L'Orient was engulfed by a spectacular explosion that lit up the whole bay. Fire, seen aboard her for almost an hour beforehand, had finally reached her stored gunpowder. The shock of the explosion caused a short lull in the fighting, and some of the dazed survivors were hauled in through the gunports of the nearest British ships, but combat soon resumed. It continued against the rear of the French line through the night, with further conspicuous pauses as ships became too damaged to steer, and exhausted crews had to make running repairs before the thunder of the guns resumed.

All through the next day the mopping-up continued, though the untouched last two ships in the French line made a bolt for the sea, with the British too battered to launch a pursuit. Other forces would capture the escapees before they could reach a safe harbour. The magnitude of the defeat was encompassed in the casualty figures. The British suffered just under 900 killed and wounded, with the dead about one-third of the total. The French reckoned eventually on an appalling 5235 killed, or unaccounted for in the fires and explosions. Of the 3000 prisoners taken, a third were wounded. Nelson had earned himself a peerage, and the adulation of the country, at the terrible cost his relentless approach to war demanded. By trapping Napoleon Bonaparte in Egypt, he had also charted in miniature the course of the great conflicts still to come.

I

REVOLUTIONARY TERRORS

Ten months before the stirring events at Aboukir Bay, the British political class had given a striking example of their bellicose spirit. In a nation that had been at war for almost five years, and which had suffered little other than reverses on the European stage for much of that time, there were discontents, and questions about the purpose of continued fighting against the new revolutionary order in France. As the new parliamentary session opened, Prime Minister William Pitt took the opportunity to rally the House of Commons to the cause of 'this happy and free nation' with an unabashed summoning of national pride:

> There may be danger, but on the one side there is danger accompanied with honour; on the other side, there is danger with indelible shame and disgrace; upon such an alternative, Englishmen will not hesitate ... we know great exertions are wanting, that we are prepared to make them, and [we are] at all events determined to stand or fall by the laws, liberties, and religion of our country.[1]

The emotive power of this argument, and the unity of the ruling elite, was then demonstrated in extraordinary fashion, as the MPs rose to their feet as one to bellow out the pugnacious chorus of a favourite patriotic anthem:

Britons strike Home!
Avenge your Country's Cause!
Protect your King!
Your Liberty, and Laws!

In a year which had seen the pride of Britain, the Royal Navy, almost paralysed by mass mutiny, this was either enormous self-confidence or the height of delusion. In retrospect, we know that the former attitude prevailed, but the years of war had shown that all was not well within the country of 'Liberty, and Laws'. Indeed, there was much evidence that those two concepts could be made to stand in direct opposition, when it suited the holders of authority. Over the coming two decades, the British state and its supporters were to maintain – to a greater degree than any other power – a robust opposition to the tyranny that ravaged the Continent from Lisbon to Moscow.[2] As this ultimately took shape as a self-consciously defined 'Grand Empire' that sought to erase and redefine almost every boundary, Britain's elites remained its great enemy, preventing its consolidation and hastening its collapse. During the later stages of this struggle in particular, that elite enjoyed, for the most part, stout patriotic support from the mass of the population. That had not always been the case, however, and nor can the British leaders' motives – at any stage in this long struggle – be called particularly virtuous. To explore them, and their consequences for all the inhabitants of the British Isles, we must begin by looking back to the point in time where the future 'Corsican Ogre' first encountered the British enemy.

*

As the autumn of 1793 turned to winter, William Pitt was approaching the milestone of a full decade in office as Prime Minister. At an age, thirty-four, when many men even of his era were still establishing themselves in life, Pitt had already secured a place in history. On his notoriously frail shoulders – caricaturists always portrayed him as little more than a stick-figure – the burden of restoring an empire to greatness had rested securely. Taking office by royal favour in December 1783, as Britain reeled under the financial and political costs of losing the American colonies, and without a majority in the House of Commons, Pitt had seen off the threat of impeachment by disgruntled and outraged opponents. He went on to win a near-landslide general election victory, and proceeded to wrestle furiously, and largely successfully, with the mammoth task of rebuilding public finance on solid foundations by the end of the decade.[3]

New challenges led on to new triumphs. At the end of 1788 Pitt's original patron and most faithful supporter, King George III, had plunged into madness, and for several months only desperate hedging had kept Pitt in office, facing off against demands to make the Prince of Wales Regent and bring the Whig opposition to power. The king's recovery brought in a period of political and diplomatic supremacy, as France collapsed into revolution in 1789, and adroit British diplomacy secured favourable outcomes (in the absence of a viable French counterweight) in a series of disputes that echoed around northern and eastern Europe. French troubles seemed only to escalate over the following years, while British influence and trading power grew, so that in February 1792 Pitt could announce to Parliament a healthy budget surplus, cut taxes, reduce military expenditure, and proclaim that 'there never was a time in the history of this country, when, from the situation of Europe, we might more reasonably expect fifteen years of peace'.[4]

Only two months later, he was proved wrong when aggressive French revolutionaries launched a war on Austria, setting off a chain of events that saw the establishment of a French Republic and the execution of their deposed king, with Prussia, Spain, Holland, the other minor states of Germany and Italy, and from the spring of 1793, Britain itself being roped into the escalating conflict.[5] The close of Pitt's first decade in office was thus met with yet another of the crises he had tackled so adroitly before. And indeed by the autumn of 1793 all seemed to be going well. France was embroiled not only in her external conflicts, but in two separate outbreaks of civil war: against out-and-out royalist reactionaries in the rural west, and spurned moderate republicans (rapidly becoming more royalist under pressure of circumstances) in the major cities of the south-east. British troops had joined the Austrians in driving French forces out of the Low Countries, and even if they had had limited success moving into France itself, a stunning blow had been struck to the south. Fearful of republican reprisals, rebel forces had surrendered Toulon, the base of France's Mediterranean fleet, to the Royal Navy.

The siege of Toulon by the French, however, was to be one of the turning points of the war. A hitherto obscure artillery officer, Napoleon Bonaparte, brought himself to political attention, and general's rank, by masterminding the assault on a key outlying fortress, placing the port at the mercy of his cannon. After their two-month occupation, the British were obliged to flee, able to secure only some of the captured ships and failing to destroy others. They left their French allies to a grim fate of reprisal and repression. Overall it was a poor substitute for the hoped-for consolidation of royalist revival throughout the south. Indeed, it placed the seal on a republican resurgence, as other centres of revolt were crushed in the same season, and France entered the winter of 1793–4 girding its loins through massive mobilisation to take the war to its external foes in the spring.

That mobilisation was the fruit of what the French did not hesitate to call Terror, a policy which in their enemies' eyes meant the unleashing of near-satanic powers of mob violence and pitiless slaughter. Through the first half of 1794, the Terror reached its peak within France. Captured rebels and suspected plotters were done to death by the thousand, while property and wealth were increasingly sequestered to serve the needs of the state and, more sinister still, long-term plans for redistribution to 'poor patriots'. All this provided British and other observers with a theatre of horror; first-hand accounts were inflated by rumour and propaganda, and augmented into cannibalistic orgies by the stunning visual talents of caricaturists. More terrifying still, as French forces pressed back into the Low Countries that spring, outmanoeuvring ineffective British troops, was the thought that French principles were already at work within Britain.

The events of 1789 in France at first seemed to have fallen as little more than a stone in the pond of British life, but as the situation deteriorated and war loomed, that stone became more like a depth-charge, its sunken explosion bringing a churning mass of discontent to the surface.[6] To think that British politics and society were placid during Pitt's years in office would in any case be a grievous mistake. Beyond the crises of war, diplomacy and regency, he had also in the 1780s had to contend with bitter strife over the nature of the expanding empire in India, whose ill-gotten loot was widely seen as corrupting the very constitution. He tried, and failed, to reconcile competing political and economic interests between Britain and its subjects in Ireland. He fought off attempts to open political life to Protestants outside the Church of England – this, ironically, after he had suffered humiliating defeat in his own efforts to reform the blatantly corrupt parliamentary franchise. The political culture of late Hanoverian Britain rested on ambiguous and contradictory foundations that would turn out to be ripe for further convulsion.[7]

Britain was a land of liberty, of 'revolution principles' laid down against tyrannous monarchy a hundred years before, a land where the major political force of the century, the Whigs, nurtured a fringe of 'Commonwealthmen' – ideologues who disdained almost all centralised power, and who could attract dukes and earls to their celebrations, as they did for a raucous centenary feast for the 'Glorious Revolution' in London on 4 November 1788. Britain was home to habeas corpus, the legal principle that prevented arbitrary detentions, and to the jury trial, which stopped the courts being the mere plaything of power. The institution of Parliament so central to the political culture was itself almost unique in a Europe of absolutist monarchies, and the appearance of public consent helped sustain a far higher burden of taxation and borrowing to fund imperial expansion than could safely be managed by other powers.[8]

The stout, booted stereotype of John Bull stood for 'English' virtues, freedom and prosperity, in sharp and deliberate contrast to France, depicted in a thousand popular images as the home of skeletal, clog-wearing, straw-eating victims of Roman Catholic despotism. But habeas corpus could be suspended, and the juries of British courts sometimes struggled to uphold their instincts for justice against the 'Bloody Code' of parliamentary statutes, with a bewildering mass of specific crimes and capital sentences. Juries' willingness to declare the value of goods stolen to be just below the threshold at which a hanging would have been mandatory was legendary, but while it may have saved lives it did little to assuage growing fears about the security of property.[9]

Other grim contradictions had erupted in 1780, when Protestant fanatics whipped up fears that secret Catholics in government were plotting a *coup d'état*. A protest march brought tens of thousands on to the streets of London, and law and order broke down in the infamous 'Gordon Riots'. As violence unfolded, the agenda switched from bizarre conspiracy theory to all-out assault on the emblems of power, with public buildings, and notably prisons, assaulted and torched. Local authorities were unwilling to requisition armed force in defence of 'papists', army officers declined to act without civilian authorisation (fearing robust legal sanctions if they did), and finally only a royal proclamation was able to unleash repression – producing several hundred deaths.

The British state ruled over its millions of 'freeborn Englishmen' (and women, and Scots, Welsh, Irish and others, too) from the heart of Europe's largest city, at the centre of a globe-spanning empire based on trade in imperial plunder and the produce of Caribbean slavery, on an island in the throes of industrialisation. The population of England and Wales, which had risen slowly from around five million in 1700 towards seven million by 1770, shot up past eight million in the 1780s, on course to add a further two million in the next two decades, and three million more in the two after that.[10] Tumultuous economic and demographic growth had seen villages turned into bustling towns in the 'industrious districts' of the north and Midlands. Birmingham, a metalworking town of craftsmen and workshops, was at 70,000 people five times larger than it had been a century before. Manchester, home to swelling ranks of cotton-weavers, had held fewer than 20,000 people at mid-century, but was now on course to top 100,000 within a few years. Its satellite towns, equally devoted to the textile trade, would by the 1801 census house almost a quarter of a million people.

London, whose population was soon to reach a million, had long been a vast metropolis, but now seemed to grow ever faster.[11] Stretching miles in every direction from its ancient heart, overhung with a sooty pall from the 'sea coal' (brought by ship from the north-east) that had fuelled its fires since Tudor times, its fringes seethed with new building, just as its heart throbbed with every variety of human activity. Districts like Kensington, Paddington and Islington, not long before almost wholly rural, had in recent years been given over to a combination of market gardens and weekend retreats for the various needs of city-dwellers, and now were on the brink of absorption into the urban mass. Islington had once been a spa, but by the 1790s little of this glamour remained, except in the name of its theatre, Sadler's Wells. Like many districts, its reputation rose and fell over the decades, marked with waves of successive gentrification and dilapidation.

Urban development was unplanned, speculative and frequently chaotic.[12] Not even the Great Fire of 1666 had persuaded Londoners to abandon the warren-like construction of the medieval city. Elsewhere around the capital, fine squares and crescents might be laid out one decade, and fall into slum conditions in the next, as fashion and other, newer developments encouraged the rich to move on, and left the poor as a landlord's only source of profit. Much housing built speculatively for the 'middling sort' of prosperous Londoner turned out to be shoddy and unsafe, accelerating the tendency of the emergent middle classes to prefer more individual suburban villas, and leaving what had once appeared to be solid townhouses to be gutted and let out as crumbling and over-crowded tenements. Spitalfields to the east of the city was one such area already beginning a decline towards the worst excesses of destitution in the century to come.[13]

Growing extremes of wealth and poverty were masked by a general sense of rising prosperity, especially in the capital. No population in Europe was as well-fed (or as inclined to overeat) as the English, and to foreign visitors the streets of London were an astonishing spectacle of popular vivacity and liberty.[14] London crowds were notoriously no respecters of persons, inclined to gather and gawp at anything of passing interest, and to pass noisy (and occasionally violent) judgment on anything they disagreed with. This cult of spectatorship was promoted by eager commercial forces, selling newspapers, pamphlets and print illustrations (the latter frequently obscenely satirical) by the ton. Prints were put on show in shop windows, attracting many to the free spectacle, but almost anything might also be exhibited for a fee. The willingness of the English to part with a penny to view items ranging from a new painting to an anatomical curiosity was the foundation of many modest fortunes, and a mainstay of a culture of unregulated public openness and engagement shockingly alien to continentals.

Less salubrious pleasures were also shared by every class, and privately run 'pleasure gardens' such as those at Ranelagh and Vauxhall wavered uneasily between park, fairground and open-air brothel.[15] Whilst theatre-going was one respectable pastime – if not without occasional raucous interruptions from the cheaper seats – many other public entertainments still bore a harsh edge of primal indulgence. The robust and gruesome pleasures of bull- and bear-baiting, dog- and cock-fighting, and their human equivalent in bare-knuckle boxing, attracted 'sportsmen' of every class; those who could afford it combined spectating with heavy drinking and high-stakes gambling. At night the city was a dangerous place, and the wise pedestrian secured the services of reliable 'link-men' to light his way home – his, for no sensible woman of the propertied classes would risk being abroad after dark. The disadvantages of city life, except perhaps for a seasonal visit, further encouraged the proliferation of rural building that also marked the age.

Colonial and agricultural prosperity had already produced a wave of country-house building in the sternly neoclassical 'Palladian' style by mid-century. In later decades this trend swelled, augmented by the sophisticated combinations of taste in interior decoration and architecture epitomised in town and country alike by Robert Adam. As a working architect, he had a guiding hand in some fifty notable urban and rural developments, as well as various churches and public buildings, but his and his competitors' designs were increasingly available to anyone with money, thanks to the commercial diffusion of pattern-books and exemplary building plans. As prosperous merchants began to hanker after neoclassical elegance as the reward for their labours, suburbs like Edgbaston in Birmingham expanded rapidly with what we now think of as prototypically Georgian detached villas and elegant streets.

As the middling sort reached out towards the rural elegance of the gentry, so some at the very top of society expanded their more substantial fortunes on newly industrious foundations. Most famously, the Duke of Bridgewater invested £200,000 in a canal from his coal-bearing hills to Manchester's commercial hub, and by

the early 1790s was making £80,000 a year as a result.[16] Especially
in the Midlands and the north-west, canals opened up the country
to trade in a generation, their aqueducts rivalling those of the
Romans in grandeur, and in their march across the landscape, sym-
bolising a country woven together by active and expanding
commercial and industrial wealth.[17]

Just as the bustling cityscape had its dark side, so too did this
new alliance of aristocrats, engineers and merchants. Changes in
agricultural techniques, crowned by the 'enclosures' that turned
medieval strip-farming into scientific practices of crop rotation in
hedged fields, had raised productivity, and helped to support the
soaring population. Led by the most advanced agrarian thinkers
amongst nobility and gentry, this process had cut away age-old
common rights, helping to propel large sections of the population
into dependence on wage labour. When demand for labour was
high, in field or workshop, this was no great hardship, but rising
population cheapened labour in some sectors, while increasing
use of machinery – still hand- or water-powered, but with steam
looming on the horizon – propelled intensifying exploitation as
more and more employers competed to recoup their investments
on plant and buildings.

Rising production in the mills of the new industries – and even in
old-established urban trades – often came in these years from driving workers into absolute dependence: on machines, and on the will
of their masters. Statute after statute crowded the books, literally
criminalising long-established forms of resistance and collective
bargaining with such masters.[18] Over all this presided the personnel
of the state, a political class comprised essentially of the aristocracy,
numbering in the thousands, its wealth based in land and tradition,
but also in the plunder of the state for profitable office. Power was
wealth, and vice versa – the king himself had chipped in to help buy
the 1784 election for his favourite Pitt, and Pitt's arch-rival Charles
James Fox had planned in detail just who should get what spoils if
he had taken power in the 1789 regency crisis.

When all was going well, this turbulent, venal, starkly unequal society could celebrate itself (and regularly did) as the best of all possible worlds. After all, even the breakaway Americans fixated, in their founding debates, on the fine qualities of the 'English' constitution. The ideological challenge posed in 1789 by the French seemed to have been smacked down convincingly by the end of 1790, when the Whig politician Edmund Burke produced his *Reflections on the Revolution in France*. This proved to the satisfaction of the British elite that such democratic practices could only end in carnage. While this jeremiad turned out to be prophetic of later events across the Channel, it also called forth a challenge at home from Burke's former friend, the Anglo-American revolutionary Thomas Paine.[19] His *Rights of Man* in its first part dissected Burke's flowery rhetoric, and in a second part published in 1792 offered a pithy summons to unmake the aristocratic monarchy in favour of a democratic republic and the outlines of a welfare state. Sold in cheap editions and reprinted by the tens of thousands, Paine's work inserted a dangerous political radicalism into the culture of popular awareness and boisterous self-expression. From supporters of both positions, a pamphlet war between 'radicals' and 'loyalists' began that would spiral on throughout the decade.[20]

With the working people of the country already bemoaning 'the hardness of the times and the dearness of all the necessaries of life', early 1792 saw a movement of 'corresponding societies' begin amongst workers and craftsmen in London, uniting first with a similar group in the precociously radical atmosphere of Sheffield, and developing into a nationwide network as Paine's message, and the deeper economic hardships of war, began to strike home from 1793.[21] Their initial goal was simple – to gain a political voice through manhood suffrage – but it implied sweeping away all the structures of the existing order, and as their numbers grew, so too did the perceived threat they posed. Local authorities became almost hysterical in their fears of mobs and conspirators.[22] Thomas

Paine, fleeing to France ahead of an arrest warrant, was burned in effigy at loyalist celebrations around the country, and an Association for the Preservation of Liberty and Property against Republicans and Levellers organised a nationwide witch-hunt of radicals.[23] Meanwhile, government began building up internal networks of spies and informers, in parallel with similar operations against the French enemy, that would grow ever more elaborate over the years to come.[24]

In the fervid atmosphere of May 1794, with the French Terror before their eyes, Pitt's government passed into law an Act to deal with 'a traitorous and detestable Conspiracy ... for subverting the existing Laws and Constitution, and for introducing the System of Anarchy and Confusion which has so fatally prevailed in *France*'.[25] Habeas corpus was suspended, licensing indefinite detention without trial. The leadership of the London Corresponding Society was rounded up, charged with high treason and interrogated personally by the king's Privy Council. John Thelwall, an educated merchant's son who had thrown in his lot with the radicals, recorded a confrontation with a panel including the Attorney-General, Lord Chancellor, Home Secretary and Prime Minister Pitt himself. He scorned to answer their questions, and his young comrade, fourteen-year-old Henry Eaton, treated them to what the *Morning Post* reported as a 'political harangue, in which he used very harsh language against Mr Pitt, upbraiding him with having taxed the people to an enormous extent'.[26]

The prosecution of these men collapsed when an Old Bailey jury could not be made to agree that their plans for a 'convention' of delegates to demand suffrage amounted to treason in its bloodthirsty medieval definition. But the jubilation of a London crowd who carried Thelwall and several others in triumph through the streets merely highlighted the strains imposed by an increasingly unsuccessful war, and by the continued influence of revolutionary ideals of liberation.[27]

The problem posed for the British state in resisting the call for change was particularly acute in Ireland, where political realities posed a perennial challenge to the libertarian self-image of the 'free-born Englishman'. Since the later nineteenth century, Ireland has been a small country compared to England – its population often no more than 10 per cent of that of the larger nation. At the end of the eighteenth century, however, Ireland held over four and three-quarter million people, well on the way to half the population of its neighbour.[28] With three million colonial subjects already lost in North America, any prospect of a further dissolution of this empire threatened the collapse of the British state.

Ruled as a satellite kingdom of England, Ireland had for centuries been the domain of a 'Protestant Ascendancy'; its parliament had been a puppet for English wishes since the 1490s, and under rulers from Elizabeth to Cromwell the Catholic population had been repressed and massacred into line. Irish Catholic rallying to the cause of James II, the monarch cast out of England by the 1688 Glorious Revolution, reinforced the perpetual English prejudice that the Irish were incorrigibly dangerous subjects. The Protestant population, descendants of seventeenth-century 'plantations' of aggressively Presbyterian Scots in the north alongside the landed gentry that owned much of the south, caused their own problems. Rebelling against unfavourable tariffs for their exports during the disasters of the American War, they succeeded in bullying the British into restoring their long-lost legislative independence – and so the Irish Lords and Commons in Dublin went in 1782 from being a conveniently tame matrix of patronage to a complicating factor in an already congested field of faction and partisanship.

The French Revolution, subsequent war and radicalisation of protest across Britain struck home with particular force in Ireland, raising new alarms and cutting across old ones. A rich tradition of conflict was coalescing by the mid-1790s around a clandestine Catholic militia that called itself the 'Defenders', and a more overt and aggressive Protestant response in the foundation of the

'Orange Order'. The intermittent fighting and relentless hatred encouraged by such groups complicated (but also deepened) the threat from another new organisation. The United Irishmen, whose leadership stretched up into the fringes of the ruling elite, saw a beguiling example in the French exaltation of their 'nation' over an aristocratic caste, and forged a strong network of both Protestants and Catholics committed, nominally at least, to freeing all Ireland from the British yoke. Pursued by the same spies and informers that harried the footsteps of the Corresponding Societies, the United Irishmen nonetheless became a standing challenge to British rule, especially as the situation of the war with France deteriorated.[29]

The end of the Terror in the summer of 1794 was far from the end of the French threat: indeed one reason that the republican politicians had felt able to rid themselves of the puritanical fanaticism of the leading 'terrorists' was that their armies were now clearly winning on all fronts. Though Britain continued with the idea of crushing the Revolution – landing a force of exiled French royalists on the coast of Brittany in 1795, with disastrous consequences – most of France's other foes were being driven to a settlement. Spain and Prussia both signed peace deals that same year, while the Dutch were overrun and converted into a pro-French republic. When – led by the new wonder-worker, General Bonaparte, who would force a favourable peace the following year – the French in 1796 achieved crushing victories against Austrian power in Italy, their thoughts turned to possible routes to a defeat of Britain, and Ireland was the self-evident first choice.

By 1796 one of the United Irish leaders, Theobald Wolfe Tone, had already been granted a French military commission, and in that year and the next abortive efforts to stimulate a national rising through an armed landing sowed panic and dread through the British and Anglo-Irish ruling classes. With the country's finances in a precarious state, a French descent on the coast of Wales by a few hundred soldiers in 1797 struck such a panic in London that the

Bank of England had to suspend payments in gold. It was a symptom of a country living on its nerves, fighting a war whose purposes were by now obscure, and in which victory – or indeed peace – remained appallingly elusive.

The democratic threat had endured through these years, intensifying that nervousness. Through 1795 the London Corresponding Society swelled by hundreds and thousands, riding on the popularity of further acquittals on trumped-up treason charges. French successes cut off traditional markets for British goods in the Low Countries, unemployment rose, and a poor harvest and a bitter winter had produced hunger throughout the land. Opposition spread far wider than just a hard core of radicals, with petitions for peace reaching the capital from many provincial gatherings, and fears widespread about the combination of harsh weather and rampant enemies. One diarist recorded in February 1795 that 'This is the hardest winter ever known. In the north the snow 12 and 18 feet deep. The poor are starving with cold and hunger, for want of trade, especially with Holland.' The poet Coleridge gave a public lecture in Bristol that month, warning that 'social confidence' was collapsing, 'our liberties have suffered a serious breach ... And shall we carry on this wild and priestly War against reason, against freedom, against human nature?'[30]

Symbolic of the apocalyptic social mood was the rise to prominence of the 'prophet' Richard Brothers, a former naval lieutenant who since 1789 had been living the life of a penniless anchorite, and producing screeds proclaiming the imminent end of the world. Financed by a range of followers, including at least one MP, Brothers' stream of words fitted into a well-developed strand of millennial and apocalyptic thought that lay just below the surface of eighteenth-century Christianity. It also actively alarmed the government.

By early spring 1795, Brothers was attracting wide public attention in London with claims that universal destruction was about to come upon the 'Babylon' capital. Declarations that this would result in the Second Coming and that 'the day is at hand when none can work', but all would eat 'butter and honey', proved too much for the authorities. Brothers was arrested in March under a sixteenth-century statute forbidding 'fantastical prophecies, with intent to create dissensions, and other disturbances within this realm'. Like the leaders of the London Corresponding Society the previous year, he was treated to a personal interrogation by the Privy Council, whom he informed of his 'immediate communication with GOD'.[31] He was simultaneously indicted for treason and declared insane, and locked away in a private asylum.

His prophecies, however, remained active in the public imagination. He had foretold that the capital's destruction would begin with an earthquake on 4 June – the king's official birthday, one reason for deeming such claims seditious. The prediction had been widely publicised, and as the day approached, it appears that many contemplated flight: one diarist condemned the inhabitants as 'disloyal, superstitious, villainous, and infamous', and the cartoonist Gillray mocked them in print.[32] Yet on that very day, when a huge thunderstorm broke over the capital, the dread seemed very much alive. A leader of the London Corresponding Society later recalled that he had been caught by the storm on his way to a meeting, and taking shelter in a hotel found fifty or sixty people waiting: 'every one in the room knew something of Brothers' prophecy, and of the time at which it was to be fulfilled ... There was a general feeling and expression of alarm.'[33]

Beyond such fears of a metaphysical apocalypse, the state of the country as pointless war continued and food prices soared seemed to cry out for change. Parliamentary willingness at the end of June 1795 to grant the newly married Prince of Wales an annual income of £125,000 (on condition he allocated £65,000 a year to paying off his £630,000 of debts) added insult to injury.[34] In July, protestors smashed the windows of 10 Downing Street while Pitt was hosting a dinner party inside, one of a series of riots that also attacked 'crimping houses' where men were supposedly kidnapped into military service.[35] By the autumn, mass meetings of the London Corresponding Society and its ilk were bringing tens of thousands to hear fiery rhetoric about the connection between corruption and starvation. As the king drove to open Parliament on 29 October a reported 200,000 thronged the streets, crying against Pitt and for peace, and brandishing loaves draped in black crepe – ominous emblems of popular hunger. When what was probably a flung pebble cracked the window of the king's carriage, it was enough to spark further repression against such 'assassins'.

Two new Acts banned a range of 'Treasonable Practices', and subjected those who held 'Seditious Meetings' to the sometimes overwrought judgment of local magistrates. These were able now, without habeas corpus, to hand down sentences of indefinite confinement almost at a whim.[36] Edmund Burke, who had denounced radical fervour even before it had arisen, saw terrible things in the continued stream of rumours and reports from ever-active (and sometimes imaginative) government spies. A majority of the working population, and as many as one in five of the electorate (a much more restricted, and supposedly respectable, body) he damned as 'pure Jacobins' – that is, revolutionary republicans on the French model: 'utterly incapable of amendment; objects of eternal vigilance'. The constitution of the body politic had to be protected from such diseases with 'the critical terrors of the cautery and the knife'.[37]

Under such rhetorical and punitive onslaughts, attempts to sustain the London Corresponding Society were restricted to an ardent hard core. Provincial counterparts through 1796 in Manchester, Birmingham, Leeds, Sheffield, Nottingham and elsewhere floundered under 'terrifying ... arbitrary proceedings' by the authorities. Nonetheless, individuals struggled on, and the scattered legal records that survive show that men were still producing outbursts of radical fervour across the country. One Scot declaimed against the law to raise a new militia: 'Why should we fight for them. If the French come they will not hurt us – they will only plunder from those who have already too much.' The magistrate who sentenced him noted that his rank as a local constable proved 'how soon the true British character can be debased by the poison of democracy'.[38]

Oppression and isolation played on many of the leaders of radicalism.[39] John Thelwall had struggled to maintain a public platform for democratic ideas, enduring both assaults and the provocations of spies who sought to incriminate him in riots and other violence. But he was ground down, and visiting the rural idyll of his friends Coleridge and Wordsworth, imagined in verse how sweet it would be to dwell 'far from the strifeful scenes/Of public life', tending a garden and discoursing on art and literature. The poets, however, coming to regret their earlier dabbling with sedition, pushed him away.[40]

The growing divide between establishment opinion and a radical fringe was intensified in the aftermath of a new general election in the summer of 1796. Though Pitt and his colleagues secured a huge majority from the largely elite electorate, this victory brought not security but new crises. French successes left the British government with little option other than to contemplate making peace, but national pride (and cold calculation) meant that London could not offer terms that the rampant republicans were willing to accept. In December 1796 a change of ruler in Russia weakened the anti-French alliance even more, causing a decisive rejection of the British mission. With recently defeated Spain turning its coat and entering the war on the French side, forcing the hasty evacuation of the Mediterranean fleet, Pitt had to call on all his reserves of political capital to raise millions in extra taxation, and no less than £18 million in a 'loyalty loan' from the propertied population. That this sum was subscribed in four days was a triumph, but the money was needed partly to fund increasingly unpopular expansions of the armed forces, which would bring their own perils.[41]

There was another narrow escape at the end of 1796, as a French invasion force, destined to link up with planned (or at least predicted) United Irish revolt, was blocked by the weather from landing in Bantry Bay. Irish authorities continued with campaigns of repression against the United Irishmen and their Defender counterparts, and amidst a rising atmosphere of alarm one tactic widely used was to ship prisoners into naval service. According to one report over 15,000 such men had been sent from Ireland between 1793 and 1796. If accurate, this figure represents over a tenth of the manpower of the Royal Navy by the latter year. Somewhere approaching a similar proportion were 'Quota Men', the products of legislation requiring local authorities to provide recruits since 1795. Such men were got by a variety of means, one of which was the sweeping of the jails, including the direct dispatch of suspected radicals and insurrectionaries from England and Scotland. Another was the payment of substantial cash bounties for volunteers, which enticed a further wave of men, including artisans and traders, to enlist to escape debts and impoverishment brought on by the harsh conditions of wartime.[42] All such men, with their diverse grievances, were expected to be tamed by the relentless discipline and isolated conditions of life aboard ship.

In February 1797 the continued potential of the Royal Navy was proved when the Mediterranean fleet sortied from its temporary refuge in Lisbon to engage the Spanish off Cape St Vincent. Outnumbered twenty-eight to fifteen, the British ships nevertheless had the advantage of well-drilled and tempered crews. The Spanish, on the other hand, had filled up their ships with soldiers and conscripted landsmen – as much as 90 per cent of many crews had never been to sea. The British commander, Admiral Sir John Jervis, earned himself an elevation to the peerage as Earl St Vincent by carrying his ships through the middle of the confused and disorderly enemy fleet, capturing four and driving the others off in panic. His subordinate, Commodore Horatio Nelson, gained fame by capturing two of those four ships, the *San José* and the *San*

Nicolás, which had become locked together in the mêlée, racing across from one to the other in a move wits dubbed his 'patent bridge'.

Though this news caused short-term rejoicing, the mood of the country remained sour. Whig opposition members amongst the ancient corporate organisation of the City of London prompted a petition to the king in March 1797 that called in bitter terms for peace. It was 'the evil instigations of your majesty's advisors' that kept the country in a war 'unparalleled in misery and destruction', ruining commerce, augmenting corruption and bringing on circumstances in which 'the very vitals of our constitution' were threatened by repression of dissent. They begged for a change of government to restore 'national prosperity and happiness'.[43] The king refused to accept the petition on the throne, which would have required him to reply to it, though he condescended to receive it at a lesser ceremony.

By the time of this rejection, the sailors of the Channel fleet, crucial to defence against France, had already begun petitioning the Admiralty over their miserable wages, unimproved for a century, and over other grievances from lack of shore-leave to poor medical treatment, deductions from rations, and inadequate pensions for crippled veterans. How far they were influenced by the currents of 'democratical' agitation has always remained a mystery, though this must clearly have played a part. The Admiralty's response was to order the fleet at Spithead, the anchorage off Portsmouth, to proceed to sea. On 16 April 1797 every ship refused the order. Britain's wooden wall had fallen to mutiny. The speed, secrecy and discipline with which the crews acted astonished government and civilian observers alike, and within days ministers agreed to meet at least some of their demands. Rejection by the sailors of this first offer led to a further, remarkable, government concession: an emergency Cabinet meeting on the night of the 21st agreed to add a sweeping royal pardon to the deal. Such was the desperation that the threatened loss of the fleet provoked.

Though this brought agreement from the Portsmouth crews to end the mutiny, as they awaited implementation of improvements they were joined by delegates from the squadron at Plymouth, and both groups began formulating new grievances, notably about the harsh conduct of individual officers in various ships. In early May the fleet redoubled its claims, demanding an immediate Act of Parliament to consolidate the sailors' gains, and the removal of such unpopular officers. The government had to pass an emergency Finance Bill, and sent Admiral 'Black Dick' Howe, a popular superannuated hero, to Spithead, where three days of discussion and reassurance brought unalloyed victory for the demands of the Portsmouth and Plymouth men. On 15 May the sailors held a celebratory banquet; on the 16th they sailed to resume blockade duty off the main French naval base at Brest in Brittany.

If the mutiny had been confined to the Channel fleet it could have been incorporated into the national story as an example of plainspoken British justice. One of the reasons the men's complaints were taken so seriously was that their conditions were palpably unjust, when rates of pay and conditions in the army had been improved two years before to overcome equally reasonable disaffection. However, while Howe's mission to Spithead was still in progress, news reached London that ships at the Nore, at the mouth of the Thames, had launched their own protest. Unpopular officers were sent ashore at once, and after news of the Spithead victory was brought first-hand by a sailors' delegation, the Nore ships proceeded to draft their own petition on 20 May. Along with all the demands of the Channel fleet, they included goals that began to sound alarmingly democratic, such as the introduction of sailors' juries into court-martial proceedings.

Ministers reacted by calling up army units to nearby towns, and asked the Admiral of the North Sea fleet, based at Yarmouth, if his men could be relied on in action against the mutineers. Within a few days, most of the Yarmouth ships mutinied too, and sailed to join those at the Nore, where they took up defensive positions that also threatened a blockade of the Thames. At the end of May such a blockade commenced, provoking some occupants of nearby towns to flee. The stakes were rising; the more radical amongst the mutineers had already had to use cannon-fire to prevent two wavering ships slipping away. Over the following ten days, with government intransigent, tensions wreaked havoc with the mutineers' unity. An attempt to put to sea on 9 June collapsed, over the next two days open fighting broke out on many ships, and by the 14th the mutiny was effectively over, the last ship surrendering the next day, along with the committee of delegates who had led the enterprise.

Over the course of the summer some thirty-six men were hanged for their roles in the Nore mutiny, and over 350 sentenced to an assortment of floggings and deportations to distant colonies.[44] With the government's recovery from its initial shock at the Spithead events, it had become clear that dangerous political grievances had been present even there. Several sailors aboard HMS *Pompée*, for example, voiced views that the refusal of peace petitions in London was because 'the great Men at the Head of Affairs ... meant the ruin of the Nation', a body which would be 'very indebted to the seamen' if their actions could force an end to the war. Beyond this general demand for peace – which would, incidentally, release many men from their enforced naval servitude – there were sinister signs of organised democratic agitation. The London Corresponding Society tried to get in touch with the Spithead men, as did the United Irishmen, though the movement ended before any real action could be taken. At the Nore however, agitation amongst Irish seamen for radical goals was present from the outbreak of mutiny. Some members of the Nore committee later claimed (no doubt self-servingly) to have opposed 'a set of damn'd rascals in the place' who held a 'violent opinion ... against the good of their king and country'.

As the mutiny began to disintegrate the committee tried to split the ships into five divisions. The first would take those who wanted an immediate surrender, the second would head out to sea, ultimately aiming to desert to France. The third would head for Scotland, for reasons not overtly explained, but perhaps to make contact with disaffected workers in the cities. The fourth would aim for Ireland, perhaps to become the navy of the United Irishmen. A fifth set was to abandon Europe and seek refuge in America. Each ship was to vote on which division to join. It was a scatterbrained and desperate plan, but it shows clearly that, of the five options, at least two and perhaps three were seditious in intent. A later petition from over 250 imprisoned mutineers bewailed the influence of the 'leaders of a dreadful Faction' in dragging them towards conflict.[45] As the mutiny broke up in disorder and fighting, many of the most ardent mutineers escaped – in one case no fewer than twenty men from HMS *Inflexible*, which had persistently been a hotbed of extreme views, stole a cutter and sailed directly for France.

In a context such as this, further efforts by the London Corresponding Society to revive public agitation were doomed. Before the mutinies, they had written to provincial groups calling for mass meetings to be held, and demands to be put forward for a change of government and a commitment to peace, annual parliaments and universal manhood suffrage. With little enthusiasm on display for what seemed a futile demand – and Sheffield radicals arguing it would be better to await a general collapse that would bring change in its wake – the London group nevertheless went ahead with a meeting on open ground at St Pancras on 31 July 1797. In response, the authorities displayed overwhelming force, mustering 2000 civilian constables and a total of almost 10,000 troops, on the spot and in nearby reserve. Magistrates on horseback summoned the meeting to disperse, and there could be no resistance. It was meagre consolation that, once again, a jury found there were no charges to answer against six arrested ringleaders. The days of mass radicalism seemed over.[46]

Meanwhile, further echoes of mutiny continued to shake the British state. During the Nore events, regiments of Guards in

London had shown 'disaffection and discontent', and a rattled Cabinet had approved an immediate rise in army pay. Despite their elite status, the Guards were notably problematic from the point of view of discipline, as many were Irish, and they lived out of barracks, free to mingle with the capital's radicals. Later in May the artillery troops at Woolwich Arsenal had to be disarmed by infantry and cavalry after striking against unpopular officers. Meanwhile in Plymouth a plot amongst sailors and marines, which included alleged plans to blow up the local arsenal and unite with freed French prisoners to 'do everything in their power to overturn government', was suppressed by the use of regular troops and local militia. The authorities unhesitatingly blamed a 'Mutinous Irish Banditti', and hanged six ringleaders – but at the end of the summer there were still several hundred marines in barracks that it was 'not thought prudent to trust' with weapons.[47] The months ahead were to show that both government and radicals still had formidable arsenals at their disposal.

2

SEDITION AND STALEMATE

With mutinous aftershocks still being felt across the country, October 1797 brought news from the Navy that seemed to put the world back on its axis. Pitt's government was still seeking peace, and had suffered something close to a humiliation in September when an envoy to France, Lord Malmesbury, had been given twenty-four hours to agree to surrender all British conquests, and was then essentially expelled. Nonetheless, it remained prepared for war.[1] Admiral Duncan, whose fleet had been ravaged at the Nore, had been able to restore discipline and resume his blockade of the Dutch fleet, which since the French takeover had significantly augmented the threat to Britain's coasts.

On 11 October at the Battle of Camperdown Duncan took twenty-four ships of the line into battle against twenty-five Dutch. This was the main strength of their fleet, which had sortied on exercise after a temporary British withdrawal. The Dutch were a much tougher adversary than the Spanish had been at St Vincent, but the end result of a pounding fight was even more emphatic. Ten of the Dutch battleships were taken, including their admiral's flagship, after the British broke through their line of battle in two places, resulting in a furious mêlée with many ships firing to port and starboard at once. Testament to the ferocity of the combat, and the effectiveness of the British gunnery, is that all seven of the captured Dutch ships in condition to be towed to England were later judged too battered to be worth repairing – a remarkable fact, at a time when many of the best ships in the Royal Navy had been taken from their foes in previous fights.

Even this victory, however, was not without its disturbing domestic elements. One reason the Dutch had been watched so closely was their reported intention to take an army north to link up with disaffected Scottish radicals in Edinburgh and Glasgow. While this plan seems to have been called off, a second reported goal was to take the Dutch fleet to French ports, there to collect an army for the invasion of Ireland. Defeat put paid to this scheme for the time being, giving the authorities in Dublin more time to undermine the United Irishmen. The London crowds, meanwhile, were offered a massive victory parade, and greeted Admiral Duncan as a popular hero. Prime Minister Pitt was less fortunate: his carriage was stoned on the way to the thanksgiving service at St Paul's Cathedral, and he wisely chose to slip away incognito as it ended.[2]

Just as national celebrations could be exposed as a flimsy covering on a cauldron of dissent, so the bellicose unity shown in the House of Commons in November 1797 was something of a façade. Earlier in the summer both Houses of Parliament had decisively rejected motions from Whig supporters of Charles James Fox for political reform and extension of the franchise. The nature and sentiments of the Whig grouping marked out the continued potential for real ideological conflict at the heart of wartime politics. Fox himself was an extraordinary figure, not least in caricature, where his formidable bulk, dark jowls and black eyebrows were an irresistible target. Entering Parliament as little more than a youth in the late 1760s, he rose rapidly to become a leading speaker and political strategist; and arch-rival of Pitt, whose rise ousted him from power in a move Fox ever after saw as little more than royal despotism.

Despite bearing the names of the two Stuart 'despots' of the previous century, Fox led a party that had long held the mantle of protectors of liberty. Some, including Fox himself, had actively welcomed the first, liberal phases of the French Revolution, and throughout the decade sought to resist what they saw as a steady slippage towards 'Pittite' tyranny. When the Duke of Portland led much of the party into effective wartime coalition with Pitt in 1794, Fox and his rump of supporters intensified their hatred, and were in return targets of open scorn.[3] The pro-Pitt caricaturist Gillray did not hesitate to depict Fox's Whigs as leading a French invasion in October 1796, with Pitt tied to a 'liberty tree' and flogged by Fox himself, Burke attacked by John Thelwall, and the Lord Chancellor guillotined as monkey-faced French troops goose-stepped down Piccadilly.[4]

Fox's political career was one of continuous paradox. Despite the connections he carefully maintained with the extravagantly louche Prince of Wales, despite the essentially aristocratic nature of his parliamentary support, despite his own somewhat rakish tastes for high living, gambling and female company, and despite his repeated failure to effectively alter repressive policy, he was, thanks to his extraordinary rhetorical talents, regularly hailed by a wide range of radical and reformist opinion as the people's champion. At the 1796 election, standing for the City of Westminster, which had a particularly wide and thus 'popular' electorate, he denounced Pitt's government for killing more men in wars than Louis XIV, and for having 'attempted the lives of more innocent men at home, than Henry the Eighth'.[5] He won the seat easily, but was almost isolated in the Commons.

The following year, replicating the act of an earlier generation of Whigs disgusted with the government's attitudes towards the American rebels, Fox led his followers in a 'secession' from

Parliament. Though this was little more than a gesture, and had the effect of clearing the way for displays of bellicose unity, Fox also reinvigorated the periodic and elusive connection that his patrician group had maintained with the plebeian radicals of the London Corresponding Society.[6] In May 1797, for example, he publicly shared radical alarm at the harsh suppression of opposition in Ireland, and called for leniency to restore confidence.

In October, in a wide-ranging public speech, Fox defended the rights of the London Corresponding Society leaders detained during the summer. Denouncing the idea that 'upon the whim, caprice or officiousness of an individual, thousands of people of this country were to be silent', he received the Society's written thanks.[7] Through the winter of 1797–8, Foxites and radicals campaigned against new proposals for repressive laws and harsh taxes, and it soon appeared that this was more than merely parallel activity. At least one organising meeting in early January seems to have brought Whigs and radicals together in London, and towards the end of that month, a huge banquet to celebrate Fox's birthday was openly attended by both groups, as hostile MPs later remarked.[8]

To such inimical observers, Fox and his supporters were leaning dangerously close to the revolutionary solutions that the radicals had been accused of advocating since 1792. In his October speech, Fox had asserted the need for radical reform and 'entire and complete change', defined 'popular convulsion' as a lesser evil than the current oppressive circumstances, and gone on to say that 'there are moments in which you are called upon to choose the least evil'. At the January banquet no less a Whig than the Duke of Norfolk, England's premier nobleman, had toasted 'our Sovereign the Majesty of the People', and made a direct comparison between those present and the Americans who rallied to Washington's leadership in the 1770s.[9] For this he was stripped of public offices, including the Lord Lieutenancy of Yorkshire, by Pitt's government.

When Fox himself expressed similar sentiments at the Whig Club, he was struck from the roll of royal Privy Councillors, and for a time at least, Pitt contemplated confining him to the Tower of London. Pitt's friend and ally William Wilberforce, writing even before these outbursts, thought the general tone of Whig speeches 'throws light, if any were wanting, upon their secession. It is my firm opinion that a conviction of their weakness alone prevents their taking up the sword against the government.'[10] This was the internal atmosphere in which Pitt summoned Britons to 'strike home', and in the months ahead, as new taxes were raised and loans subscribed to support this renewed effort, they would indeed do so: in the distant Mediterranean, to glorious effect, and in Ireland, leaving a deep legacy of bitterness and tragedy.

Ireland by the end of 1797 was approaching civil war. Since the attempted French invasion of 1796, United Irish strength had been growing, across the social scale, as independence seemed a realistic possibility. But the same threat forced the government in Dublin to abandon its (admittedly rather half-hearted) policy of neutrality and disarmament in the rising struggle between Catholic Defenders and Protestant Orangemen. The spring of 1797 saw the collision of a rising tide of Defender terror against local authorities in Ulster with a renewed and remilitarised repression. The British allowed Orange lodges to form themselves into official Volunteer corps, and these were deployed, alongside regulars and other Irish and Scots Militia units, under effective martial law.

General Lake, British commander in Ulster, thundered that 'nothing but coercive measures in the strongest degree can succeed in this country'. He explicitly tied the trouble into the United Irishmen's rise: the 'French principles' had penetrated 'the lower order of people & most of the middle class', and these 'determined republicans ... will not be contented with anything short of a revolution'. The policy was approved at the highest level. Home Secretary the Duke of Portland noted that the 'delusion' of the republicans was such that 'mercy and forgiveness' had to be put aside until the 'power of Government' had convinced them 'that there is no means of escaping justice but by throwing themselves on the generosity of the Crown'.[11]

Under cover of an official campaign to seize illicit arms, thousands of households were raided and sacked; suspects were flogged to extract confessions, houses were burned, and all manner of other outrages committed. Waves of refugees began flooding south from Ulster, while others fled to Britain, and even to America. Prodigious quantities of weapons were recovered, bolstering perception both of the threat and of its successful neutralisation.

A different kind of struggle was conducted for the loyalties of Militia regiments throughout Ireland. Government proceeded by a policy of rooting out and executing ringleaders, while pardoning those prepared to confess to having had their loyalties subverted. Thus there were four shootings and seventy pardons in Belfast, two and fifty in Dublin, and similar numbers in other regions. The United Irishmen, meanwhile, continued working to win over the troops, and cells of activists remained in place. Repression emboldened and embittered many, and through the summer of 1797 both the authorities and the United Irish leadership saw a growing republican strength across virtually the whole of Ireland. There now began almost a year of complex calculation and plotting, as all sides acknowledged that the one key ingredient for a successful uprising was an invasion by the French.

United Irish leaders in touch with the French, notably Wolfe Tone, pressed for invasion as soon as possible, but the French leadership was no longer convinced that the effort was worth it. The fleet defeated at Camperdown, seen as threatening such a move, had not been actually committed to it, though the United Irish believed otherwise. Meanwhile, the more extensive the United Irish and Defender networks grew, and the harsher was the British repression, the more voices rose for immediate insurrection: first, lest the British penetrate and break the movement, and second, because from the summer of 1797 there was a growing conviction amongst Catholics that the ongoing repression foreshadowed a full-scale religious pogrom.

This idea may have started amongst the United Irish as a deliberate strategy to encourage Catholic support against 'the murderous Orange faction now lording it through the land', as one republican handbill put it, but it soon ran out of control.[12] Splits between those who urged caution and those who wondered aloud where the French were, and how long the republican cause could survive without them, deepened in late 1797. Reports that the French were planning to invade Britain itself provoked a new realignment. As some United Irish leaders made contact with cells of radical activists in England and Scotland, amidst a continued daily toll of official and sectarian brutality, the idea of a mass national uprising began in early 1798 to gather a momentum of its own.

Rumours of a French invasion plan in the winter of 1797–8 had a solid foundation. An Army of England, in name at least, had been building up on the French coast opposite Dover, and in command of it, after smashing Austria out of the war, was the mercurial General Napoleon Bonaparte. The intention to invade was firmly enough believed by the London Corresponding Society that they actively discussed what to do when the French came; some were disillusioned enough with the militarism on display in Paris that they advocated joining the official Volunteers to resist. Others thought that volunteering would be a good opportunity to gain access to weapons for an insurrection. The point was under debate in April 1798 when police broke in and arrested the whole meeting, ending their dilemma.[13]

By then, however, decisions elsewhere had removed the invasion threat for the foreseeable future. Bonaparte's restless quest for glory was taking him towards Egypt, and a fateful collision with the equally soaring ambition of Horatio Nelson. That encounter would never have taken place, however, without a complex chain of events that linked Irish revolt to the highest levels of diplomacy and war-making.

In early March 1798, authorities in Dublin received intelligence that the United Irishmen's national leadership were to meet on the 12th, to resolve strategic quarrels, with one agent reporting the likely outcome to be 'a rising within four weeks'.[14] A massive police raid netted the majority of the leadership, and left those that escaped partially isolated from events. These were developing rapidly, as networks in several provinces could no longer resist the grass-roots pressure to take action against their oppressors, and sporadic guerrilla fighting broke out throughout the spring across areas of western and southern Ireland.

Meanwhile, to the north, the massive repression in Ulster was crumbling the United Irish strength in their former stronghold, a process aided by news from the south that the conflict was becoming overtly sectarian, driving Protestant republicans out of the movement. Though the situation remained critical, a continued flow of intelligence to the Dublin government showed that their enemies' networks had been thoroughly penetrated. With news filtering through that the French invasion threat was no longer what it had been, Pitt's government in London felt able to take a risky, but fateful decision.

The best chance of removing the pressure of French attention from Britain, and perhaps of encouraging a more productive attitude towards peace, would be to reignite France's conflict in central Europe with Austria. The Habsburg dynasty that ruled from Vienna extended its tendrils of power and influence throughout the Italian peninsula, across Germany through its continuing grip on the office of Holy Roman Emperor, and deep into eastern Europe. With the Prussian monarchy firmly withdrawn into neutrality, and Russia restricted by geography from direct approach, Austrian power was indispensable to balance the rising forces of France. However, though the Austrian armies had been militarily humiliated by Bonaparte, their political leaders had snatched at peace as a chance for gain.

Signed on the same day that the Battle of Camperdown took

place, the Treaty of Campo Formio had given formerly independent Venice and its surrounding lands to the Habsburg court to balance out French dominance elsewhere in northern Italy, and promised French assistance in gaining territory for Austria from its northern neighbour Bavaria as compensation for yielding the distant and troublesome Austrian Netherlands officially to France. From the Austrian point of view it was a classic piece of self-interested diplomacy, and clear evidence that, if the war against revolutionary France had ever been an ideological coalition (which is questionable), it certainly was no longer one by October 1797.[15]

Austria's withdrawal from the war was even more irksome, and indeed painful, for the British government. Some £1.6 million had been paid to the Austrians in loans over the previous two years for the upkeep of their forces against France, under an agreement for repayment which, for complex political reasons, the Austrian government had never formally ratified, and now seemed inclined to ignore.[16] Such an ally might seem almost more trouble than it was worth, but giving up in disgust was not an option, and diplomatic conversations between Britain and Austria continued through the winter of 1797–8. By early April, the Austrians were proposing a new alliance against the French, with the aim also of drawing Prussia and Russia into a united front.

Pitt's ministers hesitated – the proposal hinged on many contingencies, involved Britain in war for other powers' aims, and would cost millions more in loans and subsidies – but there seemed no other way forward. While negotiations persisted, the only feasible way to show direct support for the Austrians was to do as their chancellor had requested in the early spring, and send ships back into the Mediterranean. This would also offer renewed support to the Kingdom of Naples, currently under intense French pressure, but thinned out the defences against French invasion, and many advisors counselled against it.

With some evidence from Dublin that the insurrectionary threat was being contained, Pitt himself chose to roll the dice, and a complex shuffling of newly raised and experienced squadrons went on between British, Irish and Spanish waters to produce the necessary reinforcements. Meanwhile Admiral St Vincent took the initiative of sending the recently arrived Rear-Admiral Nelson into the Mediterranean. The bet was somewhat hedged initially, however, as he cruised to loiter off Toulon with only three battleships and three scouting frigates. The orders from London to send in a full fleet arrived in late May, and Nelson was reinforced to thirteen battleships and four frigates, allowing him to begin his epic chase in earnest.

Ireland, meanwhile, was in flames. Across swathes of the rural south, tens of thousands had risen in rebellion in May, as whole counties fell out of the control of the authorities. Isolated columns and garrison outposts were assailed by waves of insurgents, armed 'with pitchforks, scythes, hay knives, billhooks and other instruments of the farm and field'.[17] In late May, the authorities viewed the situation with optimism, crediting their earlier arrests with disrupting the organisation of the revolt, but by early June a wave of panic set in. 'This Treason is universal' stressed one minister, and the rebels' 'formidable numbers' were supposedly compelling even those who would rather remain neutral to join them, or to flee. 'From Carlow to Dublin ... scarcely an inhabitant is to be seen', and 'very strong reinforcements' were needed, or else Britain would be faced with the need for an actual military reconquest of the whole island.[18] Such alarm was temporary, however, for in truth the Dublin government had done a very good job of blocking the rebels' key objectives even before they rose.

The arrests of the early spring had crippled the United Irishmen's ability to offer decisive leadership. Their plans to appoint military and political commanders to each of Ireland's provinces fell into disarray, leaving rebel columns with little or no strategic direction. The rooting-out of subversion in the local Militia had stripped out a key component of the United Irish plan, which had banked on mass desertions to provide numbers, weapons and rapid military training to the civilian rebels. In Dublin itself, despite the existence of four 'divisions' each claiming between 800 and 1400 adherents, the United Irishmen failed to rise, crippled by leaders' arrests and a wish to wait for decisive French support. Their comrades in the Leinster leadership damned them as a 'cowardly set of rascals', but the authorities, and the propertied classes, had swamped the city with troops and Militia, and a rising would have been a massacre.[19] Meanwhile to the north, in Ulster, the United Irishmen also failed to rise in May, and by the time the leadership called for revolt in June, many rank-and-file had been alienated by news of sectarian massacres of Protestants by southern Catholic rebels. A few days' fighting in the second week of June restored the province to the authorities.

By this stage, the revolt had assumed its definitive, and tragic, form. Sectarian slaughter of Protestant prisoners at soon-to-be iconic sites such as Scullabogue Barn and Wexford Bridge intensified and justified ravages against the insurgents and their supporters by local Protestant Militia and Volunteers, and by a rising tide of English and Scots regiments hastily shipped in. Hunting down 'croppies', the derisive epithet by which the Catholic peasantry were known, took on the dimensions of a blood-sport in many rebellious regions. Widespread reporting of rebel 'outrages' helped harden attitudes, with the press claiming that the Catholic peasants had taken an oath 'By the blessed Virgin Mary, that I will burn, destroy and murder all heretics, up to my knees in blood. So help me God.'[20] Under the intemperate leadership of General Lake, little effort was made to restrain troops bent on massacre, pillage and rape after rebel defeats.

The last major rebel force, some 20,000 gathered at Vinegar Hill near Wexford, was shattered by military assault on 21 June, and though several thousands managed to slip away in the aftermath they were no longer a strategic threat. Their leaders

continued to hope for French intervention, but from the end of
June a combination of savage repression and the offer of an
amnesty by the newly arrived commander-in-chief General
Cornwallis broke up rebel forces decisively. By mid-July, Cornwallis
could report that operations were 'reduced to a predatory system in
the mountains of Wicklow and the bogs of Kildare', the surviving
rebels little more than a 'contemptible' grouping of 'cruel robbers,
house burners and murderers'.[21]

News of the rebellion had sent the United Irish leadership in
French exile into a frenzy, desperately lobbying the Republic for
intervention. Despite their entreaties, the French were willing to
risk only token commitments. A first expedition succeeded in landing a regiment of troops in the western region of Connaught in
August. This stirred the surrounding areas, previously quiescent,
into revolt, and for a time an army of several thousand rebels was
gathered around an enthusiastically proclaimed 'Republic of
Connaught', before crushing repression inevitably arrived. James
Napper Tandy, a longstanding radical amongst the United Irish
leadership, returned from American exile to France early in 1798,
and in September was given a small ship and a supply of arms to
land a rebel force. Arriving in a remote village in Donegal, he
remained on shore for only a few hours before learning of the end
of the Connaught effort, and fled to sea again.

News of the initial success in Connaught had meanwhile
prompted the preparation of a larger expedition of ten ships, bearing some 3000 troops. This was intercepted at sea off the Donegal
coast in October and harried to destruction by an active British
squadron. Amongst the ships captured was the battleship *Hoche*,
fittingly named after the leader of the unsuccessful 1796 Bantry
Bay invasion force. Aboard it was found Theobald Wolfe Tone, in
the uniform of a French general officer. He committed suicide in
prison the following month, after being sentenced to hang for high
treason. The intervention of the French and the Irish exiles had
done nothing but provoke further deaths – the overall toll of the

revolt may have reached 30,000 – and gave Pitt's government further propaganda ammunition by tying the Irish cause irrevocably to the French threat.

Irish revolt had also destroyed what little prospect there might have been of a Whig-led insurrection in England. In an act of noble and foolish principle, almost the whole Whig leadership from Fox downwards appeared as character witnesses in May 1798 for Arthur O'Connor, a prominent United Irishman seized in Kent some months earlier, and now on trial for treason. As revolt raged in Ireland, and O'Connor later confessed to the deeds he was accused of, their declarations that his politics were their own cast them in a grim light. Nor did it help that the Earl of Thanet was soon to go on trial himself for provoking a riot, allegedly seeking to free O'Connor after his initial arrest. With Fox's own cousin, Lord Edward Fitzgerald, a leader of the Dublin rebels, stabbing two officers as they tried to arrest him, and expiring of his wounds shortly afterwards, all these associations consigned the Whigs to irrelevance. Many, indeed, would spend the next year discreetly grovelling to power to regain their social status.[22]

The events in Ireland had unfolded through months in which, hidden from British eyes by distance and unreliable seaborne communications, the ongoing fight with France had entered a dramatically new stage. The British establishment celebrated Nelson's great and 'ever memorable' victory in fine style, notably with a rash of pro-government prints that simultaneously lauded victory over the French 'colossus' and assorted emblematic Nile crocodiles, and mocked the dashed hopes of the Whig opposition for power through national disaster.[23] As news of the Nile had made its way back to London, the British war effort had already been handed another lifeline, thanks to General Bonaparte's presumptuous actions in the Mediterranean. His seizure of Malta had touched a nerve in the quixotic (and somewhat unstable) Russian Tsar Paul I, who took the dispossessed Knights of the island under his protection, seeing their chivalric ideals as a bastion against the infection of the revolutionary spirit.

Russian diplomats were already alarmed by the French incursion into the eastern Mediterranean, a major export route for Russian agriculture via the Black Sea, and offended by exclusion from French-led plans to debate the future of the Holy Roman Empire. When cautious and protracted negotiations for a general anti-French coalition became deadlocked in the summer of 1798, the Tsar decided to throw Russia's weight into the balance regardless. He offered troops to support Austria under a pre-existing treaty, mobilised a corps to help defend the Ottoman Turks if they requested it, and sought an agreement with Britain for as many as 60,000 Russian troops to enter the fight in western Europe.[24]

Given that Austria was currently at peace with France, and still wrangling with Britain about the debts incurred in its last war, putting the Russian offer to work was very far from simple. Since it was further dependent on a substantial British subsidy, it plunged Pitt's Cabinet into months of anxious diplomacy. As an incentive to rejoin the war, £1.2 million had been earmarked for Austria in the spring: Russia could only be supported without breaking the budget if this sum could be split. Austria continued, as it had for the past years, to work for its own interests, which meant getting the greatest number of allies, and the greatest amount of cash, for the least possible commitment.

Notes and envoys flowed across Europe as summer turned to autumn, but by November 1798 the whole process had reached stalemate. Austria persuaded Russia not to accept British cash at its expense, but would not enter a war without a prior Russian commitment, which was not forthcoming without a British subsidy. Russia wanted an Austrian commitment to action before it moved, and both powers were further divided over the role of Prussia: Russia concerned that it should be brought into a general alliance, Austria happier for it to remain neutral.[25]

Into this darkness there suddenly came two points of light. A semi-official communication from Prussia opened up the possibility of cooperation, if the terms were right, on an invasion of France's Dutch satellite. This, coming at a moment when France's conquered Belgian territories were racked by anti-conscription revolts, might be a precursor to driving back the French all along the Rhine. The second glimmer of hope was a note from Vienna that Austria might be about to reopen hostilities on her own account, resisting French efforts to dominate all of Switzerland, which was currently undergoing divisive convulsions. Seeing once again the reviving hope of a general anti-French alliance, the British Cabinet prepared to offer £2 million in subsidies to the German powers, and sent the Foreign Secretary's own brother, Tom Grenville, as an envoy to Berlin with the message.

He would nearly die for the mission, wading ashore across treacherous tidal sands after his ship was crushed by sea-ice off the German coast. The money to fund such an offer had been raised through an innovation that reflected the desperate nature of the times. The recently announced budget for the coming year had included an income tax, assessed at two shillings in the pound on incomes over £200, a full 10 per cent. The tax, with enforced assessment and declarations of income, was damned by the Whig opposition as a 'plan of indiscriminate rapine', but in the continued atmosphere of war emergency, it passed through Parliament with substantial majorities over the winter.[26]

As the tax plan was progressing, British war aims were suffering a setback, thanks in no little part to the hero of the hour, Admiral Nelson. His battered ships had sailed to a rapturous welcome in Naples, all the warmer for the preceding fear of French domination of the Mediterranean: the harbour filled with a flotilla of boats, bands played from the quayside, and the wife of the British ambassador fell in a hysterical faint into the admiral's arm, crying 'Oh God! Is it possible?'[27] Notwithstanding Emma Hamilton's tendency to bestow her affections easily upon heroes, the Neapolitan situation drew Nelson into murky political waters. King Ferdinand of Naples and his vengeful Habsburg wife, Maria Carolina (sister to the executed Marie Antoinette of France), turned their thoughts towards aggressive action in Italy. Abetted by Nelson, who took it upon himself to put his ships at their disposal, they concocted a plan to drive the French out of Rome, and sail 5000 troops north to Livorno to defend Habsburg Tuscany.

Both prongs of the plan were a gamble, and the underlying quest of the queen, who was the guiding force in the royal couple, was to oblige Austria to wade in against an inevitable French counter-attack. When a curt note arrived from Vienna informing them that no such aid would be forthcoming, Nelson was a decisive voice in prompting King Ferdinand to order the attack on Rome anyway. He argued that the French were growing in strength and would advance south sooner or later, providing the choice between action and crushing ignominy. Ferdinand ordered his 32,000 troops forward in late November, but their initial success in driving back the French from Rome was followed by a decisive defeat on 9 December. By Christmas Nelson had been forced to use his ships to transfer the royal court to safety in Sicily, and by the new year Naples was in French hands. To cap the disaster, the Austrian court took the view that the whole thing had been a deliberate provocation by the British to bring them into the war, making them even less likely to agree the grand coalition envisaged from London.[28]

Nelson, perhaps driven by a growing, and consummated, infatuation with Emma Hamilton, and almost certainly influenced by the discovery that he was granted a mere barony, rather than an earldom, for his Nile victory – the official argument being that he had commanded only a detached squadron, and not a full fleet – became something of a loose cannon over the following year. After some ugly involvement in 1799 with Neapolitan politics and the executions of captured rebels, he repeatedly clashed with Lord Keith, the new commander of the Mediterranean fleet, and was guilty on several occasions of disobediences that would have destroyed a lesser officer's career. Crowning this the next year with a vainglorious, and almost openly adulterous, return to England via Vienna, Prague and Hamburg – to a hero's reception, at least from the public – put him on very shaky professional and political ground. However, by the time of his homecoming in November 1800, the ongoing war had taken several sharp turns, and he was soon to be called into dramatic service again.

Ironically, given the failures of diplomacy in 1798, a general war against France had erupted only a few months later, with Austria at the centre of it – but fighting for its own place in the power politics of Europe, not to sustain anyone else's strategic goals. Prussia declined to enter the fight, despite Tom Grenville's efforts, but the initial stunning successes of Austro-Russian armies, driving the French out of Switzerland and northern Italy (with the rest of the peninsula liberated by a Catholic peasant uprising), boosted British hopes of a sudden overall victory. This prompted ambitious plans for an invasion of the Continent, if only an army could be raised in time.

The British Army of the time was never a large force, and recent events had shrunk its effectives critically. Almost every full-strength regular infantry battalion in the British Isles was based in Ireland in early 1799, helping to contain the aftermath of rebellion. The army was still in the process of being rebuilt after an enormously costly commitment to the Caribbean in 1796, when over 30,000 troops were deployed in a massive amphibious armada (the shipping costs alone had been £1 million). Intended to contain slave revolts and seize Dutch and French colonies, this move had been planned as a lightning strike, and succeeded in many of its objectives. However, subsequent delays and confusions had left the bulk of this army ashore on the fever-ridden island of Saint Domingue through the summer, when disease took an appalling toll – some 14,000 soldiers died, and many more were rendered unfit for further service.[29]

Imperial overstretch compounded the always problematic nature of British military organisation. Unlike their enemies in revolutionary France, British ministers had to work within a system that seemed designed to hinder efficient operations. It combined centuries-old suspicion of standing armies with nagging parliamentary oversight, aristocratic exceptionalism and considerable plain corruption. The political will to introduce conscription for regular military service simply did not exist – unlike the time-honoured resort to the press-gang for the Royal Navy's defensive needs. At the highest level, responsibilities were divided and frequently in conflict. The Foreign Secretary and Secretary for War could both claim entitlement to perspectives on strategic relations with allies, and while the Secretary for War was acknowledged as the rightful planner of agreed military operations, he had to liaise with the commander-in-chief (for much of this period the king's second son, the Duke of York), who sat in the Cabinet, but answered directly to the king, not to Parliament.

Meanwhile the commander-in-chief's prerogative of controlling the army was hindered by the ability of officers to purchase commissions (and thus promotions); and by the right of senior officers to refuse to serve under others with less seniority – determined down to the very day on which they reached a certain rank. Some army units, the Artillery and Engineers, fell outside this system altogether: their equipment was managed by the Board of Ordnance, and promotion gained by strict seniority only (which left room for less wealthy professionals to rise, but only very, very slowly, and compelled the promotion of time-serving mediocrities). The Master-General of Ordnance, for much of this period Pitt's indolent elder brother, the Earl of Chatham, also sat in the Cabinet, and those under him defended their prerogatives vigorously.

In the wider field of military operations, further complexity prevailed. The Transport Board had charge of troop movements overseas, while within the British Isles the Secretary-at-War (a position distinct from, and sometimes in conflict with, the Secretary for War) had this responsibility, uneasily combined with a duty to Parliament to monitor military expenditure overall. The Home Secretary, meanwhile, administered the Militia and irregular Volunteer units, and the Commissary General controlled an apparatus for feeding and clothing troops both at home and abroad that was riddled with corruption and inefficiency. All these organs housed men who held their positions through patronage, and who abused them for graft and the peddling of influence – not least because this was the understood nature of such public offices in an aristocratic society where the concept of disinterested public service, as Pitt and some of his followers saw it, was as yet a strange novelty.[30]

Under such circumstances, it was a marvel that any effective military force could be raised at all, and the strains of six years of war, combined with the Irish emergency, were certainly evident. By June 1799, England held only sixteen line infantry battalions, and on average they contained scarcely 400 men each, against a nominal strength of over 700. Over 40,000 troops garrisoned Britain's overseas possessions, but none could be spared for offensive operations without imperilling the security of the Empire.[31]

The weakened state of British defences reflected an essential dilemma at the heart of government about the conduct of the war. On one side stood Henry Dundas, former Home Secretary and currently Secretary for War (a post created for him in 1794). A bluff Scot (and patron of many of his countrymen who entered public service through his influence) whose aristocratic colleagues mocked his inability to match their elegant prose style, he was a long-term friend and ally of Pitt, and a devotee of imperial expansion and consolidation – thanks in part to his high position on the Board of Control of the East India Company.[32] Dundas had been the guiding light behind the 1796 Caribbean expedition, and firmly argued that the war could be won on a global stage: by strangling French contact with the vital resources of the slave islands and the

East Indies, and by securing bases for British merchant fleets (protected by naval supremacy) to penetrate and dominate the markets of Latin America, Africa and Asia. Seeking to involve British forces (or British money) in continental Europe was for Dundas asking for them to be wasted, in one form or another, for the interests of faithless allies. Whatever the advantages of this view, it certainly imposed huge costs: the toll of 14,000 dead in the 1796 Caribbean campaign was added to a similar number already lost in the region since 1793, almost all to disease.[33]

Against Dundas's position stood a view articulated in debate by one of the country's veteran diplomats, Lord Auckland: 'The security of Europe is essential to the security of the British Empire. We cannot separate them.'[34] This position was shared by the current Foreign Secretary, Pitt's cousin, William Wyndham, Lord Grenville. It was a conventional view of the British diplomatic elite, and had guided policy in previous wars, but Grenville added to it an ardent hatred of the French Revolution and all its works, which he called an 'infernal system of atheism and modern philosophy' that could not be accommodated with the existing order: 'In the establishment of the French Republic is included the overthrow of all the other Governments of Europe.'

Gifted with a fine intelligence, Grenville was also cursed with a deeply clannish sense of his own aristocratic distinction – which particularly caused friction with Dundas – and little interest in the views of others. One colleague noted that 'his judgment can never be right' because he declined to see others' perspectives, and his manner could be 'offensive to the last degree'.[35] This combination of qualities led him to be a tireless advocate of a European Grand Alliance, one which could mobilise great armies to an agreed strategic plan following an equally firm political goal of destroying the French Republic, while also blinding him to the fact that potential partners in such an enterprise also had their own agendas and interests to consider – as the painfully futile diplomacy of 1798 had shown.

Despite such limitations, in the aftermath of the mass casualties of previous years' attacks in the Caribbean it was Grenville's view that prevailed in 1799; Russia was still seemingly eager for ideological war against France and Austria at least not unwilling to enter into some agreement. Although the Austrians were never actually brought to sign up to binding collective goals, Grenville's strategic planning assumed that they would cooperate in the interests of war-fighting. The plan, as it emerged in sometimes disjointed discussions through the spring, was for a grand encirclement of France.

Austro-Russian forces would continue their advance through northern Italy and Switzerland into southern and eastern France, and perhaps also threaten the Rhineland, occupied by the French since 1795. This advance would spur royalist uprisings, especially in areas of the south-east which had been hotbeds of revolt in previous years. Meanwhile, the other such hotbed, the north-western regions of Brittany and the Vendée, would be encouraged to continue and expand ongoing uprisings through rather vaguely specified British assistance. To cap this off, a joint Anglo-Russian expeditionary force would land in Holland, liberating the country from its pro-French puppet government and advancing southwards to free the Belgian territories. If all this could be achieved in a first campaigning season, the way would be open, if the French regime had not collapsed already, for a further advance on Paris in the spring of 1800.

3

UNEASY YEARNING FOR PEACE

Lieutenant-General Sir Ralph Abercromby was an outstanding example of the British officer class. Scots by birth, he had studied law in Germany as a youth, but took a junior officer's commission aged twenty-two at the outbreak of the Seven Years' War in 1756. Rising through the ranks thereafter, he also acquired an open mind and a liberal disposition, and as a colonel at the time of the American War of Independence, he declined to go on active service against the rebels whose cause he thought just. For over a decade after that, he remained in civilian life, also serving as an MP for a while, but quitting the seat to pass it to his brother after tiring of the unpleasantness of politics. Recalled to active service in 1793, he was part of the expeditionary forces to the Low Countries under the 'grand old' Duke of York that marched back and forth unsuccessfully, until finally forced to withdraw after a bitter retreat into Holland through the winter of 1794–5. Gallantly and effectively commanding the rearguard, after already having been wounded in action, Abercromby was rewarded with a Knighthood of the Bath, and raised to a major-generalship.

In early 1796, Abercromby reached the Caribbean, in charge of the British plans to finally secure control of the whole region. Tall, upright, honest and plainspoken, solicitous of his men's welfare but Spartan in his own habits (and also extremely shortsighted – he took with him as an aide his son, whose main duty was to tell him what was happening in battle), the general led a lightning campaign. Grenada, St Vincent, St Lucia, Dutch Guiana and Spanish Trinidad fell, often with Abercromby in attendance for the decisive engagements. He also made considerable efforts to resist the impact of disease on his army, moving sick men to healthier upland areas, and adapting uniforms and ceremonial habits to the blazing climate. Thus, despite leaving behind a growing toll of dead, he returned home a hero, with only a few islands still holding out against the British imperial tide.[1]

Promoted lieutenant-general at the age of sixty-three, Abercromby was appointed commander-in-chief of the army in Ireland, where his liberal sentiments clashed violently with the growing feeling amongst the Protestant elite that the rebellious Catholic peasantry needed to be pre-emptively crushed. After weeks of private dispute about the proper role for military force – he wished to restrain the growing tendency for loosely controlled detachments to prey on the population – his views burst out in February 1798 in a public denunciation of his own troops' barbarity and indiscipline. His accusations of 'licentiousness' raised the hackles of the whole political class, and he was effectively obliged to step down the following month. General Lake, who happily took over and intensified the repression, sneered at him for being 'quite in his dotage'.[2]

Abercromby's merits were far from unknown to government, however, and he was soon called on to act as commander of forces in Scotland. He was thus available to lead the first waves of British troops to go ashore on the Continent for almost half a decade, as the ambitious plans to surround and destroy the French Republic in 1799 took shape. Not least of the problems to be overcome from the British perspective was that of recruiting the army to take part in their planned Dutch invasion. The previous year an Act of Parliament had called for 10,000 volunteers from the strictly home-service Militia to be coaxed into the army for a £10 bounty. But the Militia was a power base of patronage and prestige for the leading landowners of the counties, and they had combined, with quite remarkable self-interest, to thwart this Act's application.[3] A second attempt at a slightly more roundabout route to shift men into the army (with a bigger bounty, and a signed commitment not to serve outside Europe) was much more successful, adding some 16,000 men to the colours in the summer of 1799.[4]

Plans were thus laid, after convoluted negotiation with the Russians, for some 30,000 British and 20,000 Russian troops to go ashore in Holland in late summer. The original plans, needless to say, had called for almost twice as many, landing months earlier. Ten thousand new recruits from the Militia, flush with their signing bounties, congregated on the Kentish Downs above Canterbury. Abercromby's first assault wave of regular troops was seen off by a personal visit from Pitt and Dundas, and when news of their suc-cessful landing arrived, the Militiamen were rounded up to salute the ministers with a ceremonial rippling salvo of musketry known as a *feu de joie*. While a witness recorded that 'nothing would be more brilliant' than the 'fine effect' this produced, many of the soldiers had to be dragged out of the taverns of Canterbury and surround-ing villages, and so many were plainly drunk that a planned march-past was hastily abandoned.[5]

Nonetheless, when finally put ashore, the British troops, both regulars and ex-Militia, performed well. This would not be enough to salvage Grenville's grand strategy from disaster. For reasons both political and logistical – not least that the original plans for sea-borne transport would have required the wind to blow in two directions at once – the Russians only contributed about half their allocated total of troops to the Dutch campaign. Those that did take part earned the scorn of the British for their ill-disciplined combination of ferocity and panic, ragged appearance and unscrupulous looting. More significantly, the allied force encountered Dutch troops who were only too willing to fight back, in place of the anti-French rising they had been promised, and a growing force of French regular reinforcements that battered their advance to a stalemate within weeks, despite Abercromby's sterling efforts.

One significant reason for the French strength was that Austro-Russian operations further to the south and east were coming apart at the seams, and thus failing to provide the strategic threat that might have weakened forces in the north. Despite continued victories in Italy, where Milan and Turin were captured, and early Austrian success in repelling French advances across the Rhine, the wider strategy of encirclement broke down at the junction of these two fronts in Switzerland. By August, as a consequence of failure to agree a course of action, wide gaps had opened up in the line of the Austrian and Russian armies, allowing French counter-offensives to threaten their overall position and provoking the main Austrian force to retreat into Bavaria, leaving the remaining Russians exposed. Thus by the time the landings in Holland went ahead, at the end of August, the coalition was already on the defensive, and in fact poised to break up under further French pressure. In late September a decisive defeat for the Russians at Zurich effectively removed them from further campaigning.

By the middle of October 1799, with French strength growing on all fronts, the Anglo-Russian force, now under the overall command of the Duke of York, had to admit that their strategic position was untenable, and on the 15th an envoy was sent to the French commander to ask for an armistice and an agreed withdrawal. The French at first demanded the return of the Dutch fleet, taken to England at the start of the invasion, along with 15,000 prisoners of war held there. They finally gave up the fleet and settled for 8000 prisoners, under the British threat to destroy the sea-dikes and flood huge areas. The British were given until the end of November to complete the withdrawal, which they did in good order, if not good spirits. Ministers and generals consoled themselves over the deteriorating strategic situation with the thought that they had at least rebuilt a viable army capable of overseas deployment.

As the century drew to a close, the British infantry soldier was slowly coming to resemble the figure later to march through so many representations of Napoleonic battles. Although uniform regulations were still less than rigid, the combination of shifting fashions and military practicality had already done away with the cumbrous folded cuffs and almost knee-length coat-tails of the eighteenth-century redcoat. Short jackets, cut away to waist length in front, made marching and kneeling on manoeuvres less onerous, although high-standing collars and leather neck-stocks, designed to keep heads smartly in line, were an additional discomfort. For garrison parades, soldiers retained tight-fitting knee-breeches and high buttoned gaiters, but on campaign they had switched to loose pantaloons – full-length trousers, grey in winter and lighter-weight white for summer or tropical climes. In this they had a persistent advantage over the French, whose regulations continued to insist for all but the most menial of duties on a complex arrangement of gaiters, stockings and breeches, all of which fastened about the knees, and which proved a positive hindrance on extended marches.

The wide eighteenth-century tricorne felt hat, useful for shade but easily knocked off and vulnerable to the ravages of bad weather, had been replaced by the cylindrical shako. Its name deriving from Hungarian (as did, for example, 'hussar' light cavalry), this peaked cap went through several iterations of cloth and leather, and tended to grow in height and decoration over time. The British version was always more restrained than the French, however, which broadened towards the top and was a considerable burden (although providing a neat storage solution for hairbrushes, razors and occasional loot). Of all the armies of Europe, the British had by 1800 one of the most practical uniforms, an irony given the nation's relative lack of interest in military matters.

All the considerations of practicality and smartness in uniform, were, of course, subsidiary to the real job of the infantryman, which was putting his weapons into action. The smoothbore flintlock musket had been the hallmark of infantry combat for a century, especially since the invention of the socket bayonet had allowed a razor-sharp spike to be attached around the end of the barrel without preventing the gun from being loaded and fired. While the techniques of rifling – putting spiral grooves inside the barrel to spin the bullet for greater accuracy – were well-known, the greater precision of manufacturing, routine care, and time needed to load such weapons reserved them for hunters and a very few elite units. British 'Land Pattern' flintlocks had been manufactured to official specifications since 1722. Nicknamed 'Brown Bess' (for reasons unclear) since at least the 1770s, they were an unwieldy weapon, although changes in this later period made them slightly less so. Weighing around ten pounds, with a barrel of forty-two inches in older variants and thirty-nine in others, the musket fired a lead ball almost three-quarters of an inch across (made to be slightly smaller than the actual barrel diameter, for quick loading).

From a distance of fifty yards, an individual musket had only an even chance of hitting the man it was aimed at, but four or five hundred firing together could devastate an opposing line. Eventually, at least, for statistics showed that sometimes hundreds of rounds had to be fired to secure a single enemy casualty – but such was the nature of battle. The complex routine of loading and firing a musket was drilled into soldiers relentlessly, with the intention of making their massed fire a deadly threat. Ammunition came prepackaged in paper cartridges that troops stored in waterproofed leather cases hung at their waist. After biting the top from the cartridge, crunching on the charcoal-sulphur-saltpetre mix inside, the soldier first 'primed' the flintlock action with a trickle of powder before securely closing the lid on this, upending the musket to reach the mouth of the barrel, and pouring the remaining powder and the ball inside. A long ramrod was kept in a groove under the barrel, and this was used to pound home the charge, with the cartridge-paper shoved down on top as a wad to hold it all in place. The ramrod replaced and the weapon brought up to the shoulder again, it only required the spring-loaded jaws holding the flint to be brought back to 'full-cock', and the soldier was ready to fire.

On the parade ground, experienced troops could do all this five times in a minute, but keeping up such a pace for much longer was impossible, and two rounds a minute was a more probable battle-field achievement. Tired, scared soldiers might manage a volley only every minute or two. The musket had a vicious kick, and even veteran troops reported that after firing more than a hundred rounds in a day, their shoulders were blackened and immobile the following morning. On the battlefield, of course, soldiers were also being shot at by similar weapons. The French 'Charleville' 1777 pattern musket fired a slightly smaller ball than the British, but could be no less devastating. Even if not immediately fatal, the relatively low-velocity impact of the bullet made it less likely to pass through tissues cleanly, tending to lodge and aggravate diffi-culties of extraction and infection. Such a ball hitting an arm- or leg-bone, as Admiral Nelson had experienced, was as likely as not to lead to amputation, after which survival was always a question of luck.

To stand and endure such firing – and the longer-range pound-ing of artillery that threw nine- or twelve-pound iron roundshot over a thousand yards – was regarded as the consummate mark of quality in troops, dependent as it was on a resilience much harder to maintain than mere aggressive action. When such troops then had to respond by manoeuvring without losing formation, and keeping up a rapid fire to order, the need for robotic repetition in drill to overcome fear and uncertainty was emphatic. Nervous sol-diers could too easily fire off their ramrods left in the barrel, effectively disarming themselves, or, forgetting to prime the pan, continue to ram cartridges down until, once at last primed, the musket exploded in their face.

In 1799, getting the new waves of troops beyond this 'green' state had been a notable achievement of Abercromby and his subordinates. They had fought five significant engagements – albeit no pitched battles – in six weeks, and returned with most observers acknowledging that a little more experience would make them a truly formidable force. Indeed much of the following year would be taken up with efforts to put them to use again. Months of planning went into a proposed occupation of Belle Isle, off the coast of Brittany, as a base to support royalist insurrection. This was abandoned in favour of raids in strength on Spanish naval bases, aiming to repeat the seizure of the Dutch fleet. Troops were actually landed at Ferrol in northern Spain, but withdrew when the port's fortifications seemed impregnable, and much time was then spent contemplating a similar action against Cadiz. This return to a peripheral, and essentially maritime, strategy was compelled by the disastrous course of events elsewhere.

General Bonaparte, though trapped in Egypt by Nelson's victory, had not been downhearted. French rule from Cairo had been consolidated, while in early 1799 the army advanced north through the Holy Land into what was then called Syria before admitting defeat at a gruellingly unsuccessful siege of Acre. A British naval detachment under the flamboyant Captain Sir Sidney Smith played a crucial role in denying Bonaparte the town, capturing his siege train at sea and joining the defence with their powerful and well-directed artillery. It might also be argued that the brutality that Bonaparte displayed towards the inhabitants of towns he occupied had something to do with Acre's stubborn resistance. In March 1799 he had stormed the town of Jaffa, after two emissaries sent in to call for surrender had been decapitated. In reprisal for this, not only were his troops permitted the normal pillage of the town, with the inevitable rapes and slaughter, but up to 3000 prisoners, including children, were marched to a nearby beach and systematically executed.[6]

Nonetheless, for Bonaparte, it was Smith's role that lingered in his mind, and was long to rankle with him, especially as he viewed Smith as a 'pirate'. The British officer had been in charge of the detachments that burned much of the French Mediterranean fleet during the withdrawal from Toulon in 1793, and when captured on inshore operations in 1796 had been held a prisoner for two years with the threat of criminal charges hanging over him. A subsequent daring escape aided by British spies and French royalist agents (prototype for later fictional adventures) only confirmed his nefarious reputation.[7] Defeat at the hands of such a figure may well have been formative in the later development of Bonaparte's determined hatred of 'English' power and its operations.

Meanwhile, pulling back to Egypt, and nursing an army ravaged by plague (if poisoning those too sick to move can be called 'nursing'), Bonaparte still had plenty of fight. His troops routed a Turkish assault launched with British naval support in July 1799, devastating the landing force at the same Aboukir Bay where his own ships had been smashed a year earlier. The following month, stretching his orders to the limit, he left his army and sailed on a fast ship for France with a select band of followers. News of continued political instability, and the fear that the war might be decided while he was confined to a sideshow, spurred him on, and he made himself the figurehead of a group of conservative republican plotters determined to replace the annual seesaw of elections with a more robust system. In November the plotters struck, with initially rather precarious success, but through the winter Bonaparte imposed his vision of what the new constitution should be: one that left him, as newly coined First Consul, with powers little short of a monarch.

At first this chain of events was seen as a blessing by Pitt's government. The rise of Bonaparte, already famous for his restless ambition, was taken to indicate the crumbling of the republican system, and a step towards a further popular uprising in favour of a restored monarchy. When at Christmas 1799 the First Consul despatched a personal letter to George III calling for peace, the offer was taken as a clear admission of weakness, and thus rebuffed (while also being condemned for its breach of protocol in address-ing the monarch, rather than his ministers). In a debate in the Commons in February 1800, Pitt stated that Bonaparte's 'military despotism' could not be trusted to make peace durably. Two weeks later, goaded by the opposition to declare what the aims of con-tinued war were, Pitt declared unambiguously that he sought 'security against a danger which never existed in any past period of society', and that a restored French monarchy, sweeping away any remnants of the revolutionary system, was his preferred means of achieving it.[8]

Unfortunately the campaigning season of 1800 brought not the collapse of Bonaparte's Consulate, but its vigorous consolidation. With Russia now shunning active engagement, France still faced over 200,000 Austrian troops in southern Germany and northern Italy. While equal forces of about 120,000 each faced off in the Black Forest, Bonaparte led 40,000 across the Alps into Italy to cut off the Austrian army, which was already advancing into the south-east of France. By the combination of aggression and luck that had long been his trademark, Bonaparte won a decisive victory at Marengo in June – a battle he had in fact lost, and which the Austrian commander had left to a subordinate to mop up, when French reinforcements arrived and turned the tide.

General Desaix, leading the charge of his fresh troops, had the courtesy to be shot dead, leaving all the glory for the First Consul. Within a day the Austrian commander called for a truce, and sub-sequently acknowledged his strategic defeat by agreeing to evacuate all of north-western Italy. After a brief general truce, fighting further north resumed at the end of the year, and France's General Moreau crushed the Austrian army in Germany at Hohenlinden. After Marengo it was clear that France was not going to be defeated; after Hohenlinden, with French troops only a few dozen miles from Vienna, peace if it came would be at least on equal terms, if not at Bonaparte's dictation.

Hopes of internal subversion in France faded almost as quickly. Bonaparte showed how deep his ruthlessness ran when the victorious General Moreau, enjoying his fame in Paris, was arrested and banished for becoming a figurehead of discontented salon discussion. Moreau had been higher on the list of potential figureheads than Bonaparte during the plotting of the previous year, but had personally recommended him for the role.[9] Various other plots for assassination and dethronement, including the explosion of an 'infernal machine' in the rue Niçaise in Paris in December 1800, became excuses for thoroughgoing purges of both left- and right-wing suspects, and the consular regime seemed to grow more secure with each attack.

Throughout 1800 Britain had been kept on the fringes of the conflict by strategic indecision, its troops floating around the coasts of Spain and the western Mediterranean unable to intervene effectively. Meanwhile the home front brought further uncertainty and rising problems, with politics and nature conspiring to bring something close to chaos. A run of appallingly bad weather, including both torrential rains and droughts by alternation, had led by the autumn of 1800 to a critical shortage of basic food-grains. Shortages had already been felt after the previous year's harvest, and had provoked time-honoured popular responses – after one food riot in Huddersfield in November 1799, a woman was sentenced to a year's imprisonment for seizing and selling grain to an 'immense mob ... consisting principally of women' who had invaded the market-place.[10] By February 1800, the anti-Jacobin newspaper *True Briton* was earnestly cautioning against hoarding of grains by millers and bakers during 'the present dearth and scarcity', seeing in such actions the start of a process that 'will infallibly produce the effect that is meant to be avoided'.[11]

The result of yet another poor harvest in 1800, as a senior Guards officer reported to a diplomat friend, was what 'in any other Country than this ... would be called Famine'. The President of the Board of Trade, the Earl of Liverpool, warned the Cabinet in October of the likely consequences:

> there will be Insurrections of a very serious nature, and that different Bodies of Yeomanry may possibly fight each other ... those of the Cities and great manufacturing Towns, who are adverse to the Farmers will fight those of the Country, who will be disposed to defend them.

Such events, he warned, threatened to 'shake the Foundations of the Government of Great Britain'.[12]

The onset of deep distress was sudden and shocking, and its consequences horrifically real. Prices of basic grains almost tripled, forcing families to slash expenditure on all but essentials, and thus adding a commercial slump and subsequent fall in employment to the shortage. Numbers tell part of the story: as much as a fifth of the population was in receipt of support, or 'relief', from the age-old Poor Rate system by 1801. In the previous year the death rate in Norwich, to take one example, had risen by a quarter, and much of that rise was due to the deaths of children. Hunger imposed awful choices. Three Hertfordshire families were prosecuted for 'nearly starving to death' their daughters – seen perhaps as useless mouths – while many working men went so short of food that reports of them fainting, even at the coal-face, became commonplace. Theft and vagrancy rose steeply, as did military enlistment, a traditional refuge of the desperate and marginal.[13]

Those communities not yet reduced to desperation began to seek remedies for their grievances. Across the country there were 'blockades' by rural communities to prevent grain leaving for distant markets; and in urban markets protests and seizures of food stocks for sale at lower, 'just' prices. Yeomanry, Militia and Volunteer corps, alongside regular troops, were in action far and wide, and not always with a united agenda. Volunteers in particular notably refused to muster for action against local crowds on an alarming number of occasions.[14]

In reality the situation never came to actual clashes between bodies of troops, but troops that did act found themselves the subject of aggrieved protest from local authorities. As had been the case in many previous, if less drastic, episodes of shortage through the century, local magistrates widely shared crowds' concerns that high prices and shortages were stoked by illegitimate speculation. In 1800 and 1801 many were prepared to ignore recent statutes and reimpose customary restrictions on the movement and sale of foodstuffs outside established markets, effectively surrendering to the agenda of rioters and their expression of a 'moral economy' divorced from dogmas of free trade.[15] If the authorities had taken the approach of the government in Ireland to disorder, and if regular troops had been allowed to behave in Britain as they had there, then it is quite likely that local Militia and Volunteers would have opposed them. Though ministers thundered about the illegal actions of the magistrates who appeased rioters, the basic sympathy many protests received probably prevented them becoming something much worse.

Fear of that worse outcome remained, however. Pitt's government was so concerned to reinforce the home front that it pulled out several thousand regular troops from Portugal. This exposed their ally in early 1801 to a Spanish invasion, known as the 'War of the Oranges'. A fortunately brief and relatively bloodless episode, it nonetheless saw Portugal's ports closed to British trade by the subsequent treaty for several years. The willingness to risk this highly predictable outcome is testimony to the domestic threat perceived in Britain. Instability played into the hands of a democratic opposition that continued to be active and widespread, and whose message of the perfidy of the aristocratic ruling elite chimed perfectly with the dire times.

Months before the food crisis reached its first peak in the autumn of 1800, that threat had already been demonstrated in the

most direct fashion. On 15 May 1800, George III's box at the theatre was shot at with a pistol by a silversmith, former soldier and
prisoner of war, James Hadfield. Although he pleaded insanity at
his trial, information from government spies, which could not be
publicly used without exposing them, connected him to democratic groups in the capital. Moreover, earlier on that same 15
May, in an incident hastily covered up as an accident, a serving soldier took a shot at the king under cover of a *feu de joie* at a review
in Hyde Park. Even *The Times* found the official explanation neither 'conclusive nor satisfactory', while one soldier who witnessed
the event announced the king would be 'done for' before his birthday parade on 4 June, and another was heard to declare, 'By God
he deserves to be Shot.'[16]

Rumours of London risings, led by the same Guardsmen whose
loyalties had been questioned during the mutinous events of 1797,
brought 'great expectations' to Birmingham radicals, and presum-
ably others, through the summer. By the time the shortages began
to bite, seditious and republican graffiti chalked on London walls
was such a problem that local constables were issued with buckets
and sponges for special patrols to clear it away. In Manchester the
magistrates reported that 'the Public Eye is dayly saluted with
Sedition' in the same form, and 'whether the subject regards Bread
or Peace NO KING introduces it'.[17]

In London in September 1800 handbills were posted, showing
clearly both the physical organisation of the dissidents in their production, and the comprehensive nature of their arguments:

FELLOW COUNTRYMEN how long will ye quietly and
cowardly suffer yourselves to be imposed upon, and half-
starved by a set of mercenary slaves and Government hirelings?
Can you still suffer them to proceed in their extensive monopolies, while your children are crying for bread? NO! Let them
exist not a day longer. We are the sovereignty, rise then from
your lethargy. Be at the Corn Market on Monday.[18]

Six days of rioting followed. This was national news, reported in the regional press as far away as Aberdeen, with detailed accounts of the 'immense concourse' of people 'clamouring for bread', and the various Militia and Volunteer units called upon by the Lord Mayor to help restore order.[19] Two months later, troops had to be used to drive away crowds called to Kennington Common for a similar cause. Across the country, notorious centres of 'Jacobinism' like Nottingham, Sheffield and the Lancashire mill-towns produced further examples of seditious agitation. Oath-taking and the formation of 'secret societies' was widely noted, along with claims of the stockpiling of arms, and florid reports of nocturnal meetings, masked orators, and secret correspondence being read out and burned.

The spring of 1801 brought further alarms, as the food crisis continued and the repressive legislation of 1795 expired. With habeas corpus once again in force, men who had been detained on suspicion, in some cases for several years, returned to the streets and to their old associates. A rash of newly legitimate public meetings were called, tying exorbitant prices to corruption in 'Hereditary Government'. Printed demands echoed the calls of Thomas Paine in the early 1790s for free education, protection for the elderly, and political justice above all, with a sometimes apocalyptic tinge: 'we are the sovereignty . . . Drag the constitution from its hidden place – and lay it open to publick inspection – Shake the Earth to its centre . . . '[20] Government swiftly responded by reimposing the ban on 'Seditious Meetings' and suspending habeas corpus for a further year, though reports of secret meetings continued.

The shocking force and depth of the crisis in 1800 and 1801 is all the more remarkable for passing away as suddenly as it arrived. The 1801 harvest was very good, and by the end of 1802 a humble Oldham weaver could record in his diary a trenchantly joyful account of the times:

Such a Cristmas for Roast beff pies and Ale etc as was never witnessed by the oldest person living for Such was the power

of All Famileys by the Goodness of all Sorts of Trade that one
family vied with A nother wich could Give the greatest treat
to its neighbour and nothing but mirth Glee and Harmony
was Seen during this Great Festivity.[21]

The contentment of the Oldham weavers was all the greater for
living in a country at long last at peace – a peace that Pitt had
sworn not to make, but which came after he had abruptly surrendered his office for reasons quite unrelated to the food crisis or the
French threat.

It was a pacification of another kind which brought down Pitt.
Ireland had still been reeling from the aftershocks of brutal rebellion and repression when plans began to be put forward for a
political solution to its troubles. Lord Cornwallis, Viceroy and
commander-in-chief in Ireland, a man who had faced defeat at the
hands of American rebels, and gone on to both military conquests
and new political settlements in India, saw the need for a radical
answer even as his troops were still chasing Irish rebels in remote
western bogs. The key problem of Ireland, as Cornwallis and others
around Pitt saw it, was the disastrous intertwining of politics and
religion. Power lay in the hands of a Protestant Ascendancy viscer-
ally opposed to conciliation of the more numerous Catholic
population, and granted the autonomy from Britain to maintain
oppressive relations even when it harmed the greater imperial interest. The solution of the United Irishmen to this conundrum had
been, of course, a non-sectarian and independent republic. The
British solution was Union.

The Irish Parliament would cease to exist, with revised and
enlarged constituencies sending 100 new members instead to
Westminster. The government spokesman Lord Hawkesbury, speaking in the House of Commons (as he was not a peer, but holder of
a courtesy title as son of the Earl of Liverpool), made the case for
the plan emphatically on 25 April 1800. 'The collision of contending factions' was dragging Ireland to 'ultimate destruction', but 'let

this Union take place – all Irish party will be extinguished; there will be no more parties but the parties of the British Empire.' What Hawkesbury called Britain's 'strength' and the 'constitution of her Parliament' would 'enable her to keep all such parties in subjection, and to secure to every member of the Empire the possession of its religion, its property and its laws'.[22]

Such rhetoric was all very well, but it did not answer – in fact it enhanced – the perceived threat voiced by opposition spokesmen in these debates. One, Charles Grey, had a few days earlier denounced the proposed hundred new MPs as an opportunity for the Crown to add a 'regular band of ministerial adherents', only able to win their seats in costly elections when 'supported by the Treasury', and thus fated to become the 'constant and unalterable supporters' of the holders of power. After Hawkesbury spoke, William Wilberforce, old friend of Pitt and veteran moral reformer, announced that he also feared the 'very considerable addition to the influence of the Crown' proposed. Indeed, he 'never felt his mind more tremulously uncertain than on the present occasion'.[23]

Certainly, the large sums that the Crown was prepared to expend on the process suggested the extent of the benefits to be gained. Overtly, £7500 was to be paid to each of the proprietors and patrons of abolished Irish boroughs, such proprietorship being a stark reminder of how undemocratic the existing system had been. Meanwhile, covertly, five-figure sums were spent on direct bribes and lifetime payments to Irish MPs induced to vote for the plans, alongside a very visible shower of honours and peerages.[24] These proceedings, which while concealed were yet assumed as the obvious method of working, strained the consciences of the opposition, but they could not come close to impeding the process of Union. For that, it needed the conscience of a king.

George III informed Cornwallis, as plans were advancing in January 1800, that he was 'a strong friend to the Union of the two Kingdoms'. However, he went on, he would become 'an Enemy' if the plan involved a 'change of the situation of the Roman

Catholics'.[25] Here was the rub, despite Hawkesbury's bland assurances about 'possession of its religion' for every part of the Empire. Cornwallis had always been clear that only Catholic emancipation, entitling 'papists' to political participation on the same, albeit limited and property-bound, basis as Anglicans, could hope to ease the inherent tensions of Irish society. Without it, and with the planned retention of an essentially authoritarian Dublin government answerable to Westminster, Ireland would remain little better than a subjugated colony. But for the king, this was a point he could not concede. His coronation oath bound him absolutely, and it bound him to deny entry to the body politic for adherents of the Papacy, and indeed also for any other heretics and dissenters. Though in asserting this the king contradicted the government's own legal advice on the subject, he was immovable.

This had given Pitt a conundrum to wrestle with throughout the process of Union. Irish Catholics might be disenfranchised, and most of them might be benighted peasants, but a fair proportion formed a rising middle class, and their tacit approval, at least, was important if Union was actually to end republican and nationalist agitation. Thus, from the end of 1798 on, the message had gone out to such Catholics that emancipation would come with Union, that public silence on the matter was tact in the face of the potentially mutinous Protestant Ascendancy, but that the good faith of Pitt's ministry could be relied on once the deal was done.

Legislation for the Union was consummated late in the summer of 1800, and on 1 January 1801 Britons and Irish alike awoke to find themselves in a new country, the United Kingdom of Great Britain and Ireland, with a new flag, the red diagonals of St Patrick now interlaced with the red, white and blue of St George and St Andrew. In accepting this radical shift in the nature of his realm, George III had agreed to give up the claim, asserted since the Middle Ages, that kings of England were also kings of France (it was after all only polite, when fighting to restore the Bourbons to their throne). He also demurred at the suggestion that he should become 'Emperor of the British and Hanoverian Dominions' – unfashionably refusing an aggrandisement shortly to become all the rage on the Continent.[26] George III, however, was an unfashionable man, and his unfashionable resistance to Pitt's rational views on religion and politics would now prove a decisive sticking-point.

Pitt's plan, which he shared with fellow ministers (but not the king) in the summer of 1800, was for an end to the penal 'Test Acts' which barred both Catholics and Dissenters from office. The new, broader body politic thus created would be further cemented in its unity by a revised loyalty oath for office, putting revolutionary republicanism rather than popery and heresy at the focus of enmity. Practical measures to ease the injustice of Church tithes in Ireland, and fairer pay for all clergy, rounded out a package which Pitt, with seventeen years as Prime Minister behind him, believed that the king could be made to accept.[27] But Pitt, with the burden of those seventeen years upon him, in poor general health and prone to painful attacks of gout, was forgetting that there were other politicians in the country. After the Prime Minister called a Cabinet meeting in September to finalise the proposals, Lord Chancellor Loughborough, who had deserted his Whig comrades in opposition to join the government some years before, showed his slippery character by briefing the king against Pitt's plan.

Pitt's failure over the next few months to do anything substantial to alleviate the king's growing outrage became a clear marker that this was a man no longer master of events. He cajoled the Cabinet towards continued unity with assurances that matters were in hand, while postponing a reckoning with the only man who really counted. By the end of January 1801, with Union achieved, Pitt pushed a Cabinet meeting into agreeing to put the religious proposal on the legislative agenda. A few days later the king exploded with rage at a public reception, demanding to know 'What is the Question which you are all about to force on me ... that you are going to throw at my head?' He declared unequivocally that 'I shall look on every Man as my personal Enemy, who proposes that Question to me.'[28]

Exchanges of notes over the following days revealed two men unwilling to back down from their basic positions: a king resistant on the specific point about Catholicism, but also resentful at what he felt to be marginalisation from aspects of government where he had a God-given right to be consulted; and a Prime Minister certain that he was the head of the government, and entitled to expect the king not to publicly disown his policies in advance. Despite professions of affection and loyalty on both sides a breach was inevitable, and Pitt's resignation was accepted on 5 February 1801.[29]

What followed was a truly extraordinary episode. Pitt and the king effectively agreed on a successor, Henry Addington, then Speaker of the Commons, a figure who owed his political career entirely to Pitt. Such a move led Charles James Fox to judge the whole affair 'a mere juggle' for mysterious motives. But almost all the senior figures in Pitt's Cabinet resigned with him, leaving Addington to compose a team which, by comparison, looked distinctly second-rate. Addington himself was dismissed by Dundas as 'totally incapable' of running a government, while the Whig Richard Brinsley Sheridan fulminated in the Commons about his ministers: 'the right honourable gentlemen had literally knocked out the brains of the administration'. He mocked the idea that this 'empty skull, this skeleton administration' could manage to 'overawe our enemies' and 'command the confidence of the House and the people'.[30]

To make matters worse, at the very moment that the ministers were due to change over, the king lapsed into a ferocious episode of madness, unseen since his great crisis of 1788–9. While the unspoken question of how much his recent vexations had contributed to this state hovered over them, Pitt's Cabinet nonetheless literally could not resign, as there was no sane monarch to return their seals of office to. For several months, the country was run by a bizarre parallel administration: Addington's Cabinet met without any official authority, but as de facto government, while Pitt's Cabinet met as office-holders, and were still consulted on major decisions for which their official approval was required. Since Pitt also continued to advise Addington personally behind the scenes, the whole thing seemed very like a farrago, and it was during these months of confusion that habeas corpus came, perhaps unintentionally, back into force, releasing a new wave of internal agitations. It unfortunately also coincided with a further low ebb in the fortunes of war.

The Russian Tsar Paul, already aggrieved at the lack of success of the various combined operations of recent years, had by the end of 1800 reached the end of his rather short tether. When he learned that the British were refusing to hand back Malta, recovered from the French after a lengthy siege, to his beloved Knights, the Tsar began to make secret overtures to France for a grand strategic alliance, and even issued orders to send 22,000 Cossacks through central Asia to threaten India. Meanwhile in the Baltic he lent a welcoming ear to the protests of Denmark about oppressive British insistence on blocking the access of their ships to French-controlled ports. Sweden and Prussia were prodded into joining Russia and Denmark in a League of Armed Neutrality, to threaten not only a counter-blockade against British commerce, but also the occupation of George III's German territory of Hanover, until now protected by a Franco-Prussian agreement in 1795 to 'neutralise' all of northern Germany. British ministers saw little choice but to order an embargo on the Baltic powers' shipping in late January 1801, initiating an effective state of war.[31]

At a stroke, a powerful ally had become a leader amongst dangerous enemies, and mere weeks later more bad news followed.[32] After bullying negotiations, Bonaparte's France forced Austria to sign the Peace of Lunéville on 9 February 1801. This conceded Belgium definitively to France, and also began a process whereby French possession of the Rhineland and dominance over western Germany would be officially acknowledged by the institutions of

the increasingly moribund Holy Roman Empire. It further consolidated French control of Italy, and by handing Tuscany to a
Spanish Bourbon prince, completed a bargain agreed with Spain
the previous year for the return to France of the vast territories of
Louisiana – the whole western bank of the Mississippi – given away
in 1763. (Napoleon would shortly sell these vast but currently
unprofitable lands to President Jefferson's USA, helping to open the
American 'frontier' for the next century.)[33] Following this up with a
quick military defeat of Naples, which had reinvaded Rome after
Austrian successes further north since 1799, France rounded off its
hegemony of western Europe by prompting Spain into the 'War of
the Oranges' that cut Portugal off from British trade. It would take
a striking turnaround for Britain to regain anything approaching a
favourable position from this diplomatic débâcle.

4

PEACE THROUGH WAR, AND WAR FOR PEACE

On 8 March 1801, the much-abused Aboukir Bay saw yet another decisive military event, as General Abercromby took his army ashore. After long tergiversations, the British leadership had finally decided on action to oust the French from Egypt and secure control of the Mediterranean. The benefits of recent experience of combined operations were shown as troops landing from small boats quickly shrugged off artillery fire on the beach and a hasty French counter-attack.[1] After a second victory five days later, the cautiously advancing British force reached Alexandria on 21 March, and inflicted a decisive defeat on an evenly matched French army of 12,000. French columns hurled their weight against thin British lines, in a prototype of many battles to come, and were driven off with disciplined volley fire. One battalion, the 28th Foot (later the Gloucesters), earned immortality, and the right ever after to wear a second badge on the back of their hats, by abruptly about-facing the rear rank of their formation to drive off an encircling French thrust.

General Abercromby, who had done much to instil the pride and discipline which made this success possible, was fatally wounded during a last, desperate French cavalry charge. A bullet lodged in his thigh-bone turned gangrenous, and he suffered for a week before finally succumbing.[2] It was not a good end for a man who had become a hero in his sixties and set an example for a generation of leaders who would carry his virtues forward into the new century. He was memorialised in marble in St Paul's Cathedral, captured at the moment he fell from his horse, and his widow was granted a posthumous peerage to pass on to his heirs.[3]

So clear was the significance of the victory that the government ordered an official account circulated, and read out to boost the morale of Militia and Volunteer units. The press dwelt on Abercromby's character at length, though some did not hesitate to embellish the tale of his death: the *Caledonian Mercury* appended a disquisition on the general's imprudence in exposing himself to the wholly mythical 'assiduously trained' riflemen of Bonaparte's army, specially designated to pick off Turkish generals because an Ottoman army supposedly 'flies and disperses' when its leader falls. Though this was perhaps what we would now call an urban legend, it was followed with the quite correct note that the British Army was beginning its own experiments with riflemen, and the anecdote overall suggests just how closely, and speculatively, the public followed the war.[4]

With a second British force arriving from India via the Red Sea, and taking control of Suez unopposed a few days after Abercromby's victory, the British cut off two separate bodies of French troops in Cairo and Alexandria.[5] Both would surrender after a grim summer of siege, revealing that they outnumbered the shocked British by two to one. Word of this strategic defeat made its way slowly back to both London and Paris, where the news of further startling events to the north was already being digested.

While Abercromby's troops were advancing on Alexandria, a naval task force was sailing towards the Baltic. Despite their odd composition, the combined Pitt and Addington Cabinets had agreed on decisive action to head off the threat of the Armed Neutrality. Reliable opinion gave the Russians, Swedes and Danes a combined naval strength of over ninety battleships, enough to overwhelm available British forces if allowed to unite in aggressive action. While an Armed Neutrality did not necessarily presage an all-out war, the risk was too great to accept. Admiral Sir Hyde Parker was dispatched at the head of a squadron assembled from the Channel and North Sea fleets, moving towards Denmark as the winter ice retreated. He was a prudent and diplomatic commander, and paused his ships near the Sound, between Denmark and Sweden, while political discussions took place.

Under him as deputy, however, was Vice-Admiral Nelson, no longer quite the shining hero of his Nile days, his overt liaison with Emma Hamilton having tarnished his social reputation.[6] His naval reputation as a stop-at-nothing leader of battle was fully intact, however, and he saw the Scandinavian powers as little more than an obstacle between his ships and a decisive engagement with Russia, key to restoring British dominance in the region. As talks came to nothing at the end of March 1801, Nelson led his ships through the narrow Sound towards the Danish capital of Copenhagen, where both the Danish fleet and an assemblage of gunboats and floating batteries had been hastily made ready to receive them.[7] After the refusal of a final ultimatum sent in by a frigate, Nelson took his twelve battleships into action against the city's defences on 2 April.

Although like the Nile it was a battle against a fixed enemy position, it lacked any of the dash and daring of that encounter. Three of the British ships ran aground in the shallow waters, and the remaining nine, picking their way slowly forward, were engaged more fiercely than they had anticipated – some of the low-lying floating batteries had been unobserved until they began to fire. From about ten in the morning the ships were locked in combat, anchoring about 200 yards from the main Danish line, pounding furiously, and being pounded in return with unexpected vigour. The Danes had been thought to be shy of a fight, but were doggedly determined to defend their capital. Their defiant courage caused Admiral Parker to reconsider; he was having difficulty bringing his own reserve ships up in support against the wind, and at 1.15 p.m. hoisted a signal for withdrawal.

At this point Nelson (according to later reports) gilded his own legend with the declaration that 'I have only one eye – I have a right to be blind sometimes ... I really do not see the signal.' There were good practical reasons for ignoring it: retreat would have been slow and difficult and quite likely would have seen several ships crippled under fire. Moreover, the Danish defences were at last beginning to slacken their fire, with some of their anchored vessels ablaze and over a thousand dead already inflicted. Only half an hour later, Nelson sent in a note proposing a truce. Magnanimously addressed 'To the Brothers of Englishmen, the Danes', it warned of Nelson's need to burn more of the floating batteries 'without having the power of saving the brave Danes who have defended them' if firing did not cease.[8]

Taken in by a small boat that had to skirt the raging combat, the offer did not arrive until 3 p.m., when it was accepted at once, and Nelson was able to pull out his ships having suffered over 250 killed. Eleven Danish vessels were burned, there being no way of safely getting them away as prizes. Negotiations followed, during which Nelson at one point had to remind the Danes that his ships remained in position, equipped with mortar-throwing bomb ketches, to bombard Copenhagen itself. A collapse of Danish objections after several days was occasioned by a piece of news that they kept secret from the British, and that Nelson did not learn until he had sailed his patched-up ships further east and north: the Tsar was dead.

Paul was murdered on 23 March by a widespread court conspiracy, wearied of his erratic changes of policy. He was probably not actually mad, but close enough to it for no one except his wife to try to protect him. Overwhelmed and strangled after defending himself

at swordpoint in his own bedroom, when his beloved Knights of
Malta failed to guard the doors, he was succeeded by his son,
Alexander, who immediately set in train the dissolution of the
Armed Neutrality and pledged peace with Britain. News of this,
combined with the result of Nelson's battle, is said to have brought
a cry of despair from Bonaparte, who declared 'that the blow had
come from England'.[9] British forces could now withdraw from the
Baltic with honour, their rights to police the high seas reinforced,
and French designs to dictate policy across all the continent
severely checked. The Prussians, who had occupied Hanover as
their contribution to Tsar Paul's plan, held out for a few months in
a vain hope that the territory might fall to them as part of a general
settlement, but finally agreed an evacuation in October 1801, as
events elsewhere were bringing this period of general European
warfare to a close.

Peace negotiations had in fact been going on in desultory
fashion for almost a year. The French envoy in London who han-
dled the exchange of prisoners, Louis Otto, had forwarded a
suggestion as early as August 1800 to extend a temporary military
armistice to cover a cessation of naval hostilities. Since navies
could not just halt in place like armies, in practice this would
mean lifting the blockade of both France and Egypt, and the siege
of Malta (shortly to fall to the British), with nothing offered in
compensation. It was thus refused, as were later requests for similar moves – they were little more than Bonaparte chancing his arm
on the possibility of British desperation.[10] Nonetheless, Foreign
Secretary Grenville did not categorically rule out the possibility of
discussion, and so a hesitant series of manoeuvres, between and
around the rollercoaster succession of military and political events,
continued into early 1801. When George III was finally in a position to confirm Addington's Cabinet in their posts in mid-March
1801, meaning among other things the removal of the ardently
anti-revolutionary Grenville from his ministry, conditions were
ripe for progress.

Even before news of British successes arrived, the new Foreign Secretary, Lord Hawkesbury, had written via Otto openly asking to discuss terms, and a first face-to-face meeting between the two men occurred on 21 March – the day of Abercromby's distant victory.[11] By early April, the opposing sides' views had become clear: Britain offered a general return of territories outside Europe (a proposal which included a French evacuation of Egypt); France demanded to keep Egypt, along with regaining all the other territories lost to Dundas's drive for colonial supremacy. Over the next six months, the British terms did not vary much from their opening position. Early on in discussions in mid-April, they hardened a little as the military balance tilted, so that Hawkesbury proposed retaining some of the most strategic of British conquests – but notably these were largely islands taken from the Spanish and Dutch, not from the French themselves. As a series of meetings and exchanges of let-ters proceeded into and through the summer of 1801, the French position shifted dramatically several times.

Sometimes descending to peremptory demands, often making assertions about entitlements absent from the core agenda, and reinforced by the ostentatious gathering of an encamped army on France's Channel shores, the French approach was quintessen-tially Napoleonic. It took no account of the other side's legitimate interests, asserted both grievances and supremacy as fact, and made repeated thrusts and diversions in an effort to unbalance its oppo-nent.[12] At one point the British riposted by suggesting that consideration should be given to withdrawing France to its pre-war borders of a decade earlier. There was absolutely no prospect of Bonaparte doing so, but it made the point that both sides could be absurdly demanding, if they chose.

British resilience in the face of such tactics made a sharp contrast to the Russians' eagerness to extricate themselves from ongoing conflicts on all sides in Europe. While Britain gave Russia a reasonable deal, saving their diplomatic face after Tsar Paul's reckless adventures, Bonaparte's France extorted agreement from

the over-confident new Tsar Alexander to effective French hegemony in Italy and assistance in settling affairs with the Turks, all in
return for vague noises about Russian influence in central Europe –
where Bonaparte was happy to let the Russians tangle with Prussian
and Austrian power if they chose.[13]

As these negotiations moved ahead, by midsummer the outline
of an Anglo-French settlement was growing clearer, and grew
clearer still as news began to arrive of the parlous state of the
French in Egypt. By late July the French at last conceded that
Egypt might be returned to the Turks. Momentum for a settlement
grew with news of a further defeat for a French squadron near
Gibraltar, and as Admiral Nelson, posted to the south-east coast of
England to counter the threat of invasion, led daring raids in
August to sink and burn ships of the gathering flotilla.

Even in France crowds began to expect a peace – one British
diplomat, passing through on his way to Vienna, reported that at
Calais his cheerful popular reception gave way to gloom when he
proved not to be the bearer of a treaty. Agreement came finally at
the end of September, basically along the lines suggested by the
British in April. Just as in the battle of Alexandria, daring French
thrusts had come to nothing against a dogged British defence.
Active combat ceased in October, though the final treaty was not to
be signed, after a great deal of further, largely pointless haggling
between parties of diplomats quartered at Amiens in northern
France, until March 1802.

While peace brought rejoicing, it did not end the British government's anxieties, nor many of the activities which gave them most
cause for alarm. Two remarkable trials that came to a climax early
the following year demonstrate the juxtaposition of continued internal and external problems. The first was that of Colonel Edward
Despard, which produced the last sentence of hanging, drawing
and quartering ever pronounced by an English court. Despard was
in his early fifties, the product of a landowning family, and had

enjoyed a lengthy military career. He had served in the Americas for nearly two decades, and at his trial was able to call Admiral Nelson as a character witness to attest to his patriotic and professional dedication in service against the Spanish in 1780. But returning to Britain a decade later, placed on half-pay and unemployed, Despard was led into the rising movement of underground radicalism, and particularly that associated with the liberty of his native Ireland.

What combination of new-found idealism and private grievance may have been involved is impossible to weigh, though it is notable that in the plots for which he became notorious, the rewards of rank and wealth were often held out as enticement. Nonetheless, he was clearly involved with both the London Corresponding Society and the United Irishmen at the time of their most dangerously conspiratorial operations in 1797–8, and in the latter year was amongst those rounded up for detention without trial. He remained in custody until the temporary restoration of habeas corpus in early 1801, and seems thereafter to have gone straight back to work.

The interplay of internal conspiracies and external threats in these turbulent years was impressed distinctively on the public imagination by their presentation pell-mell in the columns of national and local newspapers. The *Bury and Norwich Post*, for example, on 22 April 1801 reported on one page the following: Whig objections in Parliament to 'indecorous haste' in bringing forward repressive measures in a Sedition Bill; a detailed account of the Battle of Copenhagen; news from Jersey of menacing military movements on the French coast; confirmation of the death of Tsar Paul (from an 'apoplectic fit'); word from Paris of the Prussian advance on Hanover (and in another column of its postponement upon news of the Tsar's death); and a report from a 'Secret Committee' of the House of Commons explicitly linking the 1798 events in Ireland with continued radical conspiracy in Britain, noting that 'persons lately released from prison ... have been the most active' in new conspiracies, having 'artfully availed themselves of the high price of provisions to sow discontent amongst the lower orders'.

A month later, the text of the Secret Committee report was made available in greater detail, and widely reproduced. Its opening lines were uncompromising:

It was not to be expected that persons who had deeply imbibed the principles of the French Revolution, who were inflamed with the most sanguinary animosity against all the existing establishments of church and state; that such of them, particularly of the lower orders of society, whose hopes were instigated by the prospect of the plunder of the rich, and the partition of the landed property of the country, and who had been taught to abjure all the restraints which divine or human laws have imposed on the passions of men; should be induced, by any change of circumstances, or legal coercion, suddenly to abandon these principles, and to return to the duties of loyal and peaceable subjects.[14]

Under such circumstances, that Despard remained free for another year and a half reflects the curiously erratic nature of repression in this era. Despard's chosen field of play was amongst the Irish soldiers and disaffected workers of the capital. He circu-lated through various taverns known for their 'jacobinical' clientele, and was soon part of a network significant enough to produce its own 'constitution', a blend as before of ideals and rewards:

The independence of Great Britain and Ireland – An equaliza-tion of civil, political and religious rights – An ample provision for the families of the heroes who shall fall in the contest.

A liberal reward for distinguished merit – These are the objects for which we contend, and to obtain these objects we swear to be united.[15]

Copies of this were found as far away as Yorkshire. Information reaching ministers spoke of a clearly paramilitary organisation, with units and ranks, and of a plan for a *coup d'état*, the killing of the king, and of a national rising signalled by the non-arrival of London mail coaches, stopped by the rebels for that purpose.

Some, at least, of this may have been either braggadocio or scaremongering by one side or the other, but enough was feared for Despard and a half-dozen associates to be seized in late November 1802. He was taken at a tavern amongst a crowd of the kind of men that composed his planned rank and file. At his trial he did not try to account for his associations, merely wishing to deny the particular claim that he had 'seduced' other men to his lead. Going to the scaffold alongside six co-conspirators on 21 February 1803 proclaiming 'that the period will come, and that *speedily*, when the glorious cause of Liberty shall effectually triumph' suggested he was guilty of at least some of what he was charged with, though more moderate radicals preferred to paint him a martyr to the lies of government agents.[16] Reports from the provinces of continued secret meetings, oath-taking and the manufacture of pikes for an insurrection may have been exaggerated, but they remained troubling until overtaken, temporarily at least, by renewed external threats.

The second extraordinary trial opened on the very day that Despard was hanged and decapitated (a substitute for drawing and quartering that was judged more suitable for the sensibilities of the new century, on display in the crowd of some 20,000). Jean-Gabriel Peltier was one of the most distinguished journalists to have emerged on the conservative and royalist side of politics in France since the Revolution of 1789. His first journal had been the wickedly satirical *Acts of the Apostles*, in which he mocked reformers and radicals with self-consciously superior and obscure language, to the delight of an elite readership. Forced to flee the country after the fall of the monarchy in 1792, he had settled in London, and became the author and publisher of a series of journals, supplying news and satirical comment on the evolving French

scene to an international audience of royalist exiles and their sympathisers. By the turn of the century he and a small band of
colleagues had become a particularly painful irritant to the authoritarian government being established by First Consul Bonaparte.

While subsidising hostile propaganda was something that enemies did as a matter of course in wartime, the arrival of peace
brought demands from Paris that the 'horrors' of Peltier's press
should be stopped. A directive to French negotiators on 1 February
1802 asserted bluntly that 'Whatever the liberty of the press in
England, the government always has means at its disposal to prevent or punish such disgusting abuses.'[17] Attempts to insert into the
Peace of Amiens a formal ban on harbouring such men failed, but
the French persisted in invoking the 'spirit' of its first Article, pledg-
ing future amity, in their efforts to silence Peltier. In truth, there was
something more than a little hypocritical in British willingness to
crush any signs of dangerous internal dissent, while claiming a
total inability to act in this case, and as the French repeatedly
pressed the matter, Britain's noble defence of press freedom shriv-
elled. By July 1802 Peltier's publications had been referred to the
Attorney-General, and under a continued barrage of French
demands, it was confirmed on 19 August that there was a case to
answer for criminal libel.

At this point French efforts to ensure that action was taken
crossed with Bonaparte's increasingly arrogant approach to the outcome of the Amiens treaty. Believing – as he so often did – that he
held the upper hand, Bonaparte placed an article in the official
Moniteur journal, asserting that the British government was either
insufficiently sovereign to deal with journalists on its own shores, or
insufficiently respectful of a 'friendly' power and at grave risk of
restarting hostilities. A diplomatic interview at which the foreign
minister Talleyrand threw the suspension of habeas corpus in the
British ambassador's face, as evidence for what could be done if
government chose, compounded the offence. The declining state
of Anglo-French relations made it all the more remarkable that

Peltier was, in fact, brought to trial the following February, having in the meantime continued to circulate bitter attacks on the Bonaparte regime. By the time the court convened, crowds had gathered, amidst reports that City speculators were betting on the immediate outbreak of war, should he be acquitted.

The main charges concerned verses in which, under the paper-thin veil of classical allusion, the assassination of the First Consul was urged; echoes of these demands in prose compounded the offence, along with the masthead of the journal *l'Ambigu* itself, a cartoon of a Sphinx with Bonaparte's head, defiantly printed in a state of decapitation, when demands for Peltier's trial began to be made.[18] Despite valiant efforts by his barrister, Peltier's guilt was evident, and the jury, directed to do so by the presiding Lord Chief Justice Ellenborough, took less than a minute to return a verdict confirming it. The outcome was replete with ironies. A bilingual account of the affair, sold by Peltier on subscription, made him a fortune. Bonaparte took the result as a cue to press harder on a number of diplomatic fronts, convinced now of both the bad faith and weakness of the British – they had caved in on Peltier, what else might they be made to give up? In this he was fundamentally mistaken, as he was shortly to discover. Peltier, meanwhile, was never actually sentenced for his crimes, and continued a long and profitable career of denunciation against the man who, whatever his protestations of peaceable intent, was about to engender war in every corner of the globe.

When Prime Minister Henry Addington stood to address the House of Commons in May 1803, announcing the resumption of war with France, he did so in the red-coated uniform of Captain Commandant of the Woodley Cavalry Volunteers. It was a gesture of pride in the relatively humble Berkshire formation that reached out in a number of contradictory directions. Addington himself spoke of the mushrooming growth of Volunteer corps during the previous hostilities as an 'insurrection of loyalty', a phrase that bordered on the double-edged, given the troubles over food in 1801, and over radical politics more generally.[19] It was always a delicate task, when summoning up the strength of the populace, not to have it overflow into a demanding uprising.

The Prime Minister's appearance in the uniform of a relatively plebeian corps might also be seen as an implicit challenge to the nation's 'natural' aristocratic leadership. Addington's nickname amongst the political class was 'the Doctor', a phrase which sounds pleasant enough until it is noted that his father was a physician connected to the Pitt family, which had led him into a position of effective clientage under them. Addington entered Parliament in 1784, with the explicit support of his former childhood friend, as part of the significant majority that marked Pitt's first great triumph as Prime Minister; Pitt went on to lift him to the position of Speaker of the House of Commons in 1789, expressly because he could trust his loyalty. For the scions of the landed gentry who continued to dominate politics, 'the Doctor' would always be something of a figure of fun, not quite one of them. On the occasion of the declaration of war, the unfortunate coincidence of his resplendent entry to the Commons with the second reading of a Medicine Bill brought ribald laughter from the opposition benches.[20]

Even as he spearheaded a government that had won a tidy election victory a year before, and contemplated committing Britain and its empire once again to a global war, Addington had been reminded that for many he was no more than a bit-part player on a stage walked by giants. William Pitt had not long left the premiership when he began to regret his decision, especially as the issue of Catholic emancipation could safely now be regarded as a dead letter. Addington's management of national finances by the end of 1802 appalled him – the income tax was abolished, and new debts were incurred without specific provisions for repayment, exactly what Pitt had striven all his political life to prevent.

Even the granting of a peerage (as Lord Melville) to Henry Dundas, his old friend and ally, was taken amiss. In the early

months of Addington's premiership Pitt had become accustomed to
being consulted on such political matters, but on this, as on a growing range of issues, he was not – was one old friend now trying to
bribe another away from him? Meanwhile, Pitt's supporters began
to hint, perhaps prematurely, at a return: when in Commons
debate the Whig Richard Sheridan scorned the idea that any one
man was necessary to save the nation, George Canning, often noted
as over-eager to let fly with a polished phrase, retorted that Pitt
'must endure the attachment of a people whom he has saved'.[21]

Remarkably, Addington's magnanimity on this point (and perhaps his practical realisation of his position) extended in March
1803 to an offer, communicated to Pitt in person by the newly
ennobled Melville, to resign the premiership and serve alongside
Pitt in a Cabinet nominally headed by the latter's elder brother, the
notably untalented but conveniently figurehead-shaped Earl of
Chatham. Pitt, however, despite now suffering recurrent bouts of
ill-health, had lost none of his fire. Melville reported his view that
government now required an undivided authority in a Prime
Minister with real control, notably over the finances, and that this
person 'must be allowed and understood to prevail'.[22]

Even more remarkably, Addington then went further, offering
Pitt just such a premiership, albeit on the understanding that he,
Addington, and the majority of his Cabinet colleagues would continue to hold ministerial posts. A sitting Prime Minister, with a solid
Commons majority, and all the resources of Crown patronage at his
disposal, was offering to resign in his favour, and this was still not
enough for Pitt. At a face-to-face meeting on 10 April, with the threat
of war already ever-present, Pitt said he would enter government at
the king's request, but only as a chief minister with full discretion to
name his colleagues. Britain went to war five weeks later with
Addington still at the helm, but with the man whom Canning had
recently and poetically dubbed 'the pilot that weathered the storm'
of the 1790s staring hard over his shoulder.

*

War was not entered into lightly. From some perspectives it seems extraordinary that a government could safely contemplate a renewal of hostilities when the previous conflict had brought the country so close to financial collapse and internal disorder. But First Consul Bonaparte's continued activities had altered the political landscape, both internally and internationally. By 1802 it was becoming clear that, whatever threat Bonaparte posed, it was different in essence from that of the revolutionary contagion of the 1790s. In 1801, the French regime had negotiated an ideological peace treaty with the Catholic Church, ending a decade of revolutionary persecutions and papal execrations. Public worship returned officially to France with a great mass at Notre Dame in Paris for Easter Sunday, 18 April 1802. Meanwhile, the consular regime was also reaching out to the other great pillar of opposition, the emigrated French nobility. While the princely leaders, and some of the die-hard aristocrats, remained in defiant exile, numbers of their followers began slipping back into France, their status as legally dead outlaws expunged by official connivance. Those nobles whose exile had only ever been internal, a withdrawal to rural retreats, began re-entering public life even more visibly. Radical democratic agitation could evidently no longer look to France for inspiration, and the menace of a country broken by simultaneous invasion and insurrection faded from the scene.

Nonetheless, a threat remained, and ever more evidently. Bonaparte's aggressive style during the negotiations for peace continued both before and after the formal signing at Amiens in 1802. The Peltier affair was only one dimension of this. France undertook a series of offensive moves that had been forbidden, both implicitly and explicitly, by treaties it had signed. British authorities were deceived into concurring in the dispatch of a large French force to attempt a reconquest of rebel-held Saint Domingue in the Caribbean (and perhaps to prepare to pounce on British colonies), by assurances that the expedition would be much smaller than that which finally sailed. In Holland, several tens of thousands of

French troops due to be withdrawn according to the Treaty of Lunéville with Austria remained firmly in place, and in September 1801 carried out a military coup on behalf of pro-French, anti-democratic forces.

A new constitution for the Dutch was ratified the next month in a referendum where the three-quarters of voters who abstained were counted as 'tacit affirmations', overturning the actual majority against the imposed deal. The following year, after internal political strife in Switzerland, Bonaparte's forces again imposed a constitutional solution there that was most congenial to the interlopers, and without reference to any other powers. Meanwhile in Italy, France annexed further border territories to itself, imposed control over lands further south towards Rome, re-formed a new, expanded satellite state as the Republic of Italy, and imposed Bonaparte himself as president there in another rigged poll.

In August 1802 Bonaparte put the referendum device to work for himself again, as French voters approved, with remarkable unanimity, the proposal that he should be appointed First Consul for Life. His progress towards all the powers of a monarch, and one with seeming ambitions to become a new, continent-spanning Charlemagne, was in full flow. But the British persisted in standing in his way. A global empire had not been gained by diffidence, and against a foe who had already shown himself dissatisfied with anything short of complete mastery, the leaders of the country saw no alternative except to fight.

During the peace, French and British diplomats had continued to butt heads over the issue of Malta. The Amiens treaty foresaw a British evacuation and the return of the island to neutral status under the Knights, but as French power expanded further into Italy, the British argued firmly that they had a legitimate strategic need for a naval base in the central Mediterranean. Bonapartist propaganda would lean on these claims in future months and years to depict Britain as a shameless treaty-breaker. But French negotiators had offered to collude in British seizure of Corfu or Crete as a replacement: what would have been overt acts of aggression against third parties, whose future enmity towards Britain could only serve French interests. As with the simultaneous brutal and treacherous effort to re-enslave Caribbean rebels (a campaign of massacres that verged on genocide), the truly shameless approach to diplomacy came not from London, but Paris.[23]

It was perceptions such as these, and the real prospect of a need to defend their homeland from determined efforts at invasion, that made this moment for the British one of genuine national mobilisation. But it would be wrong to suppose that the threat of 'Boney' had brought the country together in unequivocal martial unity. When even the London Corresponding Society debated taking up arms in 1798 for national defence, it is evident that the men who flocked to the colours, in many different forms, had widely differing motivations. In the half-decade before 1803 enlistments had ebbed and flowed, with the difficulties of getting Militiamen to agree to regular service in 1799 just one part of a complex pattern. Membership in part-time Volunteer corps doubled to over 100,000 in 1798, for example, but a key reason was that such membership offered the rank and file exemption from being balloted to serve full-time in the Militia – just as Militia service safeguarded soldiers from being sent overseas.[24]

The Volunteers continued to swell through the scares about invasion that preceded the Peace of Amiens, but were disbanded (or at least robbed of public funds) by Addington's government in 1802, a move that reportedly 'very generally excited' the 'disgust' of patriotic opinion, especially amongst the many local notables who found a stimulating public role in officering such formations.[25] Many amongst Addington's ministers were set against the role of the Volunteers. Evidence from Ireland, in recent upheavals and others in the 1780s, showed that movements of armed civilians could have destabilising consequences. Senior officers inspecting formations in 1801 spoke of 'a chaos of discord and confusion', brought about in some cases by 'party influence'.[26] Meanwhile, three-quarters of units were so small that they could not be feasibly incorporated into larger battlefield formations should the necessity arise – they lacked all opportunity to practise essential tactical skills.

Addington's government hoped to remedy all these deficiencies with legislation in 1802, creating a much-enlarged Militia with both full- and part-time components, but with a more professional overall officer corps, and a clear relationship to military discipline and larger structures of control. Ministers even sought information on the Prussian system of national mobilisation, to consider how this could be done without crippling industry.[27] But under the circumstances of 1803, public opinion, and political opposition, pressed for a less innovatory, less 'foreign' solution. William Pitt, increasingly disenchanted with Addington's performance, became a loud advocate in the Commons of the revival of the Volunteers, and effectively forced this move on the government.

Pitt's old friend Melville grumbled in writing about the Pittite habit of 'doing more than can be practically done well', and the 'loose and desultory manner' in which Volunteer units were conducted.[28] But the die was cast, and by the end of the year an astonishing 380,000 men were, at least nominally, enrolled as Volunteers, in addition to a healthy strength of over 150,000 regulars and Militiamen.[29] On paper, this was a mass equal to confronting the armies Bonaparte could field. In practice, of course, there was no comparison between the Volunteers and a force of battle-hardened and rigorously drilled regulars. The government made detailed plans for the deployment of troops to fight back against an invasion force, including the national mobilisation of reserves from the north to camps near London, and ringed the southern coasts with the famous 'Martello towers', but it was clear to all that the best hope of safety from Bonaparte's veterans remained, as it had been since time immemorial, the wooden wall of the fleet.[30]

In contrast to the toleration of local initiative, and even insubordination, that marked the British preference for land-based voluntarism, the manning of the navy, as is legendary, was

distinguished by a brutal pragmatism that stood sharply at odds
with the liberties of which it was the prime wartime guardian. The
raising of the fleet to its wartime height in the 1790s of over a hundred battleships and countless other smaller craft, manned by more
than 130,000 sailors, had required extraordinary and dangerous
measures, including the sweeping of the jails under the Quota
Acts, and the wholesale enlistment of captive Irish rebels.

Underpinning these methods was the basic and long-established
practice of the press-gang. Any man who 'used the sea' (with
exemptions for crews of outbound merchantmen and a few other
categories) could be taken up – from out of a ship or a tavern,
from off the street, even out of his bed – and compelled to serve.
Coastal communities in wartime became accustomed to playing
cat-and-mouse with the Naval Impress Service that sent regular
patrols to roust out desperately needed bodies. Crews of inbound
merchant ships might be plundered of men by individual naval vessels, experiencing the sharpest of ironies at the hands of the very
men who had shepherded them to safe harbour.

The formidable Admiral Earl St Vincent, raised to First Lord of
the Admiralty, had vouched for the value of the navy in a famous
remark in Parliament during the difficult days of early 1801: 'I do
not say, my Lords, that the French will not come. I say only they
will not come by sea.' But his ruthless dedication to preserving the
wartime strength of his forces was matched by a clear-eyed commitment to retrenchment of costs upon the onset of peace, and
from the end of that year onwards, the fleet's active complement
was slashed – over half of the battleships were laid up, and an even
larger proportion of the smaller vessels, essential for protecting
trade in wartime but devoid of a role in peace. Perhaps as many as
100,000 sailors were put ashore.[31] Some were able to return to
former trades abandoned in the slumps of the 1790s, others found
berths on merchant shipping, but it was a difficult time for many.
As the clouds of war gathered again, some would be happy to re-
enlist. Individual captains, especially those that had gained a

reputation for earning rich rewards for their crews in officially sanc-
tioned 'prize money', might have their pick of experienced seamen
in such circumstances. But to return the fleet as a whole to its
peak, when the bulk of the work would be either the tedium of
convoy duty or the even worse misery of blockading the enemy
coast, the press remained essential.

It was also essential to prepare its first sweeps in secrecy, and to
move before war was upon the nation. Over two months before hostilities became official, the government struck. A message from the
king to the House of Commons, on 8 March 1803, spoke in the
light of 'very considerable military preparations' in 'the ports of
France and Holland' of the need 'to adopt additional measures of
precaution for the security of his dominions'.[32] What this meant
became clear at the seafaring strongholds of Plymouth and
Portsmouth two days later. Warrants, prepared and issued in the
highest secrecy, and delivered post-haste by special messengers,
sent swarms of armed Royal Marines through the towns and over
the many merchant vessels lying at anchor – the troops themselves
in ignorance of their orders until they were in place and the command to begin seizing seamen was issued.

Such was the vigour of the press in Plymouth that, as the *Naval
Chronicle* did not blush to report, 'landsmen of all description'
were taken up, and 'one press gang entered the Dock Theatre, and
cleared the whole gallery, except women.' At Portsmouth men and
boys alike were swept from the merchantmen, and even the water-
men who ferried passengers around the harbour, and who held
personal exemptions from the press, went into temporary hiding,
creating the 'utmost difficulty' for those seeking transportation.[33] Up
and down the country similar scenes were reproduced, the press
spreading up the coasts as fast as word of it could be carried to
local commanders.

St Vincent reinvigorated the Impress Service itself, as one Admiralty official noted, 'nominating young and active officers to it
instead of old ones', but this could bring its own problems, at least

for the individuals concerned. As the spring wore on and the first
easy pickings for the press faded away, its continuing vigour sparked
furious resistance. At Hungerford Stairs on the Thames, mere yards
from the headquarters of the Admiralty itself, angry port workers set
upon two boatloads of sailors in a mêlée that left one female
bystander grievously wounded, and some of the sailors 'cut in a
most shocking manner'.[34] The eagerness of individual ships' captains to make up their crews, under pressure of orders to proceed to
sea, led to some brutal collisions between the naval and the civil
mindset.

In May 1803, as war loomed ever closer, the frigate HMS
Immortalité – like so much of the fleet, a vessel captured from the
French – launched a raid on two East Indiamen outbound from the
Thames: large, well-crewed vessels that held official exemption
from the press. An expedition in the frigate's boats turned into an
armed confrontation, as boarders were thrust back with pikes and
iron roundshot was hurled into the boats. A naval lieutenant, exas-
perated at 'refractory and illegal' resistance, ordered marines in the
boats to open fire, killing two men. The Gravesend coroner
declared upon investigation that this was an act of wilful murder,
and the officer was tried for his life (though acquitted). It was far
from clear which side had been in the right, and the ambiguities of
the warrants under which the press operated were highlighted in an
even more appalling clash on the Isle of Portland.

The frigate HMS *Aigle* (another former prize of war) launched
a raid there in April, declaring to the local authorities that it had a
warrant duly signed by the mayor of nearby Weymouth. But the
locals denied that Weymouth's writ ran in their own, royal and
privileged borough. Some fifty sailors and marines found themselves confronting an armed crowd of over three hundred, and as
scuffles broke out, a volley from the marines shot three men dead
and mortally wounded others. One woman, Mary Way, shot in the
back as she fled, lingered in agony for seven weeks before dying.
The fighting, meanwhile, wounded sixteen men on the official

side, nine so severely that they had to be discharged from the service. No fewer than four of the officers involved were charged with murder, but acquitted on grounds of self-defence.[35] All around the country, similar defiance, if with less dreadful consequences, made the press's job an arduous one, but one in which they persisted, with the vital importance of manning the fleet always held up before them.

The flaring of war brought William Pitt back to the Commons on 23 May, to deliver a speech that was poorly recorded, but long remembered as an extraordinarily powerful performance.[36] A hostile Whig observer, Thomas Creevey, noted acerbically that the 'great fiend' had 'in the infinite energy of his style, the miraculous perspicuity and fluency of his periods' outdone all previous efforts: 'its effect was dreadful'. By this he meant that Pitt was cheered to the rafters for phrases that a more sympathetic witness noted enthusiastically: 'Bonaparte absorbing the whole power of France ... the *liquid fire* of Jacobinical principles desolating the world', along with 'an electrifying peroration on the necessity and magnitude of our future exertions'. It was also noted, ominously, that Pitt's 'lungs seem to labour in those prodigious sentences which he once thundered forth without effort'.[37] Regardless of the state of his health, the great pilot of the ship of state was still intent on taking up the tiller again in this hour of new crisis.

5

ALONE AGAINST THE EMPEROR

It was inevitable that war would begin again at sea. With Anglo-French relations in a nosedive, and Bonaparte having ordered his own mobilisations after learning of the British efforts that began in March 1803, diplomats exchanged between the two capitals began asking for their passports in mid-May, and on the 15th the Admiralty issued an order for the detention of all French vessels, in port or at sea. This order pre-empted the official decision of the Privy Council in London on the 16th to implement naval hostilities, but was made to allow forces to be prepared, after the inevitable delays in transmission, for what was now seen as imminent conflict. However, it also thus ran ahead of the final official declaration of war published on the 18th. As a result, on 18 May itself, one French ship was attacked and captured by a British frigate scouting off Brest, and on the 19th two other frigates not far away seized another vessel.[1] As official word of war had not yet passed via Paris to the fleet at Brest, Bonaparte was able to make some propaganda capital out of these 'unprovoked' attacks, but he wasted it by his own aggressive actions in the following days and weeks.

Most immediately appalling, for British public opinion, was an order issued on 22 May for the arrest and detention of all British naval, military or Militia officers currently in France. The country had seen a flood of wealthy tourists over the previous year, rediscovering the joys of a continent closed to them for almost a decade, and the customs of an earlier age would have seen them all safely shepherded homewards upon such an outbreak of war. Bonaparte's order in itself was perhaps justified, but its application proved draconian, as eager officials rounded up not just the specified officers, but all identifiably British men, women and children.

Hundreds were stricken by panic. Some managed to escape across Europe, finally taking to the seas from ports in Germany and Denmark, others resigned themselves to a brief but inconvenient period of captivity while the mess was sorted out. But it was not. A few figures able to claim some eminence and connections amongst the French elite were let go, but the First Consul declined to overrule his bureaucracy, and the mass of detainees, over a thousand strong, were by the autumn dispersed to provincial fortress towns, there in many cases to wait out the entire conflict to come in the company of growing numbers of genuine prisoners of war. This move, striking at the heart of the British ruling class – everyone who was anyone knew someone now a prisoner in France – added another dimension to the demonisation of 'Boney'.

The weeks after 18 May also proved that French plans for the outbreak of war were well-laid long before. On the first official day of conflict General Gouvion Saint-Cyr in Italy was ordered to occupy the ports of the southern coast; this he did, casually bypassing Naples, where the royal family remained in dread of his arrival until Admiral Nelson's ships appeared in June, giving at least reassurance that they could be evacuated to Sicily again if the need arose. To the north, as early as 13 May French troops in Holland were ordered into forward positions near the frontier, poised to invade George III's Hanover. This assault had been planned during the peace, with one of Bonaparte's own aides going on a reconnaissance of the territory to be conquered, and the garrison of the Netherlands reinforced to provide a strike force. After a few final preparations, General Mortier sent his troops into Hanover on 26 May, and had coerced the civilian administration into capitulation within eight days. The Hanoverian army, however, some 20,000 strong, retreated further north and east, declining to surrender until a separate capitulation was signed by its aged commander, Field Marshal von Wallmoden.

This defiance, accompanied by the news that the French had not even deigned to declare war (taking Hanover to be part of the British realm, which it emphatically was not), helped make these events another cause of grim determination in Britain to see off the Bonapartist menace. French official looting of George III's personal estates, along with a settlement which forced the Hanoverians to find 50 million francs a year to support an army of occupation – from an agricultural territory whose capital held barely 20,000 people – added to the sense of justified rage. As soldiers from the now-disbanded Hanoverian army began slipping across the North Sea, they were welcomed, and by the end of the year had formed a body of some 2000 men. The Duke of Cambridge, the king's seventh son, had been serving in this army as a general, and was forced to flee the French advance on a Royal Navy ship. He was now authorised to form a King's German Legion of up to 5000, a force which was to have a long and distinguished record in the conflict ahead.[2]

While British public opinion absorbed the news of French advances, and heard ominous reports of the massing of troops and boats across the Channel, the political class continued to reflect on its own divisions. The former Foreign Secretary, Lord Grenville, nurtured a growing detestation for Prime Minister Addington, abetted by his own insuperable conviction of aristocratic superiority, and rallied a growing band of more 'hawkish' former Pitt supporters around himself. Pitt, meanwhile, stood above the everyday fray of politics by throwing himself into the campaign of national defence. Not only did this slender, bookish and increasingly unhealthy man sign up as colonel of a Volunteer corps during the rush of enthusiasm for such bodies, but he also committed himself to forming his men into as effective a defensive force as they could be made. According to his niece, Hester Stanhope, he 'absolutely goes through the fatigue of a *drill-sergeant*', riding between musters fifteen or twenty miles apart. He also compiled extensive notes on tactical formations, as well as supervising plans for 'driving the country' – stripping it of livestock and supplies in the event of an invasion.[3]

The urgency of this task was multiplied by the location of Pitt's residence in late 1803, for he had taken station since August at Walmer Castle on the Kentish coast, his official home as Lord Warden of the Cinque Ports. This post was supposed to be a rewarding sinecure, but Pitt transformed it into a personal mission of national defence. Coupled with another office as Constable of Dover Castle, it saw him organising the equipment of some 170 gunboats stationed from Margate to Hastings, and engaged in a constant effort to prime the defences of what was indisputably the key sector of any Napoleonic invasion plan – often working, as he saw it, against official obstruction and incompetence. As fears of invasion reached a height in the autumn of 1803, and the long eighteenth-century tradition of political prints was used to rally the public with defiant messages, one in particular reflected an acknowledgment of Pitt's activity. Entitled *The Centinel at his Post, or Boney's Peep into Walmer Castle!!*, it depicted Pitt, with uniform and musket, standing guard on his walls while 'Boney', in a boat full of downcast soldiers, cries aghast, 'Ah. Begar – dat man alive still – turn about Citoyens – for there will be no good to be done – I know his tricks of old!!'[4]

Though there was every indication that Pitt was entirely sincere in his devotion to national defence – and friends noted how his health rallied as he threw himself into the task – the impression it created could not but aid him politically. In December he attended the Commons, and following a careful policy of critical support for the government, saw some of his suggestions gleaned with first-hand experience incorporated into improved arrangements for organisation of Volunteers. But as winter relieved the immediate threat of invasion, political attention turned again to Addington's deficiencies. Though his government had overseen a stunningly successful naval rearmament, with the French fleet bottled up under blockade and British squadrons already pressing in on French colonial territories, the pressure to do more continued to rise.

In January 1804 Grenville repeatedly pressed Pitt to take a stand against a government of 'middle lines, and managements and delicacies', as he put it; but Pitt did not want to alienate the members of the government's substantial majority by committing to opposition.[5] The desperation of Grenville's anti-French rage was marked by his decision, at the end of the month, to take his hawkish band of supporters into alliance with the Whigs. These were the men who had stood against Pitt all through the previous two decades; their leader, Charles James Fox, had in 1789 called the French Revolution 'the greatest event . . . that ever happened in the world, and . . . the best'.[6] It was an extraordinary indication of Grenville's detestation that he would contemplate such a move – though of course the Foxites were now rallied to the national cause, and Fox was far more of a gentleman, in Grenville's eyes, than the upstart Addington.

As winter drew to a close, with a brief flurry of royal illness injecting yet more uncertainty into the mix, Addington's position grew steadily more untenable. In what was a very difficult strategic situation, with France truly dominant on the Continent and no other power yet prepared to try their strength against Bonaparte, the failure to do more to take the war to the enemy was nevertheless treated as a personal failing. Fox remarked caustically of his perceived shortcomings that 'it is no excuse that he is a fool' – this of a Prime Minister who had succeeded in reintroducing income tax, on a sounder basis than Pitt, securing a greater income for the Treasury with a lower burden on individual taxpayers.[7] But Pitt's sense that Addington could no longer rally the nation pushed him into overt opposition – detached from the Grenville–Fox axis – late in February, attacking in detail continued deficiencies in anti-invasion planning, and going on a few weeks later to lambast a lack of strategic aggression in the navy. There was a 'very wide difference', he asserted, between Earl St Vincent's indubitable qualities as an admiral and those he possessed as an administrator, and the 'terrible activity of the enemy' was meeting 'alarming supineness' from the government.[8]

By mid-April, Pitt was writing to the king to warn of the danger he saw in allowing the present government to remain, and later in the month he succeeded in cutting their Commons majority to only thirty-seven in yet another debate on inadequacies in national defence. With Grenville in the Lords sometimes actually winning critical votes, Addington's time was up, and he began to manoeuvre to leave office on the best possible terms, which for him meant keeping both Fox and Grenville out. Pitt's preference was to form a grand coalition – a government of national unity, in effect – but while Addington's wishes might have to yield, others were more obdurate. The king himself vetoed Fox's presence in the Cabinet, though he agreed to giving him some other official post. This, however, ran up against an increasingly solid front from the Fox–Grenville opposition. They, like Pitt, but on different grounds, had been advocating an inclusive government, and though Fox himself generously offered to stand aside, his associates would not permit their other leaders to join a Cabinet based around an 'exclusion'.

William Pitt finally accepted the seals of office on 18 May 1804, first anniversary of the new war, having taken such umbrage against Grenville's behaviour that he reportedly declared that 'he would teach that proud man, that, in the service of and with the confidence of the King, he could do without him, though he thought his health such, that it might cost him his life'.[9] These were ominous notions to take into office with what was, if not technically a minority government, then one which faced much wider and more united opposition than Pitt had been accustomed to. The day he assumed power was further marked with the announcement of a new, and also ominous, development in the affairs of France, as after another carefully managed referendum campaign, Napoleon Bonaparte was declared officially to be the hereditary Emperor of the French.

Napoleon's elevation was forever to be studiously ignored by official British policy, for whom he was always 'General Bonaparte', but it nonetheless shifted the French threat even further from its original revolutionary axis towards considerations of raw power. Yet it was the ruthless exercise of that power by Napoleon's state that was to provide a route out of British isolation. After the discovery late in the winter of 1803–4 of a major plot to depose him, involving British spies, royalists, disgruntled republicans and aristocratic exiles, Bonaparte and his police had decided to demonstrate a vigorous response to such activity.

A young prince of the royal house of Bourbon, the duc d'Enghien, was living in peaceable exile in the neighbouring German state of Baden – but thought by the French authorities to be subsidised by the British to work on invasion plots. In mid-March 1804, he was snatched in a cross-border raid by French troops, summarily tried, and shot by firing squad on the 21st. In the words of Napoleon's dour police minister, Fouché, this was worse than a crime; it was a mistake. It put paid to any chance that the hitherto wavering concerns of Russia would lead to an agreement to carve up spheres of interest in Europe and the Near East with France, and indeed spurred immediate Russian protests, and ineffectual calls for French advances in Italy and northern Germany to be reversed. French arrogance in response led to a complete diplomatic break in August 1804.[10]

This was an opening for Pitt's government to restart a process of seeking a European coalition – something Addington's diplomats had laboured in vain over for the previous year. Even so, it did not immediately clarify the position of the other powers, and much of the following twelve months were marked by the same kind of hesitant and self-interested manoeuvres that had finally brought the coalition of 1799, only half united, into being. As on that occasion, much effort would be expended on all sides trying to draw Prussia into some, any, kind of commitment, only for its timid king eventually to refuse to stray from comfortable neutrality. Also as previously, both Russian and British diplomacy saw Austria as the key to an effective alliance against France, while both (and especially Russia) were keen for the Austrians to shoulder most of the military effort, and gave little consideration to appropriate recompense.

The Austrians had their own firm, and potentially disruptive, ideas about the proper roles and rewards for all parties. Amongst other things, evident Austrian greed for more German territories succeeded in making their south German neighbour, Bavaria, into a stout French ally before a shot was fired. Meanwhile, both British and Russian plans for the aftermath of a successful war envisaged a Europe in which those two powers held powerful and hegemonic roles, with Austria implicitly downgraded from its accustomed position as arbiter of central Europe and the Holy Roman Empire.[11]

The cold calculation involved in such diplomatic minuets was shown late in 1804, when Pitt's government effectively forced Spain into the war on the French side. The Spanish government, which had been glad to get out of the earlier war in 1802, and which was being bullied by France to provide expensive subsidies (while also being short-changed on French promises in various treaties), had sought secretly to explore the possibility of a British alliance. But Britain, still obsessively fortifying itself against Napoleon's invasion fleet, had no significant force it could send to defend such an ally against the troops that would pour across the Pyrenees, and judged that its interests were better served by a show of strength in a bid to get Spain to cut off its subsidies – or make it an enemy, opening its colonial territories for profitable occupation.

In an act that was very little short of state piracy, a force of British frigates intercepted the annual Spanish treasure convoy from the mines of the Americas at sea in October 1804. The seizure of a huge fortune – the underpinning of Spanish state finances – and the killing of 240 Spaniards (including civilian passengers) when one of the intercepted ships blew up under fire, left the Spanish little real choice.[12] After further agonies of indecision over what would be a deeply unpopular move, they joined the war on 12 December, ten days after the Emperor had demonstrated his utter commitment to absolute power at his coronation in Paris, taking the crown from the hands of the pope himself to place it emphatically on his own head.

That commitment – to being able to do as he saw fit, and aggrandise his empire without regard for the views of others – would finally open the way to a new coalition of allies for Britain's struggle. While Napoleon was crowning himself, Pitt's government was locked in negotiations with Russia that continued into the spring of 1805. What resulted in April was a treaty that called once again for Austria to bear the burden of providing 250,000 troops. Russia offered 115,000, and Britain helped pay for these alongside subsidising another 40,000 from minor allies including Sweden and Naples. As in the previous year's negotiations, the desired outcome of the war was hegemony for the two signatories, with both Austria and Prussia reduced to second-rank status, components of a system to block a French revival.[13] Even this version of the treaty did not represent a full meeting of minds between Pitt's government and the Tsar's, and continued haggling over concessions demanded on both sides meant it remained unratified as spring passed into summer. By then, Napoleon had begun to force the issue.

In March 1805 the Emperor showed his bullying hand again, to north and south. The Dutch, who had already suffered one *coup d'état* under his rule, had further measures of centralisation imposed on their state by force, making their independence even more nominal than before. Meanwhile, expanding his sense of dynastic grandeur, Napoleon obliged the leadership of the Italian Republic to transform itself into a Kingdom of Italy (once again flagrantly violating his 1801 treaty with Austria). After a show of offering the throne to his brother Joseph, Napoleon took it for himself, and was crowned with the ancient Iron Crown of Lombardy in Milan on 26 May. Annexing the territory of the important maritime trading city of Genoa the following month set alarm bells ringing across Europe, as did the granting of two duchies in central Italy to the Emperor's eldest sister Elisa and her husband.

News of this forms the famous opening scene of Tolstoy's *War and Peace*, as the patriotic Anna Pavlovna declares that if 'Genoa and Lucca are now just family estates of the Buonapartes', this must mean war against the imperial 'Antichrist'. Indeed it did, but only once Austria had been further assailed by the Tsar. Having grudgingly signed up to a defensive alliance with Russia in November 1804, the Austrian court had been horrified by the Anglo-Russian deal of April. The desire to reduce Austrian power in a future Europe could be dealt with by later negotiation, but the quest to reduce France to impotence struck the Habsburgs' ministers as folly. A durable balance of power was the most they thought could be aimed at, particularly one that restrained the apparent French drive to dominate all Italy and dictate the shape of a future German league. Against such quailing, remarkably crude and overt bullying from Russia, including effective threats to change sides and support a Franco-Russian division of the continent, was needed to bring an offensive Russo-Austrian alliance to final fruition on 8 August 1805.[14]

As Britain at last acquired allies on land, so at sea the scattered elements of an epic campaign were coming together towards an epochal resolution. Back in January 1805, a ferocious winter storm had driven off the blockading squadron from the French port of Rochefort, allowing Rear-Admiral Missiessy to head out into the Atlantic with five battleships, three frigates, and 3500 troops embarked. Though his Mediterranean counterpart, Admiral Villeneuve, failed to exploit a similar opening a few days later, a grand strategy for the defeat of Britain was at last under way. Missiessy headed for the Caribbean, undetected until he appeared off Barbados several weeks later.[15] He managed to raid British-held Dominica, St Kitts, Nevis and Montserrat, but lacked the force to hold any conquests. Receiving word on 14 March of Villeneuve's failure to escape, and of a possible British squadron headed in his direction, Missiessy led his ships back across the Atlantic, never receiving a later dispatch that ordered him to stay and await reinforcements. He crossed, unseen, with Villeneuve's fleet in mid-ocean, for the latter had finally slipped out of Toulon on 30 March, and reached the Caribbean on 14 May, joined shortly thereafter by a squadron of Spaniards under Admiral Gravina.

Admiral Nelson, who as Commander-in-Chief of the Mediterranean Fleet had been blockading Toulon since the start of the war, had been delayed in his pursuit by fear that the French were heading east for another attack on Egypt, and did not head west until Villeneuve was already almost in the West Indies. The French made poor use of their freedom, managing to subdue a British fortress that had been established on the almost inaccessible Diamond Rock, where it harassed ships approaching French Martinique, but accomplishing little else. The British sugar convoy they captured on 8 June brought bad news – Nelson had reached the Caribbean. Short of supplies, and with the usual grim tropical sicknesses striking at his crews, Villeneuve decided to break for home. Nelson learnt of his departure shortly after, and set off in pursuit. Heading back towards the Mediterranean, he actually overhauled the French – repeating his feat before the Battle of the Nile – but this time they were not making for the same destination.

Villeneuve's and Missiessy's meanderings were part of a grand Napoleonic plan. They should have united in the Caribbean, wreaked havoc with British commerce, and then turned for Europe, ahead of any pursuing fleet, to break the blockade of Brest, freeing another powerful squadron and allowing the six hours' domination of the Channel that Napoleon declared was all he needed to be master of England. Whether that claim was true was never to be tested, for Napoleon's general's mind made little allowance for the vagaries of war at sea. Villeneuve attempted to follow orders and make for Brest, but was intercepted by another British squadron nearby on 22 July, losing two of his Spanish allies in a confused, fog-bound mêlée before heading for safety in the northern Spanish port of Vigo. He lingered there until a lack of crucial supplies and hospital facilities forced him to head south to Cadiz, arriving on 21 August. There he would wait, watched by the Royal Navy, as the opportunity for a summer invasion slipped away, and as, indeed, Napoleon's own thoughts turned towards a new continental campaign, the army gathered at Boulogne being steadily depleted by detachments sent off towards the Rhine.

Events on land and sea now followed a remarkable parallel course. Admiral Nelson had returned to England, where he rested for several weeks amongst a public and a political class consumed with fears of invasion. News of the enemy's concentration at Cadiz arrived on 2 September, but already in the middle of the previous month Admiral Cornwallis of the Channel fleet had despatched twenty battleships to reinforce the squadron blockading that port. This left the Channel with only eleven ships on guard, and potentially at risk from the more than twenty French vessels still penned up in Brest – but the enemy's main strength needed to be engaged. Nelson set sail in HMS *Victory* after further preparations on 15 September, as the reinforcements were already arriving to the south, and finally joined them on the 29th. With further ships joining over the next weeks, this was far from the finely honed 'band of brothers' Nelson had flung into battle at the Nile seven years

before, and there was little time to work up a detailed understanding amongst them, but thanks in great part to Nelson's own 'touch',
a tradition of victory had been so consolidated amongst the captains
and crews that few had any grave doubts about the outcome.

As the British fleet patrolled out of sight of Cadiz, a detached
screen of ships keeping a careful eye on the port, forces with their
own tradition of victory were on the march across France.
Napoleon's newly dubbed Grand Army had departed its encampments on the Channel coast by late August, and by late September
was in position for a bold strike. The Austrians had decided to put
their main strength into northern Italy – partly because they saw it
as the easier route for the French to strike through Venice towards
their homelands, and partly because it offered the offensive opportunity of recapturing the rich cities and lands of Lombardy, stripped
from Habsburg control almost a decade before. A hundred thousand troops were committed to a drive towards Milan. Over 70,000,
meanwhile, took up a more defensive posture on allied territory in
south-western Germany, holding the Black Forest and the uplands
near the headwaters of the Danube – which, if undefended, offered
a direct highway to Vienna. If, as expected, the French concentrated south of the Alps, the forces in Germany, joined by a
substantial Russian force slowly making its way west, could attack
across the upper Rhine when the strategic situation seemed ripe.

Napoleon declined to follow his enemy's lead. With good intelligence of the Austrian intentions, he set 50,000 troops to restrain
the advances in Italy, while massing 210,000 from the Boulogne
encampments and the garrisons of Holland to cross the Rhine
north of the Black Forest. In late September, disregarding Prussian
neutrality, these forces cut a diagonal swathe across western
Germany; through rapidity of action, flexibility of organisation, and
the dread and disarray that their coming spread, they succeeded in
swinging behind the main Austrian force and herding it towards the
fortress town of Ulm. A series of sharp battles in the first two weeks
of October left the Austrians pinned within the fortress itself, which

came under bombardment on the 16th. With news of other nearby detachments' surrender, the Austrian General Mack capitulated on 20 October. The following day, with the Grand Army paraded in a vast semicircle before the gates, the garrison marched out into captivity. In mere weeks, Napoleon had destroyed an entire army, approaching a third of Austria's forces, and almost nothing now stood between him and a shattering conquest.

As Mack's forces marched out under the humiliating gaze of 200,000 Frenchmen, far to the south-west an even more decisive engagement was being fought. Admiral Villeneuve had at last led his ships into action. Orders issued by Napoleon on 16 September had directed him to sail into the Mediterranean, landing the troops that accompanied him in Italy, and engaging the British decisively at sea if opportunity presented itself. On this last point, Villeneuve was particularly reluctant. His crews were unskilled in gunnery, and news of Nelson's arrival offshore had unsettled his captains to the point where they had actually voted in a council of war to stay safely in harbour.

The French continued to vacillate until 18 October, when news reached Villeneuve that a replacement for him had arrived in Madrid, and would shortly continue south. Villeneuve had a long history of failing to fulfil Napoleon's ambitions for him, and dreaded the price of disgrace. With other news that six British battleships had arrived in Gibraltar to resupply, and thus that the enemy might be weakened, he ordered the fleet to sea. A sudden spell of almost windless weather, added to a continued reluctance on the part of some captains, made this a lengthy process, giving plenty of time for the watching British scout-ships to alert Nelson's fleet.

By the evening of 20 October the Franco-Spanish force, totalling thirty-three battleships, was sailing in three columns south-east towards the Straits of Gibraltar, when British battleships were sighted in pursuit. Overnight Villeneuve ordered his fleet into a single line of battle, then, as Nelson's full strength of twenty-seven battleships came in sight, ordered first a return to three columns, then to a single line again. With only light and variable winds, inexperienced crews, and a motley mix of the two nations' vessels, the result was an uneven, sprawling, vaguely linear formation. Villeneuve ordered the ships to reverse direction at 8 a.m. on the 21st, heading back to Cadiz. This manoeuvre took over an hour to carry out and left the fleet in even worse order, a ragged crescent nearly five miles long, with the slower ships sagging to leeward, closer to the shore, a dozen or so miles away at Cape Trafalgar.

Nelson's plan, which he had shared with his captains at two dinners during the preceding weeks, was the climax of the practice which had begun to emerge at St Vincent, Camperdown and the Nile.[16] Relying on the superior training and experience of the British crews, he would risk exposing his leading ships to the enemy's raking broadsides, closing in two columns to shatter their line. His initial hope was to envelop the rear half of the line and capture or destroy all the ships there, while the forward half, cut off from the flagship's signals, was without orders and could or would not turn back. To aid identification in the disorderly mêlée assumed by this approach, he ordered the ships repainted in uniform black and yellow stripes (at a time when captains were traditionally free to decorate their ships almost as they chose, if they paid for it themselves). No attention was to be paid to a formal line of battle, or any prescribed order of sailing. The fleet would fall upon the enemy as they found them. His approach was summed up in a final instruction, recognising the impossibility of accounting for all eventualities: 'No captain can do very wrong if he places his ship alongside that of the enemy.'[17]

Thus on the morning of 21 October 1805, the British fleet, divided into two roughly equal columns, approached the enemy line from the west almost perpendicularly. The winds continued to blow lightly and fitfully, meaning that the ships were sometimes moving at less than walking pace. After first feinting towards the

head of the line, Nelson leading the windward, northerly, column
turned back towards the centre, as his subordinate Admiral
Collingwood in the lee, or southerly, column steered on a slightly
converging course. At 11.45, Nelson signalled the fleet with his
immortal words 'England expects that every man will do his duty' –
words changed from his original 'confides' to spell them out in
fewer flags. Fifteen minutes later, the first British ships entered
enemy gun range, and the pounding began.

At two centuries' remove, it is hard to imagine the stone-cold
courage needed to steer into battle as the British did that day. The
'people', the common sailors, were permitted to lie down beside
their guns, which at least made them a smaller target. Officers,
including the midshipmen who might be barely into their teens,
had to answer to a different code. Honour forbade them to take
cover, and indeed obliged them to manifest complete carelessness
of their own safety, walking the exposed quarterdeck upright and in
full uniform. It was their willingness to do this that secured their
moral authority to ask the men beneath them to go into the desperate, annihilating furnace of battle, but it was not a willingness
that always came naturally. Often, it had been nurtured with an
intensity that passed through hero-worship into something
approaching selfless love.

The poet Coleridge, working at this moment as a secretary to Sir
Alexander Ball, governor of Malta, was told a story by a lieutenant
who had served alongside Ball as a young midshipman. On an
expedition in small boats to attack an enemy frigate, the midshipman had begun visibly to tremble. Ball, then a lieutenant, moved
to sit beside him in the boat, and while continuing to look in the
direction of the enemy, who were beginning to shoot at them, took
his hand and murmured: 'Courage my dear Boy! Don't be afraid of
yourself! You will recover in a minute or so – I was just the same
when I first went out in this way.' The result, according to the recipient of this gentle advice, 'was as if an Angel had put a new Soul
into me'. Knowing that he was 'not yet dishonoured' removed an

'agony' from him, and he went into action 'as fearless and forward as the oldest of the boat crew'.[18]

This was a particularly finely drawn portrait of heroic inspiration: other officers might take a more bluffly paternal approach to conduct under fire, enjoining boys not to duck in case they put their head in the way of a cannonball. But even Nelson himself was known to take care to show a personal example not just of courage in battle, but in all the necessities of naval life – running up the rigging to accompany the most junior midshipmen, for example, when they first had to tackle this awesome, dangerous, but routinely necessary feat. For all that, naval life retained a routine element of brutality – aboard HMS *Victory*, as aboard almost every other vessel except some elite cruising frigates, the lash was regularly in use to discipline the recalcitrant. Yet as the British fleet steered into action, it was welded together by its fighting spirit. One midshipman present later reminisced about:

> The delight of us all at the idea of a wearisome blockade, about to terminate with a fair stand-up fight, of which we knew the result. The noble fleet, with royals and studding sails on both sides, bands playing, officers in full dress, and the ships covered with ensigns, hanging in various places where they never could be struck.[19]

The British fleet had, almost literally, nailed their colours to the masts, a reminder of what was about to ensue. But even common sailors greeted the prospect with enthusiasm. One recalled that the enemy fleet was 'like a great wood on our lee bow which cheered the hearts of every British tar in the *Victory* like lions anxious to be at it'. An officer in another ship noted that early that day he had been awoken 'by the cheers of the crew and by their rushing up the hatchways to get a glimpse of the hostile fleet'. Their 'delight' to him appeared greater even than that experienced by men seeing 'our native cliffs' after a long voyage.[20]

Later, on the final approach to battle, with the ships rigorously cleared for action, the atmosphere was less joyful, and indeed electrically tense. Captains toured their crews, showing themselves in their dress-uniformed splendour to those already sweating, stripped to the waist, and sometimes with kerchiefs bound around their ears against the cacophony to come. Some captains made inspirational speeches, one of which struck a seaman aboard HMS *Neptune* sufficiently for him to later record it in semi-literate glory. The fate of England, Captain Thomas Fremantle declared,

> Hung upon a Ballance and their Happyness Depended upon us and their Safty also Happy the Man who Boldly Venture his Life in such a Cause if he shold Survive the Battle how Sweet will be the Recolection and if he fall he fall Covred with Glory and Honnor and Morned By a Greatfull Country the Brave Live Gloryous and Lemented Die.

Inspired no doubt by Shakespeare's *Henry V*, and with the last phrase a direct quotation from Alexander Pope's translation of the *Iliad*, this played on every heroic register.[21] Given what was about to happen, anything that helped stiffen the sinews and summon up the blood could only be welcomed.[22]

By the time it cut the enemy line, Nelson's HMS *Victory* had been under fire from four enemy ships for over forty minutes. Each enemy broadside carried between thirty and fifty guns. Even inexpert gunners could not miss such a slowly closing target. The top half of the mizzen-mast was smashed. The main wheel was shot away, and the ship had to be steered from relieving-tackles rigged to the rudder below decks. Men, including Nelson's own secretary standing on the quarterdeck, were blasted to bloody scraps. *Victory*'s captain, Thomas Hardy, standing in conversation with Nelson, lost his shoe-buckle to a cannonball that could just as easily have smashed his leg, or killed them both. A whole file of marines were cut down by a single shot. There was no way of answering the fire until the ship finally inched its way across the enemy line, firing a devastating broadside into the glittering glass stern of Villeneuve's own flagship *Bucentaure*.

The British admirals emphatically led from the front, and Nelson was pipped for the glory of cutting the line first by Collingwood, whose own hundred-gun flagship HMS *Royal Sovereign* – the weed recently scraped from its hull, speeding its passage – was under full sail. It too took three-quarters of an hour of fire from four ships before raking the Spanish Admiral Alava's *Santa Ana*. Behind *Royal Sovereign* followed HMS *Belleisle*, another of the many ships captured from the French, in this case a decade before off Brittany. *Belleisle* also took fire from four enemy ships, losing all three masts, which collapsed across the ship's sides, blinding the gun batteries. The crew endured a further forty-five minutes of helpless bombardment, refusing to haul down their colours, before other British ships relieved them. While this battle raged, the ship's captain, William Hargood, was reported to have eaten a bunch of grapes on the exposed quarterdeck, in conversation with the captain of marines.[23] Later the ship rejoined the battle, helping to blast the *Santa Ana* into devastated surrender.

As the two opposing fleets grew more entangled, the British columns slowly and steadily meshing with the rearward two-thirds of the Franco-Spanish line, ferocious fighting raged for hours. Many of the French ships carried significant cohorts of troops, and repeatedly attempted to bring these to bear in boarding actions. *Victory* was saved from one such assault from the French two-decker *Redoutable*, when HMS *Temeraire* (not a captured French ship, but named after one) cleared *Redoutable*'s decks of a mass of troops with a single broadside from the shotgun-like heavy carronades on its upper deck. The *Redoutable* was the first ship to surrender, striking its colours shortly before 2 p.m., with only 99 men left unwounded from its crew of 643. It had, however, already fired one particularly deadly shot.

Admiral Nelson, who rarely escaped battle uninjured, and who had insisted on standing on the quarterdeck not just in full dress, but in the glittering regalia of his various honours, had drawn fire from snipers in the *Redoutable*'s fighting-tops, platforms perched high on the masts. He took a musket-ball in the left shoulder that smashed through his spine. Nelson lingered below decks for three hours, and thus knew before he died that he had, indeed, won the famous victory his country needed. Accounts of his last words vary, but at least one witness, a surgeon, heard him murmur 'Thank God I have done my duty.'

That duty had created a hell on earth. The focused and inescapable intensity of violence achieved in a naval battle of this time was probably not matched on land until the explosive artillery of the First World War. For those steeled to their duty by a culture of heroism, such a day was tolerable. Others were not so prepared, and for some, including the chaplain of HMS *Victory*, it resulted in something very like shell-shock, as a later account observed:

> Such was the horror that filled [his mind] that it haunted him like a shocking dream for years afterwards. He never talked of it. Indeed the only record of a remark on the subject was one extorted from him by the inquiries of a friend, soon after his return home. The expression that escaped him at the moment was, 'it was like a butcher's shambles.'[24]

The British customarily threw their dead overboard, with an unceremonious commitment to keeping the decks clear for combat. The French and Spanish did not. After their ships had been scoured for several hours by British roundshot, grapeshot and flying debris, what had been corpses were turned into piles of indistinguishable mangled flesh and bone, the stuff of nightmares. Blood ran from every deck, staining the very sea itself. Between them the allied nations' fleets suffered over 3200 dead and 2500 wounded. Things were only a little better aboard the British ships that had seen the hardest action – *Victory* itself suffered the most, with 57 dead and 102 wounded from a crew of 821. Collingwood's *Royal Sovereign* was not far behind, with 47 dead and 94 wounded. Several of the smaller two-decker battleships had casualties of over 30 per cent, albeit slightly fewer in absolute numbers. Overall the Royal Navy suffered 458 killed and 1208 wounded. Nobody could have known it at the time, but this had been the final great fleet battle of the age of sail – and in that sense, one of the most decisive battles of all time.[25]

Fully two-thirds of the enemy fleet was taken – every ship that had been engaged by the British force – while the forward third of the line fled for harbour after a feeble effort to turn back and engage. The aftermath of the battle was chaotic, as a storm blew up, some prizes sank, others were driven ashore and in a few cases seized from overwhelmed prize-crews by prisoners and smaller vessels sallying from Cadiz. There were also later recriminations about whether all ships had been equally eager to engage, or equally rapid and consistent in their fire.[26] But this could not alter the magnitude of the triumph. Napoleon might have seized victory simultaneously on land, but he could not now turn back and threaten invasion. Until his shipyards had rebuilt a new fleet, and at the price of horrific sacrifice, Britain was safe.

With the campaigns that culminated on 21 October under way, it seemed indeed for a time that Britain was more than safe, and was in a position to triumph. With the Austrians, and promised Russians, marching in the southern half of Europe, Pitt's government made a decisive commitment further north, beginning to land the first contingents of an army intended to reach 65,000 in northern Germany. The Prime Minister also sent an offer of no less than £2.5 million in subsidy to Prussia, and by late October government circles saw it as 'almost inevitable' that Berlin would be drawn into the fight, offering the opportunity to overwhelm France along all its eastern frontiers. The Prussians would not stir at once, however, despite Napoleon's blatant provocation in sending his

Napoleon as young general, when his image was still that of a tempestuously romantic republican hero. *(Culture-images/Lebrecht)*

The siege of Acre in 1799, high watermark of Napoleon's campaign in the East, where he was thwarted by Sir Sidney Smith, the 'English pirate' who haunted his recollections. *(Culture-images/Lebrecht)*

Sir Ralph Abercromby, the elderly liberal hero who gave British arms their first military victory of the 1800s, and their last for half a decade. *(Culture-images/Lebrecht)*

A veritable cornucopia of imagery, reflecting all the cares that troubled Prime Minister William Pitt's dreams. *(INTERFOTO/Bildarchiv Hansmann/Mary Evans Picture Library)*

A contemporary print suggests that seeing off the French would be rather easier than the nation's leaders feared.
(Mary Evans Picture Library)

Napoleon in coronation regalia, one of several portraits of him in this guise, showing an almost unearthly, cold majesty. *(Culture-images/Lebrecht)*

The Imperial Family, on display in one of many Napoleonic efforts to shore up his personal rule with the lustre of a dynasty.
(Culture-images/Lebrecht)

A perceptive satire on the great contest between Pitt and Napoleon – the latter avidly carves away at Europe while British power calmly slices off half the globe. *(Getty Images)*

Charles James Fox, a remarkable combination of rake, statesman and popular hero. *(Mary Evans Picture Library)*

The grim fate of some of the Frenchmen who sought to re-enslave their Caribbean colonies. *(Culture-images/Lebrecht)*

Admiral Lord Nelson in his full regalia –
it was thus he met his death in his hour
of triumph. *(Culture-images/Lebrecht)*

William Pitt in his later years, the cares
of government written on his face.
(Philip Mould Ltd. London/Bridgeman Art Library)

Lord Castlereagh, who survived intrigue
and disgrace to become the architect of
the post-Napoleonic peace. *(National Portrait
Gallery, London)*

Henry Addington, who rose from Pitt's
patronage to Prime Minister and Peer.
(Mary Evans Picture Library)

George Canning, whose over-emotional approach to politics drove him from high office at the height of the conflict. *(Philip Mould Ltd. London/Bridgeman Art Library)*

Spencer Perceval, the shrewd lawyer and cunning politician whose rule was cut short by an assassin's bullet. *(Philip Mould Ltd. London/Bridgeman Art Library)*

Robert Jenkinson, later Lord Hawkesbury and Lord Liverpool; a cabinet minister at twenty-one, and later Prime Minister from 1812 until shortly before his death in 1828. *(Culture-images/Lebrecht)*

Lord Grenville, the ardent anti-republican Foreign Secretary of the 1790s, but later a querulous Whig critic of the Peninsular commitment. *(Mary Evans Picture Library)*

British redcoats evacuating Egypt in 1807, a scene emblematic of the stalemate that dogged warfare in the Mediterranean. *(Culture-images/Lebrecht)*

One of Goya's many images of horrors from the Peninsular War, reflecting the heavy toll that witnessing such carnage took on the artist. *(Mary Evans Picture Library)*

troops across their lands en route to Ulm. By early November the first news of that disastrous defeat was leaking through to London. Pitt reportedly denounced it at dinner on the 2nd: 'Don't believe a word of it, it is all a fiction,' but by the next day it was confirmed.[27] All was not yet lost, for Napoleon was extending himself as he moved eastwards towards the Austrian capital, and success in engaging Prussia in action could leave him pinned, with armies to north and south, poised to cut him off from France.

Soon, news arrived from Admiral Collingwood of Trafalgar, which he dubbed 'the most decisive and complete victory that ever was gained over a powerful enemy', and of Nelson's death. Pitt was so overwhelmed by conflicting emotions after being woken with the news that he broke the habit of a lifetime, forsaking his bed at 3 a.m. with his mind racing. Two days later, on 9 November, Pitt addressed the annual Lord Mayor's Banquet in London. Toasted by the Lord Mayor as 'saviour of Europe', he responded in two graceful and potent sentences:

> I return you many thanks for the honour you have done me, but Europe is not to be saved by any single man. England has saved herself by her exertions, and will, as I trust, save Europe by her example.[28]

Accomplishing this salvation grew ever more difficult, however. Attempts by the allies to draw Prussia into the war became more desperate. The Tsar himself visited Berlin in November, coming away with a commitment for a Prussian entry by mid-December if the conflict remained unsettled by then. The British government would have to bite their tongues at a deal which promised Prussia the lands of Hanover – coveted by the Berlin court for decades, and frequently dangled before them by France as well – as the price for 180,000 troops. Awaiting news of Prussian intentions put the whole Cabinet on edge throughout November and early December, and Pitt suffered a serious recurrence of his periodic ill-health. He left to take the waters at Bath on 7 December, by which time, unknown to all in Britain, the fate of Europe for the foreseeable future had already been settled.

Napoleon had entered Vienna unopposed bare weeks after the victory at Ulm, with surviving units of the Austrian forces in Germany fleeing before him. The Russians who had sought to link up with the defeated Mack had also pulled back into Moravia, in what is now the south-east of the Czech Republic. With the Austrians rallying to them, they mustered some 75,000 men, around one in three of whom were Austrian. Napoleon was in a vulnerable position. The forces to hand were barely equal to those of the allies, some two-thirds of the Grand Army being engaged in garrisoning the long road back to France. With Prussia wavering, he could easily be cut off, especially if the major Austrian forces in Italy showed any initiative. His response was characteristically Napoleonic: to gamble on a forced battle and a decisive victory.

Drawing up his forces near the town of Brno, Napoleon – after a series of feints and manoeuvres, alongside hints of willingness to negotiate – presented a picture to his enemies of an army vulnerable on its right, southern, flank. The allied leadership, which included both Tsar Alexander and Austrian Emperor Francis, was divided, but decided after a council of war on 1 December to take the proffered opportunity. Thus on the next day, 2 December, first anniversary of his self-coronation in Paris, the Emperor Napoleon lured two other emperors to their doom.

Their opening attacks were met with strong resistance, and when they had extended their flank enough against Napoleon's right, he launched a series of devastating infantry columns against their centre, splitting the allied army. With incompetence (including the drunkenness of at least one general), lack of real coordination between Russian and Austrian units, and above all with the fighting spirit of the Grand Army demonstrated in waves of infantry assaults, hand-to-hand combat, cavalry charges and surgical artillery bombardments, the allies were shattered. Over a third of their total force became casualties, and the French captured fifty regimental standards. This was the *Dreikaiserschlacht*, the 'Battle of Three Emperors', otherwise known as Austerlitz (a village behind the allied lines), and ever after to be acknowledged as Napoleon's greatest single triumph. The Russians retired towards their vast interior to lick their wounds, abandoning Austria to ignominious surrender.

A truce was agreed on 4 December, and after aggressive negotiation the Habsburg emperor was obliged to sign the Treaty of Pressburg on the 26th. This gave much of Austria's lands in Germany to French allies, and took Venetia, Dalmatia and Istria directly into the French Empire, depriving the Austrians of almost all their coastline. It led to the end of the Holy Roman Empire and gave France effectively a free hand to remould western Europe. Napoleon also used the opportunity to blame Britain for the war: 'May all the blood shed here, may all these misfortunes fall upon the perfidious islanders who have caused them! May the cowardly oligarchs of London support the consequences of so many woes.'[29]

Official news of this disaster reached Pitt in Bath on 3 January 1806, after the first vague reports in the press late in December. Hopes of a general European coalition turned to dust at once, at the point where British diplomats had still believed that the Prussians were poised to join the effort. Word following shortly after, that the Prussian minister Haugwitz had signed a deal with Napoleon that included the prize of Hanover, sealed and compounded the misery. The British expedition in Germany was evacuated without combat, but the news may have contributed to a still greater loss. Pitt was already gravely ill, reported by shocked friends as 'much emaciated, very weak, feeble and low'. He had trouble keeping any food down and was wracked with shooting pains throughout his body. He was probably suffering from the long-term complications of peptic ulcers, unknown and untreatable in his time.[30]

Pitt's illness kept him away from the grand funeral arranged for Admiral Nelson, a massive public event including three days of lying in state at Greenwich Hospital attended by huge crowds, a procession up the Thames, and a march through the City to St Paul's Cathedral. With the royal princes in attendance, the funeral procession was intended, and functioned, to rebuff with unity and dignity Napoleon's charges of perfidy and oligarchy. At the service itself, Nelson's 'touch' was marked one last time, as the sailors who had drawn his coffin spontaneously tore to pieces the battle ensign of HMS *Victory* that should have followed it into the crypt, unhindered by the array of dignitaries before them as they took their personal mementos. Seven thousand people took seats in the cathedral, while 20,000 Volunteers and 8000 regulars paraded outside, many representing the regiments that had fought with Abercromby in Egypt – to date the only great military triumph of the new century.[31]

As these events came to a climax on 9 January, Pitt was leaving Bath at last, insistent on returning to London to see what could be salvaged from the diplomatic and military wreck. Very little could, and it soon became apparent that he was a dying man. The next two weeks were taken up with false, feeble hopes of recovery and episodes of clear decline. By the night of 22 January, everyone had to admit that the end was nigh. William Pitt entered his last hours as he had spent his whole adult life: surrounded by friends, but essentially alone, wrestling with the burdens of power. His friend the Bishop of Lincoln had spoken to him in the morning, addressing the fate of his soul, but as Pitt drifted into delirium that night, another fate was on his mind. He is credited, perhaps apocryphally, with a prophetic remark upon hearing news of Austerlitz – 'Roll up that map of Europe, we shall not want it these ten years.' What is certain is that he died full of anxiety, demanding to know if fresh news might arrive from the Continent, in between delirious episodes when he seemed to be locked in parliamentary debate. His last words, uttered in what a witness called 'a tone I never shall forget', were despairing: 'Oh, my country! How I leave my country!'[32] With the exception of their distant, cool, and so far entirely ineffectual Russian allies, the British were now, leaderless, once more alone, against an ever more dominant Emperor.

6

SHIFTING SANDS

The long years of William Pitt's ascendancy had cast an equally long shadow over British politics. The vigorous partisan conflicts of the 1780s, which had grown if anything stronger and harsher in the 1790s, had been crushed by Pitt's emergent dominance as a war leader. This was marked with particular clarity from 1797, when Charles James Fox took the leadership of the opposition Whigs into a 'secession' and stopped bothering to present an active parliamentary challenge to Pittite policies he abhorred, but could not affect.[1] As late as the peace negotiations of 1801, Fox was returning only for the occasional set-piece debate, and it was not until the manoeuvres which ended the Addington government in 1803–4 that the Whig leadership could again be said to be routinely engaged in active opposition. By then, of course, Pitt's political influence was fading in other ways, most notably as his former colleague Lord Grenville swallowed his loathing of the pro-revolutionary Fox and formed a new Whig opposition. Addington's fall (compensated with an elevation to the Lords as Viscount Sidmouth) brought yet another faction into the contest for power.

Sidmouth might have been held in low regard for his origins and reputed mediocrity, but as a peer and former Prime Minister he could now claim to be a power broker.

With Pitt out of the way, a whole new landscape of political possibilities emerged. Though Fox had noted in private during Pitt's last days that his death would 'render every debate flat and uninteresting', he felt obliged to oppose a motion saluting him *post mortem* as an 'excellent statesman'. That he could gather 89 votes (against 258) showed his continued influence, even when churlishly expressed.[2] While a majority of the Commons was willing to toast Pitt's memory, they were not, however, able to support the survivors of his Cabinet in office. The very day after his death the ministers sent a formal note to the king indicating that 'some *at least*' of the opposition would need to be brought on board.[3] Grenville took charge of proceedings, and George III spent the last week of January 1806 wrestling with a deeply uncomfortable truth: Fox, whom he had turfed out of office to make way for Pitt over twenty years before, and whom he detested at every level from the personal to the ideological, would have to join a new government.

By the end of the month the urgency of the international situation, and the solid insistence of Grenville, produced the king's grudging assent to a Cabinet in which Fox became Foreign Secretary alongside four of his Whig followers. Grenville was First Lord of the Treasury (and thus Prime Minister, which remained a de facto rather than official post for another century) and brought with him three further ministers, including the Home and War positions. Rounding out what was soon declared to be a 'Ministry of All the Talents' was Sidmouth, bringing with him the Lord Chief Justice.[4] A debate in the Commons on whether it was appropriate for a senior judge to be a Cabinet minister proved an early test of the ministry's command of Parliament, and a comfortable majority of 222 to 64 showed that Pitt's followers had a long way to go to reclaim power.[5]

Two of those followers, risen from backgrounds that had both clear similarities and striking contrasts, were poised on the brink of careers at the pinnacle of politics. Robert Stewart, Viscount Castlereagh, owed his title to his father's ennoblement in 1789 as Lord Londonderry, in the Irish peerage. Then aged twenty, Castlereagh was thrown into the tumult of Irish politics by being put up the next year for a seat in the Irish Commons – a seat his family had held as influential members of the Ulster gentry until defeated in a bitter contest by a still greater local family, the Hillsboroughs, in 1783. Seven years later, it took sixty-nine days of polling, and the expenditure of a staggering £60,000, to take back the seat: a prize worth having, apparently, even if it cost the sale of family properties, libraries and pictures to fund it.[6]

In the early years of his political career in Dublin, Castlereagh flirted with a Whiggism that verged on the revolutionary, but swung back to become a firm supporter of government – a castle man, in the language of the time – by the middle of the decade.[7] By 1796 this included joining a Militia expedition in expectation of a French landing, and campaigning for the wider formation of local forces to protect against feared Catholic risings. Yet, having become a junior government minister in 1797, he was appalled, as were some of the British commanders, by the violence unleashed against actual rebels and their supporters in 1798. Castlereagh had a grandstand seat for this spectacle, as in March 1798 he had been asked to become acting Chief Secretary of Ireland – the second highest office in the land after the Viceroy. That the latter man was his uncle was one reason for the speedy ascent, but Castlereagh's administrative flair also drew attention, and the new Viceroy, Lord Cornwallis, arriving as the rebellion flared into life, rapidly learned to respect his abilities.[8]

Soon confirmed in office as effectively the Irish Prime Minister, it became Castlereagh's task to smooth the way to Pitt's solution of Union – a policy Castlereagh had come to see as desirable, or indeed necessary, some time before. This opened him to severe

charges from opponents, as he was the prime conduit for the vast
flow of blatant bribery that was used to secure majorities in the Irish
Parliament for its own abolition. Having to defend the process as
the chief government spokesman in the Dublin Commons was a
stiff test; Castlereagh passed it with notable proficiency, facilitating
his translation to a Westminster seat, and continuation in office,
after the Union. This ascent was not all to his advantage, however,
consolidating as it did a growing reputation as a cold and
Machiavellian plotter, who put up a front of bland assurance and
unapproachability behind which he machinated furiously.

In this, Castlereagh was notably different from his near-
contemporary, George Canning. He, too, came from a line of
Ulster gentry, but his early years were a far more bumpy ride to
respectability. His father had been effectively disinherited, and was
living with his actress wife in semi-poverty in London when George
was born in 1770. The elder Canning died a year later, his wife
returned to tread the boards on tour in the provinces, and for seven
years her son was dragged round lodging-houses with her. At the
age of eight, to his great good fortune, he was taken up by a far
wealthier and more respectable uncle and aunt, who guided him
back on to the tracks of advancement. Placed in the social hot-
house of Eton – his three closest friends there all went on to
become MPs (in addition to other careers in diplomacy and administration) – Canning also won academic honours sufficient to justify
his relatives' care. At Oxford his connections reached even higher,
including the future minister Lord Hawkesbury and other scions of
the nobility.[9] Family and friends alike cultivated great ambition in
him, and it was clear that he had talents to match. Unlike
Castlereagh, who excelled in the cold practicalities of administration, Canning was a natural-born parliamentary orator, as well as a
poet and wit of increasing renown. He made friends easily, though
sometimes also enemies – he found it difficult to resist the barbed
jibe, and sometimes delivered them too publicly.

Canning entered the Commons, with Pitt's assistance, in 1793, sitting for a 'rotten borough' on the Isle of Wight, one of several that sustained his parliamentary career. A devoted supporter of Pitt, he rose to junior ministerial rank rapidly, and by 1800 was Paymaster of the Forces. Like Castlereagh, he resigned when Pitt did in 1801. Castlereagh, however, returned to office under Addington in 1802, becoming President of the Board of Control. Here his efforts to supervise the autocratic Richard Wellesley, Governor-General of India, as his duties required, were largely thankless, and his acceptance of the office brought him few friends amongst Pitt's more devoted followers.[10]

As a leader amongst this band, Canning in his poetic ode of 1802 to 'The Pilot that Weathered the Storm' expressed sentiment he reiterated in debate, that only Pitt could lead the way out of continuing crisis. Allying tactically with Grenville, partly out of a shared hatred of Addington, Canning restlessly harried the government, and Pitt, towards overt confrontation, hoping for a broad coalition of national unity under the latter's leadership. In this, he was of course disappointed, and became Treasurer of the Navy in Pitt's second administration bemoaning 'shabby narrow government'.[11] Having played such an active role in bringing down Addington's ministry, it was galling for him to see members of it retained in Cabinet posts when he was still only a junior minister. Such men included his old friend Hawkesbury as Foreign Secretary, and Castlereagh, who was shortly to become Secretary for War. All this, and other manoeuvres which saw Addington briefly return to the Cabinet at the end of 1804, left Canning in a fury of resentment. Only a private dinner with Pitt in October 1805, where his grievances were aired and Pitt promised him (in Canning's own recounting) a future Cabinet seat, calmed him. Pitt's death, however, left him grief-stricken and temporarily isolated.[12] Castlereagh, too, was cast from office as the Talents took up the reins of power, and saw no easy route back.

The uneven combination of wealth, talent and connections on display in the rise of Canning and Castlereagh – including in both cases literal nepotism by powerful uncles – reflects the nature of the British political system of the age. It was highly dependent on the abilities of specific individuals (Cabinet ministers still essentially did all their own paperwork) and forced to draw those individuals from a relatively limited pool of the aristocracy and gentry; the odd exception, like Addington, stood out, and suffered for that very reason. This is one explanation why an individual with genuinely extraordinary talent, like William Pitt, could rise so young: compared to most of his contemporaries, he was little short of an administrative, fiscal and oratorical genius. But even with such talents, being the son of one of the previous generation's leading politicians helped, as it also did Charles James Fox, son of the elder Pitt's rival Henry Fox, and who had become an MP at the remarkable (and illegal) age of nineteen.

The system that could produce such precocious talents was nonetheless constrained to find places for all the sons of the powerful families that dominated Parliament and the state. An aristocratic tradition of service could render such groupings the bulwarks of public life: many families – the Gordons, the Hopes, the Pagets, the Maitlands – had sons dotted through civil, diplomatic, military and naval commands. General Cornwallis, who led Ireland through 1798, and later negotiated the final text of the Peace of Amiens, had also served as the political and military chief of British India (and before that, America), while his brother the Admiral shepherded the Channel fleet through the crisis years of 1804–5.

On the other hand, many to whom power and influence were given took it as their right. Pitt's elder brother, successor to the title granted his father as Earl of Chatham, rose effortlessly up the military hierarchy, and partly thanks to his brother's solicitude spent many years in the Cabinet as Master-General of Ordnance. Though it was remarked that he was exceptionally good at summing up Cabinet debate – according to Lord Chancellor Eldon, he '*toppled* over all the others' in this respect – he was lacklustre at best in any activities outside the Cabinet room.[13] When given any more active duties he performed them with notable indolence; hence his nickname, with a dig at his illustrious parent, 'the late Earl of Chatham'. Charles James Fox, too, had a brother in the peerage (who, dying young, left his son Lord Holland to continue the family tradition of radical Whiggery: he sat in the Talents Cabinet as Lord Privy Seal) and another holding general's rank, who failed to distinguish himself for good or ill.

Charles James Fox, it might be said, had distinction enough for any family. Even after two decades in the oppositional wilderness, he was still seen by a significant segment of what we would now call left-leaning opinion as a potential national saviour. When he entered government in 1806, he had to follow the prevailing custom and present himself to his constituency for re-election. That constituency was the City of Westminster, endowed with several thousand boisterous and sometimes riotous plebeian electors. On this occasion they returned Fox unanimously, and he was hosted at a celebration dinner for four hundred, at which he toasted the king, but closed with a rousing reminder of his Whig principles, hailing 'The cause of Liberty all over the world'.[14]

That cause had also been the cause of peace, but Fox discovered in government that it was going to be very difficult to reconcile those two goals against an opponent like Bonaparte. By April 1806, the government was forced to confront the results of Prussian perfidy, as French-occupied Hanover was passed into Berlin's eager hands. Fox as Foreign Secretary stood in the Commons to denounce such 'evil and odious' conduct, fruit of the 'pernicious counsels of France', but could not avoid the fact that it meant a step towards war with a power that had the capacity to cut off much vital trade with northern Europe. By the end of the following month, speaking on the annual Mutiny Bill which re-authorised military discipline, Fox's language showed a growing realisation of the daunting task ahead: to 'consult your popularity, and act by the dictates of public clamour' was the 'easy' way to 'become a coward and a slave' – peace, even in a country groaning for it, could not come at any price, and certainly not at the price of national honour in abandoning Europe.[15] Even the press which had execrated Fox in favour of Pitt had to remark at such words that his patriotic credentials could not now be impugned.

In the privacy of government discussions and diplomatic exchanges, too, Fox was finding the need to soften his ardent desire for peace. In March the Cabinet had written reinforcing their support for the King of Naples, now once again in British-guarded semi-exile on Sicily; in April they discussed embargoing Prussian trade, and Fox was instructed to advise France that peace could only be discussed if Russia was included – there was to be no piecemeal dissolution of the alliance. But peace negotiations there would be: Whig opinion demanded it, and even Grenville's detestation of the Revolution and its heirs had been softened by long association with such men. Besides which, the soaring increase in the cost to the country of continual warfare showed no sign of slowing. Not to attempt to escape this dire predicament would be to value national honour at far too high a price – this had been their line against Pitt.

The man they were trying to make peace with, however, continued to reveal the depths of his dictatorial nature. He had already revenged himself on the admiral who had failed to produce victory at Trafalgar. Captured in the battle, Pierre-Charles Villeneuve was exchanged back to France in early 1806, and discovered, dead, in a Rennes hotel room that April. A total of seven stab wounds to his chest made the official announcement of suicide a subject of much grim humour in the British press. There had been more outrage when a captured British naval captain, John Wright, was reported to have committed suicide in late October 1805 in prison in Paris. Wright had carried out many daring and dangerous missions to liaise with royalist agents in France (and had been Sir Sidney Smith's companion in escape in 1798). *The Times* wrote that 'They who ordered, and carried out, the midnight murders' of men such as the duc d'Enghien 'can, no doubt, explain' Wright's fate.[16] Since

Wright was, beneath his naval cover, an agent of the British secret services with a shady past, there was more here than met the eye, but it was all grist to the propaganda mill.[17]

Nevertheless, now that he seemed to be in a position to dictate terms, Napoleon was happy to discuss peace. In May 1806 he showed his growing sense of absolute, and monarchical, power by anointing his elder brother Joseph as King of Naples, and his younger brother Louis as King of the much-abused Netherlands, snuffing out for ever the last lingering remnants of the Dutch Republic that had been a world power of an earlier age. He had also set in train the formal dissolution of the 800-year-old Holy Roman Empire in Germany, carving out a new Grand Duchy of Berg for his brother-in-law Joachim Murat, and supporting various allied dukes and electors in their rise to new royal thrones: Bavaria and Württemberg, amongst others, suddenly became kingdoms at this point. In July the Emperor cemented this edifice with the creation of the *Rheinbund*, or Confederation of the Rhine, a seventeen-state association of western and southern German monarchies with France. Intended publicly as a new agent of stability in central Europe, in practice the *Rheinbund* would remain what Napoleon had probably always intended – a device for bullying minor states into subservient allegiance.[18]

In this context, in June a message from Napoleon's chief diplomat, Talleyrand, reached London, conveyed verbally by an unlikely character, Lord Yarmouth. A rank amateur in political matters, and a heavy drinker, Yarmouth had been chosen from amongst the civilian captives held in France since the end of the peace and put on parole (his family remained in France) as a suitably eminent figure to suggest the opening of negotiations – illustrating once again the limited pool of talent available to the age. Fox eagerly seized on a reported phrase of Talleyrand's, that 'we will demand nothing from you', as a signal that the current status quo would be an acceptable basis for peace. This would enable Britain to continue to defend Sicily on behalf of the exiled King of Naples, against his new Napoleonic replacement on the mainland. This was a minimum requirement for a peace with honour, alongside the retention of Malta, and some measure of movement on the bitterly resented issue of Hanover.[19]

Over the summer negotiations went on through the intermediary of Yarmouth, handicapped by his erratic behaviour, and later almost sabotaged by his clumsy attempt to tie a financial speculation to his inside knowledge of events. But even when talks were supplemented with a more experienced diplomat, Lord Lauderdale, the Napoleonic attitude to power politics proved insuperable. Napoleon wanted Sicily for his brother, and as in the previous peace negotiations, did not hesitate to offer chunks of territory belonging to other powers in exchange – Albania, for example, an Ottoman province, seizure of which might spark a long-feared dissolution of the Turkish empire. When in July the Russian negotiator in Paris was bullied into signing a peace, the Cabinet were panicked into briefly considering this option; but Tsar Alexander rejected the proposed treaty, and Fox's chance of being a European peacemaker faded away.[20]

By the time negotiations petered out, Fox, at the age of fifty-seven, had entered his last days. Indeed, doctors had despaired of him as early as midsummer, but he continued working into August. Hugely obese throughout his life, his excesses caught up with him, his body wearing out with a rapidity that shocked all who saw him. Dropsy was the contemporary diagnosis, an accumulation of fluid in the tissues that would now be called an oedema, associated with various causes including congestive heart failure. At the time the only remedy was to dig into the body to drain the worst affected areas. On one occasion in late August 1806 thirty-two pints of fluid were drawn from him, and more were taken at the end of the month. While the release of so much pressure offered temporary relief, it scarcely postponed the final decline. He died on 13 September, his last words being spoken to his devoted wife: 'I die happy but pity you.'[21] As Mrs Armistead, she had been his scandalous mistress twenty years before, but they had built an intensely happy private life together. His last thoughts of her struck a final and poignant contrast with Pitt's despair for his country: in death, as in almost everything else, Fox and Pitt were great opposites.

Fox's death left a clear gap in the political landscape for a figure to come forward as the people's champion, and at least one candidate had already staked a strong claim to the role. Sir Francis Burdett, fifth baronet of that line, was an unlikely figure to become a beacon of political radicalism. Born in 1770 to a line of Warwickshire gentry that traced their roots back to the fourteenth century, educated at Westminster School, then Oxford, and on travels through Europe, he had married in 1793 an heiress of the Coutts banking family, and in 1796 bought himself a seat in Parliament from the selection held in the gift of the Duke of Newcastle. Already noted as a handsome man-about-town, when he inherited the baronetcy the following year Burdett was, aged twenty-seven, set for a comfortable life of moderate distinction.

In that year, however, he made the acquaintance of John Horne Tooke. An Anglican clergyman of independent (though declining) means, Tooke was in his sixty-first year, and for almost all his adult life had been an outspoken constitutional radical, pamphleteer and agitator. Beginning in the late 1760s with support for popular rights during the turbulent agitations provoked by the maverick journalist and politician John Wilkes, then with support for the rights of oppressed American colonists, engagement with the early reforming years of Pitt the Younger's governments, and delight at the outbreak of the French Revolution, Tooke crowned his gadfly career by joining, and in some respects mentoring, the London Corresponding Society in its first flowering of the early 1790s. For this he was arrested in May 1794, and tried for high treason the following November – after a week's hearing, the jury took only eight minutes to acquit him, as they did his fellow, more plebeian defendants.[22]

Living on an odd fringe between well-established Whig political circles and the unrestrained radicalism of some elements of the London 'street', maintaining an effective open house at his comfortable residence bordering Wimbledon Common, Tooke became a political and intellectual mentor to the much younger Burdett. The latter was soon publicly espousing views on the historical purity of the English constitution that derived clearly from the long 'Commonwealthman' tradition of Whiggery embraced by Tooke. In the context of the turn of the nineteenth century, this was fighting talk. Fox's Whig supporters were running scared after their dangerous brush with sympathy for the Irish rebels. Groups like the London Corresponding Society and the United Irishmen, and their shadowy offshoot the United Englishmen, had been formally banned by Act of Parliament in 1799, along with all other forms of collective organisation and correspondence for political, or other, goals. 'Combination Acts' in 1799 and 1800 extended this to anything resembling trades unionism, so that even traditional associations of craftsmen became illegal when they tried to maintain working conditions or pay rates in the face of employers' pressure. The suspension of habeas corpus meant that many radical leaders were being held as 'state prisoners' without charge or trial for years on end.

It was the fate of these men that brought Burdett to prominence. Held in the grimly named, but newly built and supposedly 'model' prison of Cold Bath Fields in Clerkenwell, north-west of the City of London, the state prisoners were kept ill-fed, and in declining health, by a harsh and corrupt set of warders. Alerted in late 1798 – legend has it by a note written in blood on a scrap of paper from the flyleaf of a book – Burdett became the parliamentary spokesman for justice. Visiting the prison several times, he subsequently invoked in Parliament the plight of the 'officer and gentleman' Colonel Despard, held like a 'common felon' in what he memorably dubbed the 'English Bastille'.[23]

His campaign marched on, despite the stolid indifference of the political establishment. Committees met and dismissed his charges, and he was barred from visiting the prison, but others supplied information of outrages and abuses – at least one case of rape within the walls, and men released at death's door from malnourishment and disease. When the political confusion of Addington's administration brought in 1801 the temporary restoration of habeas corpus, Despard and his colleagues were released to radical rejoicing. By then there are signs that Burdett's thought had been hardened by experience into dangerous forms – by one account he said that winter that 'the only choice of political emancipation at present was that he and the whole of the friends of liberty should solely turn their minds to the soldiery'.[24] It is no wonder, in this context, that Burdett – and other gentleman radicals – were reportedly alarmed that their names might come up at Despard's trial for treason in 1803.

Burdett had already used the fame acquired by the Cold Bath Fields campaign to cement his place in the radical landscape. At a general election in July 1802 he stood for the Middlesex constituency, wherein the prison lay, and which had a relatively broad franchise. In alliance with more conventionally 'Foxite' Whigs, and deploying recently released prisoners to make denunciations of authority on the hustings, he secured a victory that was accompanied by large crowds of the unenfranchised raising the new cry of 'Burdett and No Bastille!'

The candidacy of a man such as Burdett for the radical cause demonstrated the paradoxical nature of the kind of gentlemanly radicalism he represented. While his name could raise dangerous crowds, it was also reported that his purple election colours were widely worn by 'beautiful, well-dressed women' supporters, and waved on handkerchiefs and ribbons from 'respectable' houses towards the throngs outside.[25] Others marched with symbolic bunches of laurel to anoint his victory. It is impossible finally to judge how far he, or men like him, desired any real social change, or merely interpreted popular discontent through a lens of political advantage. Though Burdett himself carefully spoke of the need for 'quiet, peaceable and constitutional means' to get rid of the 'odious system' of the current government, others saw his language and his associations – including travel to newly peaceful France and meetings with the impoverished exile Thomas Paine – as evidence of opportunistic mob agitation and rampant 'Jacobinism'.[26]

In the aftermath of the Despard trial, renewed crackdowns and renewed war, Jacobinism of all stripes was far from rampant in the middle years of the decade. While 'patriotic' responses such as Volunteer enrolment might have had many motivations, the general atmosphere of national siege, only partly lifted by Trafalgar before being reinforced at Austerlitz, held back the development of any movement to parallel that of the 1790s. Yet nothing had been done to address the grievances of the working men who had declared themselves for radical and republican solutions in the London Corresponding Society and its ilk. Nor had there been any measure of economic relief from the hardships of war that had become so bitterly familiar in that decade. Beneath the blanket of defensive unity, while men like Burdett and Tooke kept open tenuous links between radical ideas and political activity, older, deeper conflicts were being renewed.

The decades of war with France were also the decades at the heart of the Industrial Revolution. That event was not, as historians once liked to depict it, a sudden 'takeoff' of economic growth. Rather, over a generation, economic and social forces in British society slowly meshed with their political and imperial context in new ways, creating a unique set of conditions and ideas that made possible an accelerating series of advances in technology and organisation. Imperial conquest in India, mercantile advances in Latin America, parliamentary Acts and naval blockades: all these gave impetus to changes that steadily transformed the lives of millions. Machinery, with its disruptive potential, was the advance guard, and the scapegoat, for fundamental shifts in the conception of work itself, and in what it meant to be a worker.[27]

For a sense of the possibilities of change, and of resistance, at the start of this momentous period, we can go back to 1776, and the Somerset town of Shepton Mallet. Centre of a prosperous trade in woollen cloth, the town's specialised economy occupied several thousand people, as was the case in many other towns across Somerset, Gloucestershire and Wiltshire at the time. In July of that year, twelve spinning jennies – hand-cranked machines designed to multiply the effectiveness of spinning-wheels – were set up in the town as a public experiment. As a result, on the night of 10 July, weavers from the surrounding communities marched on Shepton Mallet, destroyed the jennies, invaded and wrecked the home of one of the innovating merchants who had sponsored them, and were finally driven off by gunfire from a troop of dragoons, leaving a man dead.

Merchants from across the county stood up in support of the productive innovation, but at a general meeting in Bath on 1 October, hedged their bets by declaring that 'they will be ready to discontinue the use of the machines if after a proper trial they shall be found in any degree prejudicial to the poor'. Local workers were unsatisfied and unsuccessfully petitioned Parliament for protection, before taking a conciliatory route and agreeing to a further trial period, providing that the jennies were kept for the inhabitants of the local workhouse. It was a further five years before jennies were brought into use in the nearby town of Frome, and there too, on Whit Monday 1781, they were smashed by a mob, accompanied by further disturbances that, again, required the posting of dragoons in the town to restore order. Partly for technical reasons, but partly also because of this spirited resistance, it was more than another decade before spinning jennies established a presence in the economy of this western woollens region.[28]

Pressure to introduce machinery was, however, intense. By the 1790s the Lancashire cotton industry was demonstrating the dramatic improvements in productivity that were possible. Though the first power-loom mill in Manchester was burned to the ground in 1791 by angry workers, the rest of the decade saw convulsive expansion. The result was a stunning fall in costs of production, and thus of produce, that opened vast new markets. The price of fine cotton yarn, which sold at 60 shillings a pound weight in 1780, had fallen to 34 shillings by 1789, and to 16 shillings only a few years later. By the turn of the century the price was under 10 shillings, and it was under 5 by 1810. By then Britain was importing twenty times more raw cotton than it had been in 1780, and exporting cotton cloth to the world.[29] In the woollen industry, those involved as employers, merchants and investors saw the possibility of vast gains. Wool, however, was harder than cotton to shift in this direction: partly because its fibres did not respond to mechanical treatment as easily as cotton did, but mostly because of its historical place in the economic and social landscape of England.

Wool had been the country's staple export since the Middle Ages – indeed the very word 'staple', meaning both raw wool fibre and chief commodity, reflects that relationship. In the mid-sixteenth century, a series of statutes passed under all three of Henry VIII's ruling children had established strict and complex rules designed to keep the trade based on high-quality, high-skill handicraft. Men, women and children worked in almost a dozen distinct trades, covering almost twenty different processes needed to turn some eighty pounds of raw wool into the thirty-eight-yard 'piece' of broadcloth that was the industry's signature product. Some aspects were simple repetitive labour, like picking the wool clean of tangles and dirt, but almost all the others required skill and judgment: from the 'scribblers' who drew out the fibres on frames to straighten them, through all the stages associated with actual spinning and weaving, to the complex process whereby woollen cloth was first 'fulled' to bind the fibres closer together, then had its nap raised and 'sheared' or 'cropped' – using metal hand-shears several feet long – to produce a fine finish.[30]

How all these trades were organised into productive enterprises varied widely: in the western counties wealthy merchants tended to coordinate the 'putting out' of work to groups of workers, while in Yorkshire's Pennine valleys more independent structures prevailed, with smaller-scale clothiers organising labour, and selling cloth to merchants at tightly regulated local market halls. In some localities, elements of machinery in manufacture had already crept in from the mid-eighteenth century, and were tolerated when used to produce lower-quality cloth.

In the later 1790s a new wave of machinery was introduced, and despite some resistance successfully began to transform the woollen industry along the lines pioneered by cotton. One authoritative observer noted that by around 1805 the 'scribbling' process had been almost entirely mechanised, displacing adult male workers with children, and cutting the time involved per piece from almost 100 hours to under 30. By the same figures, over 600 hours of women's labour on spinning the yarn had been reduced, by ever-larger and more efficient jennies, to fewer than 75. Improvements in loom technology had cut the weaving time from over 360 hours to around 250, and new 'gig-mills' cut the time taken to raise the nap for shearing from 88 hours to 12. Altogether, this reduced the demand for labour hours by some 70 per cent per piece, although, because the most highly skilled weaving and shearing trades persisted, actual labour costs only fell by some 30 per cent.[31]

None of this had happened without conflict. Female spinners, in the prevailing culture, were relatively easy to marginalise, as were the scribblers, an occupation often taken up by the elderly or infirm. As gig-mills began to encroach on the preserve of the skilled and organised shearmen, however, they responded fiercely. Gig-mills were technically illegal under a statute of Edward VI, banned for their perceived role, in the sixteenth century, in 'deceitfully' stretching finished cloth to increase its size at the expense of quality. But early attempts to mount legal challenges on these grounds failed, and even a formidably well-coordinated cloth-dressers' trade society, the 'Brief Institution', could not make headway against innovating merchants, backed by a law resolutely hostile to subversive organisations. Smouldering anger at gig-mills was reinforced at the end of 1797 when shearing-frames – which threatened to do away with the skills of the shearmen altogether – were brought in for the first time to several mills west of Bath.

One night in mid-December, over 200 men with blackened faces descended on a workshop making up shears for such frames and destroyed them, before regrouping and threatening to burn down the mill in question, at Twerton. Local authorities brought together two troops of cavalry, 200 infantry and a cannon to defend the site, and eventually rounded up over seventy men seen lurking in suspicious groups. No evidence could be gathered to charge them, however, in the face of their stonewalling silence. This initial failure of direct action forced the shearmen back on to a traditional repertoire of threatening letters and occasional strikes, but the ingress of the gig-mills, and a wider tendency to devalue their work, was accelerating in their Wiltshire strongholds.

In 1802 this stereotypically calm and rural county was wracked by events known as the 'Wiltshire Outrages'. Beginning in the spring with a series of strikes targeting larger employers and innovators, by May such incidents had escalated to the destruction of cloths being carted to market, and by June to the burning of hayricks belonging to mill owners; all done by men disguised with blackened faces. By the end of June isolated gunshots in the vicinity of employers and blackleg workers had been added to the mix. On 14 July, the imposing, new-built Staverton Mill was subjected to a half-hour peppering of shots, and the following night another mill was burnt to the ground. On the night of 22 July, the defenders of an isolated mill at Littleton were captured at gunpoint by a surprise attack, and the mill burnt down at a cost of some £8000. This resulted in a local victory for the workers, and a formal agreement not to force down their wages. Further afield in the same county, violence continued – Staverton Mill was the scene of a firefight on 28 July –

to the extent that the government dispatched the chief magistrate of London, and substantial armed reinforcements, who together succeeded in pacifying the unrest with pre-emptive arrests of suspected leaders, and vigorous patrolling by night and day.[32]

As with the more political radicalism of Burdett and his supporters, during the early years of renewed war there was a slackening of tensions in the economic sphere, partly because both sides saw the possibility of a legislative remedy. A coalition of workers from the western counties and Yorkshire succeeded in putting their situation on the parliamentary agenda in 1803, requesting clarification, and if necessary enforcement, of the Tudor protective legislation. An alliance of manufacturing employers counter-lobbied for the repeal of all such restrictive acts – though smaller employers were less keen on the total freedom this would give to capital to pursue potential monopolies. As a result, from that year, and for the next six years, the old legislation was suspended, allowing the expansion of machinery and new working practices to continue.

In 1806 a new parliamentary Select Committee finally ground into life, taking hearings from both sides, but ridiculing the economic ideas of the workers' and small employers' representatives, and opening dangerous avenues of inquiry into the illegality of the workers' associations. The MPs ringingly endorsed repeal of the old Acts, but under the pressure of wartime business, and considerable elite indifference, it was not until 1809 that the employers' victory was sealed. The historic rights of the woollen workers became merely history, and they joined others, like the cotton workers, who had never enjoyed such protection, in exposure to the gales of a global marketplace.[33]

The Lancashire cotton workers, and the other trades that shared the booming economy of the English north-west, had provided the rank and file for a sometimes awkward radical coalition since the turbulent days of the 1790s. Amongst the middling classes of merchants and professionals there were enough individuals of liberal

sentiments to form an identifiable group of 'Friends of Peace', willing to speak out against government and for more humane policy.
Irish immigrants, meanwhile, provided a base of operations for the
United Irishmen, and the social tensions of Manchester gave rise to
rumours of conspiracy and United Englishmen cells. Variously
suppressed and marginalised in the years after 1803, some amongst
the more respectable threw their energies into the crescendo of the
campaign against the slave trade.[34]

Others fought back rhetorically, keeping radical flames alive in
print. A schoolmaster from Stockport, William Clegg, in a pamphlet that unashamedly lauded the value of the French Revolution
and of Thomas Paine, had asked 'who blushes at the name of
democrat' in 1798, when such a label applied to those 'who rejoice
in the improvement of society'. In 1803, however, he had cause to
lament in verse events in France, where the glories of democracy
lay crushed 'Beneath a vain Usurper's haughty crest'. Even this
outspoken voice had changed its tune a few years later – joining
respectable petitioning campaigns for peace in 1807, Clegg published a poetic appeal to George III, 'Purge thy counsels, gracious
Sire!/ Quick the British State to save/ Bid the friends of war
retire'.[35]

Such relative politeness reflected the delicate position of those
who tried, like Burdett in London, to stand against the ruling
system during these years of continuous warfare. Two general elections in November 1806 and May 1807 stirred the propertied
'Friends of Peace' into life. One, William Roscoe, won a seat at
Liverpool with over 1100 votes in 1806, while Joseph Hanson, a
well-known regional 'gentleman radical', narrowly lost at Preston in
1807 despite polling 1002 votes from both weavers and middle-class
electors.[36] At that latter election, Roscoe withdrew his Liverpool
candidacy in the face of a rising tide of loyalist mob violence, a
grim sign of the tensions flowing through politics and society. The
subsequent victor, General Gascoyne, celebrated with remarks that
were condemned in the local press as implying that 'all opposition

to his being returned' was 'rebellion'. Election flyers put out on his behalf had gone even further, proclaiming the vote as 'A National Contest between Religion and Infidelity, the King's Prerogative against turbulent and disappointed Ambition; the purity of Protestant principles again the Fanaticism of Superstition'.[37] Events were soon to put the notion of any kind of 'purity' within the circles of power very much to the test.

7

ISOLATION AND DETERMINATION

The twin elections of 1806 and 1807 took place in the context of developments that illustrated with particular clarity the interlocking of power, morality and corruption. The general behaviour of Fox's Whigs upon entering the Ministry of All the Talents – calmly exchanging political favours with Grenville's and Sydenham's factions, and sucking up the rewards of place and patronage without a qualm – had disgusted many of the radicals who had kept open connections with them over the turbulent past decade. George Tierney, for example, enough of a firebrand to have fought a duel with Pitt years earlier, was now denounced in print as 'that greatest of Political Apostates' for taking the prerogatives of President of the Board of Control – opening the riches of India to his manipulation.[1] The Whigs in general found themselves in a particularly unpleasant situation over the behaviour of their great patron, the Prince of Wales. Despite his own notorious profligacy, both financial and sexual, the prince pounced on reports of misconduct by his estranged wife, Princess Caroline, as an opportunity to secure a divorce.

A secret 'Delicate Investigation', involving the Prime Minister, Lord Chief Justice, Home Secretary and Lord Chancellor, centred on the charge that Caroline had borne an illegitimate child several years earlier, and also revived rumours of her sexual liaisons with a number of prominent figures, from naval hero Sir Sidney Smith to the politician George Canning. The secrecy of proceedings, in this gossipy political world, was soon no more than nominal. With the child's natural mother testifying to her maternity and the subsequent adoption, and with loyal servants refusing to corroborate tales of nocturnal liaisons, nothing concrete came of these sordid inquiries, except to further lower the reputations of all involved.[2] Radicals viewed the proceedings as a shameful assault on a powerless woman, and in print condemned the Prince for failing to contain his own urges, and the Whigs for abetting him.

Two by-elections in 1806 did give concrete evidence of corruption. In the summer Honiton in Devon was, following the custom of the time, the site of a contest following the appointment of its MP as a minister. Emerging radical star and naval hero Lord Cochrane made a public stand for honesty in politics by declining to bribe the electors, and as a consequence was roundly defeated. After Fox's death, his Westminster seat was fought over in October. An initial attempt by Richard Brinsley Sheridan to step into Fox's shoes collapsed under government pressure, and he withdrew his candidacy in favour of Lord Percy – an aristocratic nonentity put forward by the Grenville faction. Amidst radical fury, the dispensing of the Percy family's cash – they were the Dukes of Northumberland, premier dynasty of northern England – secured his election despite angry scenes of mob violence at the hustings.[3] Events such as these put the seal on the radicalisation of one of the most distinctive voices of political opposition in the coming decade.

William Cobbett had campaigned with Cochrane at Honiton, and had initially thought of standing himself, as he completed a migration from anti-Jacobin advocate of war to bugbear of 'Old Corruption'. The son of an innkeeper in rural Surrey, Cobbett had educated himself while enlisted as a common soldier on the North American station in the late 1780s, rising rapidly to the rank of sergeant-major by the time of his discharge, back home in England, in 1791. After a short trip to France in 1792 – partly occasioned by fears of legal action resulting from accusations of corruption he had made against officers in Canada – he settled in the United States for the remainder of that decade, and made a career as a vivid political pamphleteer and controversialist, defending a pro-British position under the pseudonym Peter Porcupine. Further legal troubles caused him to flee to England in 1800, where his reputation led to offers of work on pro-government publications. Wishing to preserve his independence, he embarked on several short-lived projects before successfully launching a paper, the *Political Register*, in 1802, with the help of a group of politicians opposed to the Peace of Amiens.[4]

Cobbett's attitudes do not fit easily on a conventional political spectrum. His cultural preferences were essentially conservative, following earlier figures such as Edmund Burke in upholding time-honoured structures against suspiciously abstract new systems and assertions. Yet he also felt a burning concern for those, especially in rural areas, he saw being impoverished by heartless political and social innovations. In these years he struggled to retain a sense that it was worth fighting to preserve the British constitution against French and democratic innovations, while he also surveyed with growing revulsion the endemic corruption of the political world. He was still ardently advocating the national cause against France after the outbreak of war in 1803, and indeed had one stirring pamphlet distributed at government expense, but after Pitt's return to power he became increasingly convinced that the existing system was no longer true to its historic virtues.

Cobbett's vision of the political scene emphasised the power of money, particularly in the form of the national debt, to dictate an ever-rising burden of taxation and an ever-narrower concentration of office in the hands of the merely wealthy. The dominance of such people 'without any regard to birth, character, or talents', and who had often obtained their wealth through corruption and exploitation of empire, had driven him into splenetic opposition by 1805. A system which saw even Lord Melville – the ardently patriotic Cabinet minister Henry Dundas, of unimpeachable personal honesty – condoning personal speculations by his subordinates with public funds, as was shockingly exposed in the Commons in April of that year, had to change.[5]

By 1806 Cobbett had abandoned his former association with a belligerent right-wing fringe and was drawing close to equally marginal forces on the left. Old warhorses of reform like the redoubtable Major Cartwright, who had been pamphleteering since the 1770s, came into his circle of acquaintance, as did Sir Francis Burdett, smoothing over an earlier period in which Cobbett had lambasted him as an opportunistic and dangerously Jacobinical meddler. After the Honiton defeat, Cobbett could write reflectively that 'We now know that Pitts and Grenvilles and Foxes are all alike.'[6] But that attitude required frequent compromises itself, for those who opposed these factions were very far from 'all alike', and often espoused personal and problematic agendas. A case in point is the man Cobbett, Burdett and others chose to support at Westminster in the 1806 general election, James Paull. A former official of the East India Company – and thus, like most such, rich from dubiously gotten gains – Paull had arrived in England in 1804, and in Parliament in 1805, with grievances against his former superiors he was determined to air.

Claims of denied preferment were scarcely the stuff of a crusade for virtue, but Paull's inability to get a hearing in the Commons looked like victimisation, inclining him to seek comfort in radical circles, where this view was at once validated. He was thus a natural choice to stand against Sheridan, who had betrayed the radicals by doing a deal for Lord Percy to stand aside in the seat he had so recently won. Cobbett, Burdett and others threw their weight behind campaigning – Cobbett in print, Burdett through finance, and other radicals through agitation on the hustings. Paull's narrow defeat, coming in third behind Sheridan and a Tory opponent, was interpreted at a radical meeting, chaired by Cartwright, as a signal that 'the freedom of Election was violated, our Rights and Privileges were invaded, and a deadly blow aimed at our independence'.[7] That Burdett had also lost his Middlesex seat, partly through the quixotic refusal to spend his own money on the campaign (supporting another's being less morally problematic), rubbed salt into the wound.

In the 1807 election, the relationship between Burdett and Paull was played out to an extraordinary conclusion. Paull desired a joint candidacy for the two seats available in the Westminster constituency, and seems to have believed in April 1807 that Burdett had agreed to this. But while Paull was advertising a public dinner to cement the alliance, Burdett was found stating that he would not stand. Confusion soon turned to bitterness, and on the night of the dinner, 1 May, a public statement read on Burdett's behalf accused Paull of using his name without permission. The inevitable duel followed, and the men shot each other in the leg, Paull's wound being more serious. While he withdrew from active life to convalesce, Burdett discovered that he had been nominated for the poll without his knowledge by a radical committee. Amidst a general atmosphere of disgust at factional manoeuvres by all the main parties, Burdett went on to a famous victory. Paired with Lord Cochrane, together they took 8842 votes, their various opponents gaining less than 6000 between them, including a miserly 269 for Paull's orphaned stand.[8] He continued to blame hidden actions by his enemies for his defeat, and shot himself less than a year later.

As all these political dramas were played out, war continued. Indeed, with the overwhelming threat of maritime invasion lifted, a new aggression entered governmental and military calculations. Resuming the successful policy from the 1790s of securing global strategic targets, an invasion force despatched during Pitt's last months succeeded in taking control of the Cape of Good Hope (South Africa) from Napoleon's Dutch satellite in January 1806. The naval commander was Commodore Sir Home Popham, who amongst other achievements had perfected the system of signal flags that the Royal Navy used to such good effect in its battles. Besides his scientific leanings, Popham already had a raffish reputation from various adventures in the Egyptian theatre of war, and had taken an interest in pro-British forces in South America that sought support for their independence from Spain. While those he was familiar with hailed from Venezuela, Popham decided that Buenos Aires, in modern-day Argentina, was a convenient point from which to launch a British takeover of the continent.

Persuading his military counterpart, Sir David Baird, to lend him a brigade of troops, he sailed his squadron – entirely without authorisation – across the south Atlantic and up the great estuary of the River Plate, taking the city with little resistance in June 1806. Indeed, several dozen leading members of local society may even have welcomed their 'liberation' as a political and mercantile opportunity (though later reversals of fortune have hidden their identities).[9] As well as offering all the resources of a commercial hub, Buenos Aires also yielded treasure. It was the transhipment point from the silver mines of the Andes, and several million Spanish dollars were recovered, including some of the dozen wagonloads with which the local viceroy had fled towards the interior. Sending these to England on the first available ship did much to redeem the unauthorised enterprise.[10]

News of this exploit reached London in the aftermath of another moment of victory. The British troops guarding Sicily had sallied on to the mainland of Italy in late June, seeking rather incoherently to disrupt the French takeover. The only decisive engagement came outside the small town of San Pietro di Maida, where the British commander Sir John Stuart held an elevated position with his

5000 men against a slightly stronger advancing French force. As at Alexandria five years earlier, disciplined British volley-fire shattered French attacks at close range, and a final bayonet charge put the enemy to rout, leaving a third of their force killed, wounded or captured. After this the British force declined to engage the main French army, and withdrew to Sicily.

Strategically, the battle of Maida was an irrelevance, and indeed by stirring a popular resistance in Calabria brought on savage French repression against a near-helpless civilian population.[11] Moreover, Stuart arrived in Sicily to find Charles James Fox's military brother Henry (on the coat-tails of his brother's rise) waiting to supersede him in command, and resigned his position in pique. His arrival in London was garlanded with honours, however, as his victory was being celebrated alongside news of Popham's exploit. A tavern renamed the 'Hero of Maida' would give rise to a new name for an entire district, Maida Vale. The Secretary for War, William Windham, trumpeted to the House of Commons the significance of Stuart's demonstration of national military, in addition to naval, prowess:

> Glory is the only acquisition which nothing can ever take away. Ships, colonies, and increases of territory, which may be won in war, may on some other occasion be lost, but the recollection of glorious exploits can never be lost; it will be recollected in the history of the empire, it will live in the memories of future ages, and its effect will not be temporary but eternal.[12]

Not content to await the judgments of eternity, however, by late 1806 the Talents ministry had elaborated a strategy to pursue the relative advantage offered by their command of the sea in the Mediterranean. A fleet was to intimidate the Turks in the narrow straits of the Bosphorus off their capital of Constantinople, while an expeditionary force from Sicily seized Egypt. What looked like a treacherous turn against a former ally was, in the shifting sands of diplomacy and war, in fact an effort to bring peace between the Turks and Russians, which would free another Russian army to turn on Napoleon. This did not stop bombastic press rhetoric about 'the decided influence of French councils' at Constantinople's 'imbecile court', and the possibility of liberating Greece from the 'tottering authority' of 'so weak a race' as the Turk.[13] As these plans were being laid, and as the ministry continued to pick over Talleyrand's evasive proposals, they eagerly took advantage of their apparent South American triumph. Putting aside for the moment any ambition to liberate the continent, ministers focused on rushing troops to secure their new conquests. *The Times* proclaimed that 'nothing but a speedy peace can prevent the whole of Spanish America from being ... placed for ever under the protection of the British Empire', and thus providing, not incidentally, 'a never-failing market for our commodities'.[14]

Four thousand men sailed at once for the River Plate, while other expeditions, totalling around another 20,000, were readied to seize key points on other coasts from Chile to Mexico. With the first wave of reinforcements already en route, news came that a mass rising of locals, and troops rallied from the interior, had forced the original contingent of soldiers into a humiliating capitulation. Throwing good money after bad, the Cabinet amalgamated the planned expeditions, and sent a new commander, Lieutenant-General Whitelocke, to restore control. The original reinforcements succeeded in capturing Montevideo, on the north bank of the Plate, by February 1807, but by then what had looked like a stunning success was already degenerating into a fiasco.

A long-delayed assault on Buenos Aires failed with the loss of over 2000 troops, and Whitelocke would eventually be forced, in June 1807, to agree to a complete withdrawal in exchange for the return of captives. He went home to court-martial and disgrace.[15] Popham, the insubordinate instigator of the whole affair, escaped with a reprimand, perhaps not least because he could bring character references from Lords Grenville and Melville, and evidence that he had discussed a landing in the region with the late Prime Minister.[16]

Around the time of Montevideo's fall, the Mediterranean strategy also began to come apart. The ships under Admiral Duckworth that advanced through the Bosphorus, far from prompting Turkish capitulation, were almost trapped after a display of negotiation merely allowed time for the Turks to bring up more shore batteries, and only escaped after suffering 300 casualties under fire. When these ships joined the expedition to Egypt, that too moved inexorably towards failure, the troops displaying none of the élan of Abercromby's earlier expedition, and becoming themselves besieged in Alexandria for much of the year before a final evacuation in September 1807.[17] In the years to come, the Mediterranean theatre would remain largely stalemated – there were never fewer than 10,000, and sometimes as many as 30,000, British troops spread between Gibraltar, Malta and Sicily, equivalent numbers of naval personnel, and often schemes to put them to use, but never a decisive engagement.[18]

By the time of the Egyptian failure, all the other hopes of 1806 had long collapsed. On the Continent, Napoleon further consolidated his power with moves that drove Prussia – his ally in the takeover of Hanover only months earlier – into an impossible choice between total subordination and near-hopeless combat. The *Rheinbund*, and the continued presence of the Grand Army in Germany, gave the Prussian leadership few options if they sought, as they thought they must, to retain Great Power status. Demands from France for a more active commitment against Britain went on alongside diplomatic manoeuvres to isolate Prussia from other north German states. There were even Napoleonic suggestions that the prize of Hanover might be handed back to Britain for peace. After first seeking some defensive reassurance in new treaties with Russia in the summer of 1806, in the autumn King Frederick William III and his ministers declared war on France.

The result was a resounding defeat at the battle of Jena-Auerstädt on 14 October – another of Napoleon's battles where he was rescued by a subordinate, although claiming all the glory for himself – and Berlin fell without a fight on the 25th. The Prussian army was humiliated by the speed and ease of the French occupation of almost all their country, not least because they did so little to resist it, hamstrung by an elderly officer corps and outmoded models of rigid strategy. Prussian forces suffered some 25,000 killed and wounded, but over 140,000 were taken prisoner on the battlefield and in garrisons that fell like skittles.[19] As winter drew on, the remaining forces, and the royal government, retreated into the far north-eastern quarter of their state, around Königsberg, where they prepared to make a last stand with Russian support.[20] They abandoned a population that was soon condemned to support a 150,000-man occupation army, and where bitterness at the sudden defeat was so great that an epidemic of duelling broke out amongst officers unable to restrain their mutual recrimination.[21]

While resting from his victory in Berlin, Napoleon on 21 November 1806 opened a new phase in his contest with Britain. Having now taken the remaining North Sea and Baltic coastlines of Germany into occupation as a side-effect of the Prussian campaign, the Emperor could attempt new measures of coercion. The 'Berlin Decree' proclaimed Britain to be under blockade – a curious notion, given the balance of naval power, but which had the effect of banning all direct and indirect trade from the French sphere of influence with Britain and its colonies (as well as initiating a further wave of draconian arrests of British civilians caught on the Continent). The poet Wordsworth summed up the nation's unenviable position:

Another year! Another deadly blow!
Another mighty Empire overthrown!
And we are left, or shall be left, alone;
The last that dare to struggle with the Foe.[22]

To maintain that struggle, the Talents government in London had little choice but to respond in kind, issuing Orders in Council on 7 January 1807 forbidding all ships, including neutrals, from trading with the French. This growing economic warfare was one reason why Buenos Aires had been such an eagerly sought prize, as it would have opened up a whole region to British exports at a time when the country's mercantile interests were clamouring for aid.

Despite the formal conditions of warfare over the past decade, goods, individuals and information had flowed fairly freely from Britain to Europe and back, testament in part to the dependency of many states on the products of precocious British industrialisa-tion.[23] Cities of northern Europe in particular had flourished as Prussia's neutrality had cushioned them from direct attacks or close blockade. At first the results of the 'Continental System', as Napoleon's measures were known, did little harm. Indeed, when British troops seized the Danish North Sea island of Heligoland in 1807, and it became an offshore depot for goods smuggled past the French authorities, nearby cities like Hamburg that were depend-ent on trade for their livelihoods were able to continue to prosper (even if the city authorities did have to expend 1.5 million francs that year on bribes to French officials to condone the smuggling).[24] But later in 1807 Napoleon hardened his system further with the 'Milan Decree', extending punitive measures to neutrals trading with Britain, and with its colonies and captured territories around the world, threatening to totally cut off Europe's supplies of Caribbean sugar, coffee and other staples. Over the coming years, the Continental System, in equal parts an assault on Britain's trad-ing lifeblood and a brutal assertion of dominance over French satellites, would prolong and intensify economic hardship and political antagonisms across Europe and around the world.[25]

As 1807 opened in the shadow of the Continental System, British domestic politics were in no better shape than the war effort.

During and after Fox's last illness, Grenville had made efforts to solicit Canning's help in forming a new, more broadly based government. But what was on offer seemed to the latter man to be merely an effort to defuse Pittite opposition by placing him as a fig leaf on a Foxite administration. He demanded instead a full coalition, with at least five Cabinet seats for his party – a move that was rejected, for Grenville had by now wholly gone over to the Foxite Whig persuasion, and had no desire, in Canning's words, to 'wed the party' he had already divorced himself from.[26] Grenville's Whig conversion was to bring the end of his government, for further attempts to advance the cause of Catholic emancipation enraged the king through the winter, leading him in February 1807 to demand from Grenville a pledge to drop the issue. Grenville chose to resign instead, putting party principle above power – though at a point when his government risked coming apart at the seam between Foxites and the Sidmouth faction anyway. The Whig wit Sheridan remarked of Grenville's stance that he had 'heard of men beating their heads against a brick wall, but never before of their building the wall to beat them against'.[27]

George III asked the Duke of Portland, now aged, ailing and much reduced from his days as a fire-breathing Home Secretary in the late 1790s, to form an administration, and by late March an essentially Pittite government had been assembled, winning a working majority in the general election held shortly afterwards. Portland took a figurehead role, leaving policy to the men of a younger generation who filled out his Cabinet. Canning became Foreign Secretary, Grenville's earlier approaches having helped to mark him out as a leader (though old links of patronage to the Duchess of Portland, and an indirect tie by marriage to the family, may have helped also). Castlereagh resumed the role of Secretary for War that he had held for the last six months of Pitt's life, and the two men agreed on an aggressive strategy to support what was left of their European coalition. Though troops and transport ships were in short supply after the Talents' South American adventures, intervention in the Baltic seemed to offer promise, especially in the light of grim events that had closed the winter in East Prussia.

There, Napoleon had continued to harry the remnants of Prussia's army, and their Russian allies, but had overstretched the Grand Army in eager pursuit across meagre roads and in harsh, frozen conditions. Turning at bay at Eylau near Königsberg on 7 February, the army of the Russian General Bennigsen had inflicted something very close to a personal defeat on the Emperor. The French, outnumbered by some three to two by 67,000 Russians and Prussians, and attempting an over-complex offensive plan amid raging blizzards, had been fought to a grim stalemate that left perhaps as many as 25,000 on each side as casualties, with many of the wounded freezing to death in a ghastly landscape of bloodstained snow and ice. Though the French gained possession of the battlefield, they achieved no strategic end. Many of their troops were tied up besieging strongpoints further west, and with a thaw bringing flooding, rendering movement impossible for several months, it seemed as if Napoleon might have at last overreached himself.

Plans were laid by Castlereagh and Canning to get a substantial British force ashore in Swedish Pomerania, on the southern shore of the Baltic, as soon as the weather allowed, thus trapping the French, with the help of the Swedes, between two allied forces. Despite the ministers' best efforts this force did not begin to sail until 16 June, by which time, had they but known it, the opportunity for action had been lost.[28] Though the casualties of Eylau had shocked Napoleon – observers had witnessed him blenching at the carnage – he recovered quickly. A scapegoat was found in Marshal Bernadotte, whose tactical errors, it was insinuated, had led to excessive casualties, while propaganda continued to claim that the Russians were on their knees.

Any suggestion that the gloss might be coming off Napoleon's imperial ambitions was quickly pushed aside by a double-pronged political offensive. In May 1807 the Emperor inaugurated a new imperial nobility, bestowing the title of Duke of Danzig on Marshal Lefebvre – an old republican warhorse thus tethered securely to the new order. From his German base, he also ordered a grand ceremony in Paris to be held the same month, placing the sword of Frederick the Great of Prussia in the chapel of the Invalides. Led by other old republicans now showered with imperial distinctions, and surrounded by a blizzard of propaganda associating Napoleon and Frederick with both military genius and political modernisation, this cemented Napoleon's image as the crusader against an old order of French Bourbon and Austrian Habsburg collusion and incompetence.[29]

While this was taking place, better weather towards the end of spring, and the successful conclusion of several sieges along the Baltic coast, allowed the Grand Army to bring fresh forces into action. After some sharp engagements in early June, with aggressive manoeuvres on both sides, the Russians were brought to battle in an advantageous position at Friedland, only about fifteen miles from the Eylau battlefield, on 14 June. Both armies deployed infantry and cavalry assaults to good effect, but a decisive moment came as Russian forces bunched alongside a river, and French artillery was concentrated to play on them at short range, with inevitably devastating results. A further general infantry advance by the French broke the Russian line, and in their retreat many Russians were drowned, and the main body of the army effectively routed.

Tsar Alexander abandoned Königsberg, withdrawing surviving forces into Russian territory, and asked for an armistice. He was profoundly disillusioned by British inactivity in the Baltic, suspicious that Britain sought to take Egypt (while also resentful of their failure to make a greater effort at Constantinople), and feared both the economic disruption mobilisation was causing at home, and the prospect of assassination, like his father Paul, by disgruntled factions. He harangued a British envoy about the 'whole burden of the war' falling upon Russia, and observed ominously that 'this was the last act of the great drama which had occupied the attention of the world for the last fifteen years'.[30]

What this meant became clear when Alexander and Napoleon met, amidst the pomp of their armies, but alone, on a raft in the River Niemen at Tilsit less than two weeks after Friedland. Each set out to charm the other, publicly agreed peace, and left each other with a free hand in the territories they held, signalling Napoleon's unchallenged mastery of central Europe. This notably resulted in the punitive reduction of Prussia to an indefensible crescent of territories arching from Silesia to Königsberg (costing it half its population, and effectively bankrupting the state), and the creation of a French client state, the Grand Duchy of Warsaw, in what had formerly been Prussia's share of partitioned Poland. Privately, the two emperors may even have agreed to collude in the carve-up of the Balkans, and perhaps of the whole Ottoman Empire (though publicly this was limited to a Napoleonic offer to mediate a favourable Russo-Turkish peace, under threat of joint hostilities if the Turks were resistant).[31] The Treaty of Tilsit also made Russia once again an enemy of Britain, theoretically part of the Continental System, and committed to war with her erstwhile ally if a general peace was not agreed by the winter.

The summer of 1807, with news still arriving from South America and the Mediterranean of ongoing failures, was unquestionably a further low point in the British struggle against Napoleon. For Castlereagh, the strain of attempting to organise support for the Russians, and then of preparing major reforms to military organisation that he presented to Parliament in July, led to a personal collapse, and he was ill for much of the rest of the year.[32] Ministers were helpless as George III's Hanover, so long the plaything of French and Prussian ambitions, disappeared inside a new 'Kingdom of Westphalia' for the Emperor's youngest brother Jérôme. There was, however, no suggestion amongst the Portland Cabinet of giving in. Britain made much of its moral superiority on the world stage – the dying days of the Talents ministry having been crowned by the abolition, after nearly twenty years of campaigning, of the slave trade – but the coming months showed that the ruthless self-interest of the 'modern Carthage', as French propaganda put it, was still intact and vigorous.[33]

As soon as word of the defeat at Friedland reached London, at the end of June, the Cabinet's thoughts turned to Denmark. Currently neutral, with prickly memories of the attack of 1801 keeping tension high, the Danes had rebuilt a handy fleet of some twenty battleships and were in a position to close the Baltic, cutting off access to Britain's surviving northern ally, Sweden. Even before news leaked out of Tilsit, the British were laying plans to send both ships and troops, initially with the hope that Denmark could be brought into the alliance. But later in the summer it became clear that Napoleon was also intent on securing the Danes, and a significant French force was building up on their land border. At the end of July, British forces were sent into action.

A fleet sailed with orders to prevent the Danes bringing troops from the mainland to Zealand, the island where Copenhagen sat – but to do so with 'all possible civility'.[34] Twelve thousand troops already in the Baltic were joined to a further 18,000 sailing from Britain to make a formidable strike force. Diplomats simultaneously offered the Danes an alliance if they surrendered their fleet to British safekeeping, but their arrival was followed swiftly by a parallel offer, or threat, from Napoleon, and the Danish Prince Regent decided that the French menace carried more weight. Opting for a French alliance, he gave the British no choice, in their own eyes, but to invade Zealand on 16 August, and begin a siege of Copenhagen.[35]

Even some of the British commanders on hand seem to have felt this a rather dishonourable proceeding, and initially the siege was not pursued very vigorously, in hope of a quick deal after a show of resistance. No such settlement came, and by the end of August, with a British brigade having to drive off an approaching relief

column, the siege was tightened, batteries were emplaced, and a
demand in earnest for surrender was issued. Rejection was followed
by a three-day bombardment opening on 2 September, including
use of explosive mortars and spectacular (though unreliable)
Congreve rockets. The mostly wooden city burned.

With a minimum of 2000 civilian dead on their hands, the
Danish authorities begged on the 5th for an armistice. They
signed a deal two days later, sparing the city from sack, but handing over the fleet, and warehouses full of naval stores. British
opinion, glad of a victory, was less comfortable with how it had
been won. The king himself declared to Canning, 'It is a very
immoral act. So immoral that I won't ask who originated it.'[36]
There was nothing in the understood laws of war against bom-
barding a besieged city, but even former Prime Minister Lord
Sidmouth thought privately that 'British honour and good faith'
had been sacrificed to temporary expediency. William Wilberforce
noted that 'Religious people ... condemn it strongly as utterly
unjust and indefensible', even though he himself was reconciled
to the events by arguments about necessary self-defence.[37] One
general remarked that the Napoleonic jibe about a 'nation of shop-
keepers' would now be replaced with the charge that the British
were a 'nation of Saracens', neglectful of the rules of civilised conduct.[38] Whig attempts to make it a parliamentary issue were
unsuccessful, however, and quickly tainted with accusations of
partisan opportunism.

A jubilant Castlereagh meanwhile considered garrisoning
Zealand permanently, before commanders persuaded him that it
was impractical – not least because winter ice would remove the
main barrier to a French assault in overwhelming strength.[39] After
a few more weeks, the British sailed away, apparently triumphant.
The Russian government had made friendly noises in the aftermath of the Danish surrender, and had even supported
Castlereagh's garrison plan, but this may largely have been to ward
off the fear of an attack on their own naval bases further up the

Baltic. The underlying consequences of Copenhagen for the British international position were almost wholly negative.

Denmark itself, as George III had perceptively warned when the scheme was first suggested, became a firm French ally for the rest of the war. The remarkable speed with which both British naval and military forces had been gathered underlined Tsar Alexander's suspicions that the lack of help his forces received before Friedland had been the result of deliberate, self-interested dawdling. He was drawn, at least temporarily, closer into the French orbit, and early the next spring launched an invasion of the Finnish territories currently held by Sweden. British attempts to support their ally went almost farcically awry. Naval forces managed to head off a French invasion from Denmark, but there was no way of getting sufficient support in place to prevent the rout of the Swedes from Finland, which fell permanently under Russian control. A force of 12,000 British troops sent to Sweden as a near-token defence achieved nothing. Their commander, Sir John Moore, refused to accede to madcap schemes cooked up by the Swedish King Gustavus, and furious disputes ended with him fleeing back aboard ship ahead of an arrest warrant. The troops themselves never even stepped ashore.[40]

Despite this series of setbacks, outright diplomatic defeats and a growing isolation as more and more of Europe folded into Napoleon's Continental System, the Portland government was not downhearted.[41] Canning wrote to a diplomatic colleague in October 1807, justifying in harsh terms what had been done in Denmark: 'We must not disguise from ourselves – we *are* hated throughout Europe – and that hate must be cured by *fear*.' Now Britain had something that suited its interests, 'a maritime war, in our power – unfettered by any consideration of whom we may annoy', and it would pursue it, rather than a peace that would 'sanction and settle some dozen green and tottering usurpations; and leave Bonaparte to begin anew'. Canning's determination was to keep Europe unsettled, 'no kingdom sure of its existence, no spoliator sure of his spoil'. He closed with a remarkable expression of British official arrogance: 'in the midst of all this it is our business to show what England, as England, is ... whenever the true balance of the world comes to be adjusted, *we* are the natural mediators for them all, and it is only through us alone that they can look for secure and effectual tranquillity.'[42] Britain was the indispensable nation, whatever others might claim.

8

THE STATE OF THE NATION

For many in Britain, the struggle under way was not just martial but metaphysical. The prophetic tradition that had given such prominence even to the hermit-like Richard Brothers in the 1790s had embraced with even greater fervour a humble Devon farmer's daughter and domestic servant, Joanna Southcott, who by now had been issuing prophecies of tribulation and redemption for over a decade, and publishing them since the turn of the century. Having given what seemed to her followers remarkably prescient observations on the national travails of the 1790s, she was now based in London, supported by a number of respectable and independently wealthy individuals, and attracting ever wider attention. Over 14,000 people of every class had been given her personal 'seals', talismans of paper and sealing-wax, by September 1807, and it was said that these numbers rose to over 100,000 in the years to come.[1]

For a woman approaching sixty, Joanna Southcott's prophetic writings retained a remarkable erotic charge, ranging widely through a vocabulary of brides, grooms and wedding feasts, and frequently dwelling on 'spiritual marriage'. She often seems to have dreamt of Christ as a husband, once recording how his 'most beautiful and heavenly figure', with hair 'wet like the dew of the night' and skin 'white as the driven snow', joined her in bed 'in a disordered state' and bared his legs (if not more) to her.[2] Strange as some of this may seem, it fitted into long traditions of spiritual mysticism, and allied with her prophetic reputation, brought into being a veritable sect around her.

Beyond a group of over 2000 confirmed followers in London, there were hundreds in places as diverse as Sheffield, Gravesend, Huddersfield, Plymouth and Stockport, and groups of several dozen in Halifax, Manchester, Nottingham, Bristol, Leicester and assorted smaller towns. Domestic servants, labourers, a panoply of skilled workers of both sexes, and on up into the ranks of the middle classes, the Anglican clergy and even minor gentry, formed a whole society in miniature, worshipping together and awaiting the final judgment. The same forces of religious revival that had brought tens of thousands to the Methodist vision of an enthusiastic Christianity – Joanna had attended such services in her youth, before finding her more individual path – created a new church around her increasingly apocalyptic words.[3]

Joanna Southcott's personal vision became increasingly linked to her own failing health, which before her death in 1814 she would come to interpret as a sign that she was pregnant with Shiloh, a harbinger of the Second Coming. Her followers, while clinging to her particular leadership, also formed a subset of much wider circles where the spiritual significance of Napoleon Bonaparte was debated as fiercely as any matter of practical policy. Southcottian prophecy was of a particularly mystical kind, based on dreams and visions, only sometimes cross-referenced (as with the identity of Shiloh) to specific biblical texts. Other forms paid much more direct attention to the outside world, resolutely determined to read secular events as 'figures' of biblical history. One such strand went so far as to designate Protestant Britain as a new 'Israel', claiming simultaneously that there was literal historical descent from the chosen people, and that current history recapitulated the travails of the Old Testament.

When Napoleon made peace between revolutionary secularism and Catholicism, and went on to give Jews a semi-official place in his state, all manner of anti-Catholic propagandists in Britain saw implications for home-grown questions of toleration. This was often expressed in terms of 'Popery' and its supposedly natural affinity for quenching 'every spark of civil and religious liberty', blocking 'combinations against despotism' and willingness to 'hold men under an absolute subordination to an usurped power'.[4] Other writers wrestled heroically to extract the 'number of the Beast', 666, from various numerological contortions – Bonaparte as the 666th ruler of the successor states of the Roman Empire; the abbreviation 'DUX CL I' (leader, consul, emperor), and a variety of evidently necessary misspellings, of which 'Napolean Buonaparte' was the closest any got to reality.[5]

What is notable is that, while some of the foremost enthusiasts for this activity may have been, even in contemporary terms, cranks, their ideas flowed out into the wider culture. Biblical exegesis was an entirely mainstream activity, to which great theological energy was directed. In 1811, a Prime Minister and a leading parliamentary radical would be found corresponding over the 'great end' that 'an over-ruling Providence' might have in mind for Bonaparte, and agreeing that while there might be 'inscrutable purposes' at work, it was 'still our duty to resist him'.[6] From hellfire sermons to popular almanacs, the idea that Bonaparte might be in some sense a 'scourge' sent by God to punish a fornicating nation (or a slave-holding one, depending on the author's political bent) was never far away.

Loyalists and radicals alike found messages that suited them in scripture, and in the stars (astrological almanacs were some of the biggest-selling texts of the era). Some even found them in their pockets. One thoroughgoing theological assault on the political establishment associated the 'mark of the Beast' with the 'general system of bribery' that Cobbett was to label as 'Old Corruption', before going on to denounce the image of Britannia on a new issue of halfpennies as the Whore of Babylon:

> An harlot, with wet drapery from the hips upwards, and which causes the parts to be exposed; a loose garment thrown over the thighs and legs, but so as to permit them to be very *conspicuous*; the feet, arms, bosom, neck and head, completely bare, and in the very attitude of invitation ...[7]

This might seem a peculiar viewpoint in many respects, but it was published and circulated along with many others that differed only in detail (albeit that differing over details was one of the things that theological scholars did best). It would be hard to identify any immediate practical consequence of all this debate on government policy, but there can be no doubt that such policy, in increasingly difficult times, was made in a context that rang with strife over the nature and purpose of national life. Was Protestant liberty to be safeguarded from Popish domination? Did the current generation even merit such salvation? These were far from empty questions as the Usurper's hand stretched ever further over what some still called Christendom. They echoed even in the mind of one who surely has a paramount claim to be a true original of this era: William Blake.

Born into the skilled artisan class of the capital in 1757, Blake's life was marked out by engagement in the prophetic mysteries of sectarian religion, a persistent apocalyptic vision of the evils of the social order, and a prodigiously eccentric artistic talent. Trained as an artisan engraver, he had begun to study the artistic dimension of his craft at the Royal Academy, aged twenty-two, in 1779. A year later, he was caught up in the turmoil of the Gordon Riots, when arson and the opening of the prisons may have given him a real-life flavour of the End of Days. Established by 1789 as a skilled craftsman, Blake was tied into radical publishing circles that linked him, albeit for the most part indirectly, with Thomas Paine and his sympathisers. He was already also writing poetry, focusing on the demonic absurdity of state power and social custom and the potential divinity within humanity. His artistic visions, and the first optimistic prospects of the French Revolution and English Jacobinism, sustained him for some time in a belief in improvements to come, but by the end of the 1790s he plunged into a deep spiritual and artistic depression, and fled London for the Sussex seaside village of Felpham.[8]

This retreat was granted to him – as support for artists so often was in this era – by the patronage of a wealthy man; in this case William Hayley, a local landowner who wanted Blake to illustrate volumes of his poetry. Over the next couple of years the relationship became strained, as Blake preferred to work on his own poetic inspirations. In late 1803, with invasion scares throughout the region, a troop of dragoons were quartered in the village. The swaggering intrusion of the soldiers seems to have raised Blake's old hatreds of the demonic powers of authority, and in August he snapped, railing at one trooper who had intruded on the peace of his garden. What he said is unclear, but the soldier, perhaps maliciously, charged that he had used seditious words, damning the king and calling the soldiers slaves.[9] As a result, he was caught up by a system that had become thoroughly militarised, appearing before a bench of magistrates who were almost all Volunteer officers, including a duke, an earl and a lieutenant-general. He was sent for trial at Chichester, although bailed in the interim, and fled the county for London. He would be acquitted in January 1804, partly thanks to the provision of a competent defence attorney by his patron, but the experience left him further convinced of the evils of the 'Beast'.[10]

Ironically, it was at this moment that Blake rediscovered his artistic inspiration, but his originality did not endear him to contemporary opinion. In 1809 Blake mounted an exhibition of his works in rooms over his brother's haberdashery shop. The show was poorly advertised, and an exorbitant shilling was charged for admission. Those who troubled to attend came away affected, though not necessarily in a positive manner. The pieces on display included a fourteen-foot-wide representation of King Arthur's last battle which divided critics – one thought it 'his greatest and most perfect work', while the poet Robert Southey, a regular and caustic reviewer of art and literature, called it 'one of his worst pictures – which is saying much'.[11]

In the published catalogue, even Blake could not avoid playing to the public mood of hero-worship and martial valour. The first two pictures described both reflected on the ongoing war, showing 'The spiritual form of Nelson guiding Leviathan' and 'The spiritual form of Pitt, guiding Behemoth ... [and] directing the storms of war'. Nonetheless his catalogue went on to note that these were 'compositions of a mythological cast, similar to those Apotheoses of Persian, Hindoo, and Egyptian Antiquity ...' One critic recorded that these were images that 'although he has seen them, dares not describe', while the *Lady's Monthly Museum* later noted that 'we dare say they may be very fine; but they are also too sublime for our comprehension'.[12]

While he endured public scorn – the radical paper the *Examiner* later declared the exhibition to be part of a worrying national trend, 'fresh proof of the alarming increase of the effects of insanity' – Blake also remained patronised by the upper classes.[13] Even his eccentric genius could not escape the need to eat, and the funds that were able to flow from the pinnacle of society. One of the men who had sat in judgment on him in 1803, the Earl of Egremont, became a sympathetic supporter. For his wife the countess, Blake in 1808 painted a *Last Judgment*, a watercolour that one artist friend praised as 'in many respects superior to the last Judgment of Michael Angelo', were it to be reproduced on the monumental scale it merited.[14] No such grandeur was forthcoming, however. After the failure of the exhibition Blake withdrew into virtual seclusion for much of the next decade, filling his epic poem *Jerusalem* with the names and characters of those he felt had persecuted him, interwoven with his unique mythological version of the history of England.

While the storms of war caused Blake much artistic and emotional pain, for a young lady at the fringes of the gentry, these years of national trial might seem to represent nothing other than a series of purely personal and familial vicissitudes. A decade begun with a father in genteel retirement at Bath, the year of the peace marked by the refusal of a marriage proposal from a wealthy but unattractive former neighbour, that of Trafalgar by the father's death and the revelation of financial straits. Penury – reinforced by the need to maintain a lifestyle of acceptably genteel idleness – was disguised by regular donations from better-placed relatives, and a long round of visits, ending the decade with a little security, lodged along with her mother and sister in a cottage on a relative's estate. Only the fact that this particular wanderer was about to present the world with the fruits of her genius, drawing heavily on her own life to do so, distinguishes Jane Austen from hundreds who were more or less successful in the game of courtship and spinsterhood, and whiled away the wartime years in a round of alternately pleasant and tedious diversions.

Yet only a very superficial reading of Austen's novels could ignore the evidence of her acutely perceptive sense of the society around her. If she did not make wartime adventures central to her plots, they nonetheless underpinned almost everything she wrote. If Captain Wentworth had not had a gloriously successful naval career, the plot of *Persuasion* would not work; if Militia regiments were not criss-crossing the country, the action of *Pride and Prejudice* would have had to be kickstarted in a very different way.[15] Behind the domestic dramas of *Mansfield Park* lurks the reality of wealth earned from Caribbean slave-driving in a decade of war. Austen herself was saturated in the country's struggle – she had two brothers serving throughout the wars as Royal Navy officers, one of whom commanded, to his bitter disappointment, a ship sent away on the eve of Trafalgar by Nelson to lower the odds and lure Villeneuve out. She was also deeply aware of the hard edges of material wealth and greed which underlay genteel society – the themes of potential and actual degradation and subservience at the hands of others and the law run through all her works, even if they concern the fate of genteel young women instead of artisans and labourers.[16]

While Austen combined her artistic genius with a settled place in the social order, others were not so fortunate. In the same year, 1809, that Austen's penury necessitated her move to her final home at Chawton, twelve-year-old Mary Godwin faced the prospect of seeing her father consigned to debtor's prison; her family was saved from desperation only by loans from acquaintances. The father, whose publishing business was foundering, was William Godwin, who had once trained to be a dissenting minister, but since the early 1790s had been a radical journalist and author, with a claim to be one of the first philosophical anarchists in a budding European tradition. Mary's mother, who had died of agonising childbed fever ten days after her birth, was Mary Wollstonecraft, a perhaps even more significant pioneer in feminism. William's noble, but reckless, decision to immortalise his wife (they had married only five months before the birth) with an unexpurgated biographical account of her sexually active life and despairing sui-cide attempts had driven the family into near-seclusion. Young Mary grew up in a household that practised free-thinking, per-haps even to extremes, and she herself was to repeat some of her parents' adventures, en route within the next decade to fame as Mary Shelley.

The Godwins' ethos was highly unusual even in the artistic cir-cles they frequented. Poets and thinkers are noted as free spirits, immune from social constraints, but Godwin's writings show him in a very different and more ethical light than many of his fellows.

At the end of the old century, for example, the family of the poet Samuel Taylor Coleridge had associated regularly in London with the recently widowed Godwin, finding his bereft children 'cadaverously silent' in comparison to the 'rough and noisy ... rampant' behaviour of their own.[17] A few years later, while Godwin wrestled with his debts, Coleridge was occupied with determined plans to free himself from his long-suffering wife, having arrived back in England in 1806 from his secretarial duties in Malta, addicted to opium and in love with another woman.

Returning to the Lake District where he had settled alongside William Wordsworth and the latter's sister Dorothy, Coleridge embroiled them in his self-centred anguish before departing for foreign climes again for several years. Another visitor of the period, Thomas de Quincey, later famed for his *Confessions of an Opium-Eater*, recalled not only Coleridge's addiction, but that Dorothy Wordsworth had a serious laudanum habit, brought on by the strains of living alongside her brother's wife, while worshipping him in tortured platonic fashion.[18]

Coleridge, like his fellow Romantics Wordsworth and Southey, had been an ardent democrat in the heady days of the early 1790s. Yet for all their unconventionality, this grouping also retained all the markings of their social origins – like Jane Austen's, at the junction of the professional and the gentry classes. Their various dwellings in the Lake District were all houses staffed by servants, their children were brought up with genteel accomplishments, and their earlier travels and current residences had been funded by family capital, not rigorous labour. As late as 1805 Wordsworth could write with a nostalgic glow that

> *It was my fortune scarcely to have seen*
> *Through the whole tenor of my schoolday time*
> *The face of one, who, whether boy or man,*
> *Was vested with attention or respect*
> *Through claims of wealth or blood.[19]*

Yet his school had been an institution for young gentlemen, he had gone on to university at Cambridge, and had had expectations, before the muse struck him, of being placed in a Church living through family connections.

Dorothy Wordsworth, in her correspondence, was much more plain-spoken about the realities of the social hierarchy they participated in. Shortly after settling at Dove Cottage, she wrote that 'We are very comfortably situated with respect to neighbours of the lower classes', who are 'attentive to us without servility – if we were sick they would wait upon us night and day'. Meanwhile, she recorded proudly, they were 'also upon very intimate terms with one family in the middle rank of life': even if the husband, a clergyman, did have 'a very small income', his mother-in-law was a gentlewoman, and 'the daughter, though much inferior to her mother is a pleasant kind of woman'.[20] Dorothy's brother, meanwhile, was in the process of shedding his earlier dabbling in notions of human equality to become trenchantly conservative, much to the disgust of a new generation of rising Romantics that, to close the circle, would in the next decade absorb Mary Godwin into their ranks.

Outside these charmed circles of creativity, where it remained always fashionable to be penniless, but not so penniless that one actually had to work, life was harder for those who strove to make a difference in the world. For most, the poets' casual adventurism in politics and life was unthinkable. James Luckock, for example, was in 1809 the manager of a prosperous Birmingham jewellery-manufacturing workshop, earning a substantial £400 a year, and about to branch out into business on his own. Born in 1761, he had been friendly with Joseph Priestley, the renowned chemist and radical dissenter, until the latter was hounded out of the city by a loyalist mob in 1791. Luckock had his radical views: he held a good opinion of Thomas Paine, and a hatred of public debt and profligacy that brought him close to the views of Cobbett; in 1810 he authored a tract on the folly of war, one of many issued in these

difficult years. By the end of his life in 1835 his organising efforts
had brought him the title of 'Father of Birmingham Reform' from
a new generation that had seized the suffrage for the middle classes.
But he tempered all this with more conventional piety and morality. One of the fruits of his association with Priestley was the
Birmingham Brotherly Society, the prime aim of which was to train
Sunday School teachers and managers for local thrift clubs, to promote 'knowledge and virtue' and discourage 'trifling unmanly
behaviour'.

Luckock also took tremendous pride in his own orderliness and
thrift – one of the great disappointments of his later years was that
his sons would not follow him into the business he had diligently
and arduously built up. One major goal of all his more political
activities was to encourage a new generation of sturdy, hard-
working and above all manly individuals to take up the challenge of
making something of themselves. There was no space for democratical levelling in his mindset, nor for the kind of sexual equality
that marked the lives of the Godwins: Mr Luckock was a famous
public figure in his provincial stronghold, Mrs Luckock, devoted
domestic helpmeet that she appears to have been, did not even
leave a record of her first name to history. This couple may make
for a particularly striking contrast, but the rising middle classes
across Britain were increasingly insisting on a domesticity for
women that offered a more restrictive model not just than way-
ward radicalism or aristocratic excess, but even than the genteel
freedom of Jane Austen's aspirations to authorship.[21]

The mercantile middle classes, as well as beginning to shift the
landscape of social aspirations and cultural emulation, also sustained the great engine of economic activity that made the
long-drawn-out war possible. From some perspectives, indeed,
global war offered remarkable opportunities for profit. The declared
value of exports from the British Isles in 1810, for example, was
£48,438,680, a sum only exceeded once in the subsequent twenty
years. Re-exports of imported colonial produce had fallen to a

trough of only £5,776,000 in 1808, but shifting alliances and opportunities saw them rebound to well over £12 million the following
year, a figure only exceeded three times in the following two
decades.[22] In the three years 1807–9, over £40 million worth of
cotton goods alone were exported. There were more than ten thousand shiploads of cargo delivered into British ports in each of these
years, and a similar number exported, the vast majority shepherded
in convoys by the Royal Navy, such a magnitude highlighting the
arduous nature of its duties.[23]

Not all of those who strove to rise into the middle classes were content to let politics take a back seat to profits, however. One such was
Francis Place. He was raised in the artisan classes of London during
the years of prosperity before 1790. His father was a baker by trade,
but twice gambled away his shop, becoming more successful as the
keeper of a 'sponging-house', a private prison for debtors. When
Place later came to write his autobiography, he was sharply critical
of the culture of his childhood. Gambling, dishonesty and violence
fill his pages, from childhood games of 'bullock hunting' – detach-
ing a beast from a group being driven to slaughter and herding it
through the streets with sticks until it collapsed from exhaustion –
to 'Cock and Hen Clubs' where teenage children of tradesmen
and householders paired up erotically after long evenings of drinking.[24]

Apprenticed in 1785 – apparently on a whim – to a leather-
breeches maker, Place found his master to have a family essentially
made up of thieves and prostitutes, and many of his youthful
acquaintances ended on the gallows, or a boat to Botany Bay. His
apprenticeship ended in 1789, apparently as a result of a quarrel
between his father and his master, and several years of struggle to
find work ensued – the making of leather breeches was a dying
trade, and strikes in pursuit of better wages yielded only further
decline in the harsh years of 1793–4. By now a married father, Place
recorded desperate days of non-stop poorly paid piecework to make

ends meet, as involvement in unsuccessful strikes branded him a troublemaker, but also began to open his eyes to politics. He joined the London Corresponding Society in June 1794, when its leaders were already charged with high treason, and aided the fight for their acquittal with his developing talent for organisation and information-gathering. In the later 1790s he quarrelled with the more insurrectionary of his comrades, and he resigned all formal connections with his fellow radicals in 1797. Two years later he put aside even informal involvement, as he had determined on making his fortune.[25]

Abandoning the craft of his youth, Place became an entrepreneur, opening a fashionable tailoring establishment in the heart of London, a position that exposed him to some drastic contradictions. On the one hand, he became a successful shopkeeper, earning a respectable, and sometimes significant, middle-class income, employing a workforce of skilled men to do the actual tailoring, and learning how to cultivate a monied clientele. On the other, such cultivation required him constantly to be 'dancing attendance on silly people ... I knew well that to enable me to make money I must consent to submit to much indignity, and insolence, to tyranny and injustice.' He kept a well-stocked library, but when one customer was shown it by his foreman, the man withdrew his business, and took away that of his friends also – Place later noted that they would not have cared if he were a drunkard, but 'to accumulate books and to be supposed to know something of their contents, to seek for friends, too, among literary and scientific men, was putting myself on an equality with themselves, if not indeed assuming a superiority; was an abominable offence in a tailor.'[26]

Such experiences drew him back into politics, and to the radical circles of Westminster elections – he backed James Paull in 1806 before becoming disillusioned with him, something that cost him 'many hundreds if not thousands of pounds' in lost custom as his identity became known.[27] Later he was closely involved with campaigns led by Burdett, Cartwright, Cobbett and others. Tellingly, he always remained ambiguous about his own social status: living and working in 'a second floor room', 'it was not a place which many persons would choose to frequent', despite his wife's 'peculiar care ... as to neatness and propriety'. But nonetheless he was 'visited by some remarkable men ... whose visits were very advantageous to me in intellectual and moral points of view'. He kept out of the limelight, but was always very attentive to anyone of the upper classes who did deign to treat him as an equal. He wrote about one such as 'a scholar and a gentleman, a man of extensive knowledge and singularly blessed with an enlarged understanding, a noble spirit and great courage ... I was equally proud of him as an acquaintance and of myself at finding that such a man should desire my friendship.'[28] To close another circle, Place was one of those most prominent in keeping the more genteel William Godwin out of debtor's prison, but it was a friendship that ended in acrimony, and £365 of unredeemed loans.[29]

Francis Place, facing the rejection of his claims to cultural equality by those who had nothing but money and blood to recommend them, could both despise and be despised by the aristocratic clients upon whom he built his fortune. At the other end of society, there was a widespread fear during these wartime years that those whom all right-thinking people ought to despise were rising in numbers and audacity. In 1806 a London magistrate, Patrick Colquhoun, produced a *Treatise on Indigence* that identified a substantial portion of the population as both helpless and dangerous. Over a million people were, he noted, in receipt of official poor relief, one in ten of the population. In addition, there were at least 300,000 other members of assorted dangerous classes, including 100,000 '*Lewd and immoral women*, who live wholly or partly by prostitution', and 50,000 professional beggars, employing tricks from claiming military service to brandishing mutilations and 'many devices to excite compassion'.

From here Colquhoun descended to smaller groupings, including 20,000 'gypsies, and another race of vagabonds who imitate their manners', a wide-ranging catalogue of marginals adding up to another 10,000 and including '*mountebanks ... vagabonds* with dancing bears ... *low Jews*', and – described with remarkable thoroughness – the category of 'Foreign vagabonds, who also wander around the country, pretending to sell pictures, but who are also dealers in obscene books and prints, which they introduce into boarding schools, on pretence of selling prints of flowers, whereby the youth of both sexes are corrupted, while at the same time some of these wanderers are suspected of being employed by the enemy as spies.' Against such looming menaces, the note of 80,000 '*Criminal offenders*' from highway robbers to house breakers, pickpockets to sheep stealers, seems almost an afterthought.[30]

While the propertied and educated classes could entertain and horrify themselves in equal measure with the spectre of such wrongdoing, for most of the common people the first thought in these decades was for food, and for earning the money to get it. In this respect, the wartime years since 1792 represented an epochal experience. As Francis Place documents, prior to around 1790 booming industry, imperial expansion and a growing population had conspired with favourable weather patterns to keep the price of food relatively low, and wages rising. 'Real wages', those earned in relation to living costs, rose by almost a fifth for many groups from mid-century, and higher still for some: up by a half for Staffordshire potters, and almost doubling for skilled construction workers. In Yorkshire, even unskilled labourers enjoyed a rise of a third in their spending power. There were also losers – agricultural wages in southern England tended to fall – but overall these were decades of stability and prosperity, and thus of relative ease and freedom for the working classes.[31]

War brought shattering changes, not least the two periods of real hardship and quasi-famine: in 1795–6, when prices rose by a half above their long-term levels, and in 1800–1, when they more than doubled. Outside these years, however, standards of living remained deeply depressed: throughout the decade after 1801, even in the years of peace, living costs in relation to wages were more than 50 per cent up on the 1780s, and as the Orders in Council bit after 1807, they rose again to average more than double from 1809 onwards.

For the radicals of the early 1790s, the first wave of such economic changes had been experienced as a sudden crisis, and helped to make the appeal of Thomas Paine and the French revolutionary example all the more vivid. With a rapidly growing young population, it is probable that by 1807, times of real plenty were in danger of passing beyond living memory for the majority. That did not mean that such hardship was simply accepted. Even in the good times the English had been renowned for their turbulent assertions of their rights: when Benjamin Franklin first visited in the 1760s, he wrote home of witnessing 'riots in the country about corn; riots about elections; riots about work-houses; riots of colliers; riots of weavers; riots of coal-heavers; riots of sawyers; riots of chairmen; riots of smugglers in which custom-house officers and excisemen have been murdered and the king's armed vessels and troops fired at'; all in a single year.[32] As Britain settled into a long period of unquestionable hardship, the popular response was to become vividly evident, and by 1812 was to raise the spectre not merely of crime, but of real revolution.

It would take time for this to become apparent, as the various versions of British identity wrestled for dominance amidst the larger conflict. For Jane Austen, such a vision meant the opportunity for intelligence, honesty and goodness to triumph over prejudiced laws and prideful social practices (even if only on the miniaturist's canvas of her novels). For Francis Place, the birthright of a 'free-born Englishman' meant the ability to prosper and to be heard in politics, not scorned for his social origins. For William Blake, the history and spirit of the nation were to be found in a conflict between free, pure love and the confining powers of the bellicose state. For many of his contemporaries, by contrast, the spirits of nation and state were being bound ever closer together by war.

In 1805 Lord Hawkesbury had worked out in his private papers a 'league table' of exactly this 'national spirit' amongst the Great Powers, calculated on the proportion of the 'male active population' under arms in the current struggle. France, Russia and Austria he recorded at a ratio of 1 in 14, Russia more generously at 1 in 10. In the domains of George III, he noted there were some 3.75 million 'capable of bearing arms'. Crediting the regular armed forces with a very generous 386,621 members, and the various Volunteer, 'fencible' and Militia formations with just over 415,000, he noted that Britons came comfortably top of the league, with 'above 1 in 5' in service.[33] Castlereagh's reforms of 1807–8 hardened up these somewhat optimistic numbers considerably, as the new 'Local Militia' came into existence at 100,000 strong, rising to 200,000 over the next few years.[34] The country that could accommodate Austen, Place, Blake and 50,000 alleged professional beggars also mustered ever-growing numbers of men prepared to defend – for whatever combination of ideals and subsistence – the unique amalgam of liberty and hierarchy they lived under. This was fortunate for the authorities, as nothing in the external world suggested that victory, or even survival, was assured.

9

NEW HOPES AND NEW DISASTERS

In the continuing context of global war, the view of Britain's significance that Canning had so memorably articulated was shared by Napoleon himself. It was one of the elements underlying the next act of the great drama that the Emperor unfolded across the European stage, as he prepared in late 1807 to take war into the Iberian peninsula. Writing to the King of Spain about the need to force Portugal into the Continental System, the Emperor insisted that 'We can only obtain peace by isolating England from the Continent ... if tranquillity is to be restored in the world, England must be forced to make peace.'[1] Portugal had been issued with an ultimatum to cut its links with Britain in late July 1807, at the same time as 25,000 troops began concentrating on the Franco-Spanish border near Bayonne to force the issue. What seemed a simple matter of agreeing with one significant ally, Spain, to enforce his will on an insignificant enemy, Portugal, was about to see Napoleon plunge his hands, elbow deep, into a hornets' nest.

The Portuguese government spent the summer of 1807

desperately trying to avoid conflict with either Britain or France; they even tried at one point to gauge the Emperor's susceptibility to a personal bribe, while assuring the Cabinet in London of their goodwill and also strengthening Lisbon's coastal defences, against whispered British plans to spirit the royal family from Lisbon by force. While Canning and Castlereagh paused in the execution of such plans on receipt of Portuguese protestations, they did direct a force of 8000 men to Gibraltar, and instructed another 10,000 to be ready to leave the Baltic as soon as possible. Napoleon forced the issue by withdrawing his ambassador from Lisbon at the end of September, and making a public declaration through the press that the Portuguese royal family, the House of Braganza, 'has ceased to reign in Europe'.[2]

On 18 October, forces under General Junot left Bayonne to cross Spain towards Lisbon, and on the 27th, a deal was signed at Fontainebleau to carve Portugal into three statelets – one in the north for a Spanish prince deprived of territory in Tuscany only weeks before (because it had become a hive of smugglers breaching the Continental System), one around Lisbon under French control, and one in the south as a personal fiefdom for Manuel de Godoy, chief minister of the Spanish king and architect of pro-French policy.[3] With this move, Napoleon hoped to tie Spain, which he viewed as a highly unreliable ally, irrevocably into his project of domination, and clear the way for a more wholehearted attention to the east, where the Ottoman Empire still begged to be carved up with Russia.[4]

The Portuguese continued to waver as Junot's troops slowly drew nearer through the autumn, but were finally driven into the arms of the British as it became clear that nothing would stop France from occupying their state. Imposition of a strict blockade by Royal Navy ships, cutting off food supplies, aided their decision (as perhaps did the example of Copenhagen), and on 29 November the royal family, the court and the leading citizens of Lisbon – perhaps as many as 15,000 people – embarked under the protection of British warships. They took with them as much of their treasure as could be crammed aboard, and sailed to establish the capital of their empire in Brazil. Portuguese imperial territories were thus fortuitously opened to vigorous commercial penetration by British merchants, who saw exports there rise from under £1 million in 1808 to over £2 million four years later.[5]

Only a day after the evacuation Junot's forces entered the city's outskirts, and proceeded to take control unopposed. It was fortunate for them that they were unopposed, for their journey of six weeks had been an unrelenting ordeal, crossing mountain passes through worsening weather, and contending with an unremitting level of hostility from the local populations. Since the army travelled, as Napoleon's armies tended to, without its own provisions, and 'requisitioned' anything it needed as it passed, such attitudes were unsurprising. They were also ominous – the combination of reckless haste, ill-chosen routes and civilian hostility left Junot with a mere 1500 exhausted and near-ragged troops to actually take possession of Lisbon. Though stragglers did rejoin, the losses faced on a journey over half of which was through notionally friendly territory set a fearsome precedent.[6]

Napoleon's unease about Spanish politics through the winter of 1807–8 caused him to seek to intervene yet more decisively, but in doing so he tore open a whole series of fault lines within the state, until it almost literally came apart around him. Under various pretexts connected with the British naval threat and the Portuguese manoeuvres, he insinuated almost 50,000 French troops into northern Spain, and in February and March 1808, by trickery and blatant force, these units seized a number of strategic fortresses. As another force marched towards Madrid, supposedly en route to Gibraltar, and noises from France suggested that the least Napoleon would settle for was the annexation of a large slice of the country north of the Ebro river, the Spanish court exploded into factional infighting. Godoy was profoundly unpopular, but supported by the king, Carlos IV. The latter's son and heir, Ferdinand, Prince of Asturias, was backed by a significant group who wanted him to take power and oust Godoy. Between March and May, first turmoil in and around Madrid forced Carlos to abdicate in favour of his son (with Godoy flung in chains), and then French interference, promises and intrigue lured both the old king and the new on to French soil, at Bayonne.

There, in the first week of May, Napoleon personally coerced both men into renouncing their claims on the throne and giving it into his hands – an extraordinarily squalid process of bluster, bribery and bullying. Napoleon then set out to place his brother Joseph, who had proved quite successful as King of Naples, on the Spanish throne. In the imperial game of musical crowns, Naples went now to Joachim Murat, the Emperor's brother-in-law, only recently anointed as Grand Duke of Berg. Meanwhile, the Emperor's sister Elisa would shortly be promoted to Grand Duchess of Tuscany, taking over the territory acquired in the Treaty of Fontainebleau. However, by the time the transactions at Bayonne were concluded, Spain was already falling out of the Emperor's grasp.[7]

Riotous attacks on French troops in Madrid on 2 May would go down in history and legend as the 'Dos de Mayo', and the artist Goya's evocative portrayal of their brutal aftermath of executions, the 'Tres de Mayo', cemented a story of heroic popular and patriotic resistance to ruthless military assault. The events of early May did lead to uprisings across the country, and the eventual formation of both a regular military opposition and a widespread insurrectionary resistance to the French presence. But many motives were involved, from Catholic reactionary sentiment to careerist ambition, and from sheer hunger after years of economic mismanagement to fierce and sometimes divisive local and regional patriotisms.[8] All these were part of the wider story of what became the Peninsular War, but at the time what mattered most to Britain was the grand opportunity it created to make trouble for Napoleon.

For much of the previous year, Castlereagh's thoughts on global strategy had turned around reviving either liberation or conquest in Spanish America, as opportunities for positive use of troops in Europe seemed to be dwindling. Some 8000 were gathered at Cork in Ireland, readied for shipment when an opportunity presented itself, and schemes for intervention from Venezuela to the Plate were mooted.[9] The stoking up of British public opinion in favour of Peninsular intervention began early in June 1808 when delegates arrived in London from Spanish rebels in the north-western province of Asturias. The combination of heroic resistance to Napoleonic tyranny and apparently popular patriotism captured both Whig and Pittite sympathies.

More official Spanish communication, however, tempered the Cabinet's enthusiasm – it was not clear that British troops, as opposed to British arms, supplies and money, were actually wanted. On the other hand, neither was it clear who, and where, the leadership of the uprising at a national level were. Much confusion and hesitation resulted, until at the end of June both the Cabinet and their Spanish contacts agreed that the best place for a British landing was, in fact, Portugal. Still held by relatively few French troops, a longstanding friend of Britain, and with a clear government-in-exile ready to resume power, Portugal offered all the advantages that were absent from the chaos currently descending on Spain. Not least of these advantages was the opportunity to control Lisbon, which with its population of 180,000 was not only one of Europe's larger cities, but the largest and most active port on the entire Atlantic littoral, with an extensive global trade network and all the infrastructure – mercantile, financial, shipbuilding and supplies – to support it. This was to become vital in sustaining Peninsular military operations in future years.[10]

Through late June and July, the British troops originally based at Cork, now raised to 11,000, moved in their transport ships first to Corunna in north-west Spain, then south to Oporto, and finally towards the coast of central Portugal. Intelligence on the French presence changed at every stage, seemingly alternating between alarming reports of large bodies of troops and reassuring news of isolation and dilapidation. It was not until the first week of August that the advance parties of a force now numbering some 14,000 troops went ashore through heavy surf, 100 miles north of Lisbon.[11] Joining up with Portuguese forces that had been fighting an irregular campaign, and with further reinforcements arriving in batches, the British advanced south, taking first blood against a French column of some 4000 on the 17th at Roliça, and on the 21st, reinforced to some 20,000, meeting a substantial French force, under their overall commander Junot, at Vimiero. The French left 6000 men guarding Lisbon and failed to coordinate their battlefield manoeuvres effectively, leaving themselves outnumbered, and suffering 2000 casualties in an indisputable British victory.

Junot offered terms for a capitulation almost at once – the evacuation of all French forces from Portugal on British ships, with their arms and stores. For complicated reasons of seniority and precedence, there was now a veritable gaggle of British generals with their army, and between them they judged it expedient to accept almost all the French requirements for surrender, including one that was particularly to revolt British public opinion: the right of the French to remove 'legitimate property', which amounted to a licence to carry home the loot of Lisbon.[12] Before Vimiero, this might have been seen as a triumph, avoiding as it did the need for an arduous campaign of sieges and the risk of new French incursions; after, and with a new British corps under Sir John Moore about to land in the Peninsula, it had a less rosy glow. The Convention of Cintra, signed on 30 August 1808, led to an outcry in London, and a public inquiry through the last months of the year that deeply embarrassed the government.

Moore's arrival, though hailed as a glorious new stage in cooperation with Spanish and Portuguese allies, did little in the end but give British arms another legend of heroic failure to mourn. Moore himself, though a prickly character in his relations with superiors, was already a figure of renown amongst the troops. He had served under the heroic Abercromby in the Caribbean, in Ireland (where he shared the latter's distaste for operations), in Holland and in Egypt, where he was wounded in the decisive engagement.[13] He had become the first senior officer to engage with a need for light infantry on the battlefield, and was at the centre of training at the soon legendary Shorncliffe Camp in Kent. Here were shaped the men who would become the Light Division, drilled not just in tight battlefield formations but also in rapid cross-country move-ment, small-unit combat and individual initiative. Almost unthinkably for traditionalists, Moore's officers had to train along-side their men, and harsh discipline was discouraged in favour of developing a fighting spirit, so that, as he wrote, 'the officers are attached to the men and the men to the officers'.[14] Such attach-ment, including that to Moore himself, played a noble role in what followed, but to no wider good.

Hopes had been raised when the Spanish trapped a French corps and forced its humiliating surrender at Bailen in the south in July, prompting a panicky withdrawal of French armies northwards. Moore's troops advanced later in the autumn from Portugal towards central Spain, only to find the situation transforming around them. The Spaniards suffered a string of heavy defeats, while their lead-ership disputed the role the British should take, as well as more sordid but essential matters of payment and supplies. Moore's troops eventually turned north, bidding to break French supply lines over the western Pyrenees. But the French rear was guarded by the dogged and wily Marshal Soult (and Napoleon, from November, was in personal overall command, spurring him on). Trying an ambitious plan to unite an army of 30,000 foot and sup-porting cavalry and artillery, marching both from Portugal and the port of Corunna, Moore found himself manoeuvring in a moun-tain landscape as winter drew in, against an agile and able foe. Over-confidence turned to pessimism, and by the last weeks of the year all efforts focused on making a successful withdrawal.

The retreat to Corunna became a legend of grim heroism, but in truth, as chronic shortage of supplies led to the collapse of discipline in some units, it was stained with pillage and brutality. The fighting spirit of those troops that held together was expended in a series of rearguard actions fought entirely on the defensive, with no clear strategic direction.[15] In the last of these on 16 January 1809, which effectively secured the Corunna beachhead for the evacuation, a bolder stand was at last taken, and Moore himself was fatally wounded, enabling a gloss of romance, at least, to be put over what was otherwise a frank disaster.[16] The troops had been at Corunna for five days before Moore's fatal battle, desperately awaiting the arrival of delayed transport ships. When they came, they could only take the men. Stores could be easily burned or blown up, but the spectacle of grief-stricken British cavalry, forced to shoot their beloved mounts to save them from capture, was to haunt the memory of witnesses.[17]

A rising sense of alarm at the course of external war was matched through 1808 with a significant growth in real social and political antagonism at home. The national leadership of elite figures such as Burdett had been partially responsible for the relatively pacific nature of activism in recent years. Others like Major John Cartwright had refocused their ideas away from directly 'popular' agitation towards coalition-building amongst the educated and influential.[18] Moreover, there were genuinely pacifist movements, particularly amongst the manufacturing middle classes, that brought together religious objections to war with alarm at its economic impacts. Such figures took a leading role in early protests at the military stalemate. Petitions from Yorkshire and Lancashire towns in 1807–8 denounced a 'war faction' that combined ministers and financial profiteers, producing a state of eternal and universal war, 'war with all the world', 'destitute of any reasonable Object', and announced that 'Christians are commanded to *seek Peace, and pursue it*'.[19] For such groups, violent action or sedition was beyond contemplation.

One other reason for relative quiet, however, was that a signifi-cant number of the most radical and potentially violent activists had been rounded up amidst the crisis atmosphere of 1801. Sentences of seven years' transportation were commonly handed down for sedi-tious offences, and a local Oldham diarist recorded at least one such activist, John Jackson of Chadderton, returning home after such a sentence in August 1808.[20] Exactly how far such returns had a role in the rising tensions of that time is unclear, but as the nation grew increasingly war-weary, economic and political goals began to interlock.

The demand for peace was, in the face of Napoleon's Con-tinental System and the retaliatory Orders in Council, essentially economic, while many workers' demands attacked the politics of the workplace, and sought national solutions. In 1802 strike action and political campaigning by Lancashire weavers had succeeded in obtaining from Parliament an Arbitration Act, which acknowledged that wages might need to be negotiated collectively, and not simply imposed by employers. In 1808, with wages for handloom weavers reportedly falling from over 28 pence a day to under 11 pence in the previous three years, their unions and associations regrouped and petitioned for a statutory minimum wage.[21] Despite the illegality of such organisations, government at first responded positively, and a Bill for such a provision was introduced. Its subsequent withdrawal was the cue for mass meetings in protest across the region.

In ironic, if less bloody, parallel to Madrid's Dos de Mayo, cavalry was deployed in late May 1808 against crowds of over ten thousand in Manchester alone, and as news of this confrontation spread, there were strikes the following week in Rochdale, Wigan, Bolton, Stockport and their satellite weaving communities. Taking the shuttles from the looms to paralyse the industry, workers locked them away, officiously marking them with employers' names as token of their intention to restore them.[22] In June the employers offered a 20 per cent wage increase, which closed the episode – though some workers' delegates wanted to hold out for 33 per cent, a marker of their self-perceived strength. This was also on show in the notable elements of public display and ritual involved: marches parading effigies of particularly hated employers were common, as were celebrations for the return to the community of freed prisoners.

Such was the value of having martyrs that some courted imprisonment as a strategy. Prosecutors charged after one Stockport gathering in June 1808 that it had been 'an assembly ... of such as appeared desirous of being made prisoners'. Other tactics pointed to a level of coordination and discipline that could only be worrying for government. Bolton weavers 'paraded the streets very quietly' by their thousands 'by file of three in a Breast', as a diarist noted, for four days. When they returned on the fifth day, the employers were ready to yield, but the authorities, shaken by the experience, drove workers from the marketplace with cavalry.[23]

These events also illustrated another developing cross-current of political disturbance. The crowds in Manchester had been addressed, apparently spontaneously, by Joseph Hanson, the 'gentleman radical', who had been engaged over the last year in supporting petition campaigns for peace. He was arrested and imprisoned as a result, and workers later presented him with a gold cup and salver in recognition of his support, paid for by '39,600 weavers [who] subscribed a penny each'. Another manufacturer, William Dawson, was arrested for addressing a similar crowd in Stockport on the same day, and it is probable that respectable radicals contributed bail funds for at least some of the hundreds of workers detained in these events.[24] The involvement of such figures had already made peace petitions from Lancashire bolder than those from Yorkshire – the latter tended to be addressed to the king, beseeching action, while the former had called boldly on Parliament to oblige the executive to mend its ways.[25]

With the Whigs now entering a temporary eclipse, thanks to a combination of their failures in government and final rupture with radicalism, there seemed more space in politics for the slightly odd fusion of democratic demands and historical virtues that brought 'gentleman radicals' like Burdett and Hanson together with more marginal campaigners like Cobbett. Although initial talk after the 1807 general election of a new radical platform to restore constitutional liberties faded under the impact of a solid Pittite government, the eruption of Spanish revolt the following year buoyed the spirits of radicals; so did further evidence of corruption (political if not financial) as the inquiry into the Convention of Cintra ground to its unsatisfactory conclusions. The travails of the next year, 1809, were to show again both the strengths and weaknesses of the essentially moral case now being made against the holders of power.

The scandal of the Duke of York's relations with his mistress, Mary Anne Clarke, had simmered below the surface of politics for some time. Clarke came of an artisan family, abandoned by her husband, and had become a courtesan like many others. The Duke had treated her very well, setting her up in a lavish home and supporting an active social life and spending habits. Their liaison had in fact ended in 1806, largely due to the prospect of blackmail demands being made by her estranged husband, and subsequent insinuations about it in cartoons and pamphlets had made little real impact.[26] But the Duke's failure to keep up promised payments needed to maintain her lifestyle drove Clarke to consider obtaining value from the many compromising letters she held.

An enterprising journalist of her acquaintance put her in contact with Colonel Gwyllym Wardle, MP, who was seeking a route to radical prominence, belying his own background as an aggressive cavalry officer and high-living man-about-town. In January 1809, with Burdett's support, Wardle brought the scandal into the open, employing parliamentary privilege to charge that Clarke had been the conduit for a shameful series of corrupt deals, having used her sexual influence over the Duke to obtain military and civilian posts for applicants in return for cash payment. Adultery and fornication were one thing – the newspapers had a regular trade in juicy court proceedings amongst the upper classes for 'crim. con.', the sordid evidence required to secure a divorce – but mixing it with overt peculation was quite another.[27] For the next two months this news convulsed the public scene, as the Commons was forced to hold an official investigation.

For radicals on the Burdett–Cobbett–Cartwright axis, it was yet another argument for root-and-branch reform of government and representation. Though the Duke's supporters protested that the corruption charges were untrue, his relationship with Clarke was in itself – once publicly acknowledged – severely harmful, and he resigned from his post as commander-in-chief on 17 March, despite being officially exonerated. Radicals in the Commons got a boost in public prestige as many Whigs, bound by their ties to the Prince of Wales, shied away from condemning his brother.[28]

Votes of thanks flowed in from public meetings to Burdett, Wardle and others who had forced the issue: from over a dozen major towns and cities, many smaller ones, several meetings of county electors, and gatherings across the London constituencies. A dinner to launch renewed reform efforts, held in London on 1 May 1809, attracted 1200 guests, some paying up to five guineas for a ticket. Speeches and toasts against 'State frauds and abuses' were cheered, and Burdett spoke of the people's eyes being opened to the vile corruption of the 'borough-mongering faction' in power, and the 'self-evident truth' of the need for reform.[29]

The details revealed before Parliament had certainly been shocking. While some points were merely titillating – the notion that Clarke had pinned a list of names for preferment over the bed in which she pleasured the Duke particularly caught the eye of satirists – beneath them was revealed a system of thoroughgoing corruption. Clarke had plugged into existing networks that had emerged because of the frantic demand of the upwardly mobile for preferment, and the stranglehold that the office-holding elite had on appointments not just in the army, but across the official landscape. Getting relatively junior posts filled was easy but not particularly profitable, and she soon went beyond meagre measures. Working with several 'agents' and demanding sums that started at £500 or £1000, she offered a fast track to prestigious and lucrative regimental commands, and other merely lucrative positions in the military supply chain.

Clarke had also branched out into areas where the Duke's influence was more indirect, taking cash on at least two occasions in unsuccessful efforts to gain men preferment within the Church: here, as elsewhere, there were no refunds. Customs inspectorships, at home and in the colonies, were another arena of competition, and in at least one case Clarke was involved in trafficking such positions in exchange for tens of thousands of pounds in proffered loans. Other allegations spiralled into further damaging inquiries, revealing that Clarke had formed only a small corner of a burgeoning market for corrupt placements in the East India Company. Here, vast personal profits were still available, so much so that in some cases preferment had been traded directly for seats in the House of Commons itself.[30]

The evidence was overwhelming that the offices of state were in danger of being taken over entirely by those prepared to use dishonest means to keep out more upstanding rivals. The whole rhetoric of the radical assault, as figures like Cobbett had begun recrafting it, relied on a patriotic appeal to national virtues, which could only find renewed vigour from such a threat. Many of those who met by the thousands in provincial cities were members of the stout middle classes, this episode perhaps indeed, as Burdett suggested, opening their eyes to the true nature of things. Yet this new infusion of support for radical reformers was to prove only temporary.[31]

With memories of the 1790s and insurrectionary plots still vivid, many meetings focused on addressing the issue of corruption with relatively minor reforms, far from the annual parliaments and manhood suffrage that Cartwright, for example, had been advocating for almost forty years.[32] The radical claim of patriotic morality also suffered a damaging blow when Clarke, taken to

court over a £1000 bill for some luxurious furnishings, alleged that
it was Colonel Wardle who had agreed to pay for them – because
he was, she claimed, her lover. Such an allegation, from Clarke's
own mouth, served to kill any real reforming momentum, especially when it was followed up with revelations that she had been
paid £10,000 by the government not to publish her memoirs, and
suggestions that Wardle had only taken up her story to further his
own career.[33]

The year 1809 was to see two further disasters, both of which combined tragedy with farce. Each was wrapped up in the
consequences of another short-lived continental effort to resist
Napoleon's ever-growing encroachments. The Austrian Emperor
and his ministers, cowed since Austerlitz, had watched with horror
the spoliation of the Spanish monarchy, crowning as it did a series
of moves to stretch French power into every corner of Europe.
With prodding from a small but vocal faction of Prussians who
wanted to stir a general German rising, and in the belief that the
Spanish situation would prevent a decisive Napoleonic riposte, the
Vienna government – aided by £250,000 in silver forwarded by an
encouraging Canning – launched a war against France by invading
its ally Bavaria in April 1809.[34]

Germany failed to rise in support, Russia betrayed vague promises of neutrality to threaten Austria from the east, and French
counter-attacks had begun by May. Napoleon himself soon took to
the field, and in early July the Austrian army was at last decisively
beaten not far from Vienna in the battle of Wagram. This hard-
fought engagement cost the French 34,000 killed and wounded,
and began to suggest that the Grand Army, diluted by multinational
contingents, was no longer what it had once been. Nevertheless,
the Austrian defeat was real enough, had cost the British government almost another £1 million in hastily supplied subsidy over the
three months of conflict, and was prelude to a further, self-inflicted,
British catastrophe.[35]

Canning's eagerness to support the Austrian war was joined by Castlereagh's to make a positive contribution through force of arms. Thanks to his organising efforts, there were now some 40,000 troops available for deployment in Britain, and with a rapid strike called for, the short sea-passage to the Netherlands came to be seen as the best way forward. The key strategic objective was to destroy the French naval base at Antwerp on the River Scheldt, with the wider possibility of posing a significant threat to an empire embroiled to the south and the east in widely separated campaigns.

The fate of the 1799 Dutch expedition seems to have been ignored by planners, who advocated a landing on the marshy coastal islands north of Antwerp, based on twenty-year-old maps and almost no local intelligence. Delays set in, as they almost always seemed to with British expeditions; in this case not aided by the appointment of the 'late Earl of Chatham' to command. By the time the expedition sailed, on 28 July, not only had its destination been reported in the press (and thus to the enemy) for over a week, but news of the defeat at Wagram was already to hand.[36]

After landing, the troops manoeuvred slowly, with no sense of haste conveyed from Chatham's headquarters. There were misunderstandings, disputes and bitter recriminations between military and naval commanders. By the time they had secured their initial objective, the town of Flushing, French forces were already moving to strengthen Antwerp, and the first signs of a wave of disease were afflicting the British. Known as 'Scheldt' or 'Walcheren fever', after the island on which most of the troops spent the next two miserable months, it struck down a quarter of the force by early September. By the time the troops were withdrawn in October, following confirmation of an Austrian submission, they had suffered as badly as if decisively defeated in battle.[37]

The disease was probably a combination of typhus and typhoid, classic dangers in confined and unhealthy quarters, and malaria from the mosquitoes of the marshes, with a spicing of dysenteric flux from poor food and hygiene. It killed directly over 4000, and left over 10,000 more to linger on the sick list long after they should have been deployed to aid operations elsewhere. So penetrating were the effects that the army had to issue thousands of extra flannel waistcoats to 'the Regiments suffering from the effects of the Scheldt fever' to ward off the long-term susceptibility to chills they suffered. Some troops that did return to service were still reported as weakened three years later.[38]

If on Walcheren tragedy predominated over farce, British domestic politics saw farce come close to pointless tragedy. One reason for the slow preparation for the Walcheren expedition was that the army high command was in the process of recovering from the disgraced resignation of its commander-in-chief. As the Clarke affair ground on, it formed the background to the quite unrelated collapse of an entire government. Canning had been fuming at the series of military setbacks since 1807, and came to place the blame, with no real justification, on Castlereagh. With the press blaming both men for the Cintra debacle, Canning was particularly aggrieved, as he had opposed the settlement outright, and argued in Cabinet for it to be repudiated.[39] While publicly defending Castlereagh against charges of electoral corruption that briefly flared in the spring of 1809, Canning was privately agitating for him to be thrown out of the War Office.

Castlereagh's old enemy from India, Lord Wellesley, was proposed as a replacement, and Prime Minister Portland – by now almost incapacitated – was induced to agree that the change would be made at the end of the parliamentary session. By June, Canning's impatience was such that the king had to personally dissuade him from resigning, promising him undivided control of the European theatre of war, with Castlereagh sidelined into colonial affairs. This and other schemes had been discussed with a number of ministers, while Castlereagh was, of course, kept in the dark, wrestling with military problems.[40]

The tension burst into the open early in September, when Canning again tried an ultimatum on the now stroke-smitten

Portland, only to discover he was not the only machinator at work. Spencer Perceval, the only other senior Cabinet minister with a Commons seat, persuaded Portland to resign rather than give Canning what he wanted, and the Cabinet flew apart in a frenzy of acrimony, not least because Castlereagh at last got a fellow minister, Earl Camden, to admit what had been going on for months behind his back, and resigned in outrage. Soon it seemed as if half the ministry was poised to resign, or was demanding the resignations of others.

Canning made a bid for power, drawing, no doubt self-consciously, on Pitt's example in the negotiations with Addington to demand an end of figurehead government and the installation of a strong, Commons-based Prime Minister. But his naked ambition itself sufficed to rule him out of contention, while Perceval, playing his cards much closer to his chest, edged towards just such a premiership. The king's view that Canning was not sufficiently socially distinguished for the highest office, possibly abetted by Perceval's sowing of dissension between Canning and Wellesley, also played a dark role in these weeks of confused argument.[41]

Meanwhile Castlereagh had spent nearly two weeks gathering the details of just how shoddily Canning had intrigued against him, refusing to be mollified even when Perceval showed him written proof that Canning had tried to end the secrecy much earlier. He challenged Canning to a duel, and met him on Wimbledon Common on 21 September. Political duels were far from unknown: a decade earlier Pitt himself had exchanged off-target shots with the leading Whig, George Tierney, after the latter had gone too far in impugning his motives in debate. This one was unusual, however, for after the first, wide, shots Castlereagh (a noted marksman) demanded a reload, and then shot Canning in the thigh, though without doing serious harm. This was generally taken to mark a bitter undercurrent of emotional excess beneath Castlereagh's imperturbable surface, and sympathies amongst close observers lay with Canning.[42] The underhand means the latter had been pursuing could not be gainsaid, however, and both men found themselves out of office, the loss of their undisputed talents capping a run of defeats that seriously questioned the wisdom of continued warfare.

The futile and murderous invasion of Walcheren, and the acrimonious implosion of the Portland government, crowned by the spectacular news of the duel between Canning and Castlereagh, should have driven home decisively the point of elite moral and practical incompetence. The Whig *Morning Chronicle* wrote that

> The distractions of the Cabinet have at last burst into open and public violence. It will scarcely be credited by posterity, that two of His Majesty's principal Secretaries of State should so far forget the duty that they owed to their Sovereign and the example they ought to give to the country in obedience to its laws, to fight a duel.[43]

But while the radical press and parliamentarians strove to make capital from these events, perhaps their very grim nature restrained a wider public from demanding change. The autumn of 1809 also provided strong evidence that radicalism of any kind remained very much a minority persuasion. In what Burdett called bitterly 'a clumsy trick, to thrust joy down the throats of the people', the country celebrated the fiftieth anniversary of George III's accession – 25 October, also the anniversary of Agincourt – with a wide range of civic festivals.[44]

Radicals fumed as the months of government near-paralysis from the summer onwards saw a sudden flourishing of local ideas and plans to hail dynastic longevity and national unity. Some initiators were public – one was the Committee of Merchants and Bankers of London, composed of men who were very clearly doing well out of the war – but others were not, leading Cobbett to voice suspicions of 'underhand means' of government manipulation. In fact much of the work was done by one middle-class widow, Mrs R.C. Biggs, who wrote almost 300 anonymous letters to municipal and other bodies on her own initiative, seeking as she later put it to 'excite a spirit of loyal enthusiasm well calculated to counteract the pernicious effects of Mr Wardle'.[45]

Though not without government connections, including the pension on which she subsisted, Mrs Biggs' patriotic enthusiasm appears genuine, and was coupled with a belief that the occasion was the opportunity for the leading classes of the country to show their 'beneficence' to the population. Local newspapers joined in a groundswell of enthusiasm, printing readers' suggestions for celebratory events and good causes to anoint. In the case of Bristol, the press harried a reluctant council into finally calling a public meeting on the subject a few days before the official date, while a combination of popular pressure and provincial mockery encouraged the Common Council of the City of London to ignore a vocal radical contingent and press on with plans for a banquet. As the *Chester Chronicle* remarked, it was unheard-of for the Londoners to take so long 'in deciding the important question of, to eat; or, not to eat'.[46]

Civic pride and seriousness went hand-in-hand with celebration: Liverpudlians gave thanks for a half-century during which their city had risen to commercial splendour (though tactfully not mentioning the just-ended slave trade) by commissioning an equestrian statue of the king, and also founding a Society for the Prevention of Cruelty to Animals. Other cities took similar initiatives: Leeds founded a Bible Society, Newcastle upon Tyne a school for the poor. Subscriptions to provide a jubilee feast for the deserving poor were widespread, and several localities followed up with more permanent amenities, including medical dispensaries and (in Oswestry) street lighting. For those so inclined, many jubilee sermons were preached, focusing on the virtues of the British monarchy in a fashion that those of a more dissenting bent found close to idolatry, but highlighting the indisputable fact that, after the upheavals of the past two decades, Britain still stood inviolate. An anonymous song penned in Dunbar, near Edinburgh, put the matter with pithy economy:

> *For under him we sit and crack*
> *In peace and unity compact,*
> *Whilst every nation's on the rack*
> *That does nae like our Geordie.*[47]

The notion of the now half-mad king as 'our Geordie' marked one of the great propaganda successes of the age. Scorned by John Wilkes and his followers as an aspiring tyrant when he took the throne, and damned as a real one by Jefferson's Declaration of Independence, George III came to be portrayed from the 1780s as a figure of simplicity and goodness. In oft-repeated tales, he roamed the countryside near Windsor garbed as a private country gentleman, and there was a kernel of truth to the stories, told of rulers since the ancients, about meeting his people in disguise and hearing of his own virtues (and shortcomings).[48]

Compared to his variously debauched sons, George III was certainly a man of moderate indulgences, and of noteworthy sexual and domestic propriety, but he was also capable of spending £500,000, largely of public money, on neo-Gothic rebuilding works at Kew Palace, and a further £200,000 on works to Windsor Castle and Buckingham House. Moreover, he knew what he was doing with such expenditure. Tens of thousands of pounds were spent, for example, on lavish ceremonies to mark the inauguration of new Knights of the Garter on St George's Day 1805, with 'medieval' aspects of the ancient order consciously emphasised in a retort to Napoleon's new-fangled *légion d'honneur* and recent self-coronation. At his death, Pitt had had in hand plans for a 'Naval and Military Order of Merit' which would have offered rewards to all ranks. The king's sense that this was a democratic step too far was significant in ensuring that such a scheme did not come to pass.[49] George III was also capable of remarking, as the Whig Lord Holland later recalled, that the state funeral accorded to Lord Nelson in January 1806 had overstepped the bounds of propriety because 'Such national marks of gratitude ... should be exclusively paid to royalty.'[50] The combination of everyday simplicity and strategic extravagance overlay a very firm sense of royal and dynastic entitlement, but as propaganda it was highly effective.

Radicals in the capital flailed around trying to re-establish their grip on the public agenda. Some were reduced to incautious scorn. The *Examiner* editorialised about 'that foolish multitude, who devoting all their time to their backs and bellies, have none to bestow upon their head'. Cobbett drew a sharp parallel between the celebratory public illuminations in London and those held earlier in the year in Madrid for Joseph Bonaparte. Were one set genuine and spontaneous, and the other, alike in all outward appearances, the result of tyrannical domination? Did the citizens of one capital love their ruler as the others did, or were they both equally cowed by force? 'The truth is, that the people have no will in the matter. The illumination at Madrid was the act of the government and, in a less direct way, so will it be in London.'[51] Acerbic comment was their only real weapon in this fight, as official and public humour was so evidently against them. Their approach to affairs was further hindered as they were again distracted by what was, at first sight, an absurd and dangerous campaign.

For weeks in the autumn of 1809, central London was convulsed by public disturbances known as the 'O.P. riots'. O.P. stood for 'Old Prices', referring to the fact that the Covent Garden Theatre, newly rebuilt after a damaging fire, was seeking to recoup its costs by raising ticket prices and increasing the number of private boxes at the expense of general places. Nightly, performances were disrupted by stamping, booing crowds, and from the first weeks of the trouble, radicals attached great importance to it. For John Horne Tooke, the 'morals and ... liberties of the people' were at stake. Members of

Burdett's constituency committee were heavily involved, as were other radical printers and pamphleteers.

Placards were produced announcing that 'In an English theatre all should see and be seen. No private boxes'. When those ejected from the theatre tried to return, they loudly proclaimed that they were exercising 'the rights of an Englishman', and were cheered for it.[52] One reason for taking these events so seriously was that Covent Garden was at the time the only royally patented theatre, licensed to put on large-scale performances, open in London. Attendance at such events was viewed as an essential component of participation in public life – outside occasional public meetings, it was the only forum in which people came together as an audience. Charging extra for what was at the moment a monopolised position was construed by protestors as an unjust tax.

The changes at Covent Garden also showed dangerous and corrupting foreign influences – a certain Madame Catalani having been brought in to make artistic innovations that included, it was said, employing relatives in place of deserving English artistes. Finally, the provision of additional private boxes struck at the heart of the radical protest against a closed elite breaking down older, organic social relationships – something particularly dear to Cobbett, but part of a long tradition of radical argumentation. Corruption was also feared here, especially of the sexual kind so recently exposed. Newspapers wondered about the opportunities for 'the whole progress of seduction and sensuality' that boxes provided, while placards in the crowds put it more bluntly: 'No private boxes, for high bred doxies'.[53] The theatre's management had by December to give in and lower prices, especially after a court case in which convictions for assault and false imprisonment had resulted from their attempts to keep order.

In comments which reflect his interesting priorities, Cobbett thought this a patriotic victory good enough to offer a measure of compensation for Napoleon's crushing of Austria at Wagram. However, it also resulted, for the first time in some years, in revival of a real 'anti-Jacobin' anxiety about the relations between radicals and the mob, which led on to more problems for radicalism in the following year.[54] Their renewed attempts to defend the rights of freeborn Englishmen were to meet with a reborn authoritarian determination from the new government of Spencer Perceval and its parliamentary majority. This vigour was aided by the fact that a new hero, whose reputation and triumphs would soon rise high above the squabbles of politics, had already begun his ascent to greatness.

10

THE SEPOY GENERAL AND THE SPANISH ULCER

Arthur Wesley was a product of the tight-knit world of aristocratic patronage and nepotism that governed Britain in this era.[1] He was born in 1769 into the long-established Anglo-Irish Protestant gentry: his grandfather had entered the Irish peerage, and his father had been raised to an earldom therein, but the family had little wealth or distinction. Arthur's elder brother Richard, who inherited the title of Earl of Mornington in 1781, did the real work of raising their profile, securing the patronage of the Duke of Northumberland to enter the Westminster House of Commons for the rotten borough of Bere Alston in Devon in 1784. Here, as part of Pitt's first majority, Mornington made his way in government circles, joining first the Treasury, and then in 1793 the Board of Control of the East India Company. An intimate of the Prime Minister, he had been a dinner guest in July 1795 when rioters smashed the windows of 10 Downing Street, and was hit by one of the stones. His bruises were a small sacrifice for the distinction he was rapidly earning his family.

Nine years younger and in Richard's shadow, Arthur progressed slowly, spending several unhappy years at Eton, followed by a spell in the mid-1780s at a school for young gentlemen in France, from which he returned much improved. Richard's friendship with the current Lord Lieutenant of Ireland secured an army commission for Arthur in 1787; and he spent the next few years first as a military aide-de-camp in Dublin, and then as an MP on the government side in the Irish Commons (gaining his seat, naturally, through further exercises of patronage and favour). As was normal, he continued to rise in military rank by purchasing new commissions, becoming a captain in 1791, and successively major and lieutenant-colonel in 1793 – the latter with funds borrowed directly from Richard, and at the age of twenty-four, showing how little real military experience was needed to rise to significant rank. With war against France now under way, Arthur led the 33rd Regiment of Foot to join the Duke of York's forces fighting in Flanders, arriving in the summer of 1794 at a point when the French were advancing in overwhelming strength. Small defensive actions were all that he fought, before the troops were withdrawn after the winter of 1794–5.

Still a member of the Irish Commons, and returned again at a new election in the spring of 1795, Arthur had high hopes of an appointment in the Irish Cabinet. Disappointed to be offered only a lower job as Surveyor-General of Ordnance, he resumed command of his regiment; he would have led it to the West Indies, but the ships were turned back by a storm, and the troops were subsequently committed as reinforcements to the British presence in India. Promoted to full colonel (by seniority this time), Arthur Wesley arrived in Calcutta in February 1797. After spending some months on an abortive expedition to the Spanish Philippines, he found himself at the end of the year with renewed hopes for advancement: Richard, Earl of Mornington, had been appointed Governor-General of India. Soon to augment his Irish title with a British peerage, around this time Richard amended his spelling of the family's name to its supposedly 'original' and more grandiose form: his brother dutifully followed, and became Arthur Wellesley.

As forces were gathered in southern India over the next year to counter a perceived threat from the Sultan of Mysore, Arthur was raised over the heads of several senior generals to be chief advisor to the allied army of the Nizam of Hyderabad. He acquitted himself well during the conflict that followed, commanding brigade-level forces in defensive and offensive actions culminating in May 1799 in a brutal fight to capture the fortified city of Seringapatam. Nonetheless, his appointment as governor of the captured fortress and its surrounding territories was undoubtedly a personal decision of his brother. After some further tergiversations about seniority and influence, Arthur missed out on the chance for glory in Egypt in 1801 due to ill-health. The following year, however, he gained promotion to major-general and was appointed to command an army against the Maratha Confederacy, whose expansionist empire in central India clashed with British imperial claims. In formal charge of this campaign, as commander-in-chief in India since 1801, was the same General Lake who had been the terror of the Irish in 1798.

While Lake conquered Delhi to the north, defeating a Maratha army led by French officers, and subjugated the blind and helpless Mughal emperor, Arthur took on the enemy in their heartlands.[2] Winning two significant battles in late 1803 – including Assaye, where his force of 4500 had been outnumbered some six to one – he was instrumental in forcing the Marathas to a peace settlement the following year. He earned a Knighthood of the Bath for his services. Still a mere thirty-six years old, Sir Arthur Wellesley, KB, returned to Britain, as did his brother, in the spring of 1805. Not long after, he had a first meeting with Castlereagh. It began as a prickly encounter – Richard Wellesley having been recalled under something of a political cloud for his disregard of instructions from London – but ended with the minister developing a healthy regard for the general's military and political acumen.[3]

Having left Europe when Napoleon Bonaparte was no more
than one of the French Republic's more dashing generals, Sir
Arthur returned to a continent dominated by the figure of the
Emperor. Joining the major expedition of troops to northern
Germany that Pitt hoped to use in conjunction with Prussia to
crush the French, he came home again without seeing action after
Napoleon's triumph at Austerlitz. Still not entirely committed to a
military role, he also served in this period as MP for two different
Westminster constituencies, and when the Portland ministry took
office he followed the new Viceroy, the Duke of Richmond, to
Dublin and became Chief Secretary for Ireland. With the Irish
Parliament only a memory, this was no longer the near-prime-
ministerial role on which Castlereagh had anchored his own
political rise, but it plunged him into the machinations of politics
and patronage. He also married Kitty Pakenham, with whom he
had fallen in love in the early 1790s, only to be rejected by her
family at the time for his lack of prospects. She was no longer the
beauty she had been, and years of absence had also dimmed his
affection, but he honoured a promise.

Military duties still called to him, however, and thus in 1807
Wellesley both gained elevation to the Privy Council (entitling him
to address as 'the Right Honourable') and served as a brigade commander during the siege of Copenhagen, driving off a relief column
in a skirmish at Køge. Military prowess and political connections
conspired to secure him command of a force held at the Irish port
of Cork in early 1808, preparatory to an expedition against Spanish
America, when the events of May 1808 opened up the Iberian
Peninsula as a sphere of action. Castlereagh's esteem, which had
helped secure the Cork posting, put Wellesley at the head of an
advance guard of troops moving into Portugal. Castlereagh had also
advised him privately to press ahead with action, before more senior
men arrived, and it was he who led at the victories of Roliça and
Vimiero.[4] He also who put his name at the bottom of the infamous
Convention of Cintra, nearly ending his career there and then.

The very sclerotic nature of the system Wellesley was rising through, and which had placed him in that position, also saved him from disgrace. As plans were in train to raise the British force in Portugal to perhaps as many as 35,000, it had been recognised by the Cabinet from the start that Sir Arthur could not remain in overall command. He had only been a lieutenant-general since April, and plans to appoint either the Duke of York or the Earl of Chatham were mooted, to much political controversy. With troops under Sir John Moore ordered from Sweden to Portugal, the more senior Sir John could not serve under Wellesley, but Moore was also too junior a lieutenant-general to take overall command.

Seniority ruled all. There were some 130 lieutenant-generals in the British Army – enough to have commanded a force of at least 1.5 million. With perhaps only a twentieth of that number actually enrolled for regular service, and with generals combining long possession of rank with other political roles, finding officers with a suitable level of seniority, experience and competence was a conundrum. It was not entirely resolved by the Cabinet's decision to send Sir Hew Dalrymple to take command after Wellesley's initial landings – Dalrymple was the thirteenth most senior of the 130, and had a great deal of political experience of Spain (he was governor of Gibraltar when the revolt of 1808 began), but he had never commanded an army in the field. Sir Harry Burrard was designated as his deputy, also with considerable seniority and noted as an able subordinate, but not as an independent commander.[5]

Burrard reached the army in Portugal first, as it drew up to face the French at Vimiero on 21 August 1808. He left Wellesley in command for the battle, but intervened to prevent any advance afterwards – fearful of reported French cavalry superiority, disbelieving accounts of French numerical weakness, and anxious to avoid being cut off from seaborne relief. Only the next day Dalrymple also arrived, the army's third commander in two days. By this time it was too late to pursue the enemy, and only hours later came the proposal from the French for a truce. Wellesley,

seeing himself demoted to third-in-command, did not object to the
French proposals as an independent and victorious commander
might have done, and went along with his seniors' caution and
willingness to take whatever kind of victory was offered. He also
went along with the mischievous French suggestion that the initial
document containing the terms should be signed by him, not
Dalrymple.

Wellesley soon left for home and briefly resumed his post as
Chief Secretary for Ireland, while press and public opinion were
convulsed by anger. Canning was driven to denounce Cintra as a
'disgrace and disaster' in writing to Spencer Perceval, while
Wellesley's advocate Castlereagh considered 'how we can best save'
him from disgrace, seeing him as '*the instrument* which of all
others' might redeem 'any faults which he himself or others have
committed'.[6] A government Board of Enquiry sat towards the end of
the year, and succeeded in fudging out a half-hearted approval of
the Convention and ending the prospect of action against its signatories.[7] The disgrace ended Dalrymple's career, and stripped
Wellesley's of any lustre from Vimiero; he remained, however, officially unblemished, and also well clear of the heroic failure that was
Sir John Moore's campaign of 1808–9. As a general with an effectively unbroken record of victory, Sir Arthur Wellesley was soon to
be in demand again.

British forces had all but abandoned Portugal in the early months
of 1809. A few thousand troops remained encamped near Lisbon,
their transport ships very obviously anchored in the Tagus, and had
already begun to attract hostility from locals who expected them to
flee at the first French advance. Meanwhile, orders from London
sent 4000 men from Lisbon to the Spanish port of Cadiz, with the
aim of turning its location, on a highly defensible spit of land, into
a redoubt for the war in Spain (and, perhaps, also controlling the
colonial trade, three-quarters of the country's, that passed through
it). Arriving in early February, they discovered that the Spanish had

not been consulted about the occupation of their city. A month of wrangling failed to overcome suspicions about the motives for this move, when only the previous year the French had insinuated themselves into their then-ally's fortresses to such fatal effect. British commanders finally gave up the effort, and withdrew to bolster the Portuguese defences.

In early March the troops, confined aboard transports for a month, arrived back in Lisbon, joined by another 4000 sent direct from Britain to Cadiz who had equally been denied entry. Thus there came to be, effectively by accident, a tidy little army building up on the Tagus. With public and political opinion turning against the Spanish – tales circulated widely of their callous indifference to the fate of Moore's troops, while the Cabinet fumed at their unwillingness to open South American markets and their unending demands for material support – Portugal returned again to favour.[8]

One reason was the Portuguese willingness to put their military efforts in the hands of the British. From the beginning of the year a scheme to attach a significant number of British officers to the rebuilding Portuguese army had been put in place, and Wellesley was first spoken of in connection with desires expressed in Lisbon that he might return in command of this force. After a predictable period of vacillation about abilities, seniority and politics, the appointment went to Major-General William Beresford. Although not a man noted for his transcendent abilities, Beresford had a working grasp of Portuguese, and had recently been present as a liaison to the Lisbon administration, where a somewhat turbulent Regency Council ruled on behalf of the absent monarchy. This commitment, together with the Cadiz fiasco, strengthened an argument in Cabinet repeatedly and forcefully put by Canning that Portugal was the place to fight back against the French, and Wellesley the man to lead British troops there.

Wellesley himself joined in with a memorandum on 7 March,

advocating a plan to build up a significant combined Anglo-Portuguese force and to use the whole country as a redoubt to take the war into Spain. Weeks of further delay and debate ensued – Canning wrote of his 'constant daily, and nightly, uneasiness' at the prevarications – before on the 26th Castlereagh conveyed to the king the Cabinet's official recommendation of Wellesley for the command. George III acquiesced the next day, though not without further grumbling at 'so distinguished a command' going to 'so young a lieutenant-general', and suggesting a more senior figure be appointed if the army was later reinforced.[9]

Wellesley arrived in Lisbon on 22 April 1809. Twenty thousand French veteran troops under Soult had advanced from Corunna southwards as far as Oporto, chief town of northern Portugal, where they were currently resting after an arduous winter drive against stubborn partisan resistance. Secure in the city, but cut off from Spain by Portuguese irregulars infesting the countryside, the French were ripe for engagement. Moving north to meet them with some 17,000 troops, supported by 6000 of Beresford's untried Portuguese, Wellesley succeeded in early May in a bold strike across the Douro river, shattering French plans for a steady, organised withdrawal, and prompting instead something approaching a rout. After a week's hard pursuit, Soult's men abandoned their cannon and heavy equipment, scattering across the frontier by any paths they could find.

News of this, alongside the stirrings of Austrian power not yet cut short at Wagram, cheered the Cabinet, and encouraged them to agree to a request Wellesley had submitted weeks before, to extend his initial pessimistic instructions to defend Portugal to cover potential offensive operations into Spain. Their new instructions were still couched in tones of deep caution, allowing him to advance 'provided you shall be of the opinion that your doing so is material in a military point of view, to the success of your operations, and not inconsistent with the safety of Portugal'.[10] The stakes of a move into Spain were high, and also reflected the concerns and dilemmas of all the campaigns to come.

Wellesley moved his headquarters to Abrantes in central Portugal as spring began to ripen toward summer, and he hoped for the opportunity to advance decisively – the course of the Tagus inland affording a direct route to Madrid, albeit through rough and arid country. If the Spanish leadership could offer serious cooperation, the large but widely dispersed French forces in the country might be driven into a withdrawal towards the Pyrenees. But armies could not move without supplies, and supplies – at least for a British army, which did not intend to plunder allied territory – could not be had without money. Wellesley harassed the Cabinet with demands for the hard cash needed. He had been forced to borrow £10,000 from the merchants of Oporto, and that had only been a tiny stopgap. Money was also needed directly to appease his soldiers. Unpaid bodies of troops had already begun to pillage the countryside, threatening an effective dissolution of his fighting force.

Some £230,000 in assorted coin was finally despatched, reaching Abrantes on 25 June, but such an amount hardly sufficed for even immediate operations – Wellesley had asked seriously two weeks earlier for a commitment of £200,000 a month in gold, but always had to make do with much less. In the years to come, extraordinary international manoeuvres, some of them coordinated by the remarkable continent-wide banking network of the Rothschild brothers, would be needed to turn the British government's paper credit into the gold and silver of American mines, shipped through the Spanish and Portuguese colonies to buy beef, beer and bread for Wellesley's redcoats.

Leaving Portugal also plunged the British army into the complex world of Spanish politics.[11] The country having risen in rebellion for a wide assortment of motives, factionalism and personal ambition combined with fundamental disagreements on politics to keep distrust and inefficiency amongst the military and civilian leaderships at a steady simmer. The Spanish were proving themselves capable, on the right occasion, of ferocious resistance. While the

British were retreating to Corunna at the end of 1808, the city of Zaragossa was enduring a siege by overwhelming French forces: after the walls were breached and stormed at the end of January 1809, it took a further, astonishing, twenty-three days of merciless house-to-house fighting to quell the population.[12] More generally, where Prussia in 1806 (and Austria, both before it and shortly to do so again) had collapsed into almost instant submission under the Napoleonic hammer-blow, Spain continued to keep over 160,000 troops in the field against the empire, almost a year after the first invaders arrived.[13]

Such examples, however, were the high points of a very complex landscape of politics and culture that shaped Spain's ability to wage a wider war. Any brief summary of the issues involved can read like a caricature, but it is unavoidable to note that personal greed, corruption and self-seeking were rife, while a culture of sensitive personal honour often overruled counsels of prudence and basic honesty, and an aristocratic indifference to the taking of pains resulted in a slipshod administration and an ill-disciplined military, prone to heroic advances and scandalously panicky retreats. It would also be fair to say that the British could suffer from almost all these sins, with sometimes only the personality of their commander as a counterweight. Tall, slender, tanned and whipcord-tough from daily hours in the saddle, famously terse, occasionally irascible, he was the military embodiment of the idea that genius is an infinite capacity for taking pains. His plain coat and hooked nose would often seem to be everywhere, his scribbled orders covering every eventuality. He was far from superhuman, of course, but his troops would come to love him, not least because he always took very great care only to expose them to danger when necessary, and when he did, was usually in the midst of it with them.

The Spanish, however, did not have their own Arthur Wellesley, a fact which was to cause them a near-infinity of problems.[14] When the first British troops crossed into Spain on 3 July 1809, they soon encountered many of these in very stark particularity. Grandiose promises that Wellesley's army would be supplied by their allies turned out meaningless in a country already scoured by French and Spanish forces alike. Wellesley's first meeting with his Spanish counterpart, Gregorio García de la Cuesta, on 11 July also brought political intelligence of discord between his supporters and their civilian leadership. Promises that all this would be papered over produced agreement on an advance, and by 22 July the allied force reached the vicinity of Talavera, two-thirds of the way from the frontier to Madrid, where they ranged up against a French force under Marshal Victor.

The Spanish resisted British pressure for an attack at dawn on the 23rd, and disagreements also took up that day, during which the outnumbered French marched away to join much stronger forces to the east under Marshal Jourdan (with King Joseph in attendance). Wellesley, deeply discontented, refused to follow: his troops had been unfed for two days, and he lamented that it 'is ridiculous to pretend that the country cannot supply our wants'. He also wrote that it was 'impossible to do business' with Cuesta, and that 'all are dissatisfied with him' even amongst the Spanish officers.[15] He may have hoped that a sharp defeat for the Spanish would topple the general and bring a more amenable attitude to cooperation. In any case, the 33,000 Spaniards moved forward alone, stumbled upon the outposts of a French force now raised to some 46,000, fell back, and rejoined their allies in a defensive posture chosen by Wellesley just north of Talavera itself – and it is said that Sir Arthur had to literally beg Cuesta to put his troops in a practicable position.[16]

That indignity was compounded when the reconnoitring Wellesley had to flee pell-mell from French skirmishers on the 27th as the armies drew up, a covering British brigade having allowed itself to be ambushed while resting in the sweltering heat. That evening, the first French probes against Spanish outposts panicked the whole Spanish front line into opening fire – a vast volley of 10,000 muskets – at which sound 2000 of the rawest troops panicked and fled, pillaging the British baggage train as they went. A rapid French attempt to exploit this disruption with a night attack on the British left flank was driven off with several hundred casualties. After a brief respite, as dawn broke the British were assailed by the first of three massive columns of French infantry advancing under heavy cannonade.

The column attack was a hallmark of the era, an innovation of the revolutionary French (though adopted later by their continental foes and allies) that made for rapid movement and concentrated weight of numbers. When a battalion formed column, it remained wider than it was deep – some fifty to sixty men wide by around twelve deep – and in this sense was very different from a 'marching column', perhaps four abreast, in which troops would move on a road. The advantages of an attacking column were that it kept the whole mass of the unit in closer contact, and allowed it to be shepherded forward by its officers and NCOs over rough ground much more quickly than a long line. Battalion columns could be formed up one behind the other to traverse a battlefield, with the general idea that they should fan out to assail the enemy line as they grew closer. Ideally they would form into line as they entered musket range, and be able to deploy their firepower and bayonets to greatest effect, but this was sometimes difficult to achieve under fire. Against unsteady troops, like many of the Spanish, it was possible to cause the disintegration of an enemy line simply with artillery fire and the advance of columns. Against Wellesley's forces, however, things were different.[17]

Talavera brought to fruition a generation of change in the British Army. Built up from the experience of commanders like Abercromby and Moore, the innovations were most intense in the Light Division trained at Shorncliffe, but spread much more widely through the force. At their heart was an attention to drill and battlefield discipline quite traditional in its rigour, but implemented much more thoroughly than had been possible in earlier eras. The relative concentration of the army in England after 1803, under fear of invasion, had allowed time for intensive and long-term training that succeeded in cementing the intricate manoeuvres required to implement complex tactical schemes without delay, or indeed chaotic disintegration. To form a battalion from line into square, for example, for defence against cavalry, involved some six hundred men, in eight companies, marching by half-companies in a series of more than a dozen separate (but simultaneous) evolutions. Performing this under fire, and with the actual threat of charging horsemen, required a very thorough inculcation indeed.

Simply to control troops in line under fire was no easy task. Wellesley was amongst a group of leading British commanders who had moved from a three-rank system (still asserted in the official drill manual) to a two-rank line. This enabled units to cover more ground and 'fill' a battlefield more efficiently, but it made the line a terribly fragile thing, especially under artillery fire. This was one of many reasons why Wellesley preferred to conceal his main body of troops behind the crest of a ridge wherever possible, sheltered on the 'reverse slope' from too hard a pounding. The two-rank line also allowed all the troops to fire on the enemy in relatively coherent formation.

One of the persistent underlying problems on the battlefield was that men performing the intricate series of operations needed to load a flintlock musket tended to drift apart, quite literally in search of elbow room. Although in theory a three-rank line was a rigid formation, the men standing almost shoulder-to-shoulder, and a few feet from those in front and behind, after more than a few minutes' firing it could resemble a straggling mob, and it was frighteningly easy, in the choking fog of powder smoke, for troops at the rear to fire into the ones in front. A two-rank line, especially if the front rank knelt, reduced this risk considerably. It also made it easier – if not always easy – to stop the troops firing and prepare them to move. This was often noted by commanders as a real problem, with soldiers understandably feeling safer when actively using their weapons and enveloped in a cloud of self-generated fog. One of the Peninsular army's great achievements was to be able both to stand and fire under threat of attack, and to cease fire and charge in a controlled fashion.

Both the attacking style of the French, and the more defensive line formations, made extensive use of a variety of innovatory light infantry and skirmishing tactics, which extended combat beyond the simple clash of column and line into more of a crescendo of engagement. The French had since the mid-1790s deployed *voltigeurs* (literally 'acrobats' or 'flutterers') and *tirailleurs*, sharp-shooters, who flitted across the battlefield in a large number of small teams to disrupt enemy preparations, and ideally to pick off officers and unsettle the line before it met the column. British light infantry practice went a stage further: a small number of units were equipped with rifles, which unlike the smoothbore muskets were accurate to several hundred yards, and could be used for deliberate sniping of officers, gunners and other key figures. More generally, a British line would be fronted by several waves of skirmishers, deployed much like the French in small groups and extended lines, with the similar goal of breaking up the momentum and leadership of an advancing force. As the two forces grew closer together, such units often fought out an intense and individual battle, before withdrawing hurriedly as the main contingents came within range to engage.

Thus it was in the first attacks at Talavera. Redcoat lines that sheltered, or even lay down, behind the crest of hills leapt up again and again to drive in the heads of the columns with shattering volleys of musketry, and after two hours the French pulled back. A brief truce to gather the wounded, which saw red and blue uniforms mingling peaceably by streams fouled in blood, was ended by signal guns, and further heavy attacks in column ground towards the centre of the British position. Four thousand French, supported by artillery, were devastated by sustained bombardment and infantry volleys, leaving their cannon in enemy hands as they fled.

Yet another even larger advance was in the course of being beaten back when several thousand British troops of the Guards and the King's German Legion took themselves off (or were taken by their officers) into a reckless advance of their own.

French guns and cavalry assailed them, threatening to sweep into the gap opened, until Wellesley plucked battalions and brigades from all along his thin-stretched line to hold it together. Again, the discipline of drill allowed for rapid action and improvisation. The prodigal attackers rushed back to re-form behind the reinforcements, and the line held. A movement of the British light cavalry against French infantry on the northern flank of Wellesley's line also resulted, through a reckless enthusiasm endemic to the arm, in over-extension and heavy casualties, but it succeeded in clearing the immediate danger. Artillery duels continued until dark, and under its cover the French withdrew, abandoning their wounded on the field, along with a significant number of cannon.

Talavera was a savagely hard-fought battle. The bombardment that preceded the second great attack, falling on troops who lay down for want of any other shelter, was observed by a young ensign in the Guards. He wrote home of seeing 'courage beyond what I could have conceived' as men coolly removed wounded or dead comrades, and returned to their accustomed places. Although these were the men whose advances later put the battle in danger, at the moment of engagement they had been steadfast. Most battalions obeyed their orders to fire a single volley as the French columns came within fifty yards, and then charge with the bayonet. Those that did not, instead performed an even cooler feat of valour, as the same officer later wrote: 'On their approaching within two hundred yards we were ordered to advance without firing a shot and afterwards to charge this we did as became British officers.' This and other battalions did not open fire until the French were already quailing at their advance, and the enemy's precipitate retreat had then brought on their own dangerous lunge forward.[18]

Throughout the fighting, strategic hilltops and ridges changed hands several times, and numerous regiments burnished their record with defiant stands and hand-to-hand combat. Generals and staff officers fell alongside common soldiers, and even Wellesley was hit, though unhurt, by a spent bullet. The French lost some 7000 killed and wounded, the Spaniards, mostly kept out of the fight, around 1200. The British casualties amounted to some 5500, a quarter of their whole force. No further advance was possible, and indeed news that Marshal Soult was advancing from the north to threaten his communications forced Wellesley to move backwards to cover the flank. To do this his army had to face the harrowing decision to leave behind all their wounded who were unfit to march – some 1500 in all. Cuesta's Spaniards were entrusted with the care of these men, but when a new French thrust threatened, the general abandoned them, marching to find safety again in Wellesley's company.

Fortunately for Wellesley's peace of mind, Cuesta was soon removed from the scene; a vast man who travelled to battle in a mule-drawn carriage and had to be hoisted on to a horse by four assistants, he suffered a stroke and resigned on 12 August. The French took good care of the wounded, but bitterness against the Spanish, compounded by lack of supplies and transports continually promised, pushed Wellesley into withdrawing towards Portugal, slowly and circuitously, as the blazing summer wore into autumn. For his footsore and hungry troops, it cannot have felt like the aftermath of a famous victory.

Such a victory, though, it was. Wellesley himself later that year called it 'the hardest fought of modern times', and when news arrived in England that 40,000 French had been driven from the field by half that number of redcoats, there was rejoicing.[19] With the shame of Cintra definitively extinguished, Wellesley could be rewarded with the peerage he might have had for Vimiero. He became Baron Douro in recognition of his feat in driving Soult from Oporto, and was simultaneously raised another step to a viscountcy for his new victory. His brother William, who had stepped into his shoes as Chief Secretary for Ireland, was asked to find a title, time being pressing. Scouring the map around the village of Wellesley in Somerset, to which their ambitious elder brother had pinned their origins, he settled on the pleasingly similar name of a nearby town. The man who had begun life as plain Arthur Wesley, was now, as he was to pass into immortality, Wellington.

Britain needed good news in the late summer of 1809, for the first transports of the vast armada sailing for Walcheren had left port even as the British lines were being battered at Talavera, and the first indications of looming disaster amidst the Dutch marshes were evident as Wellington was being heralded. The Portland government, wracked by Canning's ambition and Castlereagh's resentment, was collapsing as its armies at either end of Europe suffered and withdrew, and there was no clear sign that Spencer Perceval, whose close political game brought him the prime ministerial prize Canning had grasped for, had the talent to use it to the country's profit. A desperate political quest for distinction in the Cabinet, with so many figures ruled out by personal and political disputes, led to an assortment of tergiversations – and odds from political wits of twenty to one against the administration's survival until the new parliamentary session. Richard Wellesley, who had been sent out as ambassador to the Spanish patriots' ruling council, or Junta, in Seville, had only arrived after Talavera, but was recalled within months to take up the reins at the Foreign Office. With William in Ireland, the Wellesleys' influence was increased still further by the dispatch in the new year of yet another brother, Henry, to take Richard's place.

Such a rise in the family's fortunes did not go unnoticed – and nor did Richard's sordid efforts to eject his wife, a former courtesan, from the family home, while he carried on with what many regarded as a common whore. His combination of this self-indulgence with a seemingly growing indolence – in contrast to the energy he had shown in India a decade before – soon led Wellington to write in exasperation that 'I wish that Wellesley was castrated; or that he would like other people attend to his business and perform too.'[20]

As sick soldiers continued to straggle home from Walcheren into the depths of winter, and opposition pressure rose for an inquiry, Wellington was caught up in the swirl of partisan malice: there was sniping that Talavera had been fought for a title, and a belief amongst the Whigs that, as one put it, 'The Wellesleys will now be beat if they are attacked properly.'[21] Uncertainty remained into the early spring of 1810, with hearings in the Commons itself about the Dutch debacle, and only the resignation of the 'late Earl of Chatham' (after the inevitable long delay, and a violent argument in Cabinet in which Richard Wellesley harangued him into an impossible position) saved the government from a decisive defeat.

The situation on the ground in the Peninsula throughout these months was little less gloomy. Wellington's army withdrew steadily (and in some cases unsteadily, with outbreaks of looting ferociously punished), first towards the border, and then back into Portugal itself. Many officers assumed that, with news of Walcheren and the Austrian surrender on hand, they would soon be shipped home. With the government itself unsure on this point, such pessimism was unsurprising. Many more, even of the highest ranks, took the opportunity to disappear either into the fleshpots of Lisbon, or home on leave. Despite his best efforts, Wellington could not prevent the granting of such leave to men with their own political connections to exploit, but it hindered all efforts to keep the army fighting fit.

Late 1809 meanwhile showed that, if there was to be a continued resistance in Iberia, British troops would be more important than ever. The Spanish had gathered large forces in the hope that victories, however temporary, would stiffen future resistance as the French, freed of the Austrian distraction, turned on them again in the new year. The capture of Salamanca in late October was a good start, paralleled further south by the advance of a second 50,000-man army. But French reinforcement in the north led to a retreat that turned into a rout for no good reason except the inexperience and lack of confidence of the troops, while at Ocaña in the south, French veterans outnumbered three to five smashed the Spanish on 19 November. Six weeks later, massive French armies swept into Andalusia, driving the Junta from Seville by the end of January 1810, and leaving Cadiz, on its long defensible spit, the only remaining safe base for the Spanish government in its homeland.[22]

Through all this, Wellington watched, waited and worked. As early as September 1809 he had been to Lisbon, and had ridden the countryside all around for several weeks, sometimes in the company of his chief military engineer. By late October he knew exactly what he was going to do to resist the coming French tide, and how much work would be needed, setting the task in train with detailed plans in his own hand. Failure to share these with the government led to considerable anxiety through the winter, and awkward correspondence in which the precise degree of danger that the troops should be exposed to before being withdrawn was juggled fruitlessly. By March 1810, as the campaigning season loomed, Secretary for War Lord Liverpool felt driven to write privately to Wellington with the message that he 'would rather be excused for bringing away the army a little too soon' than run any undue risks in prolonging its presence.

Wellington fumed in writing to his brother William about 'publick Instructions which authorize a fair manly line, & private hints which direct one which would disgrace us for ever'. More officially he asked for either detailed instructions to follow precisely, or the simple confidence of government, so that 'if I am to be responsible, I may be left to the exercise of my own Judgement'.[23] This the Cabinet, somewhat sheepishly, agreed to. Wellington did in fact have carefully thought-out plans for both evacuation and seaborne redeployment of his forces, if it came to that, but he had no intention of allowing it to.[24]

The campaign of 1810 opened slowly. Napoleon himself abandoned his earlier intention to descend personally on the Peninsula
like a thunderbolt, giving himself over instead to the unedifying
process of divorcing the Empress Josephine so that he could marry
into the cowed Austrian imperial family. The wedding to the
eighteen-year-old Archduchess Maria Ludovica – great-niece of
Marie Antoinette and granddaughter of the furious counter-revolutionary Maria Christina of Naples – who became Empress Marie
Louise on 1 April 1810 in the chapel of the Louvre, marked yet
another stage in Napoleon's decisive distancing from the politics of
the 1790s. Two weeks later, however, he appointed a scion of that
era, Marshal André Masséna, to head his Army of Portugal.

A shopkeeper's son from Nice who had become a senior NCO in
the pre-revolutionary French army, Masséna rose under the revolution to the rank of colonel by 1792, and to that of major-general by
the end of 1793. Playing a critical role both in the 1796–7 Italian
campaign, and the fighting of 1799–1800 that secured Napoleon's
European dominance, he fought in almost every major engagement south of the Alps, before going north in 1809 to help crush the
Austrians. As Wellington himself noted wryly upon his arrival in
June, Masséna was nicknamed the 'Spoilt Child of Victory'.[25] But
he was also by now fifty-two, Duke of Rivoli and Prince of Essling,
and more interested in the spoils of victory than its dangerous glories. While he still had the energy to support a famous mistress, who
accompanied him on horseback, and in full uniform, he would be
leading no charges.

The peculiar logistics of Spain were also making themselves felt
in full. By a crude count, Wellington was outnumbered by the
French more than ten to one. Things were far from that simple,
however. The French might have swept through Andalusia only
months before, but they now discovered that it took a garrison of
70,000 to prevent the region's countryside coming alive with partisans. It took almost twice as many more to secure the centre of the
country and the main lines of supply and communication across

the Pyrenees. Masséna led an army, on top of all these troops, that numbered in theory over 130,000, but a full third of these were needed to guard and garrison his rear, and more would be dropped off at every stage of the advance.

The French belief that the British led only 24,000 of their own troops, and scarcely more Portuguese whose quality was negligible, helped them overlook potential difficulties. But in fact Wellington had over 30,000 of his own regulars, rising by another third as the season developed, and an equal number of Portuguese regulars over whom General Beresford and his British officers had sweated for a year. Adding in further bodies of uniformed Militia and the traditional peasant levies of the *Ordenanza* made the combat far more equal than it looked to Napoleon, as he complacently instructed Masséna against haste: 'I do not wish to enter Lisbon at the moment, because I could not feed the city', therefore 'spend the summer months' on taking the frontier fortresses, 'go methodically to work'.[26]

This Masséna did. His second-in-command, the dashing Marshal Ney, led the advance on the northerly of the two key routes across the Portuguese frontier. The fortification on the Spanish side, Ciudad Rodrigo, was surrounded on 2 July, and surrendered eight days later. Wellington concentrated his available forces in response, but his reluctance to commit his still raw reinforcements to a headlong relief dash was much criticised. It was justified by the narrow scrape experienced by his elite Light Division, who for all their skills only just managed to escape from an over-eager commitment to battle as the French approached the Portuguese fortress town of Almeida. Masséna was now seen at his most 'methodical', as logistical difficulties hindered the French from launching a formal siege until 15 August.

Though this sluggish behaviour gave Wellington some breathing space, it was counteracted by a stroke of pure chance. Only hours after beginning bombardment on 26 August, a French shell touched off a trail of gunpowder left by a leaking barrel. It led straight to the main stockpile inside the cathedral, which erupted volcanically, killing some 800 of the Portuguese defenders and devastating the centre of the town. Survivors prevailed upon the English governor to surrender with such haste that all chance of favourable terms was lost, and the supply stockpiles of the town were yielded immediately to French plunder. There was panic in Lisbon, where the Regency Council threatened to remove Beresford from command of their troops, and demanded Wellington commit to saving the north. On 7 September he threatened instead to leave the country if either kind of interference persisted, while continuing to gear up for exactly the kind of campaign he had envisaged.

A week later, the French came forward again, spending the next ten days wandering on back roads, thanks to bad maps and weak intelligence, and perpetually harassed by the *Ordenanza*, whom they in turn treated as brigands and slaughtered indiscriminately. But by the 25th the two armies were at last converging, and the French discovered the British waiting for them on the Serro do Buçaco (or Bussaco in English usage): a 'damned long hill' as one staff officer pithily put it, nine miles of steep rocky ridge stretching north–south across the French line of advance from the east.[27] Wellington had 52,000 men in place, in almost equal numbers of British and Portuguese battalions, but he concealed many of them, as was his wont, behind the crest. It was a rather thin line nonetheless, and looked positively fragile to Masséna and his generals. It was difficult to get artillery into an effective position to bombard the high ridge, and impossible to deploy cavalry. A more prudent commander might have looked to make an outflanking manoeuvre, but convictions of superiority outweighed such 'methodical' considerations, and at dawn on 27 September, with autumnal fog still shrouding the positions, the French attacked.

The first blow was to the centre of the line, as four French battalions surged upwards, following the line of a cart track that cut the ridge in two. Their job was to break through, wheel north and begin to roll up the enemy, but they were smashed back by General Picton's Third Division. A mile further north, a stronger thrust of eleven battalions, scrabbling up the rocky slopes, had the good fortune to chance on a weak point, and skirmishers were soon sprinting to the summit. Wellington himself was on the spot and directed artillery on to the French flank, while Picton rallied disordered troops to strike back into the gap. As Portuguese battalions poured in the regular volley-fire the British had taught them, the colonel of one Irish regiment rallied his men from the front, as leaders had since the time of Caesar: 'Now, Connaught Rangers, when I bring you face to face with those French rascals, drive them down the hill – don't give the false touch, but push home to the muzzle!' His men's oblique plunge into the French flank sent the enemy reeling down what was not much less than a cliff. Four allied battalions had driven off nearly three times their number. Wellington declared 'I never witnessed a more gallant charge' as he rode by, hard-pressed to manage the expanding battle.[28]

The French attack, now an hour old, continued to hammer Picton's division, a third wave climbing the slopes between the wreckage of the first two attacks. The weary allied troops were forced back, and French skirmishers again swarmed the crest, with no nearby forces seeming ready to repel them. But Wellington had not wasted the days his men had waited, and the track that ran along the western side of the ridge had been widened and shored up for just such an event. As the French had revealed the axis of their attack, he had summoned his Fifth Division from further south to move up as a reserve. General Leith led the first battalions at the double into position just as the French crested the ridge, and suddenly renewed volley-fire once more sent blue coats tumbling back downhill.

The centre of the ridge was now effectively secure, but a new French hammer-blow was falling to the north, where Marshal Ney had launched his corps forward as he saw the first attacks crest the ridge. In what was almost a replay of those events, the first thin lines of British and Portuguese skirmishers were driven in, and the French toiled towards what seemed an unoccupied summit. One small man on a horse stood before them, General 'Black Bob' Craufurd of the Light Division. Dark both in features and in moods, he was another, like Abercromby and Moore, who had seen the best and worst of British systems in the Empire, Ireland and elsewhere. After dabbling in reformist politics, he found his calling in the relentless perfection of light infantry tactics.[29] Now, at the critical moment, he bellowed out 'Avenge the death of Sir John Moore!' and 1800 of the men Moore had trained at Shorncliffe rose from their silent wait on the reverse slope.[30] Volley-fire smashed the French front lines – at no more than ten paces, some witnesses said – and the British went home with the bayonet, battering the French, yet again, back down the slope.

One more French attack was sent in, eleven battalions against a flank held by only four Portuguese battalions, but the formerly despised troops stood stoutly in their volleying lines and no headway could be made against them. By the middle of the day the battle was over. British and Portuguese forces had suffered 1252 casualties (though only 200 killed), split by some strange quirk exactly equally between the nationalities; the French over three times as many. It was a solid victory, proving to a new generation of British troops that they could see off the French, and to all observers that the Portuguese were a force worthy to stand alongside the redcoats.

From Oporto to Bussaco, Wellington had defeated no fewer than five of Napoleon's marshals on the field of battle in little more than a year, fully a quarter of the elite grouping the Emperor had anointed to surround his throne with military glory. This was no mean feat for a man French propaganda had scorned as a mere 'sepoy general', fit only to lead Indian colonial troops.[31] This last victory was only a defensive one, however, and a good part of Masséna's army had not even been committed. On the next day Wellington learned that his northern flank had been turned by the

French rather quicker than he would have liked, but he never intended to make a final stand, and after nightfall deceptive fires were lit brightly along the ridge while the first battalions slipped away west and southwards in a carefully planned retreat.

Withdrawal took Wellington's troops through the city of Coimbra, mingling with a stream of refugees who had failed to take earlier advice to flee. There was again a little looting, met with a little hanging, but nothing compared to the whirlwind of pillage the French inflicted on the city as they arrived shortly after. Even graves were smashed open to loot for jewellery, and the university was ransacked despite Marshal Ney's attempts to keep order. That some of his fellow generals, notably Junot, pillager of Lisbon, joined in did not make the task any easier. As they headed on south, the French left 5000 sick and wounded in the city's hospitals under a token guard. Scarcely was the army out of sight when Portuguese militia rushed in. The fate of the wounded was grim, and more significantly, Masséna was cut off from supply and communication. He was about to suffer another very unpleasant surprise.

11

THE SORROWS OF WAR

While the Portuguese leadership in Lisbon panicked, ordering ill-considered arrests of supposed French sympathisers and loading treasure on to ships on the Tagus, Wellington pushed on with the next stage of his plan. The French, he knew, were confident – he had captured dispatches in hand that boasted of how Masséna had turned his flank and put him in 'full retreat' – but he was leading them into what he hoped was a trap.[1] The first inkling the French had of this came on 10 October, when they captured a cavalry patrol on its way back, the men said, to 'the Lines'. Four days later, Masséna himself was at the forefront of the French advance when a final breakthrough of British outposts revealed what those 'Lines' were. A force of 10,000 Portuguese labourers had toiled for a year under British engineers, transforming the landscape over a rectangle almost thirty miles square, buttressed by the ocean to the west and the wide Tagus to the east. One hundred and fifty-two separate, but interlinked, fortified positions had sprung up to bar the way to Lisbon. Towns and villages had been walled against assault. Naturally steep slopes had been dug out into unclimbable 'scarps';

interlocking fields of fire had been cleared and batteries erected and dug in. Thousands of local militia had been drafted to man the cannon, and sailors to work signal masts linking the whole scheme.

The first and longest of these 'Lines' ran for twenty-nine miles, and was the only element of the defences that the French ever actually saw. Had they penetrated, at great cost, over and between some of the forts, they would have found a second, twenty-two-mile line of equally formidable strongpoints, and beyond that, another, and then another final series of defences around Lisbon and its beaches. And while their troops attempted to assault or bypass each fort, under the withering fire of its neighbours, they would have faced the attack of Wellington's whole field army – for these men were not tied up in garrisons, but kept free for a decisive counter-strike. How much of this vast system Masséna perceived or guessed at, as he rode in a personal reconnaissance along the front all the way to the sea on 14 October, we cannot know. But he 'methodically' declined to try the strength of the Lines of Torres Vedras, and a month later, pushed by shortages and sickness, withdrew his forces some forty miles to the north and dispersed them into winter quarters.

Intriguingly, a letter published in the *Caledonian Mercury* from 'an officer in Lord Wellington's army' gave away the secret of the Lines in July 1810. Not only did this openly list the strength of various British corps, after a colourful account of the natural beauties and priest-ridden people of Portugal, but observed that 'If Masséna enters Portugal with such odds as he now threatens, we will probably abandon our present positions, and concentrate our forces between Villa Franca and Torres Vedras.'[2] A second letter on the same page even listed individual regiments by name, noted their deployments, and commented on the difficulty of moving artillery into particular locations. Published only three weeks after it was written, this could have been on a desk in Paris only days later. It is no wonder that Wellington became notorious for telling no one what his actual plans were.

Wellington's hope at this point was that the terrain of central Portugal had been sufficiently scoured at his orders that the French would be unable to endure there longer than a few weeks. Forced into a winter retreat with a starving army, Masséna might be utterly destroyed. Alas for such plans, much of the population, less accustomed to war than those on the frontiers, had not withdrawn bag and baggage inside the Lines. Some hoped to hide their crops away from the French, or at least to leave a little something buried against their return. Those foolish enough to remain in person soon found out how ruthlessly 50,000 French veterans could go looking for supplies.

Wellington had hoped to see the French retreating in six weeks; thanks to their torture of the population, they lasted six months. Under such circumstances, disaster loomed within the Lines. The British had neither the money nor the will to directly support the tens of thousands of civilians who had fled south at their command, and the Portuguese government showed no greater inclination to do so. In a notably harsh winter, those who had sought safety from the French starved by the thousand. Few blamed Wellington for this – it was all part of the horrors of war, and clearly the French occupier carried the main responsibility – but it was an ugly situation. The months of inactivity called into question political support for the war at home, too.

News of Bussaco reached England only hours before Masséna reached the Lines. While ministers talked it up as a great victory, opposition Whig leaders were less sure – Lord Grey was reminded too much of Talavera, and the ominous retreat that had followed. Exaggerated claims of 10,000 French dead and expectations of a second, decisive engagement gave way slowly to disappointment, and confirmation of Whig suspicions. Lord Grenville, once a fire-breathing advocate of continental engagement, was now a thoroughly pessimistic observer. Writing on 1 November 1810, he thought the whole project of peninsular commitment 'desperate and wicked; it puts to hazard our safety, failure may involve us in ruin, the utmost success cannot, I am confident, insure to us the least permanent advantage'. His colleague Grey replied a week later in full agreement: complete victory was one thing, and might be worth it, 'but a doubtful or indecisive victory, and protracted operations, I should think little less ruinous (I am not sure they would not be more so) than an immediate defeat'.[3]

Some in the press echoed such ambiguous private doubts publicly: the *Morning Chronicle* commented that 'Whatever our success may be, we ought never again to enter into military expeditions abroad, yet having committed ourselves, the utmost diligence ought to have been used to call forth our whole strength seasonably to give effect to our interference.' Following this up with suggestions that a series of cavalry regiments be landed on the northern coasts of Spain 'to assist in intercepting the communication with France' indicates just how troubled (or simply confused) were those who tried to keep a critical perspective on events.[4] The *Aberdeen Journal* expressed to its readers a quite different, but perhaps equally misleading set of views, that this was 'a grand and most interesting crisis, upon which, perhaps, the fate of Napoleon himself may hang'.[5] From an army confined to a thirty-mile square in the far south-western edge of the Continent, this was a very great deal to hope for.

As winter dragged on, with very little news indeed from Portugal (which did not stop the press printing acres of speculation, including accounts of battles that turned out to be wholly fictitious, and private letters full of valuable intelligence),[6] political eyes were instead fixed on the fate of the king, and how that might shape the fate of the war. George III was sinking into the madness that would darken his last decade, probably tipped over the edge by the agonising death of his daughter Princess Amelia from erysipelas, a disfiguring bacterial skin infection, on 2 November 1810. His health for the rest of that year was marked by episodes of raving mania, and physical symptoms so severe that his life was thought to be in danger.

As in earlier attacks, ministers tried to carry on, until a regency became unavoidable. The Prince of Wales was still generally assumed to be a friend to the Whigs who had cultivated him since his youth, and a sneering retort to a proud Richard Wellesley about his brother after Bussaco – 'Masséna has quite outgeneralled him' – suggested this remained the case.[7] With a Regency Bill debated in Parliament, and Grey and Grenville leading discussions about a new government, it seemed by the end of January 1811 as if the Wellesleys would soon be sharply out of favour, and perhaps out of the Peninsula.

The Prince's relationship with the new generation of Whigs was not the close personal one he had enjoyed with Fox and Sheridan, however, and he was wary of changing the government when some doctors' reports indicated that his father could be on the road to recovery, and would change it right back. When he became Regent in February, therefore, he kept the Perceval government in power, citing 'the irresistible impulse of filial duty & affection to his beloved and afflicted father', while reserving the right to alter his decision in new circumstances.[8] As it would transpire, the opposition had lost their last, best chance to alter the course of the war. That did not mean, however, that Wellington was about to triumph.

On the Spanish side of the war, there was little to show that French dominance would not eventually be established. It is true that famous guerrilla leaders like Espoz y Mina in Navarre and El Empecinado around Guadalajara and Madrid had shown that they could keep thousands of French soldiers on the run, but it was not evident that these heroics were more than a nuisance at a strategic level.[9] Some columns of Spanish regular forces could still move around the country: General Ballesteros's regulars helped boost resistance to Soult in Andalusia, and further troops were similarly employed in Extremadura and Asturias. Others raided from the sea with British assistance: in Catalonia a whole brigade of German conscripts was wiped out in September 1810 by the combination of a seaborne landing and troops force-marched through nearby mountains.[10] Even larger operations were planned and carried out: in February 1811 two Spanish divisions and one British were landed behind the lines of the French besieging Cadiz. However, the outcome of this attack – Spanish and British units separated, the latter coming under ferocious attack by an outnumbered enemy, and unable to secure victory in the absence of support from their allies – points to a recurrent problem. The Spanish command was still riddled with political and personal divisions, and in some cases, as in the Cadiz fiasco, in the hands of men who can only be called cowards and liars.[11]

Lacking direction, unity and firmness of purpose, the Spanish were repeatedly pushed back in strategically significant areas. Initiative remained persistently with the French: thus as 1810 drew to a close, Soult rounded up 20,000 men from his Andalusian garrisons and pushed into neighbouring Extremadura, seeking to relieve the pressure on Masséna and potentially threaten Lisbon from the east. Even outnumbered and in appalling wet weather, the French succeeded in driving Ballesteros's troops over the frontier and surrounding the fortress city of Badajoz. When a further 15,000 Spaniards under Mendizabal appeared, but failed to attack immediately, Soult assailed them with just 7000 of his own men. Only 4000 Spaniards escaped, while the French lost a mere 400, and a few weeks later secured the surrender of Badajoz. Soult's operations had knocked around 20,000 Spanish troops out of the war, and captured a site of immense strategic value, along with a mountain of supplies. Wellington noted that 'this recent disaster has disappointed and grieved me much', and 'would certainly have been avoided had the Spaniards been anything but Spaniards'.[12]

While Spanish attitudes, French triumphs and British scorn all compounded the tricky question of what Wellington should do in 1811, it was still not evident at the beginning of the year that the Cabinet wanted him to do anything beyond saving his army. Before news of Bussaco arrived, Lord Liverpool had already written to warn him that the rising numbers of British troops committed to the Peninsula were a temporary measure and 'must be reduced as soon as the *present exigency* will admit of it'. Although the Cabinet was briefly tempted, before news of the Cadiz fiasco, to switch to a more expansive view, early in 1811 caution was reinforced by news of the spiralling cost of operations.

The campaign of 1809 had cost less than £3 million, but that of 1810 more than £9 million. Much of that expenditure had been in the closing months of the year, and there was no sign of the rate dropping. It was 'absolutely impossible to continue our exertion upon the present scale', according to Liverpool, without fiscal ruin.[13] As it transpired, it was not impossible, once certain political arguments had been won – hard bargaining by Richard Wellesley even produced a doubling of the British subsidy to the Portuguese government, after his brother's bitter complaints about the impossibility otherwise of keeping their army in the field. But as Wellington's men watched and waited for Masséna to move, it was only as spring began to arrive that it became clear they would be allowed to follow him even as far as the frontier.

Masséna moved, at last, on 5 March 1811, breaking camp under cover of fog and making for the passes that led via Almeida and Ciudad Rodrigo back to Spain. As Wellington's troops followed, discovering in a series of sharp actions that the French still had fight in them, they witnessed the devastation wreaked by the desperate troops, the famine left in their wake, and frequent evidence of murderous atrocity: 'half-consumed skeletons of human beings on every side', and killings showing depraved imaginations 'beyond everything horrid'. As Masséna's men exhausted the last of their supplies, and stragglers began to drop out through sickness and fatigue, some were trampled by their pack-mules where they fell, their comrades too weak and indifferent to move them out of the road. Others lingered by the roadsides long enough to meet an even worse fate, as one soldier recorded: the Portuguese peasants routinely stripped them naked while still alive, then stabbed, beat or stoned them to death, 'the very bodies of the dead were kicked about as if they had been footballs'.[14]

In the course of this campaign, another soldier had an encounter that revealed the grimly personal face of combat. Rifleman Edward Costello recalled in his memoirs shooting a persistent Frenchman during a skirmish. Moving forward as the enemy withdrew, he found the man dying, and 'an indescribable uneasiness came over me, I felt almost like a criminal'. Pausing to give the man some wine from his canteen, Costello made an even grimmer discovery: the soldier had remained at his post to defend his older brother, a sergeant, lying with a shattered leg beside him, and now sobbing with grief. Forced to move off by the demands of combat, Costello returned that night to find both men 'as naked as they were born, perforated with innumerable wounds, no doubt administered by the Portuguese. I turned back to the camp, but in a very poor humour with myself.'[15]

After more than two weeks of retreat, Masséna suddenly ordered his crumbling army to turn east, seeking to link up with Soult's forces. It was a move that would have taken the army into utterly barren terrain, and Marshal Ney, who had shown tremendous personal valour in command of the rearguard, refused the order. Like Masséna, Ney had risen to greatness through the revolutionary wars. He was the son of a cooper from Lorraine, and had abandoned an early career as a notary to join the cavalry in 1787. Seeing action from 1792 onwards, he soon became an officer, and then by 1796 a general. His early years of service were in Belgium and Germany, fighting and winning a series of engagements through almost every campaign until the climactic battle of Hohenlinden in 1800. Although he had never served under Napoleon, the Emperor recognised his talents, anointing him as one of the select band of marshals he created as military pillars of his new imperial regime in 1804. Ney proved a worthy choice, and was central to the leadership of the Grand Army in the days of its greatest victories in 1805–7.

Ferociously brave, and frequently wounded, Ney had all the best qualities of a fighting leader. Like many of the marshals, however, he rankled at subordination to anyone but Napoleon.

Masséna, however, was equally proud and determined. For his disobedience, Ney was stripped of his command and sent away in disgrace, and for a few days the army experienced further disintegration as it tried to advance over goat tracks, until the order was given on 29 March for the troops to resume their northward march. The detour gave the British the opportunity to close with them, and Masséna turned at bay at Sabugal, not far short of the frontier, on 3 April. After their appalling experiences of the past six months, his troops proved astonishingly resilient, blunting the attacks of the Light Division for several hours, but the imbalance of forces, and of supplies, proved decisive. By noon the French were again moving as fast as they could towards Spain, leaving the garrison of Almeida as their last foothold in Portugal.

Falling back on Salamanca, Masséna found supplies and reinforcements in plenty, and by the end of the month, again showing his men's extraordinary powers of recovery, was able to come forward once more with 48,000 troops.[16] Wellington was blockading Almeida with fewer than 40,000, having sent a third of his army southwards under Beresford to resist Soult around Badajoz. From hectic advance, Wellington was once again thrown on the defensive. The first days of May saw the French come upon him in an extended position, his left, northern flank guarding Almeida, his right the road to Portugal. In the centre, the village of Fuentes d'Oñoro descended in labyrinthine terraces to a rock-strewn stream.

This was the exposed anchor point of a line that was otherwise well protected by Wellington's customary reverse slopes. On 3 May, furious fighting for the village resulted in gruesome stalemate – so much so that on the 4th, both sides observed an informal truce as they retrieved hundreds of dead and wounded, almost literally wedged into the narrow streets and alleys. On the 5th, Masséna attempted an outflanking on Wellington's right, where the raw Seventh Division had been posted in open country two miles from the main line. Attacked in overwhelming force, it was in severe danger of being overrun when Wellington sent the veterans of the Light Division to retrieve it. A brave decision strategically – it sacrificed a hold over the road to Portugal to maintain the blockade of Almeida – it was also an occasion of heroic military prowess. Infantry and artillery manoeuvred in and out of square and column, shuffling back towards safety under constant attack by cavalry, the iron discipline of drill their only protection. Even that could not prevent a mauling until their own horsemen came up to assist in the relief.

Meanwhile, Masséna's other wing came on into Fuentes again, attack and counter-attack alternating until bodies were once more piled through the streets. At least twice the French nearly succeeded in capturing the whole position, and as at Bussaco, a wild charge by the Connaught Rangers was decisive in forcing back the final attack. The aftermath of hurling two well-disciplined and motivated armies at each other was recorded by a commissary who accompanied the British forces:

> it was quite a common thing to see an English and a French soldier with their bayonets still in each other's bodies, and their fists convulsively grasping the butt ends of their muskets, lying on top of each other. At one spot I saw seven, and at another five, French officers killed by bayonet wounds.[17]

At the close of the day, the French still held some of the lower houses, but their momentum was exhausted, as were much of their supplies.

The British frantically threw up new field fortifications over the next few days in expectation of attack, but on 10 May the French instead withdrew. Masséna scored a small victory by successfully extracting the garrison of Almeida from under the eyes of the distracted (and incompetently led) covering force. On the night of the 10th the fort's defences were blown up, while the troops fled, fighting off disorganised attacks until they reached safety, and the rest of Masséna's army, near Ciudad Rodrigo.

After a brief pause to recuperate, Wellington divided his army again, marching with two divisions southwards to join Beresford's operations against Badajoz, which he judged a greater prize than Ciudad Rodrigo. Beresford's forces had invested the town on 8 May, suffering in foul weather, with insufficient engineers and indecisive leadership. Morale weakened precipitously, and the siege was going nowhere when a week later Soult approached with an army of 25,000. Beresford lifted the siege and stood to face him at the village of Albuera with an army of 35,000, made up almost equally of Anglo-Portuguese and Spanish divisions. What followed was a pitiless slaughter. Soult attempted a daring outflanking manoeuvre, and only delays caused by the terrain prevented the allies being taken by surprise. The battle as it developed was a series of desperate actions as attacks arrived piecemeal, and defenders alternately stood firm or were forced to march from flank to flank to meet them. Contrary to earlier experience, the Spanish regulars behaved impeccably, as did the British and Portuguese, but their leaders lacked Wellington's finesse. Counter-attacks went in prematurely, units were cut off and overwhelmed, critical points were reinforced too little or too late.

One officer of the 66th Foot wrote home of the terrible experience of being at the heart of such chaos:

> We fought them till we were hardly a Regiment ... in this shattered state our Brigade moved forward to charge. Madness alone would dictate such a thing, and at that critical period Cavalry appeared in our rear. It was then that our men began to waver, and for the first time (and God knows I hope the last) I saw the backs of English soldiers turned upon [the] French.

The regiment rallied, but worse was to come:

> Our Colours were taken ... the 2 Ensigns were shot under
> them; 2 Sergeants shared the same fate. A Lieutenant seized a
> Musket to defend them, and he was shot to the heart; what
> could be done against Cavalry?[18]

Holding the colours – the large regimental standard – was the job of the most junior officers, sometimes mere boys of fifteen or sixteen. It was a harsh introduction to the reality of battle, especially as the capture of such flags was a point of honour for attackers. The French capped their regimental standards with metal eagles granted personally by the Emperor, and the British were just as eager to seize them when the chance presented itself. Losing the colours was a perpetual dread: the officer above concluded that, despite words of praise from their general, the regiment could look forward to 'scandal' in the mouths of the 'malicious World'. At Fuentes d'Oñoro, one colonel, later sent home in disgrace, was rumoured to have ordered the colours burned at the start of the battle, so fearful was he of their loss.

Such an action illustrates the terrible strains that command in such fighting placed on men. Though, like the naval officers at Trafalgar, the maintenance of a cool outward demeanour was carefully cultivated, it came no easier to soldiers than to sailors. Colin Campbell, later to become one of the greatest British generals of the 1850s, was a sixteen-year-old ensign on his first active service when his unit came under artillery fire at Vimiero in 1808. His captain led him by the hand to the front of the regiment, and walked him up and down in sight of the guns, until he grew calm. It was, he later said, 'the greatest kindness that could have been shown to me at such a time, and through life I have felt grateful for it'.[19] When so much of Wellington's style of fighting in particular relied on a long wait, often under fire, for an enemy attack, the ability to show before the troops that you were neither afraid nor agitated as you shared their dangers was a vital attribute of an officer. Colonels rode before their regiments, always above all enjoining calm as the route to safety. 'Steady' was the watchword, and then 'old Harry himself' – the Devil – 'can't touch you'.[20]

The French approach was rather different – their junior officers were notorious amongst the British for the vociferous way in which they rallied their men to the attack. Sometimes leaping ahead of their advancing columns, even waving their hats atop their swords for added emphasis, they were part of a culture of military valour in which reckless bravery in the attack was the prime route to promotion. Though they could be equally dogged in defence, their commitment to the attack had been turned into a rhyming couplet, *L'Empereur recompensera, celui qui s'avancera*, 'the Emperor will reward he who takes himself forward'. Even generals could be heard on occasion bellowing this exhortation. It was one reason why a French officer was statistically almost half as likely again to become a casualty as one of his men. For the more phlegmatic British, the chances were better: they were only a quarter more likely to be killed or wounded.[21]

In the carnage of a battle like Albuera, this differential disappeared: in the most heavily engaged units, officers and men alike suffered up to 40 per cent casualties. Still, the allies had the advantage of numbers, and eventually this, and their discipline, told. The French retreated, leaving behind over 7000 casualties, but they also left behind an enemy too exhausted to pursue, and in some cases too depleted even to bury their own several thousand dead. The stress was almost too much for Beresford, whose dispatch after the battle treated it as a disastrous defeat. When Wellington read it, he said it would have 'driven the people in England mad' and ordered a staff officer to 'write me down a victory' – which, strategically, it was.[22]

Albuera would prove to be the last victory of 1811, however. Hampered by inadequate artillery, Wellington's attempts to besiege Badajoz collapsed in early June after two bloodily unsuccessful assaults. News that the failed Masséna had been replaced by the more vigorous Marshal Marmont, who brought some 35,000 troops south to link up with Soult's reinforced 25,000 in mid-June, caused Wellington to raise the siege and withdraw to defensive positions across the Guadiana river. There, after some initial feints, the French would keep him penned for the summer, soon feeling confident enough to split their forces again and resume the suppression of internal resistance that was so much of their customary activity in Spain. An effort to blockade Ciudad Rodrigo later in the year was similarly aborted by a cautious Wellington as the French threatened to riposte in strength. Despite renewed expressions of confidence from government, and a steady flow of new reinforcements – so that by October 1811 his British troops reached a nominal peak of 57,000 (albeit with 17,000 sick) – the balance of forces remained against renewed offensive activity by Wellington's army, until some decisive shift should happen elsewhere.

That shift occurred to the north, as the complex mesh of Napoleonic ambitions, British resistance and Russian suspicion fomented further conflict. In December 1810, Napoleon annexed to France the whole of the former Kingdom of Holland, the coastal strip of Germany as far as Hamburg, and beyond to the towns of the old Hanseatic League on the Baltic. It was a stereotypically Napoleonic move against the persistent smuggling to and from Britain that undermined his Continental Blockade: ruthless, violently imposed, and utterly without regard to a balance of power. Right at the heart of the annexed region was the Duchy of Oldenburg, whose heir was married to the Tsar's sister, and whose independence had been guaranteed at Tilsit. Even before news of this reached St Petersburg, Tsar Alexander had been chafing under the restrictions that allegiance to France imposed on Russia's trade, and at the end of the year authorised massive increases on customs tariffs for goods crossing the land frontiers, while lowering them for seaborne trade. It was as close as he could come to challenging the Continental System without an open breach.

The news about Oldenburg pushed Alexander into contemplating actual war. Offers were made to woo Napoleon's Polish satellite by giving it Austrian territory, swapped for recent Russian conquests against the Turks in modern-day Romania. The Prussians, humiliated in 1807 and fearful of further annexations, considered an alliance, but backed off as they had done so often before. War did not come, but it was these signs of renewed unrest that helped prompt the British government to be more determined in their Peninsular policy as 1811 opened. Small official overtures to Russia – the return of several hundred prisoners of war amongst them – continued a thaw that by August 1811 had Napoleon publicly fuming, denouncing Russian intentions at a diplomatic reception for his birthday on the 15th.[23]

For a few weeks in the autumn, it seemed as if France would attack Prussia as a stepping-stone to the east, before Napoleonic threats broke the Berlin government's spirit and they submitted to an alliance. Austria sniffed the wind, and decided by the end of the year that its interests were best served by signing a similar, if less subservient, deal. Napoleon was laying the groundwork for what he hoped would be a similarly ritualistic humiliation of Russia, beaten back into the French fold by the assembly of a massive army, and the infliction of a quick and crushing defeat. To facilitate this, at the end of 1811 he called back from Spain the Imperial Guard units serving there, along with Polish units that could bolster his claim to be an advancing liberator. Over 25,000 of the best troops in the Peninsula were withdrawn.[24]

With continued successes in Spain behind them, including in May–June 1811 the siege and capture of the vital north-eastern port and stronghold of Tarragona, such a withdrawal need not have been problematic for King Joseph and the various marshals. A shift to a slightly more defensive strategy could have continued to hold Wellington, the guerrillas, and assorted regional armies at bay. Napoleon, however, insisted on renewed offensive action, and a drive on the region and city of Valencia, on the eastern coast. Initial setbacks in September 1811 persuaded the Emperor, controlling the conflict from afar in Paris, that troops had to be directed into the region from across Spain, and a complex shuffle began that seriously depleted the forces holding down the north-west, west and south. Valencia fell on 8 January 1812, after a campaign that cost the Spanish over 20,000 casualties; some of the richest lands of the country (and their vital revenues) were now in French hands.

It was a disaster, but it was also the high point of French control. Notwithstanding Napoleon's complacent belief, communicated to Marshal Marmont, that 'the English army is not ready for any important operation and will undertake none before spring', Wellington was poised to strike.[25] On the day Valencia fell, his army appeared before Ciudad Rodrigo. Entrenching for a siege was a nightmare. The ground was snow-laden, the streams half-frozen, and the troops' digging tools pitifully inadequate, thanks to profiteering contractors at home. Soldiers huddled in their great-coats or buried themselves in snowbanks, trying to keep warm. Nonetheless, by the 19th, sufficient progress had been made, with the walls battered to a 'practicable breach' into two places, for the attack to be ordered.

Launching an attack on a besieged fortress reduced combat to its most elemental. After the mathematical precision of entrench-ments and bombardments came the moment when an army had to force physical possession through a breach often only a few yards wide. Not for nothing were the first men sent in known as the 'Forlorn Hope' – though the phrase itself was a mistranslation of the Dutch *verloren hoop*, 'lost troop'. In the 95th Foot, the Rifles, survivors of a Forlorn Hope attack were allowed to wear a distin-guishing arm-badge: the only strictly military decoration for valour awarded at this time in the British Army. Defenders of a breach were well prepared: men with stacks of double-shotted muskets stood in position to pour rapid fire into the attackers, others were primed to hurl hand grenades, larger bombs made from powder barrels, and firebombs of flaming tar. Such a place became, for minutes or hours of struggle, hell on earth.[26]

At Ciudad Rodrigo, as they had so often before, the Connaught Rangers went in with cold steel – though their heroic colonel was blown up by a mine detonated at the wrong moment by their own engineers. 'Black Bob' Craufurd led the Light Division into the inferno of the breach, and received an agonising and fatal wound to the spine. The town fell swiftly, and was swiftly pillaged, while officers raged, as they always did, in some cases struggling to restore discipline with sword-flats and musket butts. Order returned by daybreak, and led to the execution of a number of recaptured deserters, shot over the graves they had been made to dig. Five of the original eleven were pardoned for previous good character at the graveside, though one went mad with terror.[27] The assault cost over 1000 casualties, but it pleased the government so much they raised Wellington to an earldom as soon as the news arrived. The Spanish went one better and made him a duke. Unchallenged by the overstretched French, Wellington rested his forces for over a month before moving south in early March 1812, aiming to repeat his feat at the larger fortress of Badajoz, besieged now by the British for the third time.

Badajoz was garrisoned by over 4000 French, and a significant number of *afrancesado* Spanish sympathisers. The governor, Philippon, was a skilled and cunning defender, who made the most of the already formidable defences with various ingenious contraptions of fire, explosives and cold steel. After investing the fortress on 16 March, Wellington learned on the 29th that Marmont was marching towards Ciudad Rodrigo, threatening to undo his men's sacrifice. By 6 April, Easter Sunday, he knew he had to throw his forces into an assault, or risk gaining nothing from the campaign. The troops all knew that the siege had not advanced far enough to overwhelm the defenders. This would be a bitter and ferocious fight. Witnesses spoke of the 'indescribable *something*' in the faces of the men picked to lead the storm.

When the assaults went in at ten that night, an unexpectedly flooded ditch made the approach to the breaches torturous in itself, and some men drowned without even seeing the enemy. Great beams studded with sword-blades blocked the breaches, and troops reportedly pressed their own comrades down on to them as they struggled to surmount the chaos. Barrels of gunpowder rolled from the walls by the hundred, their explosions lighting up the night, and a witness wrote that the 'exploding mines cast up friends and foes together, who in burning torture slashed and shrieked in the air'.[28]

If there was something worse than a hell on earth, then this was surely it. The attack on Badajoz foundered in the breaches. After suffering more than two thousand casualties for no gain, Wellington ordered the survivors to pull back. As the ghastly carnage reached a climax, he had thrown his hopes behind a subsidiary assault against the opposite side of the town. Here, too, men perished by the dozen, as they fought to scale the walls with ladders that were too short, or which collapsed under their packed weight, casting them on to their comrades' bayonets below. But weight of numbers, and awful, inhuman determination, won through: a few men got over, the foothold was widened, and before the defenders concentrated at the breaches could rally for a counter-attack, they were taken from behind.[29] Overall British casualties for the siege amounted to 4670, of whom over 3700 fell in that one terrible night.

The troops who had girded themselves for the slaughter now took their customary revenge. The orgy of pillage, rape and murder that followed appalled many observers of the officer class, who recalled it as 'wanton cruelty', 'horrid excess' and 'scenes ... too dreadful and disgusting to relate'. On more than one occasion, officers who tried to restore discipline, or just to save civilians from an awful fate, were shot or stabbed to death.[30] Such behaviour might seem to justify Wellington's notoriously dyspeptic view that his army was made up of 'the scum of the earth', enlisted to get access to drink and to avoid the consequences of fornication. But Wellington also called them 'fine fellows', and it was never entirely clear if his judgments were merely intended to shock.[31]

Certainly the common soldier was something of an outcast in society, especially until the Portland government did away with lifetime enlistments that had tended to make the army a refuge of desperation. However, as their letters and memoirs show, a significant sample of Peninsular regulars were literate and reflective men, and there is no reason to suppose that their illiterate comrades were any less capable of humanity. Common soldiers came from every corner of the British Isles, and enlisted for many different reasons. Poverty was certainly a decisive factor for many, and helps account for the over-representation of the Irish and Scots, who added up to over half of all soldiers, even in many nominally 'English' regiments.[32] Others joined for adventure, and perhaps even through patriotism – the bounties that helped to shift thousands from the Militia to the regulars were not large enough in themselves to have persuaded the genuinely reluctant, when the horrors of war were well-known.

In the army men found comradeship and care, the regimental system explicitly setting out to bind them into an extended family.[33] Even if this was cut across by the inevitable failings of incompetent, cowardly or brutal individuals, it was nonetheless real. For some the regiment went further, and produced genuine family. Female camp-followers might in many cases have been only nominally the 'wives' of individuals, but in other cases they were devoted helpmeets who shared their husbands' hardships on campaign. Military life, despite its evident dangers, could still be a shelter from a civilian existence that offered not much greater opportunities for survival, when the scales were weighted by disease, poverty and economic disruption. It certainly absorbed more and more individuals. Despite annual losses, to all causes, of around 10 per cent, the army grew steadily towards a quarter of a million as the war years ground on.[34]

Whatever combination of circumstances drove men to the extremes of behaviour witnessed in the aftermath of a siege, it could not be justly claimed that such soldiers were a marginal group of deviants.[35] Some of those who observed the carnage at Badajoz reflected the complexity of possible attitudes. One Rifles officer noted without evident disapproval that 'the men were permitted to enjoy themselves for the remainder of the day'; another observed that they exercised 'the immemorial privilege of tearing the town to pieces'. One cavalryman thought that in the light of their losses 'the Survivors richly deserved the liberty of plundering the Town', and another wrote with some insight that 'the dead and dying in the breach were the most shocking thing ever seen, and perhaps a little plunder was necessary to drown the horror'.[36]

Wellington himself viewed that horror by the cold light of the next morning, astonishing his staff, and some of his harder-hearted generals, by weeping as he surveyed the tumbled dead before the breach. He wrote to the Cabinet in praise of the 'gallantry' displayed, adding that 'I greatly hope that I shall never again be the instrument of putting them to such a test.'[37] Two days later, ferocious action by his provosts finally restored order to his army. With Ciudad Rodrigo and Badajoz secure (and Marmont falling back cautiously on Salamanca), he was free at last to contemplate a real offensive. After four years of war in the Peninsula, the tide was beginning to turn.

Wellington's travails on the Portuguese frontier were only part of a war that remained effectively global. The Royal Navy was not idle after Trafalgar – indeed the French lost more major warships in battle during the four years after 1805 than they had on that fateful day. These losses – twenty-three battleships (and thirty frigates) in a long series of minor engagements – continued to be offset by a frantic building programme, so that Napoleon still had a fleet of over seventy battleships at his disposal in 1812, with almost half as many again under construction everywhere from the Baltic to the Adriatic.[38] Although crewing such vessels efficiently was quite another matter, the British fleet was under constant strain from the need to observe and blockade this perpetual menace. It met that strain, however, and with the enemy's main naval strength bottled up in Europe, was able to go decisively on the offensive elsewhere.

With Spain and Portugal as allies, South America no longer posed to Britain the military conundrum it had done before 1808, and operations outside Europe took on the appearance of a giant mopping-up operation. An Anglo-Brazilian task force had gained control of French Guiana by January 1809, and almost immediately afterwards the French Caribbean stronghold of Martinique was seized in a campaign that lasted only weeks. In the middle of the year, Spanish troops with British naval support secured the surrender of the remaining French foothold on Saint Domingue/Haiti, and the final French island in the West Indies, Guadeloupe, was taken in February 1810 in a crushing eight-day amphibious blitz.[39]

On the other side of the world, naval forces based out of India spent much of 1809 and early 1810 subduing Dutch resistance in the Moluccas – the original 'spice islands' of Indonesia. Later in 1810, in a dramatic seesaw campaign of succeeding triumphs and disasters, a British force captured the French Indian Ocean possessions of Mauritius and Réunion, eliminating the last significant base for French privateers and commerce raiders outside Europe.[40] In August–September 1811, a major British force overran Dutch Java, leaving the allies in possession of all Napoleon's former overseas territories.[41]

Even before all these victories, the commitment of the Royal Navy to a global reach was shown in Nagasaki, Japan, in October 1808. HMS *Phaeton*, a frigate captained by Captain Fleetwood Pellew, the aggressive, twenty-seven-year-old son of an admiral, sailed into the port in search of the Dutch traders licensed to dock there, who maintained Japan's only link with the outside world. Not finding them, Pellew instead demanded food and water from the nonplussed local officials, bullied them into compliance, and sailed away the next day. Behind him, he left six dignitaries who committed ritual suicide out of shame at their humiliation, and three local interpreters who were ordered to drown themselves for their part in the exchanges. The long arm of the British Empire could bring the sorrows of war to the most unlikely places.[42]

Closer to home, the power of British naval forces, and of British money, was shown in intriguing fashion by the maintenance of a blockading fleet in the Baltic throughout these years. Theoretically surrounded by the enmity of Denmark and Russia after 1807, and from 1810 of Sweden too, a force of battleships, frigates and smaller vessels carrying up to 17,000 men was nonetheless kept in the region. It was largely provisioned by the willingness of nominal enemies to supply fresh meat (often on the hoof) and other goods, paid for with the rock-solid credit of the British government.[43]

The consequences of global war were many and overlapping, and sometimes unpleasantly unexpected. The continued economic wrestling match between the Continental System and British powers of blockade enriched smugglers and corrupt officials across Europe; it encouraged new and sometimes unexpected routes for overseas produce into British and continental markets, once again strengthening the long reach of empire. Thus, for example, British ships had moved some £2.7 million worth of goods to and from the Mediterranean, Caribbean and South America in 1807; thanks to the ruthless control exerted over access to their new Spanish allies' dominions, that total was raised to between £9 million and £13 million in each of the following five years – over a quarter of all British overseas trade in that period.[44]

Such control was resented by the Spanish themselves, and contributed to the less than happy relationship sustained between the two governments. The global control asserted by the Orders in Council also made the United States, deeply dependent on Atlantic trade, profoundly uneasy. The USA's official response had been a series of Embargo Acts, setting retaliatory limits on trade, that were widely evaded but bitterly felt. Within Britain, the aggravated competition for narrower channels of profit ran alongside the desire for intensified productivity, and each compounded the other; expensive machinery had to be made to pay. Workers' wages suffered as food prices rose, all too visibly a result of legislative protection for landowners and aggressive blockade. That aggression extended ever further towards a new confrontation with the Americans, their distrustful commercial relations compounded by the Royal Navy's habit of impressing English-speaking sailors wherever they were found – even aboard US national vessels.

A further Non-Intercourse Act passed in Washington in 1809, and taking full effect after further disputes in early 1811, effectively banned all trade with Britain. Over £11 million worth of goods, mainly textiles, had been exported across the Atlantic in 1810; the figure for the next year crashed to under £2 million. Disastrous economic depression loomed – in Yorkshire's West Riding alone, it was reckoned that by the end of 1811 £1 million of goods lay unsellable in warehouses, and over a third of manufacturers were put out of business.[45] As 1812 had opened with events in the Peninsula on a knife-edge, so it would develop in spectacular new dimensions of conflict. Before the year was out Europe would be convulsed by the Grand Army, Britain would find itself facing a new war for control of the oceans, and England would see the rise of an 'Army of Redressers', bringing insurrection to the Pennine hills.

12

THE UNCERTAIN TIDE
OF VICTORY

Spencer Perceval is an almost forgotten historical figure, but he stands at a number of intriguing crossroads in the evolution of British society. He was the younger son of an Irish earl's second marriage, and thus at the very fringes of the networks of patronage and entitlement that dictated so much of the structure of public life. Born in 1762, he had a London childhood thanks to his father's political career – he was briefly First Lord of the Admiralty in the mid-1760s – and attended Harrow School before going to Cambridge. At both places he showed a strong interest in evangelical Christianity, something that was to be a marked element in his private life and public persona. Entering adulthood with only an annual allowance of £200, not even enough for the life of a modest gentleman, he settled on a legal career, and was called to the bar in 1786. After a few years of struggle, during which he also eloped against the wishes of disapproving parents, he began to accumulate official positions and opportunities through his family and political connections.

After assisting in the prosecutions of Thomas Paine and John Horne Tooke, Perceval came to Pitt's attention, but turned down a first offer of political office in Ireland because his legal career was now flourishing, and he needed the money. His wife had already by 1795 produced four of an eventual thirteen children, twelve of whom, remarkably, survived to adulthood. Family connections propelled him towards a political career, however, when in 1796 an MP cousin succeeded to an earldom, and Perceval was called upon to stand in his relative's place for the seat of Northampton.

In the Commons Perceval established a reputation as a fierce defender of Pitt and enemy of Foxite radicalism, while continuing to work as a barrister – in 1797 he prosecuted one of the London Corresponding Society leaders for sedition, in connection with the naval mutinies of that year. From 1798 he entered the circles of government legal administration, serving successively as Solicitor to the Ordnance, Solicitor-General, and by 1801 Attorney-General, the Crown's highest legal officer. This was now under the Addington government – as an opponent of Catholic emancipation, Perceval had declined to follow Pitt out of office. However, he remained sympathetic to his old chief, and avoiding policy disagreements was kept in post when Pitt returned to government in 1804.[1]

A slight figure physically, noted for his extraordinary pale complexion, his modest and moral home life and his diligent industry, Perceval in his life might seem to echo Pitt. Indeed, with his noted evangelical zeal, he was in some respects an even more strait-laced figure. However, he was also a man who had established a successful legal practice at the heart of metropolitan political and social intrigue, and – as an extraordinary episode in the months after Pitt's death showed – possessed a ruthless side, and some bizarre connections.

One of the great events of the new Talents government in 1806 was the 'Delicate Investigation' into the reputed adultery of the Princess of Wales, undertaken thanks to pressure from her alienated husband on his Whig friends in power. Although the inquiry's official conclusions acquitted her of the main charge, they remained critical. Perceval was foremost amongst Pittite politicians in coming to Princess Caroline's defence, and drafted a response of over 150 pages which pointed the finger of blame at the Prince of Wales. Known as 'The Book', with connotations of shattering revelations within, it was common knowledge that he was threatening to publish this in the winter of 1806–7 when the Talents ministry collapsed, and he re-entered government in the more senior position of Chancellor of the Exchequer.

What was less commonly known was that Perceval had already had 5000 copies of 'The Book' printed. Even less commonly known, but apparent from government papers secret at the time, is that Perceval was paying £400 to a man called Thomas Ashe to dig up political and sexual dirt on a variety of political opponents.[2] That Perceval should even know Ashe is extraordinary – a former army captain fallen into penury and disrepute, he was a sometime pamphleteer and journalistic hack. Given some of Ashe's other connections, it positions Perceval on the brink of a dark sinkhole of iniquity that connected high society to the lowest of criminal enterprises, and to the most dangerous of political radicals.

Amongst Ashe's connections, for example, was Davenport Sedley, a professional extortionist who profited from various individuals' embarrassing connections to sexual scandal. Typically operating by presenting evidence of a muckraking volume about to come off the presses, Sedley made a steady income from 'suppressing' such publications for cash. An Irishman who had been jailed in the turbulent years after the rebellion of 1798, he also had shadowy links to the United Irishmen and other British radical groups.

Ashe was also connected to another even more remarkable figure, who went by the name of Jonathan King, known as 'Jew King', and whose real name was Jacob Rey. A Portuguese Jew by origins, who had reputedly begun his business life as a common boot-black, King had, through extraordinary efforts, become a qualified attorney, a merchant, banker and money-lender. A scholar who wrote treatises on subjects from theology to mathematics, who had been prominent in radical Whig debating circles in the 1790s, a financial supporter of the London Corresponding Society, and a man of fashion whose marriage to a dowager countess gave him a social entrée to aristocratic society, King was a dramatic example of the possibilities for social climbing in London's metropolitan culture.

He was also, by reliable repute, a blackmailer, swindler, card-sharp, fence and, in the words of the radical memoirist Francis Place, 'an atrocious villain'. He sponsored muckraking journalism, ran dishonest gambling-houses, and held power over courtesans and rakes alike by drawing them into debt. Some who knew him thought he was an unprincipled revolutionist, others that he was a government spy: for some, it was not inconceivable that he was both, always in his own interest. King himself later wrote vividly of the corrosive antisemitism that underlay his apparent welcome into society, and which might perhaps have occasioned some of his more disruptive actions in response: Jews faced 'every neighbour's enmity' and 'hatred', aroused by the very 'acuteness and suspicions' they were forced to adopt by their marginalised and vulnerable position.[3]

Regardless of motive, King was definitely connected to the scattered remnants of violent revolutionary radicalism that had survived from the 1790s, and also to the blackmailing of high-society figures. Furthermore, such activities crossed over into events which had become public news. The suppressed memoirs of Mary Anne Clarke placed King firmly behind Colonel Wardle's campaign against the Duke of York, and claimed that other professional blackmailers had been paid by him to scour for further dirt. Some of this found an outlet in two newspapers, the *Independent Whig* and the *British Guardian*, that were instrumental in rolling such events into a continuing narrative of the evils of 'Old Corruption' – but which were also partly financed by King's empire of criminal and semi-criminal connections. Even an independently wealthy radical such as Sir Francis Burdett could not avoid association with this world, which was also criss-crossed by real and suspected government spies.[4]

Given that Spencer Perceval clearly had some insight into the operation of that same world, it is perhaps not coincidental that his assumption of the prime ministerial office at the end of 1809 came through somewhat murky manoeuvres (though there are no provable connections). It is known that suppression of 'The Book' continued to involve him in paying, from the public purse, sums of between £50 and £1500 as leaked copies continued to surface, as well as making both promises of preferment and obtaining court injunctions to obtain silence.[5] It is perhaps also no coincidence, therefore, that his years of power saw an intensified crackdown on the public visibility of the political critique that welled up from the radical underground, obtained by silencing a series of notable individuals.

In February 1810, the chair of a radical debating society, the British Forum, was brought up before the bar of the Commons for daring to advertise a debate questioning the chamber's right to exclude spectators from sessions discussing the Walcheren fiasco. Despite his apologies, he was committed to Newgate prison for contempt of Parliament. Sir Francis Burdett began a campaign of furious speeches and publishing, denouncing this act as contrary to Magna Carta itself. Raging through the early spring, it seemed at points that this issue might lead to a government defeat, but on 6 April after an all-night sitting, their forces rallied, voting that Burdett had libelled the House and should be detained in the Tower of London for the remainder of the session.

A weekend intervened before the order was carried out, and Burdett's friends contemplated using the ancient powers of *posse comitatus* to raise a body of 1200 volunteer constables to prevent his 'illegal' apprehension. Angry crowds of several thousand were reported to be harassing passers-by who would not declare in Burdett's favour, and bodies of cavalry galloped to and fro dispersing the most menacing groups. Government over-reaction and muddle raised the spectre, it was said, of 50,000 troops descending on the city to keep order – though in the event only a hundred volunteers turned up for the radicals' *posse*, there was no confrontation, and Burdett went into custody peacefully.[6]

Polite radical opinion further idolised him there: he received daily visitors, including deputations from various societies, and congratulatory addresses from across the country, that from Manchester and Salford bearing 18,000 signatures. Less polite radicalism also saluted him, and the government received regular reports of pro-Burdett and anti-government graffiti and handbills – 'Soldiers fight for Burdett' was one pithy example, while another went in for menacing doggerel:

> When the LION gets out of the Tower
> How Happy will ENGLISHMEN BE,
> He'll the RATS of the NATION DEVOUR
> And Britons, from Thraldom set Free – !!![7]

Due to be released on 21 June, Burdett seemed primed for greatness: on the day itself, a crowd said to have been half a million strong lined the route from the Tower to his home, prepared to cheer him. But all ended in anticlimax: what else some of the crowd might have been prepared to do troubled Burdett, and claiming a concern for public safety (that perhaps concealed a concern for his own), he left the Tower instead by boat, out of sight of the crowds. His mentor Tooke had warned him once before to avoid 'the proceedings of a mob, especially of a mob in your favour': any appearance of leadership could, since the Gordon Riots of 1780, lead to a charge of high treason.[8] Suspicions that agents provocateurs lurked in radical ranks doubtless added to this caution, and to a certain amount of rancour that followed.

By the time the dust of this episode cleared, radicalism had been struck another fearful blow. William Cobbett, convicted of seditious libel for an article published the previous year condemning brutal punishments in the Militia, was sentenced to two years in Newgate prison, and a fine of £1000. A 'special jury' of government supporters, empanelled under long-standing but hitherto rarely used powers of the Attorney-General (but which Prime Minister Perceval was intimately familiar with), had taken mere minutes to hand down the conviction. In the course of the following year, a series of other radical writers and publishers were given similarly draconian sentences. In a deliberate campaign of intimidation that went on into 1812, Perceval's government in total issued over forty of the 'ex officio informations' used to start such actions, over half of which were brought to trial, the others being held as a threat to induce their targets' future silence.[9]

Curiously, this assault on radical subversion took place at the same time as a striking rise in judicial attacks on sodomy and buggery in London. From one or two a year, trials increased in number to almost thirty in 1810, with a smaller peak the next year. Whether this was a deliberate policy or the outcome of a 'moral panic' at alleged depravity (and sodomy was seen as an eminently 'foreign' vice), men convicted of such offences were placed in the pillory and pelted by eager crowds with offal, rotten fruit, dead animals, blood and dung. At least one such prisoner was permanently blinded and battered half-dead by the experience. With the capital shaken by several bank failures and rising unemployment, there were noted to be 'many thousands of half-starved, discharged clerks, skulking about London', and a series of widely reported sodomy trials certainly served to distract public attention from any political criticism.[10]

While this wave of alarm had no clear long-term effects, the ruthless campaign of Perceval's government against Cobbett and his ilk succeeded in turning around the general perception of the relationship between government and its radical opponents. What had begun in 1809 as a radical drive to exploit scandal amongst the elite came to be characterised as a scandalous series of acts of disrespect and outrage committed by the radicals themselves. As the tide of warfare in the outside world began to turn, and the radical argument of dangerous incompetence lost traction, their essentially political campaigns began to drift back towards their default state of rumbling discontent. New sources of anger and resistance, however, with deep roots in society and economy, were already stirring.

In April 1812, Wellington's army broke free at last from the mountainous shackles of the Portuguese frontier. Raised to new heights of manpower, and employing that strength with grim ruthlessness, the redcoats were now ready to carry the war once more into Spain. The cost of this effort was measured in one sense in the men slaughtered or mutilated in the ghastly ditch at Badajoz, which had almost sickened Wellington himself of war. It was measured in another sense by the conflict it provoked in England, where this same month saw scenes not wholly unlike another war. On 8 April, as Wellington's provosts still battled to control the rampaging soldiery, in faraway Manchester thousands gathered to shout down a bid to offer a loyalist address to the government. When a full-scale riot broke out, it marked the overturning of the authorities' prior ability to raise the urban populace against radicals. As one radical later recalled, 'We had no more Church-and-King mobs after that!'[11]

Across the Pennines, the very next day a force of some 300 attackers destroyed a woollen-mill near Wakefield. On the night of the 11th, a smaller but equally determined band of around 150 attacked Rawfolds Mill near Brighouse. The owner, William Cartwright, had put in place defences only a little less devilish than those of Badajoz, including spiked rollers and a barrel of sulphuric acid, to back up a contingent of soldiers and armed employees. The attackers peppered the building with musketry, while under its cover a party of men with hammers and axes braved the defenders' counterfire to assail the mill's main doors. Driven off, they left behind two mortally wounded comrades. One was John Booth, nineteen years of age and a clergyman's son. Local folklore recalled that he was harassed on his deathbed by the parson, a militant Tory, to reveal his comrades. At last he beckoned him forward. 'Can you keep a secret?' 'Yes, yes, I can,' replied his interrogator. 'So can I,' said Booth, expiring.[12]

What history records as the Luddite movement had entered its most desperate and dangerous phase. Its origins reached far back in time – back in one sense to the sixteenth century, when Tudor monarchs had set out the rights of skilled cloth-workers to protect the quality of their work. Back in another sense to the 1770s and 1780s, when machine-breaking was the response of communities threatened with displacement, and back, certainly, to the 1790s when machine-weaving began to transform first the cotton and then the woollen trades. It had a direct link to the alternately legal and violent campaigns of the West Country shearmen and their Pennine cousins, seeking a parallel to the cotton-weavers' Arbitration Act but getting instead, between 1803 and 1809, the erosion of their old rights, and the scorn of those they petitioned. As early as 1806, the committee of MPs charged with examining the workers' grievances concluded instead that 'such Institutions' as their unions were 'still more alarming in a political, than in a commercial view'. With English Jacobinism still a recent memory, the shearmen's 'so efficient and so dangerous' ability to act with 'facility and secrecy' helped prompt the suppression of their claimed rights.[13]

In this new era of economic blockade, a different group of workers were first pushed into organised insurrection. Framework knitters, who made fine woollen and silk stockings on 'frames' that allowed for work without intrusive seams, had flourished in the eighteenth century. As long as knee-breeches remained in fashion for men, and as long as women enjoyed more discreetly wearing decorated legwear, the stockingers' skills were in demand. It was a trade that still, in 1811, employed 50,000 people, mainly in a triangle around Nottingham, Leicester and Derby. By then, however, plain hose were in fashion – and indeed, long trousers for men, removing all aesthetic consideration from the trade.

Export markets suffered under the Continental Blockade and the Orders in Council, and employers were engaged in a race to the bottom to cheapen production in pursuit of dwindling demand. Tricks such as manipulating piece-rates, offering undervalued payments-in-kind, increasing charges for materials and 'rent' for frames, and inducing the under-employed to work cheaply were applied. The two key grievances that helped create a movement for resistance, however, were 'cut-ups' and 'colting'. The former risked the end of the framework knitters' industry, by replacing their particular skills with the confection of seamed stockings from flat cloth; the latter was the displacement of skilled tradesmen by women and teenage boys – either 'surplus' apprentices or, worse still, semi-skilled hands taught rudimentary techniques on the job.

Framework knitters were an established, and in their eyes honourable, trade. Their 'Company' possessed a charter granted by Charles II, and although its organisation had largely lapsed, they had succeeded in 1787 in securing a minimum-wage agreement that lasted for twenty years. When this began to break up, the Company was revived to fight back, and journeymen knitters paid £1 13 shillings and 6 pence to join: a month's wages in the good times, and more as rates declined, marking the value they attached to the organisation.[14] By 1811, wages were a third below their 1807 level, and legal remedies – including an effort to sue the merchant hosiers as an illegal combination – had been turned aside by authority.

The Framework Knitters' Company persisted throughout the Luddite era in seeking legal redress: delegates travelled to London, met with other trades, lobbied MPs (handing out free samples of fine-quality workmanship, paid for by collections) and presented their claims to Lord Sidmouth, the former Prime Minister Addington, serving in the Cabinet in early 1812 as Lord President of the Privy Council. A Bill was even put to Parliament, thanks to radical sympathisers, embodying protections for skilled workers in the clothing trades. When it fell, Sidmouth himself remarked in the Lords that he 'trusted in God that no such principle would be again attempted to be introduced in any Bill brought up to the House'.[15] The craftsmen's arguments were cogent, literate, reflective and persistent, supported by collections and petitions signed by thousands, and entirely without political traction. In such circumstances, the resort to direct action was only to be expected.

The first outbreaks came in response to the further crash in trade caused by the United States' Non-Intercourse Act in the spring of 1811. One March night, after a large crowd demanding 'work and a more liberal price' had been driven out of Nottingham, cheering crowds surrounded gangs of men who smashed stocking-frames in the nearby village of Arnold. For several weeks nocturnal attacks persisted, despite military patrols. Attacking the stocking-frames on which their livelihood depended has always seemed the most self-destructive and foolhardy dimension of the 'Luddite' action, but of course they did not attack the frames of the more friendly and reputable employers, concentrating their efforts on punishing those who undertook abusive practices and demonstrated hostility to workers' claims.

After these spring episodes, a more refined Luddism emerged again in the autumn of 1811, and for four months from November held the East Midlands in a state of permanent alarm. Almost at once it became an armed conflict – a stockinger named John Westley was shot dead as he participated in an assault on a hosier's premises at Bulwell on 10 November. His comrades retrieved his body, then resumed the attack, breaking in and wrecking the frames. Three days later a similar force, armed with everything from axes to muskets, destroyed seventy frames in one attack at

Sutton-in-Ashfield. By the end of the following month the *Leeds Mercury* published a report from Nottingham declaring that there was 'no parallel in history, since the troubled days of Charles the First', for the 'Insurrectional state' of the country.[16]

Attacks were occurring across the region, often in several places on the same night. Men went masked and armed, with regular systems of sentries and signals; it was supposed they had sworn oaths of obedience and secrecy. Reports of raids specifically for gathering arms, and of wide fund-raising in artisan communities, were also spread. One correspondent noted that Luddite 'inspectors' were able to summon stockinger communities to meetings, regulate wages, take collections for the support of workers laid off by frame-breaking, and 'discharge' unapprenticed or female workers, attaching signs to their workplace to declare 'Let this frame stand, the colts removed'.

Others noted that employers who fell in with Luddite demands – by goodwill or force – put up printed signs declaring that 'This frame is making full fashioned work, at the full price'. Luddite leaders kept discipline, offering rewards for the denunciation of informers; on one occasion they returned goods looted from a mill with a long note recording that those responsible 'have been punished for their vileny for one of them have been hang'd for 3 minet and then Let down agane'. This letter, ending with the message that 'I ham a friend to the pore and Distrest an a enemy to the oppressors thron' and signed 'General Ludd', appeared in the Nottingham press in early February 1812, and in the *Leeds Mercury* a week later.[17]

By this stage, there were already rumours abroad that Luddite delegates had been in contact with aggrieved workers in Manchester, Bolton and Stockport, as well as with Yorkshire croppers at their famous Shears Inn, high in the Pennines between Leeds, Bradford and Huddersfield. Another alarmed informant spoke of men from Carlisle and Glasgow meeting Luddites in Lancashire. Such news was often second-hand, and doubtless sometimes mere speculation. The officials and magistrates who had been using informers to keep tabs on workers' agitation since the days of the Corresponding Societies all noted that this new movement was unusually secretive. The Duke of Newcastle, who shortly advocated martial law as a solution, noted that 'no one dares impeach' – that is, lay charges against anyone in their own name – 'for fear of his life', and a local vicar and magistrate indicated that 'the class of men to whom we are obliged to look for information' were 'in general very unwilling to give it'. There were rumours that arms were being purchased illicitly from Birmingham manufacturers with foreign funds, while *The Times* reported a 'state of war'; it is evident that Luddism had thoroughly frightened the propertied classes.[18]

Even before real violence had spread beyond the Midlands in February 1812, fear of it produced a ferocious Frame-Breaking Bill in Parliament, imposing the death penalty as 'exemplary punishment' for anyone damaging 'machines or engines' used in the stocking trade. Passed through the Commons with opposition only from the tiny minority of stalwarts of radicalism and Whig humanitarianism, it met in the Lords the impassioned objections of the poet, Lord Byron. In his maiden parliamentary speech, Byron invoked the misery of working communities near his own family home in Nottinghamshire, 'squalid wretchedness' worse even than he had seen in 'the seat of war in the Peninsula' or under 'the most despotic of infidel governments'.

Is there not blood enough upon your penal code that more must be poured forth to ascend to Heaven and testify against you? How will you carry the Bill into effect? Can you commit a whole country to their own prisons? Will you erect a gibbet in every field, and hang up men like scarecrows?

His eloquence rolled on, declaring that only a jury of 'twelve butchers' could convict men driven to these acts of desperation, 'meagre with famine, sullen with despair ... about to be torn forever from a family which he lately supported in peaceful industry, and which it is not his fault that he can no longer so support'.[19]

The Bill passed the Lords without even a formal vote. In some respects it was no more than a gesture – for almost a hundred years, thanks to the 'Black Act' passed against nocturnal poaching gangs, going armed and disguised had been a capital offence, as it was to write the kind of threatening letters that accompanied Luddite campaigns as they had many disturbances before. The law did not lack for tools to put down Luddism. Yet in the early months of 1812, it seemed to spread ever wider. Yeomanry cavalry galloped across the Midlands, as Militia detachments stood-to nightly, and by January 1812, 3000 regular troops had already been committed to that one region, announced by the Home Secretary to the Commons as 'a larger force than had ever been found nec-essary in any period of our history to be employed in the quelling of a local disturbance'.[20]

In a country so long at war, it was unsurprising that the Luddite movement took on so many contours of an armed insurrection. The great Volunteer recruitments during the years of invasion scares had thoroughly militarised the young male population, and provided many with additional income. When the Portland gov-ernment in 1807 did away with the ruinous cost and destabilising influence of so much bottom-up soldiering, replacing it with the smaller, more closely controlled Local Militia, those laid off did not forget what they had learned. Striking weavers who paraded in columns in Lancashire in 1808 were one public sign of this martial pride. More clandestinely, every episode of unrest thereafter saw reports of 'arming and drilling' and the keeping of military disci-pline amongst the insurgents.

From Nottingham in February 1812 came reports that 'frame-breakers' fleeing a house were intercepted by what witnesses took at first to be a military patrol, but turned out to be Luddite reinforce-ments, 'armed and dressed in soldiers' greatcoats, one of whom was dignified with a large staff, and, it is supposed, he was the commander of the party'.[21] When Luddism reached Yorkshire in these same weeks, it did so with the full panoply of this military array, as press reports emphasised:

> As soon as the work of destruction was completed, the Leader drew up his men, called over the roll, each man answering to a particular number instead of his name; they then fired off their pistols ... gave a shout, and marched off in regular military order.[22]

The Pennine communities of the West Riding produced many of the most flamboyant expressions of earnest revolt. Here a whole way of life was threatened – that of communities which had built up since the sixteenth century a thoroughly unusual combination of material prosperity and social independence through their relatively decentralised manufacturing trade, where all shared, more or less, in the opportunities provided by a combination of smallholding agriculture and craft skills.[23] The croppers, whose skill lay in the subtle manoeuvring of the huge shears to finish the best-quality cloth, were now in an emblematic dilemma. Their work, so very difficult to do by hand, requiring enormous strength combined with deep concentration and dexterity, turned out to be appallingly easy to reproduce with a properly calibrated shearing-frame. Their relished independence, and their pride, marked on their bodies by their hardened musculature, and by distinctive calluses on their wrists, was being brought to nothing. Their fightback was more militant than elsewhere, and evoked all the rhetoric of earlier movements for liberty and equality, each of which had flowed through their houses in print and speech, and clearly had not been forgotten.[24]

In Leeds, 'General Ludd Commander of the Army of Redressers' authored a leaflet that recalled how the 'brave Citizens of Paris' had toppled their monarchy 'in Sight of 30,000 Tyrant Redcoats' in

1792. Now it was time in England 'to come forward with Arms and help the Redressers to redress their Wrongs and shake off the hateful Yoke of a Silly Old Man, and his Son more silly and their Rogueish Ministers'. Declaring that 'all Nobles and Tyrants must be brought down', the leaflet went on to urge recruits to join with 'above 40,000 heroes ... ready to break out, to crush the old Government & establish a new one'.

A letter to a Huddersfield manufacturer was more specific – a party of 300 would come to destroy 'those detestable Shearing Frames' in his mill; any 'Trouble' would lead to the burning of the building as well, 'and if you have Impudence to fire upon any of my Men, they have orders to murder you'. The recipient was warned that '2,782 Sworn Heroes' were in the Luddite 'Army of Huddersfield', and 'nearly double' in Leeds. The letter also named towns from Halifax to Manchester and Glasgow, and asserted a link to 'the Papists in Ireland' who 'are rising to a Man', an insurrection which would draw off the soldiers currently 'Idle in Huddersfield and then Woe be to the places now guarded by them'.[25]

However exaggerated this rhetoric may have been – and it was very much exaggerated – it showed a wide political awareness. The letter noted by name as a leader in Lancashire 'the brave Mr Hanson', the gentleman radical lauded in 1808 after imprisonment for supporting striking weavers, and all the places it listed had experienced disturbances of one kind or another in recent months and years. Combined with widespread reports of nocturnal marches, secret arms caches, oath-taking ceremonies, and a first series of impressively well-organised raids on shearing-frame sheds, all this was enough to cause many more timid manufacturers to dismantle and lock away their dangerous machines, and to spread the word that they had done so.

By early March 1812 Yorkshire Luddism appeared triumphant, and the movement seemed to be spreading west. Stockport in Lancashire experienced a major riot on the 14th, which included elements of classic protest about prices, and the looting of food shops, along with attacks on local authorities, the destroying of machinery in a mill, and the ceremonious burning of the contents of the mill owner's house. Cavalry and infantry had to charge to disperse the crowd.[26] Luddite determination to consolidate their gains by destroying the power of manufacturers to resist led in April to the iconic battle at Rawfolds Mill, and on 18 April a pitched battle at a mill near Saddleworth saw five Luddites shot dead. Reports continued to flow in of larger and larger rebel bands gathering, and some spoke of a general rising in early May.[27]

A new stage in Luddite activity seemed to be marked by the assassination by gunfire on 27 April of William Horsfall, a mill owner who had sworn to 'ride up to his saddle-girths' in Luddite blood.[28] In the week of the Rawfolds attack, government had been told of riots of various kinds in major centres including Birmingham, Manchester, Coventry and Sheffield, and in a dozen other places from the Midlands to the Scottish border. The Home Office, at last recognising that these were no ordinary riots, asked for and got a major force of regular troops committed to the safety of the north. There was already grave concern that this would not be enough – riots were reported by the end of April in Bristol and Plymouth as well as Carlisle, Leeds and Sheffield, and in distant Cornwall miners struck and marched on towns demanding cheaper food.

On 4 May Lieutenant-General Sir Thomas Maitland, just returned from six years as governor of Ceylon, marched troops into Manchester, the vanguard of a force of around 7000 under his direct command, added to another 6000 under generals in the Midlands and West Riding. He also ordered the mobilisation of another 12,000 Local Militia in Yorkshire, and a similar number west of the Pennines.[29] In total, this surpassed the count of British regulars currently serving directly under Wellington – though most of those here were not regulars, and much of Wellington's strength was not British. Nonetheless, such a major deployment is signal evidence for how seriously the government now took this threat. The calibre of the man appointed to counteract it is likewise noteworthy.

Maitland was a prime example of the British ruling class, its reach and its connections. An MP and royal Privy Councillor, son of a Scottish earl (and brother of the Lord Lauderdale who six years earlier had tried to negotiate peace on behalf of Fox), Maitland was warrior, diplomat and imperial administrator all in one. He had fought the French in the Caribbean in the 1790s, negotiated with rebellious Haitian former slaves, and would go on in 1813 to become governor of the vital strategic fortress-island of Malta, and later of the Ionian Islands. He brought both overt force and experienced political guile to the suppression of the 'native unrest' he found in the north.

While Castlereagh, recently returned to the Cabinet, verged on the hysterical in Parliament, announcing that without new repressive laws, 'all the army of the empire could not afford protection and safety to the King's faithful subjects' against Luddite 'depredations', the man soon nicknamed 'King Tom' took a cooler line. High wartime prices, and the continued slide in wages, were behind much of the agitation, he declared after careful investigation. Beyond such factors, the unrest existed 'without either, any definite Object, or distinct End'. Clearly, for the Luddites, there was a 'distinct End' of economic survival in mind, but Maitland meant to refute other, wilder hypotheses in wide circulation. While some, including his second-in-command General Acland, were taken in by informers' tales that coupled Luddite oath-taking with republican plots, French invasions, assassinations and Catholic Irish armies, Maitland took a careful, grinding approach to restoring order.[30]

This seemed to have come not a moment too soon, as on 11 May Prime Minister Spencer Perceval was shot dead in the lobby of the House of Commons. The assassin, John Bellingham, was a Liverpool merchant, immediately reported as having Luddite connections. Even as he was taken into custody, a mob crying 'Burdett for ever' tried to drag him from the coach, and cavalry had to clear a path to Newgate prison.[31] As news spread around the country, there was a distressing lack of national grief: 'the *Mob* expressed *Joy*' in Bolton, a crowd in Nottingham 'paraded the town with drums beating and flags flying', and in Stoke-on-Trent 'A man came running down the street, leaping into the air, waving his hat round his head, and shouting with frantic joy, "Perceval is shot, hurrah!"'[32] From Macclesfield, Leicester, Liverpool and elsewhere came similar narratives of popular rejoicing. Within the week, Bellingham was tried, hanged and handed over for medical dissection, a mark of infamy. The information that he had a purely private grievance against the government, after suffering uncompensated cruelties at the hands of the Russian state for several years, and was not of particularly sound mind, could not overturn the disturbing perspective of a country on the verge of dissolution.[33]

Resting his army on the Spanish frontier, Wellington was only dimly aware of this rising tide of unrest, but he had his own political problems to deal with. Richard Wellesley, whose priapic indolence had not quenched his political ambition, made a disastrously bungled attempt to persuade the Prince Regent to make him Prime Minister, and quit the Cabinet in mid-February 1812. Wellesley went on to humiliate himself the following month by heralding a great speech attacking the government in the House of Lords, then failing to deliver it at the critical moment. Perceval's assassination might have been another opportunity for him to ascend, but he insulted Perceval's memory in print in *The Times*, ensuring that the existing ministers refused to serve with him when the Regent asked him to form an administration. Lord Liverpool ended up in early June leading essentially the same Cabinet as Perceval, after almost a month of aimless circling.[34] All this, on top of perpetual difficulties with supplying money to the army, created a troubled backdrop for what was a very promising situation.

With Napoleon's rising demands for troops for the east, the French position on the Peninsula began to look at least potentially fragile. Wellington consolidated his hold on the frontier zone in May by sending the only subordinate general he really trusted, Sir Rowland 'Daddy' Hill, to capture a critical bridge, severing north–south road links west of Madrid. Meanwhile, various Spanish forces were encouraged, with the added prestige of Wellington's recent victories, to launch diversionary offensives to the south and east, alongside continued naval raiding activity on the northern coasts. Wellington had the choice of striking south-east and rolling up French forces from Andalusia towards the centre, or more boldly aiming directly east, where a victory would force evacuation of the south in any case.

He chose the latter, and on 13 June led some 28,000 British, 15,000 Portuguese and several thousand Spanish on the most ambitious march he had dared make since the approach to Talavera, three years before. Only four days later, the city of Salamanca fell amid scenes of rejoicing, though a French garrison in three fortified convents held out for another ten days of fierce attacks. The French 'Army of Portugal' appeared under Marshal Marmont in the midst of these operations, challenging Wellington to attack by parading a force of 35,000 before him. Wellington's refusal seems to have given Marmont an exaggerated impression of his caution, leading him into a fatal overconfidence a few weeks later.

Auguste de Marmont had perhaps the most conventional rise to prominence of all Wellington's great opponents. The son of an ex-officer from the minor nobility, destined for a military career, he had encountered Bonaparte, five years his senior, while studying mathematics in the early years of the Revolution, before meeting him again as a junior officer at the siege of Toulon. The newly promoted General Bonaparte took him on to his staff, and he served in this capacity through the campaigns (and the political manoeuvres) of the next seven years, until given the opportunity to command the artillery at Marengo in 1800. For this he was made a major-general, but he was not sufficiently distinguished to become one of the first wave of marshals in 1804. He did command a corps in the Grand Army of 1805, and subsequently served as governor of the newly acquired territories of Dalmatia. From here, he played a key role in repulsing Austrian attacks in 1809, and at last acquired his coveted marshal's baton. His campaigning had not been faultless, however, and there were whispers in the army that only his long friendship with the Emperor had prompted his elevation.

With Napoleon himself reported still not to be entirely sure of his prowess, Marmont had a great deal to prove when he was summoned from his command in Illyria to replace Masséna. So far he had failed miserably to protect the frontier fortresses, but now he saw a chance to force a decisive combat on his own terms. Withdrawing northwards behind the nearby Duero river (the Spanish stretch of what became the Douro in Portugal), Marmont was followed by Wellington's forces, while also receiving reinforcements that brought the two armies nearly equal in strength. There followed, through the middle of July, a brilliant and deadly chess game. Once again, armies capable of horrific atrocities when let loose demonstrated remarkable discipline and stamina when held on a tight rein.

Marmont slipped around Wellington's flank on the 15th, recrossing the Duero and threatening to cut him off. The Anglo-Portuguese forces pulled back smartly and efficiently, maintaining contact with the enemy, and then both armies marched, and marched, each watching for a mistake that would give a decisive advantage. The days were baking hot, the nights freezing, and they moved over a near-treeless plain, almost 100,000 men on short rations, near exhaustion, and forced on occasion to loot graveyards for enough wood to burn in their bivouac fires.[35] Marmont's confidence, despite having the slightly smaller force, paid dividends as Wellington gradually drew back towards Salamanca, constantly on guard against outflanking.

On 21 July, Marmont again pushed hard, taking his troops across the Tormes river and forcing Wellington to follow to keep his lines of communication open. Thus on the 22nd, the two armies stood to the south-east of Salamanca, and Wellington took the decision to begin a withdrawal, ordering the heavy baggage away from the city towards Ciudad Rodrigo. Wellington's troops were between the French and the road west, but the French, priding themselves on always marching a little faster than the more heavily encumbered redcoats, set out to sweep round them to the south, setting up the prospect of both cutting off the army and seizing its baggage. As the British raced to prevent this, the morning's marching was therefore hard and fast.

Both forces headed towards a group of rocky hills known as Los Arapiles, the French securing the southerly Greater Arapile, the British the northerly Lesser. Then the pattern of the march swung west as the French sought the decisive outflanking, and the British brought their formations into an east–west line to head off the attempt. Marmont persistently stretched his troops' formation, pressing each division ahead as the British appeared to be settling into a defensive line. By the end of the morning his extended position could easily have been considered dangerous, but the fact that the British did not then attack gave him further confidence; the leading elements of his army raced away, as fast as tired men can race, further to the west, while the British now faced them from the north along the ridge extending from the Arapiles.

Wellington had not been taking up a defensive posture, however. Despite ordering the baggage away as a precaution, he had remained hopeful of securing a decisive engagement, and now saw the opportunity. He was gnawing on a cold chicken-leg when news of the French extension to their left was brought to him: tossing it over his shoulder, a quick glance through a telescope confirmed the situation. 'By God! that'll do,' he announced, and told his Spanish liaison officer quite simply, 'Marmont is lost!'[36]

Galloping from his post on the Lesser Arapile, Wellington quickly reached his secret weapon: the Third Division of foot, which he had ordered to march south from its flanking position near Salamanca, and which was now in a position to give him a crucial advantage against the French left flank. Marmont, from the Greater Arapile, had seen something of this movement, but fatally assumed that it was preparatory to a British withdrawal to a further defensive position to the west. He ordered his troops to press on, taking the leading elements out of his sight and his control.[37] As soon as Wellington detected this, he ordered the Third, and the rest of the army, to attack. In a classic successive or 'echelon' attack from their right wing through to the left, the British and their allies fell on the French. A lucky shot by British artillery grievously wounded Marmont just as hostilities began, and his second-in-command fell shortly after, so the French were leaderless at the decisive moment. Each division was already critically engaged, however, so this absence had less effect on the outcome than might be supposed.

The charge of the Third Division was particularly decisive. Command had recently devolved on Wellington's own brother-in-law, the somewhat emotional Ned Pakenham, who now had the order from the peer's own lips to attack and 'drive them to the devil'.[38] Under him were some of the army's most experienced troops, including the ferocious Connaught Rangers, still mourning the loss of their colonel at Ciudad Rodrigo. This battalion took the centre of the charging column, flanked by two other distinguished units, the 74th and 45th Foot, and by Portuguese dragoons who first pinned the enemy before the infantry closed on them. The French had only time for a single volley before the rolling fire of the British line took charge, followed by the decisive bayonet assault. Smashing one French division to pieces – it suffered 50 per cent casualties – Pakenham's men went on to turn the flank of the formations desperately resisting in the French centre.

The French, of course, fought back hard. Those on the right, atop the steep escarpment of the Greater Arapile, threw back the assaults of the Fourth Division, which then was confronted by a large body of fresh troops coming up from the French reserve. But Wellington also had reserves, and the Sixth Division stormed in to support a final push that saw two French corps broken. Long before the summer daylight faded, the French were crushed, only one of their divisions involved managing to retreat in good order; many other units simply disintegrated in flight eastwards. They lost 14,000 men, including 7000 prisoners, and many dead. Nine hundred allied troops perished and another 4000 were wounded, including four generals. One British general, Le Marchant, died in his moment of glory, leading a decisive charge of heavy cavalry that completed the rout of the French left. Wellington himself was struck, not for the first time, by a spent musket-ball, another reminder of the extent to which senior officers shared their men's peril at the decisive moments of this war.[39]

Rather typically, a lazy error by a Spanish general, failing either to keep a garrison at the strongpoint of Alba de Tormes or to demolish the bridge there, allowed the fleeing French to escape complete annihilation. Wellington called off efforts at pursuit on the 25th, giving his almost shattered men the chance of their first rest since early June. It was well deserved, for what the French called the Battle of Los Arapiles, and the British the Battle of Salamanca, threw Wellington and his army into an entirely new light. The French General Foy, the only divisional commander to lead his unit intact from the field, called him 'almost a Marlborough'; a man hitherto known largely for 'prudence' and skill in defensive positioning 'has shown himself a great and able master of manoeuvres'.[40]

Amongst his own troops, Wellington's reputation soared higher, and higher still over the next few weeks as they moved forward at a determined pace upon Madrid itself. King Joseph fled with his government, troops and civilian hangers-on to Valencia, and on

12 August 1812 the allied army entered the city in triumph, securing a huge stockpile of supplies, and marching on a carpet of flowers. Amidst the fervent rejoicing (some of which we might suspect was to offset the inhabitants' peaceful acceptance of their new king since 1808), the only problem that Private William Wheeler reported 'was to be kissed by the men'. He coped, however, finding compensation in young women he observed to be 'the most bewitching and interesting little devils I have ever seen'.[41] In a purely military sense the capital was of little significance, though it did prompt Marshal Soult to begin to evacuate Andalusia two weeks later, raising the long and futile siege of Cadiz. The symbolic liberation of both the established and the temporary capitals crowned a season in which much had changed across Europe, and the world, leaving the wider conflict suspended in the balance.

I3

MADRID TO MOSCOW

On the day Wellington's men entered Madrid, Napoleon's Grand Army left Vitebsk, already over 250 miles inside Russia, heading ultimately for Moscow, another 300 miles further east. The campaign had begun with almost 600,000 men under the Emperor's command. The final advance began with 182,000 remaining. The master of all Europe, spurred on by his refusal to acknowledge an equal in the Tsar, or to renounce an inch of conquest to the British, was marching his empire into the ground.[1]

After their countries had begun to draw apart diplomatically in 1810, Tsar Alexander and Napoleon had seemed to toy with the idea of war for the next year. Alexander, as well as listening to voices that said obedience to Napoleon had been ruining Russia's economy, had desires to play the liberator – up to a point. Where Napoleon had established a Grand Duchy of Warsaw as a Polish satellite, Alexander imagined a larger Polish kingdom – but with himself as king, generously giving the Poles a semblance of national autonomy within the Russian Empire. He also listened to some of the same voices of German nationalism that had prompted Austria to rise disastrously in 1809: Russian war plans involved a lunge forward into central Europe, and the construction of a grand coalition with Austria and Prussia to restore the balance of power – a 'balance' which, as in previous Russian plans, would be tilted decisively their way.

Both Russia and France blustered through 1811, ordering military build-ups, but also probing for diplomatic leverage, as the real costs of war were obvious to both sides. Russian determination to keep options open even went so far as to reject British offers of alliance, because they were not financially generous enough – Russian diplomats asserted that Russia had already effectively 'saved' the war effort in the Peninsula by causing the diversion of troops to the north.[2] By late 1811, Napoleon had decided that war was inevitable. The build-up of the enlarged Grand Army continued steadily, while much normal diplomatic activity was effectively suspended.[3]

As late as April 1812, Russian diplomacy was putting forward suggestions for new treaties embodying various compromises that would only slightly reduce Napoleon's military dominance between the Baltic and Poland. All this was to no avail, and thus Russian mobilisation also proceeded apace. Three waves of conscription since 1810 had brought some 350,000 recruits into the armies, which nominally stood at around 490,000. Many of these were engaged in an ongoing war with the Ottoman Empire, and only some of those involved would be released by a last-minute peace deal on the eve of Napoleon's advance. Russia could nonetheless project having over 200,000 men operating in its western regions in summer 1812.[4]

Having such resources at their disposal meant that, even in early 1812, the Russian ministry felt able to plan on a 'forward' war, stimulating risings in the name of religion, monarchy or nation in Germany, Italy and France itself, and bringing Austria and Prussia into an alliance that would cleanse central Europe of the French menace. By the spring of 1812, as Napoleon assembled his army,

and moved forward in May to his advanced headquarters in
Dresden, such plans were shown up as unrealistic. At Dresden the
Emperor ordered the crowned heads of central Europe to pay him
court, and they did.[5] As one observer wrote, 'only by being there
could one possibly imagine the cringing submission with which a
crowd of princes' greeted Napoleon at his morning *levée*. He was
the 'king of kings', gazed on as he went by with 'a mixture of admi-
ration and wonder'.[6] Napoleon increasingly insisted on being
addressed as 'king and emperor', using the pretext of his kingship of
Italy to reintroduce the monarchical title to everyday use.[7] Even as
his self-conception seemed to grow more backward-looking, his
capacity to continue to overturn the European order grew. With
vast forces assembling at his forward bases, there seemed nothing
he could not do.

In the backwash from this stunning advance, Russian plans
became more cautious. Austria and Prussia were locked into the
Grand Army, committed to offering 50,000 troops between them
as auxiliary corps. Acting defensively now seemed the only realistic Russian option, and War Minister General Barclay de Tolly
articulated new schemes to meet Napoleon after he had crossed
the frontier. As the Grand Army moved towards its start lines in
early summer, intelligence of the true size of the force assembled
against them caused Barclay and the Tsar, not without anguish, to
agree the necessity of retreating before the oncoming human
behemoth.[8]

One version of such plans, overseen by a perhaps over-
imaginative German officer, Ernst von Pfuhl, had one army of
some 100,000 retreating before Napoleon into a prepared series of
fortifications on the Dvina river, 200 miles inside Russia, there to
pin the Emperor as Torres Vedras had pinned Masséna; meanwhile
a second army, and swarms of Cossack raiders, would cut the
French off from the rear. The Dvina lines were in fact built, but
proved of unsatisfactory quality, and would probably have been a
deathtrap, allowing Napoleon the freedom to destroy the Russian

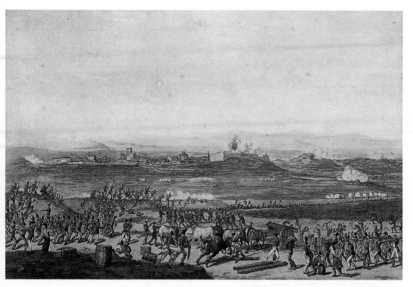

A contemporary view of the siege of Badajoz – such prints were avidly sought after as windows into an otherwise distant and uncertain conflict. *(Culture-images/Lebrecht)*

Wellington viewing the breach at Badajoz – a sanitised image that merely hints at the true horror. *(Culture-images/Lebrecht)*

The Luddite menace: the assassination of William Horsfall that triggered ruthless repression. *(Mary Evans Picture Library)*

Marshal Masséna, the 'Spoilt Child of Victory' humiliated, and driven from his last active command, by Wellington's resistance. *(Culture-images/Lebrecht)*

Marshal Soult, the 'Duke of Damnation', perhaps the most stubborn and wily of all Wellington's opponents. *(Culture-images/Lebrecht)*

Marshal Marmont, whose over-eagerness gave Wellington the chance for his first great attacking victory at Salamanca. *(Culture-images/Lebrecht)*

Joachim Murat, Napoleon's flamboyant, fearless cavalry commander, whose marriage to the Emperor's sister gave him a throne, but not the wits to keep it. *(Culture-images/Lebrecht)*

The apocalyptic burning of Moscow, prelude to the nightmarish odyssey of the retreating Grand Army. *(Mary Evans Picture Library/INTERFOTO/Bildarchiv Hansmann)*

Napoleon's Grand Army being ground into oblivion on the retreat from Moscow. *(Culture-images/Lebrecht)*

Sir Philip Broke, self-effacing heroic captain of HMS *Shannon*. *(Culture-images/Lebrecht)*

Wellington as a newly-minted duke in one of several iconic portraits by Thomas Lawrence. *(Derek Bayes/Lebrecht Music & Arts)*

Another Wellington icon: a scene of his post of danger at Waterloo. *(Culture-images/ Lebrecht)*

The end of the wars: General Bonaparte as an object of curiosity aboard a Royal Navy ship. *(Getty Images)*

The end at home: riotous protest flares in 1815 at high prices and protectionist Corn Laws. *(The Granger Collection/Topfoto)*

The aftermath: the Peterloo Massacre of 1819, in a caustic contemporary image. *(Getty Images)*

forces in detail. With the problems of this scheme on display, but little else constructive coming from his staff, Alexander, determined to act as commander-in-chief, took refuge in delay. His advanced headquarters at Vilna in Lithuania played host through the spring to a series of balls and entertainments, while warlike pronouncements took the place of decisive plans.[9]

Napoleon's pronouncements, meanwhile, were couched in a tone of regret and liberation. His official propaganda spoke of the campaign as the 'Second Polish War', a follow-up to complete the work done by establishing the Grand Duchy of Warsaw in 1807. The Poles and Lithuanians subjugated by the Russians since the 1770s would be freed, to form new, friendly buffer states driving the Russian menace decisively out of the peaceable politics of a Napoleonic Europe. The enhanced conscription necessary to raise his new army – even though only just over a third of the soldiers were actually French – had led to the kind of grumbling that a police state becomes well aware of, and should always do its best to suppress.[10] So Napoleon went publicly to war with the notion that a rapid, decisive military engagement would, quite literally, show Alexander who was boss, and pave the way for further years of peace.

There are suggestions, however, that wider ambitions – some so wide as to be almost maniacal – were at work. By the time the French reached Vilna, Russian headquarters decamping smartly before them, Napoleon was declaring in private that he would 'thrust back into their snow and ice' the 'barbarians of the north', so 'they will not be able to interfere with civilised Europe' for a generation. This violent tone was always absent from public declarations, but quite familiar to those who listened to him in private.[11] Others reported that the cause of Polish independence was embraced in a mood of pure cynicism – informed opinion in Napoleon's court agreed that the Poles who had lived in 'anarchy' before their partition could never be more than a subservient satellite.

Further reports, from a variety of observers, indicate that Napoleon linked in his mind the Russian problem with the continued resistance of Britain. One account from late 1811 spoke of the Peninsular War as 'a maggot gnawing away at him', but that 'a great blow' to put Russia 'on its knees' would 'by extension settle the fate of Britain'.[12] Napoleon's own Police Minister, the revolutionary survivor Joseph Fouché, later recalled begging him to seek peace, only to be told that 'there is no crisis', it was a 'purely political' war: 'Spain will fall as soon as I have annihilated the English influence at St Petersburg.' In Fouché's account, besides going on to describe Europe as 'a rotten old whore with whom I may do as I please', Napoleon spoke exultantly of the future prospects for deeper unification of the continent, and ultimately of making Paris 'the capital of the world'. This may be a later invention, but others noted his high spirits – he was enjoying life with his new wife, the father for the first time of a legitimate son and heir, and as the Dresden reception proved, did indeed seem capable of anything.[13]

Perhaps for this reason, rumours swirled amongst the military leadership that the Emperor's old dream of emulating Alexander the Great and seeking glory in the east had returned: Russia might literally be a stepping-stone to a descent on India.[14] He is supposed to have told an aide-de-camp that 'Alexander left from as far away as Moscow to reach the Ganges,' and to have ranted about the 'English pirate' – Sir Sidney Smith – who had foiled his march through the Holy Land in 1799. Now he planned 'to take Asia in the rear so as to attack Britain'. Once Russia had been subjugated, its southern frontier on the Caucasus would be an ideal jumping-off point for a march through Persia onwards to the Indus. The 'mere touch of a French sword' would collapse 'the framework of mercantile grandeur' that was British India – and with it, the position of perfidious Albion in the world.[15]

If there was a hint of madness in such schemes, they nonetheless reflect an appreciation that all the tensions that beset Napoleon's

Europe did relate in various ways to his obsessive inability to make peace on anyone else's terms – and thus to make peace with a British elite still convinced, as Canning had put it after Tilsit, that they were 'the natural mediators' of Europe and sole guarantors of 'secure and effectual tranquillity'. Moreover, there was no madness, at least not initially, in Napoleon's actual plans for the Russian campaign. Weeks before it began, he outlined his intentions to the Austrian chancellor Metternich. French troops would need to advance no further than Minsk or Smolensk; if Russian surrender had not already been secured, Napoleon would base himself for the winter at Vilna, organise a Lithuanian puppet state, and feed off the country until the Tsar was worn down.

If the Russians did offer battle for Vilna – only fifty miles inside their territory – he was confident of victory. If they went further, as he expected, and sent their more southerly forces westwards towards central Poland, he would catch them between the wings of his army and crush them. All this was sound strategy, and the Grand Army seemed well equipped for such a campaign – huge supply depots were assembled in East Prussia, and fifteen specially augmented transport battalions crossed into Russia with the troops, their thousands of wagons loaded with provisions. The twenty-four days' rations that the men set off with were far more than had been carried by other Napoleonic armies, with the prospect of more being brought up as they moved.[16]

Nonetheless, all these plans immediately proved inadequate. Many of the soldiers (some of whom had no idea where they were headed, writing home about 'Egippe' or the 'Great Indies') had no real rest in their forward positions, stepping out into Russia after a march that had begun in central Germany, or for some, in France itself.[17] Less than a week after the official launch of the campaign on 24 June, many troops had already been put on half-rations. For some, the endless round of forced marches broke their spirit, and there were widespread reports that such men – teenage boys in many cases – shot themselves rather than go on. Such was the chaos that probably only 350,000 troops actually advanced with the main armies, though they dragged with them perhaps as many as 50,000 civilian officials, camp-followers and family members.[18]

Freakish weather, including blizzards, thunderstorms and freezing overnight temperatures, saw thousands of irreplaceable horses dropping dead of cold, and perhaps as many as 25,000 men already dead or missing by the time Vilna fell on 28 June. There was no firewood, and men were quickly reduced to eating raw meat. There was no fresh running water, so they drank out of stagnant pools, or ditches that already contained the corpses of men and horses. Disease began to run wild. In their desperation, the troops became avid pillagers. 'Clouds of marauders' left the camps each day as the march began, sometimes returning with their loot, sometimes falling victim to outraged locals, and provoking an intensity of reprisal that collapsed any chance of raising the population against their Russian overlords.[19]

Meanwhile, with the Russian armies in full retreat before them, even the ardent efforts of general and marshals to drive their men on, at the cost of further casualties to sickness and exhaustion, were to no avail. Unseasonal cold was now replaced by all too seasonal baking heat, but Napoleon abandoned his cautious schemes of waiting at Vilna, and ordered a further advance in early July. The army was so large, despite its losses, and so dispersed over the countryside, that the Napoleonic virtues of rapid coordinated movement proved impossible to replicate.

Clumsy efforts to envelop the Russian army at Vitebsk failed, and the French found themselves on 28 July in possession of a provincial capital that was, as a general noted, 'of less use than the smallest towns in Germany' – poverty-stricken, and already stripped of anything of military value.[20] It did offer a defensible position, with nearby river-lines, and marked the conquest of all of pre-partition Lithuania; for a few days, Napoleon halted and appeared satisfied. But as stragglers and supplies began to come in, despite the effective loss already of half his army, he grew impatient.

The Russian forces were concentrating at Smolensk, 100 miles to the south-east, and on 12 August he set off in their pursuit. Five days of hard marching later, the Emperor again fumbled his plan of attack, leading only to two days of indecisive combat, and a further withdrawal of the Russians eastwards. Storming the city itself cost over 7000 casualties for no strategic gain.[21] Following doggedly, the French had lost another 50,000 men to disease and straggling by the time the Russians finally turned to fight in early September at Borodino, some fifty miles west of Moscow.

Under the pressure of continued retreat, Tsar Alexander had replaced his 'foreign' commanders on 20 July with the very Russian Mikhail Kutuzov, yielding to chauvinistic sentiments in the court, and a feeling that, if something were not done, he might share the fate of his assassinated father. Kutuzov promised action, but continued the retreat until he found a reasonable defensive position. The army had suffered its own losses in the many days of forced marching, and at 121,000 was outnumbered even by the much-reduced Grand Army. But yet again the French failed to show their winning qualities.

There was no effort at encirclement when battle was joined at Borodino on 7 September, just a series of hammer-blow frontal assaults which the Russians proved adept at resisting. Though they retreated, having suffered an appalling 44,000 casualties, they did so in good order, leaving behind 30,000 French killed and wounded. When Napoleon conquered Moscow days later, less than one-sixth of his Grand Army remained under arms with him, and he shortly found that he had in fact defeated himself. The city was burned beneath him, his troops continued to wither, and the Russians' strength, in regular forces and guerrillas, grew. On 19 October, after desperate and futile efforts to contact the Tsar, and days in which he sat, slumped and silent, for hours on end, Napoleon began the retreat from Moscow.[22]

Everything he had done conspired to make the situation worse.[23] The wounded had not been withdrawn, but kept at forward hospitals. Throughout his long advance, Napoleon had ordered a continuous stream of replacements to come up to the front, rather than consolidating at depots. Thousands of civilian followers had been lured ever deeper into Russia. During late September and early October, the road west was essentially open as the beaten Russians withdrew southwards to lick their wounds. The Emperor could have ordered a staged withdrawal, consolidated forces in safety at Smolensk or Vitebsk, and wintered in a way that would have kept his forces in being. Even leaving Moscow a few days earlier might have made a critical difference.

Leaving behind the vast quantities of loot taken from Moscow would certainly have improved the situation, but as it was, Napoleon dragged with him out of Russia an overburdened and often poorly dressed column of men, women and children that at its best straggled across fifteen or twenty miles of road, and on bad days extended well over fifty. The Russian armies, still defensively led by Kutuzov, made a series of attempts to block or cut the column, and on each occasion the Emperor, his marshals and the men they led performed valiantly in forcing a passage. But the weather grew worse, the soldiers starved and straggled, Cossacks snatched up foragers – sometimes selling them to vengeful peasants who grimly tortured them to death – and the Grand Army slowly died on its feet.[24]

One episode that has long stood out occurred at the Berezina river, east of Minsk, at the end of November. With Russian forces threatening an encirclement, and a sudden partial thaw creating a treacherous water barrier, it was a moment of real crisis. From the Dutch engineers who waded up to their shoulders in ice-strewn waters to build improvised bridges out of torn-down peasant shacks, to the troops who formed valiant rearguards, and fought off Russian attacks on both banks, heroism was on display on many sides. But the underlying situation was one of undeniable horror. Hundreds drowned, and as the Russian armies approached from the east, they assailed the thousands of civilians and stragglers huddled at the rear of the French column with relentless artillery fire. Panic, and a terrified rush for the bridges, resulted.

After the survivors had fled, one engineer officer on the Russian staff observed a scene that could have been repeated, with variations, hundreds of times:

> The first thing we saw was a woman who had collapsed and was gripped by the ice. One of her arms had been hacked off and hung by only a vein, while the other held a baby which had wrapped its arms around its mother's neck. The woman was still alive and her expressive eyes were fixed on a man who had fallen beside her, and who had already frozen to death. Between them, on the ice, lay their dead child.[25]

Ten thousand non-combatants and perhaps 15,000 soldiers were lost in this engagement alone, and the worst, coldest weather was yet to come. There was no campaign more 'Napoleonic' in the grandeur of its conception than the march on Moscow, yet none less 'Napoleonic' in the clumsy and imprudent way that it evolved. Nor was there any clearer sign of the unforeseen consequences of military action: if Napoleon had not been so visibly assembling such a mighty army, Alexander might have been tempted to attack in 1811 or early 1812, and gone down to defeat on the Emperor's familiar central European battlegrounds. Had any of the Russian plans proved successful, their armies would have encountered the French sooner, in better condition, and would probably have been soundly beaten. The Grand Army's very immensity, driving its foes into constant retreat, led it into catastrophe.

It is tempting to say that there was a similar ironic hubris afflicting the British state by 1812. Five years after Canning's determined statement of world hegemony, his former Pittite colleagues were still certain of their indispensable place in the global order. News of the victory of Salamanca seemed to counterbalance very nicely the

fear of Luddism, and by late summer the flood of troops into the
north had contained any active threat. The Prince Regent granted
Wellington a further step in the noble hierarchy, to a marquessate,
and Parliament voted him a gift of £100,000. One minister recorded
that in the jubilant aftermath, Richard Wellesley felt able to drive in
an open carriage through the London crowds – something he
might only have done at peril of his life a few months earlier –
while the 'fickleness' of the 'mob' was displayed when they broke
Sir Francis Burdett's windows. This was felt to be merited after an
ungracious, and ill-informed, speech in which the radical had
declared that Wellington's victory was no great achievement, as he
had outnumbered the enemy three to one.[26]

The symbolic treatment of Burdett reflected a wider collapse of
radicalism at this point, ironically when it had been making
renewed progress. Over the previous two years, figures in the Whig
opposition had resumed meeting with some of the stalwarts of democratic campaigning, including the redoubtable Major John
Cartwright – by 1812 in his seventy-second year. Motions for reform
of Parliament and the franchise had been put to the Commons –
one in 1810 getting 115 votes – and large meetings of the kind of elite
reforming constituencies not seen since the 1780s had been held. In
1811, the first 'Hampden Club' was formed, explicitly targeting the
propertied elite with a two-guinea joining fee, and invoking in its
name the parliamentary reformers of the 1640s.[27]

Major Cartwright also founded a Union for Parliamentary
Reform with a lower subscription, speaking of it as a 'House of
Commons' compared to the 'House of Lords' in the Hampden
Club, and expecting that it 'will have the greatest influence in
recovering our liberties'.[28] Cartwright used the opportunity of trav-
elling to witness Luddite trials in Lancashire as the starting point for
a series of 'tours' that brought his message to the provinces in
person. Those trials, however, and the shocking events they followed, quashed all hope for building a truly broad constituency for
reform. So fearful of radicalism was propertied opinion that

Cartwright himself was asked to leave the Hampden Club in May 1812 to ensure its survival.[29]

In the latter half of 1812, the nation in general, apart from sullen Luddite strongholds, experienced relief, as a great burden had been lifted with the repeal of the draconian Orders in Council. Achieved on 23 June, partly because Perceval's fortuitous death removed a stubborn obstacle, repeal followed a determined campaign of petitioning from the manufacturing and mercantile classes, and especially from the wide areas threatened with unrest because of the depression of trade. This measure combined with prospects of a good harvest to promise renewed prosperity and cheaper food in the coming months.

Unfortunately, while the ruling class proved at last able to listen to the British population about its sufferings for the war effort (at least when that message came in the form of polite petitions, and not from mere workers), the repeal came just too late to avoid another serious entanglement caused by arrogant disregard for others' opinions. On 18 June 1812, supported by votes of both Houses of Congress, President Madison of the United States declared war on the United Kingdom. It was to be a war of follies and embarrassments on both sides, beginning with the issues and attitudes that produced it, extending to its opening when a primary grievance had just been resolved, and ending with a battle fought after peace had already been signed.

In the longer term much of the blame fell on British attitudes. Taking the view that natural-born allegiance could not be altered by signatures and certificates, the Royal Navy had not hesitated, throughout the wars of the past two decades, to impress English-born seamen from American ships regardless of what citizenship they claimed – and indeed sometimes acted as if it did not recognise the USA as a sovereign nation in such matters. The Orders in Council, furthermore, claimed a control over the high seas and the destination of neutral vessels that the Americans forcefully rejected in principle – though in practice their retaliatory practices of embargo and 'non-intercourse' were petulantly self-harming.

Despite British and French measures penalising trade, the American merchant marine had almost doubled in size, to nearly a million tons, in the previous decade, and many in the mercantile states of New England were doing very well out of circumventing the various blockades.[30] Such constituencies had no appetite for war in the first place. The fact that news of the repeal of the Orders in Council, arriving weeks after the declaration of war, gave no pause to the American war plans shows that there were other motives at work.[31]

'War Hawks' in the American Congress, mostly from the new states already formed by expansion into the Ohio Valley and towards the Mississippi, were set on a vision of further imperial development. Convinced that Britain secretly subsidised the Indian war-bands that challenged settler colonisation, they had a vision of opening their frontiers to unlimited prosperity by driving the old imperial power out of North America altogether, and simultaneously seizing Florida and the Gulf Coast from moribund Spain. Building on the 'Louisiana Purchase' a decade earlier, this would give an entire continent over to the United States. In this light, while declaring war on the British Empire had a tinge of madness to it, declaring war on, and for, Canada was a piece of ruthless *realpolitik*.[32]

However, thanks to a sustained reluctance to fund a military establishment, the USA in mid-1812 had fewer than 12,000 troops under arms, of whom almost half were raw recruits. Even reinforced with local militias, this made ambitious plans for a two-pronged attack towards Quebec and the Great Lakes settlements unachievable. There were energetic clashes around Lake Erie, but this was a region held by vigorously loyalist settlers – in some cases, heirs of refugees from American persecution of such 'Tories' in the 1780s – and two separate attacks from the south in the summer and autumn were driven off by combined forces of British regulars, Canadian militias and Indian allies.

Nowhere were there more than about 4000 men in action on both sides combined, and their manoeuvres would have been mere skirmishes in Europe. Nonetheless, the humiliation of the Americans who were forced to surrender in August, yielding the territory around Detroit to British occupation, was intense.[33] It was further compounded by French refusal to treat their entry into war with Britain as anything significant at all – Napoleon declined to afford any preferential treatment to American ships, or even to pay much attention to events across the globe (though he had the excuse of the Russian campaign to distract him).[34]

Unfortunately for the British, humiliation was about to descend on them. Not long after news of events on land had reinforced the perception that they faced only a more vigorous form of the petulance that had marked trade policy, *The Times* had to report a 'disaster' of a 'nature with which England is but little familiar'.[35] One of the Royal Navy's frigates, HMS *Guerrière*, had been battered into surrender in a single-ship duel with the American vessel USS *Constitution* – technically its equal, although in fact a much more sturdy ship carrying heavier cannon.

If this had been an isolated incident, it could have been written off: the *Guerrière* was heading into port for a refit, and was suffering the ill-effects of long service. However, two months later HMS *Macedonian* met the USS *United States* in mid-Atlantic. Consistently unable to outmanoeuvre the American frigate to bring his broadside to bear, the British Captain John Carden had his ship shot to pieces beneath him in an hour of brutal combat. Two months after that, HMS *Java* was intercepted off the coast of Brazil by the *Constitution*, and suffered a two-hour pounding in which over 150 were killed and wounded, and the ship left a dismasted hulk that was, like *Guerrière*, burned by her captors as not worth saving.[36]

To lose not one, but three ships in what were unquestionably fair fights was both unheard-of and profoundly unsettling to British opinion. Nobody had stood toe-to-toe with the Royal Navy, and beaten it, in living memory. When French frigates slipped out of port, as they still occasionally did, they could count on being hunted down like dogs. When there were passing upsets – such as the disastrous 'Battle of Grand Port' in the conquest of Mauritius, which saw two frigates sunk and two others captured – there were always other factors at work, in that case including shore batteries and dangerous shoals, and victory always came in the end.

In the material calculus of war, these defeats meant little, even when accompanied by a further handful of duels between smaller ships that ended in the Americans' favour. The US Navy had barely half a dozen vessels able to face a British frigate, and only three of the ferocious calibre of the *Constitution*. By the beginning of 1813, the Royal Navy squadron based at Halifax, Nova Scotia, had been increased to eight battleships and fifteen frigates, and a formal blockade of the American coast reached as far south as the Chesapeake. By mid-1813 it reached the Mississippi. Depredations by American privateers on British trade had been noticeable in 1812, their sudden proliferation snatching up, by some figures, almost 10 per cent of the British merchant fleet.[37] This could not be sustained, however – in later years half of all merchant ships captured by the Americans were retaken at sea before reaching port – and could almost be called a nuisance compared to the damage the Royal Navy could inflict by its hostile presence.[38]

If Britain had not granted licences to American ships to deliver flour to the Peninsula – almost a million barrels were shipped in both 1812 and 1813 – American overseas trade would have already been effectively strangled.[39] Indeed, when it became possible to ship supplies from the Baltic to Spain, and the American licences were withdrawn, US exports fell from $25 million in 1813 (already half the 1811 figure) to only $7 million in 1814. Sending flour to feed the enemy's troops in wartime might seem bizarre, but it was not uncommon. Napoleon had expressly modified his Continental System in 1810 to allow crucial imports from Britain to France – and only to France, aggrieving Russia and others further – which the British were happy to supply. The Emperor went further and established a closed 'city of smugglers' at the Channel port of Gravelines, hosting (under armed guard) hundreds of men and their ships who could bring him the goods, and the information, the British government tried to safeguard.[40] In the American case, ex-President Jefferson commented that a harsher attitude might lead to harsher reprisals, and invasion: 'We had better feed them there for pay, than feed and fight them here for nothing.'[41]

There is more to war, and politics, than a mere material calculus, however. Whatever the larger practicalities, there is no doubt that the Royal Navy had become complacent in its superiority. Years of blockade had made their crews vastly superior, man for man, to the often overcrowded and almost untrained French – especially when the best French seamen sailed privateers, lightly armed predators of merchant shipping, but rarely in a position to do more than run from naval vessels. Relative superiority and absolute excellence are two different things, however, and the latter easily fell prey to a sense of the former, especially when regular gun drill was so profligate of resources carefully husbanded by the Ordnance Board, and destructive of a kind of spit-and-polish perfection that was increasingly taking root.

The Royal Navy after Trafalgar was in danger not just of thinking itself invincible, but of becoming fashionable, and thus at risk of being officered by men more concerned with social advancement than professional competence. The swelling ranks of naval officers – from around 3500 in 1805 to over 4500 after 1812 – certainly contained some who were there more through family connections than merit. 'Interest' had always played a role in promotions and appointments, and there might be some evidence that it was outweighing professional skill in these years. Of the Navy's 498 smaller vessels – brigs, sloops and cutters, commanded by the youngest and most swiftly promoted officers – more than 35 were lost to storms and shipwreck in 1812.[42] Some of this was undoubtedly the unavoidable toll of the elements, the risks of which served to keep most officers thoroughly competent. But there were ominous signs in the defeats of 1812 that a rot had begun to set in.

Such a rot suddenly seemed to strike Wellington's army – and what was worse, the great man himself – in the autumn of 1812. After the rapturous reception in Madrid, and leaving his southern flank still guarded by 'Daddy' Hill, Wellington took just over 20,000 men north, more than halfway to the French frontier. What the French still called the 'Army of Portugal' had recently pushed west as far as Valladolid, and he sought to cut them off. Wilder plans of forcing a French withdrawal to the Ebro river were mentioned in his correspondence, though some of this may have been for political consumption in England.[43] The French withdrew north-eastwards at his approach, and he pushed his army on after them to the stronghold of Burgos. Already dangerously over-extended, with major French forces, including Soult's men pulled out of Andalusia, moving around to the south-east, Wellington found himself besieging this formidable fortress with some of his weaker troops.

The First Division's officers had begged for a chance at glory, having been in reserve at Salamanca, and he had yielded rather than bring the Third Division or the Lights, who had swept into Badajoz and Ciudad Rodrigo. With the Spanish yet again providing short rations and ineffectual military support, Wellington's men made almost no headway – breaches in the outer defences led to sharp French raids to beat off the engineers and repair the damage, and only three heavy guns had been brought along. Repeated savage fighting and gallant assaults brought only mounting casualties.[44] A hundred siege guns lay near Madrid, but before they could be brought up the siege had to be abandoned – on Trafalgar Day, 21 October – as superior French armies threatened to surround the attackers.

What followed was a desperate retreat in search of safety, made more desperate by mismanagement from Wellington's subordinate generals, and indiscipline in the rank and file. Heading for

Salamanca, and reuniting with Hill's troops on the way, the British were passing through wine country in the weeks after the vintage. Soldiers gorged themselves on vats of new wine – 12,000 were supposedly dead drunk in the town of Torquemada, some left lying in rows like the dead on a battlefield. Private Wheeler recorded seeing men shooting holes in thousand-gallon vats, then 'fighting like tigers' up to their knees in the fountaining alcohol.[45]

While this indulgence afforded a temporary relief to some, all too often the army merely suffered – the Connaught Rangers, for example, being issued on one occasion with raw beef, but no firewood. Mixing with ration biscuits in their packs, and turning to a vile paste as they marched, it inflicted dysentery on those brave or desperate enough to eat it. Worse than all this was a resumption of other bad habits. Spanish peasants were murdered in significant numbers by marauding soldiers, and regular hangings by the provosts could not prevent what one witness called 'the old trade . . . killing and slaying, and capturing our daily bread'.[46]

Torrential autumn rains battered the army, and soon the men were wading through mud, while the French, who reoccupied Madrid on 2 November, continued to snap at their heels. On the 16th, the armies passed the Salamanca battlefield, and it seemed for a moment as if the French might force a rematch on the now outnumbered allies, but Wellington pulled them back smartly. After an appalling error by the quartermaster-general, the army marched twenty miles out of its way as it neared safety at Ciudad Rodrigo. Partly as a result, French skirmishers cut off and captured Sir Edward Paget, recently arrived commander of the First Division, and Wellington's much-needed second-in-command. Other generals disobeyed routing orders direct from Wellington and had to be rescued by the peer himself, who in his cold fury remarked with dreadful understatement, 'You see, gentlemen, I know my own business best.'[47] Some likened it to the retreat to Corunna, while others said it was much worse. Over 6000 men were killed, wounded or captured.[48]

A lack of real vigour in the French pursuit – armies under Soult, King Joseph and others together totalling well over 60,000 – prevented a much worse disaster; the allies' situation was aided by a successful Spanish attack on Bilbao in the north which diverted some attentions in that direction, and, of course, by the constant, exhausting oversight of Wellington himself, riding horses into the ground as he shepherded the army home. That exhaustion was perhaps partly responsible for the unusually stinging rebuke he issued in writing to his subordinates after they reached safety on 19 November: 'this army has met with no disaster', yet had gone completely to pieces. There had been 'no privations which but trifling attention on the part of the officers could not have prevented'. He demanded 'minute and constant attention to orders' in future, and ended with a particularly mean-spirited dig at the troops' slowness in cooking food. Forbidden, unlike the French, to loot Spanish houses for wood, and forced, again unlike them, to carry heavy iron pots in place of light tin kettles, the troops, especially those of the Light Division, felt this blow keenly.[49] It was a depressing way to end a campaigning year that had begun with costly and splendid victories, but ended almost back at its starting line.

14

IN THE BALANCE

The year 1813 opened with a decisive indication that the British state had dealt with Luddism to its own satisfaction. In the past six months the north and Midlands had been criss-crossed by troops, new laws had been passed against machine-breaking and seditious oath-taking, thousands of pounds in reward money had been offered, and hundreds of defenders of order had been sworn in as Special Constables. These included military officers leading patrols, thus empowering the army to make arrests, a decisive step beyond the norms of earlier conduct and towards a genuine martial law.[1] General Maitland, and some of the senior officers under him, had adopted plain clothes and pseudonyms to meet with spies and informers, and the lines between civil and military power had been thoroughly blurred. As a result, hundreds of actual and potential insurgents had confessed to Luddite allegiances, giving up the names of others in a cascading process of carefully blended persecution and amnesty.

Now, to mark the conclusion of this campaign, the elegant Georgian building known somewhat anachronistically as York

Castle hosted a trial by Special Commission of Assize.[2] The York Commission opened on 2 January, with the space outside the castle thronged by hundreds who had walked or ridden from the Luddite West Riding. Such bodies had already sat at Lancaster and Chester the previous summer, dealing with dozens of defendants caught up in the diffuse Luddite-related rioting that marked events west of the Pennines. The Lancaster Commission proved particularly ruthless, ordering eight executions, including that of fifty-four-year-old Hannah Smith, for stealing potatoes, and of Abraham Charlson, aged sixteen, who went to his death on 12 June 1812 calling for his mother.[3]

The first case heard in York showed the broad-brush approach taken by the authorities, as four men, three of them coal miners, were sentenced to death for acts of burglary that required considerable imagination to be clearly defined as Luddism. But the prosecuting counsel made it clear that the 'dreadful disturbances ... amounting almost to a state of actual rebellion' justified this labelling.[4] The court met again on the 6th, for the trial of three croppers implicated by turncoat witnesses in both the Rawfolds Mill attack and the murder of William Horsfall. One witness offered dramatic testimony that after the former events one defendant had remarked that they had 'lost two men, and they must kill the masters', going on to describe nocturnal wanderings with loaded pistols that stopped short of directly witnessing the killing, but were damning nonetheless.

A parade of defence witnesses who offered assorted alibis did little to shake the prosecution case, especially as the Treasury Solicitor had been in correspondence with local military officials two weeks earlier about the mode of execution that would be both most secure and most exemplary. Found guilty after twenty-five minutes' jury deliberation, the three men were sentenced to hang, and their bodies then to be handed to the local medical school for dissection.[5] The sentence was carried out in front of York Castle two days later.

The Special Commission continued to meet for another week,

sentencing a range of defendants to transportation, and fourteen more in total to execution – three of those sentenced on its first day (one of the original four having his sentence commuted), five more for the Rawfolds attack, and six for other episodes of violence and robbery. On 16 January they were hanged in two batches of seven, before and after noon.[6] They went to their deaths like martyrs, not criminals, refusing to confess their 'crimes', and instead singing hymns together and 'praying most loudly' until the fateful moment. The funerals were allowed to take place in the men's home communities, and crowds reportedly lined the road from York to see them on their way.

The burials were closely watched by the authorities to take the temperature of local opinion, and an official summarised the mood as 'sullen silence ... occasionally interrupted by acknowledgements of having done wrong: not, it appeared, from a sense of the enormity of their crimes; but because they had failed in accomplishing their object'.[7] Whatever their continued grievances, under military occupation many in Yorkshire chose to take advantage of a royal proclamation, made two days after the mass executions, offering a pardon for those who would confess to Luddite oath-taking. In the process of taking declarations, much fishing was done for further information on Luddite organisation, but little new came to light. Nonetheless, General Maitland soon felt able to report that 'the spirit of Luddism is completely extinguished'.[8]

Much had been done that would never be forgiven, however. Ben Walker, the workmate who turned King's Evidence to condemn the assassins of William Horsfall in return for a promised reward of £2000, ended his days an outcast, begging on the streets of Huddersfield: not least because he was never paid his blood-money, the government arguing that he was not the first to provide evidence in the case. He was a dreadful example of how a government by now deeply experienced in the use of spies and informers could use up and cast aside those whose utility was merely temporary.[9]

*

Meanwhile, in France, the population was absorbing the news that Napoleon's Grand Army had been used up and cast aside. Assailed by Russian attacks, and with temperatures dropping ever further below freezing, the Emperor abandoned his army on 5 December 1812, as he had abandoned his troops in Egypt more than a decade before. Fleeing westwards under cavalry escort with a small band of companions, destroying several vehicles en route, Napoleon reached Paris during the night of 18 December. Only two days earlier, the news that all was not well in Russia had burst on the French public with the release of the 29th *Bulletin of the Grand Army*, admitting to the abandonment of Moscow and the privations of the troops. Attributing the losses to bad weather rather than gross strategic mismanagement, and ending with the note that 'The Emperor's health has never been better', it was a perfect example of his solipsistic self-regard.[10]

One reason for his flight – alongside the pressing need to raise new armies – was a threat to his power from within. News had recently reached him that in October 1812, imperial officials in Paris had briefly been hoodwinked by Claude François Malet, a retired general with republican sentiments, who forged letters showing that Napoleon had been killed in Russia.[11] For a few hours, it seemed as if Malet's plan to arrest leading loyalists and install a republican provisional government might work, before he was recognised and seized by a more alert officer. Napoleon was outraged not so much by this attempt as by the fact that the hereditary succession he had worked so hard to create did not seem to have crossed anyone's mind upon news of his 'death'. The renewed impression that the safety of his dynasty hinged on his person alone, and on his victories, was to colour the events of the year to come.

It was abundantly clear that radical action was imperative. Napoleon had ranted to observers as he passed through Warsaw that 'I have always beaten the Russians. They will not dare to do anything ... they will hang around at Vilna, while I go off and raise 300,000 men ... all that has taken place is nothing: it is a mere

setback, the result of the climate. The enemy is nothing: I beat
them everywhere.'[12] However, even before he reached Paris, the last
French survivors staggered out of Russia, and kept heading west.
The Emperor had nominated two commanders in his absence,
both family members (and perhaps chosen more for that relationship than for actual merit). His first choice, his brother-in-law
Joachim Murat, abandoned the remnants of the army and returned
to his Kingdom of Naples to recuperate.

Murat, the son of an innkeeper, who had risen from the ranks to
lead General Bonaparte's cavalry in the Italian and Egyptian campaigns, was an exceptionally fearless commander of horsemen,
though there were some who said his courage sprang from the
inability to grasp the concept of danger. His suitability for independent senior command was certainly dubious – his aggressive
response to the uprising in Madrid in May 1808 may have helped
lose Spain for the Bonapartes. His command in Russia of a vast cavalry corps of some 40,000, intended to drive the enemy back by
speed and surprise, had achieved little except to kill thousands of
horses and scour the countryside clean of forage. The order he
gave for a general retreat just before his own departure paid no
attention to an order of march, or any other administrative details,
helping to ensure the final disintegration of the Grand Army. The
new commander, Napoleon's stepson Eugène Beauharnais,
Viceroy of Italy, did what he could to rally the troops, but Russian
pressure drove him back.[13]

The Emperor had ordered a position to be held near Vilna, but
by the early weeks of 1813 the French (barring garrisons in a few
fortresses) were back at the Oder river, having abandoned all of
Poland and East Prussia. From some perspectives, the Russian
advance itself was reckless – of the 110,000 troops who had
launched the main pursuit, only some 28,000 remained – but it
seized a moment. Prussian villagers had scorned the retreating
Napoleonic troops who had tried to repeat the acts of requisition
that had supplied their advance. At the very end of the old year, the

Prussian General Yorck had defied the timid counsels of his own king, signed a deal with the Russians, and marched his corps back from near Riga into East Prussia as liberators.

This was just one of many signs that Tsar Alexander took to indicate that his hour had come to save Europe. Having experienced a religious conversion of some intensity during the troubling months of the summer, he now saw himself as empowered to rebuild a Christian continent free from Bonaparte's demonic Jacobinism. Besides, as he remarked, 'After so disastrous a campaign in Russia, and the great reverses which France has just met with in Spain, she must be entirely drained of men and of money.'[14]

This, however, was not entirely the case. Napoleonic France had raised military conscription to a fine art.[15] For well over a decade, since the 'Jourdan Law' of 1798, annual cohorts had been obliged to register for military service. A well-entrenched local civilian bureaucracy kept track of young men as they reached maturity, and older ones who had been granted exemptions in years of less urgent demand. A *Gendarmerie* of former veteran soldiers patrolled the villages and highways of the Empire, making evasion if not impossible, then certainly much harder than almost anywhere else.

Napoleon had but to say the word, therefore, and new armies did indeed spring into existence. One hundred and fifty thousand men had already been called up from the 'class of 1813' in the autumn. In January the 'class of 1814' was summoned a year early, along with a further 100,000 previously passed over in the years since 1809. The National Guard, formerly a purely internal-service militia, gave up another 100,000. Another 15,000 experienced leadership cadres were withdrawn from Spain, the navy was scoured for gunners, even the *Gendarmerie* had to yield some of its younger men to serve as cavalry. Not counting reinforcements arriving from existing units stationed in Italy – perhaps as many as 40,000 in itself – Napoleon's empire stood up a force of over 400,000 men in these months, as if out of thin air.[16] Many remained as raw recruits in depots, and the difficulty of finding them uniforms, arms and equipment was enormous, but 170,000 were ready for action at encampments near Frankfurt by Easter 1813.

As that year's campaigning season opened, Europe was on a knife-edge, and the British government sought desperately to tilt the balance their way. Late 1812 had been a fruitful season for the Cabinet under Lord Liverpool. The new Prime Minister, born Robert Jenkinson, was yet another example of hereditary political distinction: his father, the first Earl of Liverpool, had risen from the minor gentry to serve in Cabinet throughout the Pitt and Addington administrations, and acquired his earldom in 1796. This allowed him to pass on the title of Baron Hawkesbury (acquired ten years earlier) to his son Robert as a 'courtesy title', while the latter continued to sit in the Commons. Here, Robert had been a minister since 1793 (aged twenty-three), rising to become Foreign Secretary under Addington, and he remained thereafter in Cabinet continuously, except for the brief Talents administration. Named Baron Hawkesbury in his own right in 1803, and inheriting his father's earldom in 1808, he had a wide experience of different ministerial offices, and a smooth insider's approach to mollifying potentially disruptive internal opposition. This was to serve him very well, as he remained Prime Minister until 1827.

In 1812, Liverpool had gone swiftly to work in the wake of Wellington's glory at Madrid. A September general election had reinforced the government's moral authority and shown how little the travails of Luddism affected the views of the political class. Indeed, ministers had the satisfaction of seeing half a dozen of the Whig opposition's leading speakers defeated in open contests, and forced to take seats for the 'pocket boroughs' of wealthy supporters. When Parliament opened in November, attacks from the alienated Canning and Wellesley, both of whom had hoped for office after Perceval's death, came to nothing. They had seized on Wellington's stumble at Burgos to blame government parsimony, but their momentum faded as his correspondence resolutely failed to back them up, and Castlereagh, newly returned to government, offered impressive defences in the Commons. News as the year ended that Wellington had at last been offered operational command of the Spanish armies put an end to fears of collapse in the Peninsula, and allowed the Cabinet to concentrate on events further north.[17]

Ministers had never given up hope of finding new cracks in the Continental System, and even before the invasion of Russia had been actively working to make peace with Sweden. Swedish politics had taken an intriguing turn in recent years. Forced by Russian invasion to give up its Finnish territories in 1809, the increasingly decrepit Swedish monarchy submitted to Napoleon. One king was deposed by *coup d'état* in that year, replaced by his aged and child-less uncle. The first, Danish, candidate to become designated successor as Crown Prince died of a stroke in May 1810 barely four months after arriving in the country. Casting around for another candidate, the Swedish court settled, not without dispute, on the French Marshal Jean Bernadotte, well-regarded in the country because he had treated captured Swedish soldiers humanely during an earlier Baltic campaign.

Bernadotte was a man who had risen from humble origins as a private soldier to revolutionary glory as a general by 1796, and War Minister by 1799. He was married to the sister of Joseph Bonaparte's wife, who had for a short time in 1795–6 been Napoleon's own fiancée. He thus felt himself both equal in talents to the Emperor, and entitled to respect as a member of his family. Napoleon, how-ever, while making him a marshal, had long seemed to scorn him. Made a scapegoat in the press for failure at Eylau, Bernadotte was also criticised for failure to act appropriately in the Jena campaign, and actually removed from command in the field during the Wagram campaign – officially for an unauthorised retreat, perhaps unofficially for seeking to steal the Emperor's glory by publicising the valour of Saxon troops he was leading. He had every reason to look with an appraising eye at the offer of monarchy held out to him.

The fact that the Emperor seemed to treat the Swedish offer as a joke when it was raised with him may further have inclined Bernadotte to accept. In November 1810 he became Crown Prince Karl Johan, heir to the throne, effectively regent, and commander-in-chief of Swedish forces. Napoleon was inclined, naturally enough, to treat the new ruler as a puppet, but his seizure soon afterwards of Sweden's last possession on the southern coast of the Baltic in Pomerania led to festering resentment. By early 1812 a British diplomat was having discussions in Stockholm about a possible alliance. Bernadotte's demands, including the cession of a Caribbean sugar-island and a free hand to invade Danish-held Norway as compensation for the loss of Finland, were excessive, but communications continued. After the invasion of Russia, an Anglo-Swedish peace was rapidly signed, with the promise of £500,000 in aid if Swedish designs turned from Norway to a landing in northern Germany. This proved a sticking-point, and the relationship developed no further until the following year.[18]

British relations with Russia were almost equally problematic. The two nations were still technically at war when Napoleon invaded, and although a peace was rapidly agreed, followed by the despatch of 100,000 muskets, little else was quickly settled. The envoy sent in the late summer was General Lord Cathcart, who was both sufficiently distinguished and competent for such a post, though some dubbed him 'rather stupid'. The fact that he had led the 1807 expedition that burned Copenhagen, outraging Russian opinion, nonetheless clearly reflected the British elite's disinclination to take genuine account of others' views. Despite this potential handicap, Cathcart was able to take the lead in securing agreement that Russia, Sweden and Britain were all now, at least in general terms, on the same side. He brokered a meeting between Bernadotte and Alexander as early as August 1812, at which Alexander gained such a positive impression of the Crown Prince that he spoke of placing him on the throne of France. There were a few small matters to clear up before that might become a possibility, however.[19]

As the Prussian king's terrified outrage at General Yorck's actions had shown, Napoleon was still diplomatically supreme in central Europe. However deluded some of his suggestions in early 1813 might have been – that Britain might accept a deal involving the independence of Portugal and Sicily, but not Spain and Naples, for example – in other respects he was firmly in charge.[20] The states of the *Rheinbund* might have groaned as they absorbed news of the losses in Russia, but their rulers shrugged and recruited new soldiers at the Emperor's order without overwhelming difficulty. Austria, meanwhile, whose troops had retired from Russia in a conspicuously pacific manner, suffered a barrage of typically Napoleonic bluster and coercion. One set of diplomatic instructions from the Emperor ordered his envoy to 'Play upon the family connection. The emperor, my father-in-law, is intelligent, moderate, and sensible: he has felt the full weight of a French invasion, and I have no doubt that today he wishes to continue faithfully to adhere to me.' If court intrigues should lead Emperor Francis astray, the veiled threat in this passage was to be brought into play a little more overtly.[21]

Ironically, neither Francis nor his leading minister, Metternich, believed at this stage that Napoleon could be overthrown, though the latter fondly hoped that the Russian catastrophe might lead to a more balanced disposition of power on the continent. Austria even rejected Prussian overtures in January 1813 towards a possible joint 'armed neutrality', though this caution could not prevent the first great crack in the imperial system. In February, abandoned by fleeing French troops and seeing growing numbers of Russians on their territory, spurred on by military discontent and the urgings of reformers, the Prussian government signed the Treaty of Kalisch binding itself to an alliance with the Tsar, and agreeing to put 80,000 troops, and a supporting militia, into the field against Napoleon. All this happened before Britain could open any formal diplomatic relations with the central European powers at all, though informal links to Prussian leaders did lead to the dispatch of a modest amount of artillery and military supplies at this point.[22]

While the storms of war threatened to break out once more over central Europe, the Iberian Peninsula was still wracked with its own conflict. In the early months of 1813 Wellington had had to endure the frustrating experience of being first acclaimed in Cadiz as a liberating hero – and named *Generalissimo* of Spanish forces – and then discovering that the contentious politics of the Spanish brought this title to virtually nothing. Intensely riven between the idealistic, almost Jacobinical, and to the British insufferably and unjustifiably arrogant *Liberales*, and the minority of more socially amenable, but often ferociously reactionary *Serviles*, the Cadiz government and its parliament, the Cortes, also had to pander to the self-regard of a chauvinistic press, and individual military leaders whose views of their own merits far exceeded any practical basis.

In the background hovered other disputes, notably an imperious Spanish desire for British assistance in subjugating various South American colonies inclined to revolt, against British wishes to continue trading with such places, especially as this helped defray the huge costs of subsidising the war in the Peninsula.[23] Thus, while Wellington made well-informed suggestions for structural and strategic reform, almost all of them were ignored, and in some cases overturned, in favour of actions more suited to appeasing Spanish egos or party prejudices.[24]

Fortunately the overall situation stood in the allies' favour. Weakened by the demands coming from the north, the French position was becoming precarious. In 1811, the French in Spain had mustered some 291,000 troops, outnumbering all the allied forces by more than 120,000. Two years later, French numbers had fallen to some 175,000, and the allies mustered 200,000. Weight of numbers was having its inevitable effect.[25] The still optimistically named Army of Portugal was pulled back to help guard northern Spain's strategic supply lines, while in early spring King Joseph and his government withdrew from Madrid, leaving only a military garrison, and leading a huge train of civilian and administrative staff to a new temporary capital at Valladolid.[26]

As usual, these orders came from the Emperor himself, who continued to control the conflict from afar based on unreliable reports, prejudice and arrogance. Withdrawing most of his marshals to help in Germany, he made Joseph commander-in-chief of the armies in Spain: something the latter had long sought, but even with the assistance of the competent Marshal Jourdan as chief-of-staff, was not really equipped for. Believing Wellington's forces to amount to no more than 50,000, Napoleon continually asserted that Joseph had them safely outnumbered.

The Anglo-Portuguese army, however, numbered over 80,000, and in contrast to previous years was currently suffering from relatively few sick. The troops had effectively been rested since the arduous retreats of November 1812, as well as receiving considerable reinforcements, and major improvements to their order of march. The infuriating heavy iron cookpots had been replaced with light kettles, and the space they had taken up on pack-mules filled with new tents. For the first time in all their years of campaigning, Wellington's redcoats would not have to scrabble for shelter or sleep under the stars. Though this led to a somewhat imprudent decision to order the troops to march without taking their heavy greatcoats – much regretted when torrential rains periodically burst out – the sense that their material needs were at last being taken seriously did much to boost morale in a force already taking heart from the news of Napoleon's setbacks.[27] General Picton – himself a gruff and occasionally foul-mouthed individual – reported that a cheerful mood infected even the phlegmatic Wellington. As he led his troops across the frontier into Spain once again in late May, he turned and waved his hat, crying out 'Farewell Portugal, I shall never see you again!'[28]

While this was recorded with hindsight as a prophetic token of victory, one may speculate that it was a statement that the

Portuguese would have heard with a sigh of relief. Doughty allies though they had proved, the cost was terrible. Agriculture had been crippled by the scorched-earth policies of 1810–11, and by the conscription each year of tens of thousands into the armies. Overall economic disruption was profound: the country's prime colonial market for manufactured goods, Brazil, had been usurped by the British, and as early as 1811 over a third of industrial concerns were winding down or already closed.[29] Wellington himself had written the previous year that 'Great Britain has ruined Portugal by her free trade with the Brazils' – costing £1 million a year in lost customs revenue, as well as destroying private fortunes dependent on the trade.[30] The Regency Council was soon condemned to pay its bills by printing paper currency, as the heavy taxes on the peasantry – up to one-third of income by some reports – simply did not yield enough to support the army, even with an annual subsidy of over £2 million from London.[31]

In some areas the resultant misery had turned the population into little more than bandits, posing a major hazard even for their supposed allies.[32] Whether attacks were prompted more by desperation or resentment is unclear, but resentment would be understandable at many levels. A peaceable French occupation would have been unpleasant, but unlikely to have led to the drastic loss of 250,000 people – one in twelve of the entire population – that Wellington's campaigns produced. So demographically and economically crippled was the country that the population did not rise significantly above its pre-war level until the late 1830s, and it would carry the burden of a bloated and parasitic military officer class into the next century.[33] Nor could it be said that the British had treated the country well even in print. Letters home, diaries and memoirs dwelt incessantly on the sloth, superstition, untrustworthiness and filth of the inhabitants. Much evidence indicates that British officers and men regarded themselves as having more in common with their 'civilised' French enemy than with the savagery they perceived as lurking in the civilian population.[34]

Nonetheless, despite all this, Portugal provided around a third of Wellington's army (and in some future engagements, Portuguese infantry would outnumber British).[35] When the sick-list, reserves and other detachments are included, this force rose to almost 100,000 in the course of the 1813 campaign. It was an army he used carefully and secretively with a grand strategy in mind.[36] The state of intelligence about military movements was drastically tilted in his favour. The French were so deprived of useful informants that Wellington was able to bring a cumbersome and strategically vital bridging-train on its wagons up to the front lines without any word of it reaching Joseph's forces. Meanwhile, not only were the Spanish guerrillas regularly intercepting all manner of vital French communications, but since the summer of 1811 a brilliant staff officer, George Scovell, had made steady progress on breaking their codes.

Scovell cracked not only the substitution codes used for operational communications between armies, but by 1812 also a new number-based 'Grand Cypher' intended to keep strategic communications with Paris secure. Messages sent to and from Joseph's headquarters, often by three, four or half a dozen different couriers, usually got through, but many of the copies not only now came into British hands, but were read as easily as if they were in plain language.[37] Scovell's success was a leading example of the more professional approach being taken to 'staff' tasks in the army, after the recent formation of the Royal Military College and Adjutant-General's department.[38] Thanks to this, and to networks of intelligence officers that rode out, sometimes with partisan groups, but sometimes alone, to procure vital first-hand information, Wellington was equipped to lead a campaign that took shape with an extraordinary lack of contact with real enemy forces.

Wellington set off initially with a force of 30,000 under 'Daddy' Hill towards Salamanca – as so often before – but after he had fooled any observers by this display of his presence, he left Hill's force and cut sharply back north-west, to where his main force of some 60,000 was advancing through terrain considered in previous campaigns to be impassable. Thanks to the condition of his army, Wellington could push them over 200 miles of steep, dry mountain terrain, crossing through the desolate Tras-os-Montes of north-east Portugal into the Cantabrian mountains, using his pontoon bridges to straddle rushing torrents, and executing a massive flanking manoeuvre with four separate columns of troops around the French armies. The latter had withdrawn from Valladolid and Madrid towards Burgos, shadowed by Hill, and continuously alarmed at the vague reports of other movements which were all that could be obtained.

Wellington's cavalry threw a wide screen around his main columns, so the looming presence of the enemy was clear, but only clear enough to intensify the feeling of threat. So effective was this strategy that on 13 June Joseph's forces abandoned the citadel of Burgos, blowing up its fortifications with a great explosion heard in the distant British lines, and continuing a retreat north-eastwards that soon carried them across the upper reaches of the Ebro river, and three-quarters of the way from Valladolid to the Pyrenean frontier.[39]

The deteriorating French position had also allowed Wellington to shift his supply base from the distant ports of Portugal to the much nearer harbour of Santander, enemy activity in north-western Spain having been all but extinguished by rampant partisans. As the year wore on, this would cause difficulties for the Royal Navy, which escorted over 400 convoys in support of Wellington's troops during the Peninsular War. By late 1813, ships were compelled to operate perilously inshore in the notoriously stormy Bay of Biscay, rather than taking the safer open-water route to Lisbon. Nevertheless, and despite some severe grumbling from Wellington (inclined like many Britons to expect miracles from the navy), regular convoys were brought through.[40]

Thus, though Wellington's troops suffered occasional shortages, and might well complain about the constant daily marches, they continued their advance across the Ebro in fighting trim. Joseph's army, gathering in previously detached units as it pulled back, still numbered over 60,000, and a week after the destruction of Burgos took up defensive positions in a narrow valley that stretched to the west of the Basque town of Vitoria. Here the only feasible approach for Wellington seemed to be straight up the valley – heights to the south were impassable, and the River Zadorra ran along the rugged north flank, turning to also shield the western end of the French position. A staggered array of defensive positions seemed to secure them from attack, and information from patrols that only half of Wellington's forces were to the west suggested another long out-flanking was in progress. This would still give the French several days' repose, and with new forces due to come up, might provide the opportunity for a counterstroke.

The French, however, had misread the land to the north. Dismissing it as unsuitable for moving large bodies of troops, they were caught in near-disarray on 21 June when Wellington launched an attack from both west and north. The missing half of his army had swung through the hilly passes and descended towards the Zadorra, which with a series of bridges and fords was not the defin-itive obstacle the French had assumed. When Wellington opened the fighting with the troops on his right, most south-westerly flank, the French hurried reinforcements there, fearing Wellington might encircle them. But this was a feint, albeit a fiercely fought one. Cutting the French off from retreat to the north was a bold plan, but with over 75,000 troops Wellington had the manpower, and the vision, to attempt it. Like any battle, things did not go exactly as he would have wished. The Fourth Division, thrusting from the west, became locked in fierce fighting with the French forward posi-tions. The Light Division, posted at the 'hinge' between the allies' western and northern arms, came under heavy counter-attack, and the commander of the Seventh Division, which should have been in position to support them, instead seemed ready to continue an already sluggish outflanking manoeuvre.

General Picton of the Third Division, fuming at his orders to follow and support the Seventh, broke loose. Leading from the front in a surge across the bend of the Zadorra, crying out 'Come on, ye rascals! Come on ye fighting villains!', Picton broke the French front line, which withdrew hastily to a second position near the village of Ariñez.[41] Rifleman Costello of the 95th recalled seeing the Connaught Rangers deploy from column into line and advance for this attack. The French opened fire on them at 'three or four hundred yards', causing enough casualties for the line to halt and close up its ranks. The Rangers then advanced a further fifty yards 'and in turn gave a running fire from their whole line, and without a moment's pause cheered and charged up the hill against them'. Strikingly, while the Rangers covered all this ground, the French failed to complete the reloading of their muskets, and were forced to come 'immediately to the right about, making the best of their way to the village'.[42]

Meanwhile, an even deeper outflanking manoeuvre was in the hands of General Graham leading the First and Fifth Divisions, descending from the northern hills several miles away on the other side of Vitoria itself. But there were critical delays in getting these attacks moving. As the French retreated stubbornly back down the valley towards Vitoria, selling every inch of ground dearly, they ought to have been surrounded, but Graham's men, meeting their own share of resistance, could not push across the Zadorra fast enough. Eventually, with all the rest of the army pounding on them – including more artillery than Wellington had ever before been able to bring to a battlefield – the French broke, fleeing directly eastwards from the town along a narrow road towards Pamplona.

The allied army's attempts to pursue them through broken terrain were ineffectual – partly because of the ground, partly through ill-advised piecemeal cavalry attacks, but mostly because the troops' eyes had fallen on one of the largest collections of loot a battlefield had ever seen. On the military and political side, the French left on the field 151 of their 152 cannon and over 500 wagons of artillery supplies, as well as spare uniforms, boots and other equipment in huge quantities, and the documentation of Joseph's monarchy. They also left behind the royal treasury, with literally millions in gold coin, and much more in other forms of treasure – the king's personal art collection came into Wellington's safekeeping, and was later granted to him by the restored Bourbon king.

The troops, British, Portuguese and Spanish, as well as camp-followers, wagon drivers and even local civilians, descended on the long lines of abandoned baggage in a joyous fury of pillage. In many cases what was stolen was itself the loot of shameless occu-pation, and the finery of pampered mistresses (and the 500 high-class prostitutes that travelled with the French headquarters). Over 3000 vehicles packed with clothes, furniture and everything else, down to pet parrots and monkeys, were there to be ravaged, while the civilian *afrancesados* who had opted to leave with Joseph found themselves abandoned to less-than-tender mercies.[43] Many picaresque tales would be told of what followed, along with notes of chivalry as individuals plucked women and children from the mêlée. Uglier scenes also took place, of course, as men fresh from battle found strong drink and turned to violent squabbling over trinkets or women.

Rifleman Costello seized an 'exceedingly heavy' case which proved to have £1000 of gold and silver in it, but had to threaten fellow soldiers with his weapon to bring it to safety (he entrusted most of the money to the regimental quartermaster and other offi-cers). One senior officer, Sir James Kempt, put a guard on a wagon he believed to contain gold, only to discover the next morning that it was full of blacksmith's supplies.[44] Official buildings, shops, and even private homes in Vitoria itself were also put to the sack, as the longest day of the year drew very slowly to a close.

Wellington, naturally, was infuriated. He had wished to march in pursuit of Joseph the next morning, but the troops were still recov-ering from twenty miles of marching and fighting, as well as their orgiastic night. Those still fit spent much of the 22nd buying and selling loot in a huge spontaneous market. Over the following days attempts to catch the enemy were fraught with mistakes, and in the end the French took some 55,000 men safely back over the western flank of the Pyrenees. Joseph was forced by his disgusted brother into private life, but his men were soon ready for action again. Congregating at Bayonne, they were once again reinforced – to almost 85,000 – and handed over by Napoleon to Marshal Soult. The man who had harried Sir John Moore to his death, who had been forced out of Oporto at a run, but returned so many times to threaten British flanks, and had lived like a king as viceroy in Andalusia, was Duke of Dalmatia in the Emperor's arcane system of honours. 'Duke of Damnation' the redcoats called him, for good reason.

Nicolas Jean-de-Dieu Soult had been a private soldier in 1789, having enlisted four years earlier at the age of sixteen. Son of a legal notary, his father's early death had impoverished the family, sending Nicolas into the ranks in search of preferment. Made sergeant in 1791, and an officer shortly after, revolutionary campaigns led to a lightning rise. By 1794 he was a brigadier-general, having shown valour in the republican victory at Fleurus, and after five years' campaigning in Germany in 1799 he became a major-general. He fought in Switzerland and Italy, and despite a defeat leading to a brief period of captivity was made one of the commanders of Bonaparte's 'consular guard' in 1802. Although many veterans of the German campaigns affected to despise the new head of state, Soult wisely allowed himself to be cultivated. He commanded the camp at Boulogne where much of the future Grand Army was trained, and after becoming a marshal led a corps in the victories at Ulm and Austerlitz – for which he always felt he deserved more credit than he got.

A masterful organiser of troops before battle, he was sometimes careless of their performance in actual combat, and often failed to be sufficiently flexible when faced with a determined foe. One area where he did excel was in plunder, amassing a huge fortune, and a distinguished art collection, from the Andalusian territories under his command. Like many of Napoleon's marshals he had developed a titanic ego, which led him into disputes with King Joseph and his fellows, further hindering military operations. Now, freed from royal supervision, he could hope to strike a decisive blow against Wellington.

Outside Catalonia, which formed effectively a separate theatre in this war, only Pamplona and the port of San Sebastian remained in French hands after Vitoria. On 25 July the British tried for a first time to assault the latter, and failed miserably. On the same day, Soult's refreshed troops appeared at the passes above Pamplona, and descended with overwhelming force on the screening detachments posted there. Even the bluff Picton was nonplussed, and forced into withdrawal. Once again, the aftermath of British victory was proving bitter. Two weeks earlier, Wellington had had to report that over 12,000 of his army were still stragglers, absent without leave somewhere in the Spanish countryside, while rainy weather proved the folly of abandoning the men's greatcoats, and ensured that almost a third of the forces present were out of action through sickness.[45] Nonetheless, decisive leadership saved the day.

Wellington appeared to rally the troops retreating under Soult's attacks, and near the village of Sorauren on 28 July they withstood three massive waves of assault. It was 'fair bludgeon work' in Wellington's own words, but it opened another opportunity. On the night of the 29th, Soult tried to disengage his army and strike westwards, aiming to divide the allied forces, but as soon as dawn broke on the 30th, Wellington launched his men in a rapid attack on the withdrawing, and hence disordered, French. Soult having ridden on ahead to join a different wing of his army, there was no one to give overall leadership; the resultant rout scattered the French across the foothills of the mountains, leaving their generals with no more than 35,000 men. Soult pulled back across the Bidassoa river into France within days, abandoning San Sebastian, their last stronghold, to renewed siege.[46]

By late August batteries were emplaced, and pounded two breaches in the walls. On the 31st, troops clambering along the shoreline of a tidal estuary under enemy fire began their assaults, to face absolute carnage. French defences battered the attackers with fire and shot: many fell wounded only to burn to death. One witness, hobbling back from the breach with a leg wound, found the first line of trenches a scene of horror:

> It was literally filled ... with the dead and dying ... one was making the best of his way minus an arm; another his face so disfigured ... as to leave no trace of the features of a human being; others creeping along with the leg dangling to a piece of skin; and, worse than all, some endeavouring to keep in the bowels.[47]

As at Ciudad Rodrigo and Badajoz, the ferocious courage of the assailants eventually overcame the defenders, and as also at those sieges, what followed was in some sense inevitable, all the more so as many officers had been killed or wounded in the storm. Pillage, drunkenness, rape and murder were consummated by fires that, unfought, devoured most of the town. It was commonly said afterwards, and Wellington repeated it in writing, that the inhabitants had in part earned their fate by cooperating with the French, but real evidence for this is scanty, and it scarcely absolved those responsible for the crimes. Opinion in the Spanish press was understandably outraged, and even went as far as accusations that the destruction was a deliberate effort to hinder the post-war development of trade in rivalry to British ports.[48] Exaggerations aside, the bitterness of this episode, as the Anglo-Portuguese army turned its attention to an invasion of France, reflected the turbulent complexity of this legendary campaign.

15

ENDGAMES

Wellington could only contemplate invading the Emperor's domain thanks to a remarkable series of clashes in central Europe. So great were the stakes, so diverse the interests and so erratic some of the leading players, that it seemed as if the continent was trapped on a seesaw, until a final, decisive tilt. The early spring of 1813 showed signs of a complete rout of Napoleonic forces. In mid-March a flying column of Russians, led by a German general, occupied Hamburg after its abandonment by the French. This seemed to open up all of north Germany to the allies, and indeed made it much easier for the British envoy, Castlereagh's half-brother Sir Charles Stewart, to reach the Russo-Prussian leadership in Berlin in late April. Bearing offers of millions of pounds in subsidy, he was very welcome, but had scarcely begun to discuss the substance of a real alliance when the dread news of Napoleon's advance arrived.

Even before the Emperor took the field, the allied gains of the spring had been reversed. Russo-British support for Swedish aggression over Norway helped alienate Denmark, which returned to the

French fold, and assisted Marshal Davout in a rapid reconquest of Hamburg; he was to garrison the port, and defend it ferociously, all through the year ahead. Germany, meanwhile, had not responded to the call of Prussian reformers to rise against its leaders in a war of national liberation – and the call itself alienated some otherwise pro-Russian rulers, while pushing others, including the King of Saxony, firmly back into the Napoleonic camp.[1]

The significant battles of the spring were fought on Saxon territory, and were marked by a series of notable deaths. Kutuzov died of pneumonia on 28 April, leaving the Russian command to an assortment of increasingly squabbling generals, while one of Napoleon's longest-serving and closest associates, Marshal Bessières, was killed by a cannonball in a skirmish on 1 May. General von Scharnhorst, one of the great figures of the Prussian reform movement, was fatally wounded in the fighting that developed over the following days around Lützen, a 'meeting engagement' of increasing forces funnelled in from each side that ended with over 100,000 French and 73,000 allies in action, and the latter being pushed into retreat. Napoleon's army, having suffered some 20,000 killed and wounded, and desperately short of cavalry, could not follow up and turn retreat into rout, but did occupy the cities of Saxony as the allied command argued over lines of withdrawal – north towards Prussia, or south-east into Russian Poland? They finally agreed to make a stand at Bautzen, east of Dresden, and the Emperor's forces caught up with them on 20 May.

This was again a major battle – the allies now had some 96,000 in the field, the French 115,000 on the first day, joined by another 80,000 on the second. But both sides approached it with politics as much as tactics in mind. The allies needed to keep their southern flank in contact with the Austrian territory of Bohemia, to keep open the possibility that the still neutral power might join them. Napoleon, more brutally, sought to swing round on them from the west and north, and drive them to a position where they had either to surrender en masse or violate Austrian territory in retreat – thus (he imagined) bringing the Austrians back to his camp. Marshal Ney was supposed to lead the northern wing, but after the Emperor's forces had already been engaged for a day of heavy fighting, Ney's manoeuvre failed. Through his own misunderstanding, and perhaps the general inexperience of his troops, his strike pushed the allies eastwards instead of south, and they retreated in good order, still keeping open their flank to Austria, leaving behind a further 20,000 French casualties and a similar number of their own.

The battle left both sides demoralised. Barclay de Tolly, who had taken over Russian command once more, argued that retreat into Poland was the only salvation of the battered army. Napoleon, meanwhile, struck by the loss of General Duroc, another close confidant – and more generally by 40,000 battle casualties and a sick list of a further 90,000 – called off any pursuit.[2] Some clearly thought that fighting could not continue. Marshal Macdonald (a French-born descendant of Scottish Jacobites) wrote that 'We had done enough to retrieve the honour of our arms . . . France and the army earnestly longed for peace.'[3] Initial French suggestions of armistice were shunned by the prickly Prussians, but on 2 June Austria re-entered the political fray with a carefully timed suggestion of a general truce, with negotiations to follow under Vienna's mediation. Two days later, the armistice of Pläswitz (or Pleiswitz, and sometimes Pleswitz) took effect; it was to last for ten weeks, during which a whole other, political, war was won and lost.

Austria's Chancellor Metternich had seized the opportunity to propose a truce out of a firm conviction that victory for either side in the current, essentially Russo-French, continental war would be a disaster for the dynasty he served. Should either power establish, or re-establish, a hegemonic position in Europe, the Habsburgs and their lands would be sidelined. Perhaps worst of all would be a replay of Tilsit, with both powers agreeing to split the continent and make Austria no more than a buffer state. As early as January,

Metternich had remarked to the Russian ambassador that 'all the calculations of Austria and other poor intermediaries must be directed at how not to be *wiped out*'. The vision behind the furious politicking that followed was in some senses quite idealistic – that France might withdraw behind the Rhine and Russia the Vistula, leaving Austria, Prussia and the *Rheinbund* or its successor as genuinely neutral powers between them, constrained to 'equilibrium and durable tranquillity' by mutual guarantees.[4]

Against this was set, however, both Tsar Alexander's new personal sense of messianic destiny and Russia's long-standing pursuit of hegemony, expressed as far back as the negotiations with Pitt's government in 1805. British willingness to tolerate a forcibly pacified continent, if its maritime interests were acknowledged and freedom to trade guaranteed, also stood against Metternich's more complex goals. So, from another direction, did Prussia's increasing focus on revenge and aggrandisement back to its pre-1806 state. Both Prussian and British leaderships distrusted Metternich, the former seeing his schemes as threatening their rise, the latter suspecting it was a ploy to save the man who was, after all, still Emperor Francis's son-in-law.[5]

Napoleon himself tilted this delicate situation away from any outcome that might have saved him. On 26 June, as Austrian, Prussian and Russian envoys were already setting down the outlines of a defensive alliance for peace, Metternich met Napoleon at his residence in Dresden, the Marcolini Palace. Each man later offered rather self-serving accounts of the conversation, but if Napoleon perhaps did not rant quite as much as Metternich claimed – or say, ominously, maniacally, that 'A man like me troubles himself little about the lives of a million men' – he did decisively spurn the idea that he might join that general alliance, and made it entirely clear that the current armistice suited his war-making purposes.[6] Napoleon seems to have rejected as incomprehensible the idea of establishing a peace not based on a trial of strength, and alternated between threatening a new Tilsit and offering to restore lost Austrian territories, assuming that somewhere beneath the veneer of principle, that was what Metternich really wanted.

When on the 27th Russia, Austria and Prussia signed the Treaty of Reichenbach, it contained relatively moderate demands for the exclusion of Napoleonic power from eastern Europe and the Baltic, to be put forward at a peace congress in Prague. Were these to be rejected by France, however, this would lead to war, with 150,000 Austrian troops committed alongside the same number of Russians and 80,000 Prussians, and the open possibility of harsher demands in the future. Remarkably, Metternich succeeded in getting French acceptance at least of the initial idea of a congress – there had been some allied hope that Napoleon would reject even that, forcing Austria into war on Russo-Prussian terms – and even managed to insist that the armistice be extended beyond its original end date into early August to accommodate both discussion and Austrian rearmament. It is fairly clear that Metternich hoped not to have to fight Napoleon.

Napoleon, however, clearly intended to fight. As one officer in his army recorded, the weeks of truce spent in Saxony were filled with 'preparations for a new campaign'. The west bank of the Elbe was fortified, strategic fortresses reinforced, massive stockpiles and hospitals established, while 'whole corps ... made up of young soldiers full of enthusiasm and goodwill' arrived continually from France. This might have been arranged in order to secure a strong negotiating position, but as he went on, 'We knew the Emperor well enough to know that, once he found himself at the head of such a large army, it would indeed be difficult to extract the least concession from him.' Within his own army there were reportedly 'widespread recriminations and complaints' about this inflexible character, but the military preparations continued.[7]

When the peace congress opened at Prague in July, it rambled on to no purpose. Napoleon sent one of his closest advisors, General Caulaincourt, to represent him, but neglected to give him credentials to actually negotiate. Rejecting reports of the impressive numbers that Austria had mobilised, and that Russia in particular was receiving as reinforcements, Napoleon had chosen war. The truce expired on 10 August, and two days later Austria formally acceded to military alliance with the other powers, mollified for its abandonment of pacifism with the nomination of its leading general, Prince Schwarzenberg, as commander-in-chief.

Britain had been tied by formal alliance to Prussia and Russia since 14 June. The costs of this, though suspended during the armistice (and even then Stewart found himself obliged to advance £100,000 for the immediate needs of the Prussians), were huge. With £2 million already committed to paying in its entirety for Sweden's war effort, another £2 million was offered to be split between Russia and Prussia, plus a further £500,000 to support Russian warships currently sheltering in British ports. Russian hopes of a further £5 million in interest-bearing bonds were also to end up as a further direct payment of £2.5 million over the next year, after negotiations on the nature of the bonds proved too complex.[8] Opposition disquiet, some of it on principled grounds, some based on alarm at the generosity to Sweden and the indecisive military situation, emerged in parliamentary debates in June, but neither the Whigs nor an angry and embittered Canning could make much impression on a Castlereagh who was on top form, even without heartening news such as that of Vitoria which arrived in the following weeks.

Such good news was vitally important, for it underpinned the huge outlay that the government was committed to making on the war. This effort absorbed more and more of the economy; the proportion devoted to private consumption had fallen from over 80 per cent in the early 1790s to less than 65 per cent by 1814.[9] The customary raising of temporary revenue through selling interest-bearing bonds to the public was being strained to the limits of its capacity. Having borrowed £16.6 million in 1811 and £25.4 million in 1812, they proposed to borrow £38.4 million this year.

This met the shortfall in an overall budget in which expenditure, as outlined in March, rose to £72.1 million from £58.2 million in 1812. Almost £30 million was now being spent on the army alone, up by almost a sixth on the year, as well as over £6 million on general subsidies, and additional specific grants to Portugal and Sicily.

While much of this borrowing came from domestic wealth invested in the various bonds issued as part of the National Debt, some came from a flight of capital from the embattled Continent – compared to which, Britain represented a much safer haven for investment. Apart from borrowing, the government also raised customs duties by 25 per cent, and planned for rises in receipts from general taxation as the economy expanded on renewed continental trade. Exports were running at some £48 million in 1814, up by almost a sixth on the figure of a decade earlier – and double what they had been in the mid-1790s, and almost four times the rate of the 1780s (testament to the potent combination of global maritime dominance and industrialisation).[10] There was thus no great difficulty in raising these sums, so long as lenders retained confidence, but the increases were clearly unsustainable in the longer term – a point that would arrive as soon as it looked as if Napoleon might win, or indeed force a continental peace that would not let Britain safely disarm. Then bankruptcy might loom. The stakes of conflict had never been higher.[11]

How much of a gamble both sides were taking was demonstrated unambiguously by events in Saxony in late August. Outnumbering the French by three to two, the allies had agreed a strategy of attacking Napoleon's subordinate corps in strength, while avoiding battle with the Emperor himself until his forces were worn down. Initially this seemed to be working: Bernadotte confirmed his change of allegiance by leading 80,000 Swedes and Prussians to beat Marshal Oudinot's 60,000 men south of Berlin on 23 August, and three days later Marshal Macdonald's 100,000 were beaten by a similar number of Prussians under Marshal Blücher in a dramatic (and

accidental) engagement during a thunderstorm on the Katzbach
river in Silesia. On this same day, Schwarzenberg, with 200,000
men, and the three allied sovereigns observing, attacked the forces
of Marshal Saint-Cyr occupying Dresden.

The first day of combat was indecisive, but on the second
Napoleon appeared on the battlefield with reinforcements. The
import of his presence was shown clearly by events. Still outnumbered almost two to one, the French nonetheless managed to turn
the allied left flank, trapping a whole corps against a flooded river
and capturing over 15,000 men. Overall allied losses amounted to
some 38,000, four times those of the French. Had the Emperor not
been stricken with violent stomach pains, he might even have managed to encircle the panicked allies. But Napoleon had not
managed to turn the tables. A French pursuit led by General
Vandamme caught up with rallying enemy forces at Kulm in
Bohemia on 29 August. The 36,000 French pressed an attack
against inferior numbers, but on the following day massive reinforcements approached from several directions, leaving them again
outnumbered two to one. Vandamme was captured along with
some 10,000 comrades, while other formations had to fight their
way back to safety.

Napoleon's initial strategic goal of this campaign had been to
capture Berlin, in the belief (profoundly optimistic, as 1807 should
have shown) that it would take Prussia out of the war.[12] Oudinot's
forces had been attempting this when defeated by Bernadotte, and
after pausing to regroup, the Emperor sent Marshal Ney with
58,000 men to try again. Advancing along a single road, partly
because he feared his novice troops could not be kept together
otherwise, but partly also out of haste, and severely lacking in cavalry for reconnaissance, Ney walked into a major allied force at
Dennewitz on 6 September. The battle developed as the strung-out
French arrived piecemeal, not helped by the superseded Marshal
Oudinot neglecting to cooperate fully with his new superior.
Pressed hard by the allies, the French were forced back, leaving

over one-sixth of their forces as casualties. Whole formations of
inexperienced troops were routed in chaos, in some cases even
before contact with the enemy.

Even after Kulm and Dennewitz, Napoleon did not recognise
that a defensive posture might now be needed. He continued to
attempt strategic manoeuvres to outflank or divide the allied forces,
but to no avail. Carefully exploiting their superior numbers and
reconnaissance to avoid him, Schwarzenberg's subordinates
harassed the detached corps of the marshals through September,
while Napoleon was obliged to pull back from Dresden to Leipzig,
shortening his lines of communication and abandoning the east
bank of the Elbe. His German coalition began to crumble. Bavaria,
amongst his staunchest allies since the essential part his victories
had played in elevating it to a kingdom in 1806, pulled out and
signed the Treaty of Ried with Metternich – the self-interested calculations, and prospective rewards, involved were complex, but
the abandonment of the Empire was clear.

Even within the army there was dissent. Marshal Macdonald
reportedly had an angry exchange with the Emperor after his
defeat: when Napoleon demanded to know what he had done with
his army, the Marshal retorted, 'You no longer have an army: there
is nothing left but a few unfortunates dying of starvation ... You
have lost everything: your only hope is peace.'[13] The massive scale
of the operations made Macdonald's claims both true and false.
Constant countermarching in bad weather by inexperienced troops
led to tens of thousands of disease casualties, further aggravated by
the exhaustion even of the great supply stockpiles hastily accumu-
lated over the summer weeks of truce. Whole units collapsed, and
stragglers thronged the countryside, while the base hospitals were
swept with epidemics that made evacuation with wounds almost a
death sentence in itself.

Yet the allies were almost equally suffering, and Napoleon still
had nearly 200,000 soldiers under arms as October opened.[14]
Rational calculation would have suggested that, with winter

approaching, either a commitment to negotiation or a steady withdrawal west of the Rhine to regroup was the best approach. The Emperor, however, was a gambler, not a philosopher, and attempted to launch another offensive against the forces of Bernadotte and Blücher to the north.[15] As he did so, Schwarzenberg advanced from the south towards Leipzig, forcing Napoleon to pull back to the city to defend his base, and allowing the Prussians, Swedes and Russians to follow. By the end of the second week of October, more than 400,000 allied troops were closing on the city from north and south. There was still time to evacuate westwards, but the situation seemed to offer Napoleon the decisive battle he craved, and he settled his troops in defensive positions ringing the city.

A first series of onslaughts from both directions on 16 October, involving some 130,000 allied troops, was fought off with major casualties. On all sides, the rapidly raised armies lacked the tactical finesse of previous years. Massive batteries of artillery – the allies eventually deployed over 1500 cannon – substituted for subtlety of manoeuvre, and deep attacking columns sustained by their very bulk replaced the vigour and speed of earlier offensive styles. The results began to foreshadow the awful slaughter of later industrialised wars, as units advanced into a meatgrinder, absorbing huge casualties and overrunning defenders with sheer weight of numbers.

On 17 October there was relatively little combat, though one cavalry action proved that the French were now decisively inferior in that arm. Both sides rested and received reinforcements. While the French were joined from the west by a corps of 14,000 men, the allies received over 140,000 from the east and north-east, so that when fighting resumed on all sides on the 18th, the balance of forces had decisively tipped. Steadily driven back towards the town of Leipzig itself, especially from the north (for Napoleon was in the south, and his presence remained inspirational), the French did not break, but gave ground under enormous pressure. Fighting went on for over nine hours before failing light and exhaustion drew it to a close. During the day, a contingent of Saxon troops some 4000 strong had defected to the allies, and the situation of the remaining forces had at last become clearly unsustainable even to the Emperor.

Overnight and into the next day, the able-bodied survivors began to evacuate over the remaining bridge westwards across the Elster river. Marshal Oudinot commanded a rearguard that fought ferociously from house to house to delay the allies as they flooded into the town, and his reward was to be forced into a desperate escape as the bridge was blown up prematurely by French engineers. As a result the Polish leader Poniatowski, made a marshal by Napoleon the previous day, was drowned trying to flee, and over 15,000 of the rearguard were forced to surrender en masse.

As the allies consolidated their hold on central Germany, they could do little immediately to pursue Napoleon. They had suffered over 50,000 casualties in the battle, and faced the same menaces of disease and weather that the French did. These, however, did most of their work for them. Napoleon recrossed the Rhine into French territory in early November with some 70,000 men. A further 40,000 straggled home in the following weeks. All these forces continued to be ravaged by disease, notably typhus. Meanwhile, another 100,000 men were left trapped in major fortress towns, as far east as Danzig and Stettin on the Baltic, all of whom had surrendered by the end of November.

The Battle of Leipzig, the largest battle fought on European soil before the twentieth century, went down in legend as the 'Battle of Nations', where in particular the mission of German liberation was consummated. The 40,000 dead and wounded, and over 30,000 prisoners, it cost the French were undoubtedly significant. The remarkable irony of the campaign of 1813 is that Napoleon's huge army – at its height it may even have exceeded on paper the 600,000 assembled for the invasion of Russia, though only a little more than half that number reached the front lines – would have been destroyed even without that great engagement. Disease and hunger ate it away from within, and Napoleon held it in being, far from home and without realistic prospect of success. What is perhaps even more remarkable is that this crushing defeat settled nothing, either for Napoleon or amongst the allies. As victory for them seemed to loom, the question of what to do with, and after, the Emperor grew only more vexed.

As the allied armies began to penetrate the alien soil of France, untouched by invaders' boots for almost exactly twenty years, so British diplomacy began to penetrate once again, after almost as long, the foreign soil of Continental political practice. Both manoeuvres would prove more fraught than anyone expected. The diplomatic class of the European powers was made up of men drawn from an international elite, accustomed both to complex multi-levelled interactions and to necessary compromises and changes of allegiance. To take a leading example, Karl Philipp, Prince Schwarzenberg, currently commander-in-chief of the allied armies, had also led the Austrian auxiliary corps that had invaded Russia alongside Napoleon in 1812, and before that had been sent to Paris, tasked with negotiating the marriage treaty between the Emperor and the Habsburgs in 1810.

Before all this, however, Schwarzenberg had led troops in every campaign against France between 1793 and 1809. After the disaster at Moscow, Schwarzenberg (carefully instructed by Metternich) had secretly negotiated a peaceful withdrawal of his forces from Russian territory, and then a further evacuation of the Grand Duchy of Warsaw, the latter against explicit instructions from, and assurances to, Napoleon. Yet the Emperor welcomed him back to Paris in the spring of 1813 as an ally and peace envoy, and Schwarzenberg (according to Napoleon) also assured him upon his departure that his troops stood ready to rejoin the imperial cause.[16] None of this made him anything less than a figure of honour and renown.

The individuals who made up this elite were men who had crossed borders at will in pursuit of advantage and distinction. Metternich himself was the son of a Rhineland noble who had become an Austrian diplomat, and while following in his father's footsteps, was also thus far removed from any sense of loyalty to homeland or people. At Metternich's side throughout his diplomatic adventures of this era was Friedrich von Gentz, born to the Prussian service nobility, but who had abandoned his monarch to accept payments from both the Austrians and the British as a ferociously anti-Napoleonic publicist in the years after 1800, before officially entering the Habsburgs' service after their defeat in 1809.

Other leading players on the German diplomatic scene included Heinrich, Freiherr vom Stein, who until its abolition had been a Knight of the Holy Roman Empire, and in Prussian service. Exiled under Napoleonic pressure in 1809, for declaring a wish for a German national rising akin to that in Spain, he took refuge in Austria until 1812, and then fled to Russia, becoming both a bellicose advisor to the Tsar and an intermediary with his old Prussian master (sometimes against the wishes of the timid king). Now, he was charged by the allies with administering the territories they had liberated from Napoleon's German satellites. Meanwhile, the Prussian government was now led by Karl August von Hardenberg. A Hanoverian by birth, in Prussian ministerial service he had been a voice for compromise, and even alliance, with Napoleon in the early 1800s, before converting to nationalistic views akin to Stein's, and helping to persuade his adopted king to join the allied cause in 1813.

On the Russian side, the situation was even more complex. Alexander's key military commander Barclay de Tolly, although born a Russian subject, was of mixed Scots and Baltic-German ancestry. The Russian foreign minister (though somewhat overshadowed by the Tsar's personal diplomacy) was Karl Nesselrode, the son of a Count of the Holy Roman Empire who had entered the Russian diplomatic service. Born in Lisbon (and baptised into the Church of England at the British Embassy there, the only available Protestant chapel), he had been educated in Berlin while his father was posted there, before serving briefly as a naval midshipman and army cadet, and then entering the diplomatic corps in time to help negotiate the Tilsit treaty.

The Russian diplomatic and political elite had always drawn on German expertise, but the vicissitudes of the previous decades had also brought some extraordinary individuals into the Tsar's service. These included Carl Andrea Pozzo di Borgo, a Corsican who had once been a revolutionary associate of the Bonapartes, breaking with them during the Terror and serving the British military occupiers of the island until 1796. Fleeing French reoccupation, he lived in Vienna until entering Russian service in 1804, but was driven out of it by Napoleon's continued enmity after Tilsit. Periods of further exile in Vienna and London followed, until renewed hostilities caused the Tsar to recall him. He had been instrumental in the new alliance with Sweden, and was a permanent voice resisting compromise with his old, and very personal, enemy.

Alongside him, a rising star of the Tsar's diplomacy had an even more extraordinary route to distinction. Ioannis Kapodistrias was Greek, born on Corfu when it was a Venetian possession, and trained as a doctor, despite having a noble background. When the Ionian Islands were taken over by revolutionary France in the late 1790s, he remained at his medical post, but joint occupation by Russian and Turkish forces in 1799 saw the creation of a 'Septinsular Republic' in which the young Kapodistrias, at twenty-five, became a government minister. Noted for popular reforms, he was forced to flee by renewed French occupation in 1807, and entered Russian service two years later. A committed and idealistic liberal, at the same time he dutifully served his autocratic master and rapidly rose to prominence. At this point, he was working to ensure a safe disentanglement of Switzerland from the mesh of Napoleonic obligations.

Set against men like this, with long experience, mutual acquaintance, broad perspectives and subtle minds, the British diplomatic leadership seems almost farcical.[17] General Cathcart had proved a safe pair of hands, but with little initiative, foresight or real ability. Sir Charles Stewart seemed to have little but his family connection to recommend him. Having served as a cavalry officer in the Peninsula, this was clearly where his heart remained. A colleague spoke of him as 'a most gallant fellow, but perfectly mad', and in the campaigns of the autumn, he had probably spent more time careering around joining in the fighting than in serious negotiation – so much so that he had been wounded in action at Kulm.[18]

Stewart's diplomatic shortcomings were so evident that they were even noted by the man sent to negotiate with Metternich: George Gordon, Earl of Aberdeen, who at twenty-eight, and with no previous diplomatic experience and a poor command of French, its routine language, was not an obvious candidate for the role himself. He was at least widely travelled, and a personal associate of first Pitt and then Castlereagh, with some experience of politics in the House of Lords, but he confessed in a letter to a 'feeling approaching contempt for the whole diplomatic profession in general'.[19] Taking an instant mutual dislike to Cathcart, and looking down on Stewart's antics, Aberdeen – much to his physical and emotional discomfort – found himself in the autumn of 1813 effectively on active military service, when he had expected to be a court envoy,

Stricken with something he diagnosed as cholera, horrified by the sights and smells of battle's aftermath, and thoroughly off-balance, Aberdeen was wooed ruthlessly by Metternich. At first cautious in his letters to Castlereagh – 'yet it may be, after all, that he is only a most consummate actor' – he was soon won over completely, denying that the chancellor was a 'formidable personage', asserting that he was 'heart and soul with us', and advocating strongly for more financial and political support for Metternich's schemes. At the same time he managed to give away the British position on the fate of the Kingdom of Naples, allowing Metternich to do a deal with the flamboyant Joachim Murat for the latter to keep his Napoleonic crown in return for peace, while his Bourbon rival – Britain's client for over a decade – was left with only Sicily. These negotiations, consummated late in 1813, but under way even while Murat was still commanding Napoleon's cavalry before Leipzig, showed how much the British had to learn about what Aberdeen referred to as 'Foreign modes of acting'.[20]

There was even more below the surface of that idea of what was 'Foreign'. Nobody could justly accuse the British ruling class of being prudish, especially not with that seasoned debauchee the Prince Regent in charge, but the frantic entanglement of sexual and political lives that seemed to occupy the Continental mind came as a positive shock. Over the last year, one of the intriguing signs of Napoleon's fall from influence had been the rallying of a number of aristocratic *grandes dames* to the side of the allied leaders. Tsar Alexander managed not to allow his messianic religious conversion to interfere with acceptance of the worship, and favours, of a wide range of ladies. At times it had also seemed as if one of the primary reasons for Metternich's choices about the location of various conferences was the access to such ladies' bedrooms that they afforded.

The chancellor was no dry stick, but a man of considerable personal vanity, and remarkable amorous success. As ambassador to Paris between 1806 and 1809, an elegant and charming figure in his mid-thirties, he had bedded every Parisian beauty that was willing, and a great number had been. These included Laure Junot, duchesse d'Abrantès, perhaps the leading hostess of her day. They possibly also included the Emperor's sister Pauline Bonaparte, a legendary sexual adventuress, and definitely included his other sister Caroline. Memories of what was a brief but intense affair may have played a role in Metternich's willingness to safeguard her husband, Murat, in his Neapolitan possessions.[21]

The British leadership should not be painted as either saints or fools. Sir Charles Stewart was as adventurous in his social life as he was on the battlefield (and Wellington would prove, when circumstances allowed, a notable ladies' man), while the Cabinet had acted swiftly and decisively to assert support for the restored Dutch leadership when Napoleonic rule there collapsed after Leipzig. This, in cynical European eyes, was about securing themselves a compliant satellite in control of the ports from which invasion had been so often feared, even if ministers declined to speak in such terms.[22]

Yet Britain continued to experience problems with European ways. Metternich in November 1813, with Aberdeen's unwise compliance, sent Napoleon an unofficial peace offer that would have given him France's 'natural frontiers' on the Rhine and Alps, and hinted at British relaxation of their maritime dominance. The Emperor toyed with this, playing for time as ever; the result was political outrage in London (and from the other allies), furious arguments between the British envoys and their various hosts, and finally a plea from the Continental powers (delivered in person to the Cabinet by Pozzo di Borgo) for a single high-profile plenipotentiary to join the diplomatic circus and bring unity sadly lacking in British efforts to date.[23]

The names of Richard Wellesley and George Canning had been mentioned by Metternich, showing how out of touch Europeans could be with the realities of British politics, for both men were entirely out of favour. The situation was such that only real eminence connected to practical powers would suffice. Thus, on Boxing Day 1813, Castlereagh took leave of his Cabinet colleagues after a last, detailed briefing meeting, and travelled to Harwich, with his family, to take ship for the Continent. Three days of dead calm, followed by three days of raging storms, saw them eventually pitched up, somewhat bedraggled, at The Hague. Further midwinter travel ordeals ensued as the minister raced ahead of his family, one concern in London being that some ghastly deal might be done before the British perspective could be reinforced. Castle-reagh arrived at Basle on 18 January 1814, to play a crucial role in everything that followed.[24]

The military situation, meanwhile, continued to provide the necessary context for all diplomacy. Wellington's armies had crossed the French frontier at the beginning of October 1813, and though the advance had been held up at least as much by polit-ical uncertainties as by dogged French resistance, by the end of the year Soult's army had been pushed back across several river-lines to the vicinity of Bayonne.[25] The viciousness of the Franco-Spanish attitude to war had followed the allies, with the Spanish troops who made up as much as a quarter of the forces engaging in ferocious bouts of pillage and murder. As soon as the first advances were secured, Wellington solved this problem by marching them all back, under arms and in formation, safely on to Spanish soil, and leaving them there. Paradoxically, allied success further north caused him another problem: many of the King's German Legion deserted as their Hanoverian homelands were liberated in late 1813, to the extent that some units became unusable.[26]

The usual fierce Wellingtonian orders against plunder made his men surprisingly welcome amongst a French peasantry accus-tomed to being extorted by the 'requisitions' of their own passing troops – and hundreds of thousands had passed by the western Pyrenees in the past five years.[27] No stern words could deflect the winter weather, however, and for two months further advances were precluded by torrential rain. The campaign resumed on 14 February 1814 at breakneck pace. Bayonne was bypassed and its garrison left hemmed in by a covering force, while over the next two weeks Soult's men were repeatedly outflanked and driven back by rapid and complex river-crossing manoeuvres.

The army that Wellington had devoted so much time, care and anger to nurturing was repaying him with almost flawless success.

The tempo of engagements was higher than at any other stage of the war, causing the French some 19,000 casualties in six months, at the cost of over 16,000 Anglo-Portuguese. Wellington, so successful in safeguarding his men when defence was the priority, now did not hesitate to buy strategic advantage with lives.[28] Even receiving a painful wound to the thigh from yet another spent bullet did not slow him down; by the end of March 1814 he had harried Soult far inland towards entrenchments at Toulouse, and was on the way to liberating Bordeaux.[29]

Behind him, Spain was reverting to political chaos, a pot vigorously stirred by Napoleon when he signed a treaty on 10 December 1813 with the imprisoned Bourbon king Ferdinand VII, restoring his kingdom in return for peace and the expulsion of the British. Though this deal was repudiated immediately by the political leadership of the Spanish Cortes, Napoleon went on to deliver Ferdinand to the Spanish frontier on 24 March, in the hope that this action would unleash the many thousands of French troops still in Catalonia to rejoin the imperial cause. It did not, though it did end the experiment in constitutional liberalism that Spain had been enjoying since 1812. Ferdinand, the Spanish people's *rey deseado*, 'desired king' since 1808, turned out to be a ferocious political and religious reactionary, whose policies over the coming decades sank his country into stagnation, and cost it almost all its overseas empire.[30]

Napoleon's gamble on Ferdinand was one part of a multipronged attack (he also released the pope, a prisoner since 1809) that despite its diplomatic dimensions remained essentially military. Defeat at Leipzig unleashed another round of conscription demands, seeking to suck out another 120,000 men from the already thoroughly drained 'classes' of 1809–14, and summoning an unprecedented 160,000 from the 'class of 1815'. By the end of the autumn another 300,000 were being demanded from all classes back to 1803, and yet another 180,000 for internal service as National Guards.[31]

All this, and a doubling of tax demands alongside it, was impossible, and self-destructive. In the end, only some 65,000 new recruits were produced, at enormous political cost. Reports arrived from the Belgian territories, part of France for almost a generation, that a return to the old Austrian allegiance was being demanded, and French officials prudently evacuated themselves on to safer soil. Theatrical propaganda in Paris, depicting the ravages of Cossack invaders, was roundly hissed, and satirical insults began to be voiced in the streets without fear. Efforts to stimulate the revolutionary patriotic spirit of 1793 – a remarkable ideological turnaround by any measure – met with little success, and by the end of the year even the subservient placemen of Napoleon's tame legislature were coming as close as they dared to demanding immediate peace.[32]

What to do when peace arrived continued to occupy many minds. Even the British, who had envisaged a Bourbon restoration as the ideal solution since the 1790s, and were currently hosting the prospective king, were not committed to it as a policy. As late as November 1813, Wellington had said in political correspondence that Napoleon was 'probably as good a sovereign as we can desire in France', if his aggression were reined in.[33] Castlereagh two months later echoed the point that negotiation with the Emperor remained possible. Yet Napoleon fought on. He agreed, yet again, to a meeting with allied diplomats to discuss peace terms, sending the ever-faithful General Caulaincourt to Châtillon in late January 1814. He was joined there on 3 February by the other representatives, one each from Austria, Russia and Prussia, and all three of the British envoys (thus leaving Castlereagh a free hand to deal with the sovereigns and ministers at headquarters). But even as he dispatched Caulaincourt to this meeting, the Emperor also made arrangements for a regency in civil government, and on 25 January left Paris to join his army.[34]

Under an assortment of marshals, various French forces, none of them more than a few tens of thousands strong even on paper,

faced the invaders who had, over the course of the winter, tenta-
tively breached the French frontiers. Schwarzenberg's largely
Austrian forces formed the southern flank of this advance, currently
occupying the plateau of Langres to the west of the Vosges mountains, while further north the Prussian Marshal Blücher's Army of
Silesia, with substantial Russian components, had conquered the
Rhineland. The French were outnumbered at least four to one by
some 350,000 allies, while their former satellites in Germany were
busy raising new armies and militias against them to augment the
reinforcements that continued to arrive.[35] Napoleon took charge of
only 45,000 men at Châlons-sur-Marne, initially facing the
Austrians. The situation seemed hopeless.

What followed was the last heroic gasp of the old General
Bonaparte, the man who had stormed through Italy, conquered
Egypt and trapped the Austrians at Ulm. On 29 January, the
Emperor's army took Blücher's forces by surprise, winning an
engagement at Brienne. Three days later there was a setback, as the
hugely outnumbered French were forced to retreat from battle in
blizzard conditions, but in mid-February they returned, fighting
three engagements in five days between the 10th and 14th that
drove Blücher's forces into a general retreat. Turning on the
Austrians, who were already pulling back, Napoleon then inflicted
defeat on them on 18 February. Allied headquarters, which had
come forward to Troyes, was driven into a fifty-mile retreat to
Chaumont.[36] Ministers, diplomats and crowned heads suffered all
the indignities, and not a few dangers, of a rout. Ironically, the
envoys sent to Châtillon sat out this débâcle in tranquillity, guarded
by French National Guardsmen under the cloak of their diplomatic status and Caulaincourt's duties as host.

Napoleon's army criss-crossed north-eastern France, fighting like
demons for a cause that, for a moment, no longer seemed lost.
When Schwarzenberg requested an armistice (even before defeat
on the 18th), Napoleon screwed up his note and threw it aside. By
24 February he was in Troyes, Tsar Alexander at Chaumont was

talking of asking for peace terms, and King Frederick William of Prussia was actively and emotionally defeatist. Castlereagh reported drily that such views were 'strongly tinctured with the demoralising Influence of a rapid transition from an advance made under very lofty Pretensions to a Retreat of some Embarrassment, and of much Disappointment and Recrimination'. Napoleon put it more bluntly: 'They thought the lion was dead and it was safe to piss on him.'[37]

The death of the lion also featured in an intriguing vignette of the difference between British and French society played out at this moment. Whereas reports of Napoleon's demise in 1812 had been the pretext for General Malet's attempt at a political coup, the deliberate spreading of false news of the Emperor's death was now the key element in a fraudulent financial coup on the London stock market. Conspirators disguised as military officers spread news from Dover to London of Napoleon's death and subsequent peace on 21 February, allowing their collaborators to profit from the sale of over £1 million of government bonds as their value soared. The naval hero and radical MP Lord Cochrane was later convicted of having orchestrated the plot, along with his uncle and his financial agent, though he would protest his innocence for the rest of his life, and was effectively exonerated almost two decades later.

Napoleon's continued good health, and good fortune on the battlefield, may have robbed some gulled investors of their profits, as it robbed assorted monarchs of their dignity, but the larger game was still heavily stacked against him. On 19 February, he had instructed Caulaincourt to demand the 'natural frontiers' of the Rhine and Alps as a minimum condition for peace. This was at least more realistic than the first instructions the general had arrived with, which called, amongst other things, for the retention of the Kingdom of Italy under its current viceroy, the Emperor's stepson Eugène Beauharnais, and an independent Grand Duchy of Warsaw. These were rejected out of hand by the allies from a position of strength at the beginning of February, but to Caulaincourt's discomfiture, he discovered at the end of the month that all Napoleon's campaigning had changed nothing.

Panic at allied headquarters soon passed, and at Châtillon – with Castlereagh now in personal attendance to supervise discussions – the minimum allied position remained a withdrawal of all French power inside its frontiers of 1792, in return for a partial restoration of overseas colonies. Not long afterwards, the allied chiefs decided that Napoleon was not negotiating in good faith (or rather, that it was no longer worth pretending that he was), and in mid-March the talks were formally broken off with the assertion that they had been 'terminated by the French government'.[38]

By the end of March, it was all over. On the 9th, after heavy prompting by Castlereagh, the other powers were at last persuaded to join a mutual and binding alliance in the Treaty of Chaumont. Not only did this harden their mutual line against Napoleon, but it bound them to 'reciprocally engage not to negotiate separately with the common Enemy, nor to sign Peace, Truce, nor Convention, but with common consent'. It also went further, imagining a long-term settlement: 'The present Treaty of Defensive Alliance having for its object to maintain the equilibrium of Europe, to secure the repose and independence of its States, and to prevent the invasions which during so many years have desolated the World, the High Contracting Parties have agreed to extend the duration of it to twenty years.' Though beneath this veneer lay the shadow of various ambitions, it also offered the prospect of lasting peace of a kind that the old Europe of contesting dynasties had not imagined.[39]

Faced with this evidence of allied unity and determination, Napoleon fought on, defeating Blücher at Craonne on 7 March while outnumbered two to one, and attacking Schwarzenberg two weeks later against odds of almost three to one. France, however, crumbled. Refugees clogged the roads of eastern France, terrified of the advancing Cossacks. Wellington's advances in the south encouraged Bordeaux to declare for the exiled Bourbons on 12 March, and the marshals who faced the enemy when the Emperor was elsewhere began to put up less and less resistance. Meanwhile in Paris, Talleyrand, the former aristocratic bishop become revolutionary politician, then Napoleon's chief diplomat – who had resigned in 1807, secretly encouraged the Tsar to resist the Emperor's megalomania as early as 1808, and yet retained, through his extraordinary wiles, a position of influence – was hard at work shaping the future. If France was to regain her status after Napoleon's fall, it meant establishing an independent ruling dynasty, and showing that Emperor and Empire were not necessarily one. Talleyrand defied imperial orders for the political class to quit the capital as fighting grew near, and readied himself to be the arch-mediator of the looming crisis.

On 29 March, Blücher's and Schwarzenberg's forces were united before Paris. Heavily outnumbered French forces attempted resistance the next day, but signed a capitulation of the city in the early hours of the 31st. Later that day, fulfilling a pledge to his messianic self-image, Tsar Alexander rode in to take possession of the city, and fell into the twin clutches of his quixotic chivalry and Talleyrand's wily cunning. The latter successfully persuaded the Tsar to lodge in his own town house, while having himself elected by the surviving legislative body to head a provisional government the following day. Releasing France's soldiers from their oaths to the Emperor, this government, thanks to Talleyrand's persuasiveness, was allowed to recall the Bourbons, putting aside Bonapartist schemes for a regency, and the prospect of a puppet of the Tsar being enthroned.

Napoleon tried to rally an army at Fontainebleau, but in the first days of April was told by his own marshals that abdication was his only choice. One of the few to fight on, true to his nickname as the Duke of Damnation, was Soult in the south. Wellington was forced to defeat him yet again in a bloody battle outside Toulouse, the day before news of the abdication arrived.[40] Attempting to sweeten the bitter pill with a show of magnanimity – and thus also to reinforce Russian influence in France – Alexander personally agreed a deal for the Emperor's exile to the Italian island of Elba. This was alarmingly close, for Castlereagh and Metternich, to France, Italy and Murat's Neapolitan kingdom, but the Tsar insisted on upholding the treaty he had put his hand to, and Napoleon sailed (on HMS *Inconstant*) before the end of the month.[41]

The extraordinary leniency with which the allies were prepared to treat their defeated enemy – compared to the way in which Napoleon had treated them – is shown by the armistice agreed on 23 April 1814. French troops by the tens of thousands would be peacefully repatriated from the fortresses they still garrisoned across Germany, Italy and Catalonia, and the allies would evacuate France. No military occupation was envisaged, and no reparations. With the long war at last ended, a kind of political rapture overtook the allies gathered in Paris, perhaps not entirely disassociated from the delights afforded by the world's greatest city of pleasure. One of the many French officers in allied service wrote that 60,000 prostitutes were in constant demand, 'without counting the decent wives of civil and military officers', and 'millions' were being spent on them.[42]

The other pleasures of the city were also soaked up, including the magnificent collections of art assembled in the Louvre under the name of the Musée Napoléon. Though much of this was the blatant loot of campaigns stretching back to 1796, a consensus amongst the allied leadership about its unique value as a unified collection kept it safe, renamed, naturally, as the Musée Royale. Those German leaders who were less inclined to rhapsodise over French cultural superiority, having felt their military boot for over a decade, were compelled, temporarily at least, to yield to more refined sensibilities. Prussia on 17 May attempted to break the genteel consensus with an assessment that France had extorted 169,785,895 francs from her in the previous years of occupation, and should pay it back. Castlereagh sharply retorted that Britain was not asking for a penny of the £700 million he claimed had been invested in the war (a sum a hundred times larger), and after some acrimony the matter was buried.[43] At the end of the month the Treaty of Paris signalled the disintegration of Napoleon's empire, but the rebirth of France – granted its 1792 borders, plus a further eight districts on the northern and eastern frontiers that added to strategic security, and the return of the majority of its overseas colonies.

16

RECKONING AND RETURN

Castlereagh could afford to be magnanimous about the economic costs of war. Though defeat, or stalemate, had threatened bankruptcy, victory brought domestic joy and global supremacy. The latter would endure, even if the former was short-lived. In the early summer of 1814, the allied sovereigns and their generals were acclaimed by London crowds on a collective state visit. Thousands of people had picnicked along the Dover road to watch their carriages arrive, and wherever they went they were mobbed by enthusiastic spectators. Some played up to their welcome – Blücher, accompanied by Sir Charles Stewart to translate, became a great favourite for his willingness to drink the health of gatherings and make rabble-rousing speeches.

Others, including the crowned heads, soon found the public attention both wearing and alarming – it was far from the respectful distance that they expected from their own peoples. Even Blücher was jostled by invasive crowds when he went to have his portrait painted by the artist Thomas Lawrence. The Tsar, despite some efforts at serious political conversations – with Whig figures,

Quakers and antislavery activists, for example – showed an unwillingness to acknowledge the public, and an inclination to make disparaging remarks about the sights he was shown, that left an increasingly unsavoury impression.[1]

Behind the scenes, a nasty diplomatic row that combined the marriage plans of the Prince Regent's daughter with Russian rivalry for influence over the Dutch and their soon-to-be-restored colonial empire also soured relations. This was a hint that Alexander's political magnanimity towards France, like Castlereagh's, was based on an assessment of his own strength and freedom of action. If for the British this meant a determination to hold on to global power, for the Russians it meant a free hand to absorb the Grand Duchy of Warsaw and dominate the continental scene. As such tensions rose closer to the surface, the allied leadership began to realise that some serious haggling still remained to be done. A diplomatic congress at Vienna had already been planned, and Metternich had hoped after the signing of the Treaty of Paris that it would be a brief formality – there would be, he wrote home, 'less to negotiate than to ratify' there.[2] But instead the opening of the congress itself was pushed back into the autumn, and it would prove to be an epoch-making marathon.

As the Europeans contemplated the new battles of peace, Britain was still at war. Though the conflict with the United States had never escalated beyond being an unpleasant distraction for the global empire, the early naval defeats had produced considerable anxiety. The honour of the Royal Navy had been salvaged by a remarkable single-ship duel, both noble and horrific, on 1 June 1813. HMS *Shannon*, an undistinguished thirty-eight-gun frigate, but one captained by a dedicated officer, Philip Broke, who for seven years had worked to bring the crew to a fine pitch of perfection in gunnery, set out deliberately to entice an American warship from Boston. Showing itself off the coast without any consorts, the *Shannon* succeeded in inviting an attack from the USS *Chesapeake*, a ship of approximately equal strength, though crewed by men with far less experience of working together. So keen was Broke for the combat that he had gone as far as preparing a formal letter of challenge, promising a single combat 'to try the fortunes of our respective flags'.[3] It did not reach the *Chesapeake*, which had already begun to move out, watched by crowds from on shore, and accompanied by various civilian vessels confident of victory. A dinner was prepared in the city to greet the returning heroes.

About twenty miles offshore, at 5.30 p.m., the two ships met. The *Chesapeake*'s Captain Lawrence encouraged his crew with cries of '*Peacock* her!', recalling another in the Americans' string of victories. Broke's style was quieter, prohibiting cheering after a short address that played on 'the stuff *British* sailors are made of', and ended 'Remember, you have some hundreds of your brother sailors' blood to avenge!'[4] Closing directly, the ships exchanged two broadsides before colliding, leading to a mêlée of attempted boarding and general firing. The opening salvoes of the well-drilled British crew were devastating, but the Americans fought back valiantly.

The decks became a blizzard of shot, splinters and falling debris, within which men fought with the dreadful face-to-face weapons of a boarding action: cutlass, pike and axe. Broke himself led a boarding party, and suffered a serious head wound from an enemy's blade. The ships drifted apart again, but the Americans were demoralised by the loss of their captain, struck by a musket-ball, and overwhelmed by continuing fire from the *Shannon*. In little more than ten minutes the fighting was over, though its close was marked by the tragic slaying of the *Shannon*'s first lieutenant, hit by his own ship's cannon-fire as he struggled to lower the *Chesapeake*'s ensign. The British secured their captured foes with particular ease, one lieutenant noted, 'as the *Chesapeake* had (upon deck) some hundreds of handcuffs in readiness for us'.[5]

Captain Broke's own official letter, written from his hospital bed in Halifax, Nova Scotia five days later, declared that 'No expressions I can make use of can do justice to the merits of my valiant officers and crew', and observed that 'I have to lament the loss of many of my gallant shipmates, but they fell exulting in their conquest.'[6] His own wounds would prevent him ever serving at sea again, though he remained in the navy as a highly regarded gunnery expert, and would die an admiral at a ripe old age. A witness to the captured *Chesapeake*'s arrival in Halifax glossed the aftermath in less conventional terms than those Broke chose. Manned by a hard-pressed prize-crew, the ship still bore the internal marks of what had befallen her:

> The scene was one never to be forgotten by a landsman ... The coils and folds of ropes were steeped in gore as if in a slaughter-house ... Pieces of skin, with pendant hair, were adhering to the sides of the ship; and in one place I noticed portions of fingers protruding, as if thrust through the outer wall of the frigate ... Altogether, it was a scene of devastation as difficult to forget as to describe ...[7]

The ferocity of the fighting can be gauged from the fact that the two small ships between them lost more men in this engagement than the whole British fleet at the Battle of St Vincent, and more than fell on the *Victory* in the carnage of Trafalgar – over ninety dead and well over a hundred wounded, around two-thirds on the American side. Captain Lawrence died of his wounds while the ships were still returning to port, all his lieutenants already having perished in action. He was buried with full military honours, and a sombre sense of the cost of the fight permeated opinion in Halifax, where there was little overt rejoicing. For British opinion, which exulted in the victory in greater safety than Broke's fallen comrades – and which was of course spared confrontation with the butchery involved – it was a price well worth paying to prove their navy's worth. Broke was given a baronetcy, the freedom of the City of London and a 100-guinea ceremonial sword, while his surviving subordinates were promoted.

The end of European combat operations in 1814 brought an immediate effort by the British government to close down the American war. While diplomatic negotiations opened, both sides put forward aggressive claims for territorial and other concessions – showing, in the British case, that their European magnanimity was partly the product of indifference, not virtue, and in the American, a wholly unrealistic appraisal of the continuing economic impact of blockade. British military aggression intensified considerably; some 20,000 troops, many of them Peninsular veterans sailing directly from France, were sent to open a series of new fronts. There was bitter fighting around the Great Lakes through the summer and autumn of 1814. An invasion-thrust into upstate New York was repulsed in September, but British dominance further west was by then almost complete.

Eastwards, along the shoreline of the Chesapeake Bay, British amphibious forces meanwhile operated with near impunity, most famously burning the public buildings of Washington, DC in late August, having captured the White House with places already laid for dinner.[8] A repulse from the defences of Baltimore the following month furnished the Americans with material for their future national anthem, and the destruction in general bred American anger both with their own government and the enemy, making the war more futile and intractable rather than less. As the diplomats, meeting in Holland, slowly worked their way to a treaty that basically declared a no-score draw, a British force of some 6000 launched an over-ambitious attack on the city of New Orleans. Soundly defeated in battle in early January 1815, with fatalities including General Pakenham, Wellington's brother-in-law, the troops had fought a nation with whom peace had already been signed, on 24 December. It was a pointless end to a pointless war.[9]

By the time of the fiasco at New Orleans, another pointless war was brewing. At points through the winter it seemed, indeed, as if Europe would see open conflict between the victorious powers.

Vienna had become a whirlpool of intrigue and espionage – most of the latter political, much of the former sexual. With increasingly tedious ceremonial public events wearying even the stoutest courtiers, everyone from the Tsar downwards seemed to be taking the opportunity to fornicate. Any woman who was remotely attractive was fair game to the aristocratic seducers, and though some resisted firmly, there were many, professionals and amateurs alike, willing to use their sex for financial and social gain. In that respect, they had at least an advantage over the many male petitioners who flocked to the city, who all too often found they had no call whatsoever on the sympathies of the powerful. Thousands of private claims for compensation were afoot. Some represented the grievances of individuals, businesses or estates looted by various rampaging armies, others the fate of the dignitaries of the Holy Roman Empire robbed of their social position by Napoleon's *Rheinbund*. For many there was to be no assistance: not least because when it came to territory, all the powers had their own designs.

Austria was already by the Treaty of Paris guaranteed its old territories in Lombardy, and possession of the Venetian prize granted by General Bonaparte back in 1797. Metternich was happy with the return of various south European provinces swept into the Empire, and content to see the distant Belgian lands become someone else's problem, though he hoped to secure a dominant position in the politics of a future Germany, and a small slice of Poland. Prussia, whose territories had seesawed violently in extent and significance since the 1790s, was insistent on regaining at least some of the Polish territories it had seized in the old century, only to lose in 1807. It also sought a powerful position in western Germany, to counterbalance Austria and insure against French revenge.

Russia, meanwhile, wanted all of the former Grand Duchy of Warsaw, and to be acknowledged as the arbiter of Europe. Nobody else wanted this, and all the Tsar's transparent assurances of goodwill and religious humility could not disguise the dangerously unbalanced nature of the continental settlement Alexander was grasping for. The haggling that ensued was ferocious, and quite literally came down to disputes about how many thousands or hundreds of thousands of people, with their capacity to be taxed and conscripted, should be parcelled out to each power. Calling such figures 'souls' could hardly disguise the material greed, and disregard for anything resembling self-determination, involved. With all this, and the servants paid by the police to go through the waste-paper baskets for information, one can almost understand the resort of rulers, courtiers and diplomats to so many welcoming beds – though, of course, the sex began even before the arguments.

While all this was taking place to the east, France was trying to come to terms with its new master. King Louis XVIII, a hugely corpulent figure with no discernible virtues beyond some old-fashioned good manners, had lumbered into Paris from English exile, and had barely been restrained from taking the country back to the 1780s. Although Talleyrand and other more liberal figures prevented the total repudiation of constitutional rule – on the grounds of the likelihood of civil war – the king and his returning aristocratic advisors insisted that the 'Charter' produced in June 1814 should explicitly state that it was 'granted' by royal grace, not the product of national sovereignty.

Word of plans to refurbish the Palace of Versailles, symbol of absolute monarchy, and possibly even for the king to reside there in future summers, sent a shudder through a generation that still remembered revolutionary liberty and equality. Re-establishment of an aristocratic set of royal Household Troops alienated the still powerful military leadership, while apparently passive acceptance of France's reduced status produced sentiments on the Parisian streets that French arms had been 'betrayed', that the 'natural limit' of the Rhine must be regained, and even that 'at least Belgium will be ours in two years'.[10]

Overt royal Anglophilia, with British visitors accorded special rights of recognition at court in gratitude for their country's hospitality, had by the autumn produced a venomous stream of public satire, and open political abuse, showing that Napoleon's belief in the 'English' as the key enemy was widely shared, and the current humiliation deeply resented. The appointment of Wellington (since May 1814 a duke) as British ambassador to France pleased the Bourbons, whom he had actively welcomed in the south, but few other Frenchmen.[11]

Some were offended by the Duke's casual approach to protocol – once appearing at dinner in a mud-spattered hunting outfit – while others objected to his notorious success with the Parisian ladies. Being a frequent guest of the new dynasty at court, and close advisor to ministers concerned to use British influence against Russia, while also conducting a semi-public affair with the Italian-born Giuseppina Grassini, once Napoleon's official 'First Singer' and lover, made it look to embittered Bonapartists as if Wellington was enjoying far too many of the victor's spoils. Amidst swirling rumours of assassination plots, he was recalled, for his own safety and the stability of the capital, after a few months, though he did not actually leave until January 1815, when it conveniently became necessary for him to take over from Castlereagh as chief British envoy in the Vienna maelstrom.[12]

By the time Wellington left, Bonapartists were actively anticipating their Emperor's return. Aiming for reconciliation, the Bourbons had done little to purge society of Napoleon's followers, even at the higher levels of government. The army was still in the hands of his marshals. The indefatigable Soult had even become War Minister at the end of 1814, claiming a royalist conversion. Some, such as Davout, had retired from the scene, but Ney, 'bravest of the brave', was still on active service, as were Marmont, Masséna, Jourdan, Oudinot and others. Overtly, at least, such men seemed to have made their peace with royalty. The officer corps of the swollen Grand Army had been radically reduced, however, and there were thousands of officers surviving on meagre pensions available to fill the cafés of the capital and elsewhere with seditious talk.

This was seconded in the salons of the formidable hostesses who had ruled society under the Empire, and pined for dazzling greatness to replace the sad mediocrity of Louis XVIII and his aged companions. A leader amongst these was Napoleon's stepdaughter Hortense, who as wife of his brother Louis continued to claim the title of Queen of the Netherlands (despite the Emperor's own dethronement of her husband). In early 1815 Hortense's favourite flower, the violet, became a symbol of Bonapartist expectation – that the blooms which return in the spring would herald the Emperor home.[13]

Napoleon himself brooded through the winter on Elba, surrounded by a thousand of his most faithful troops, but with little else to do but plan new flowerbeds. He was deprived of his wife and child, who had been carefully secured by Austria – in more ways than one, for Marie-Louise was quickly seduced by a handsome aide dispatched for the purpose by Metternich himself. With France refusing to pay the generous pension agreed by the Tsar (and lobbying for him to be moved somewhere more remote and secure), Napoleon had much to be aggrieved at. Given his gambler's approach to war and politics, an escape was all but inevitable, and given the short distances involved, even the nervous watchfulness of the Royal Navy (now of course rapidly being stripped down to peacetime levels) could do nothing to prevent it. On 26 February 1815, the Emperor's British overseer having left for the mainland to consult a doctor, seven small vessels slipped out of harbour. They landed near Fréjus on the French Riviera on 1 March. What followed is summed up in a legendary piece of doggerel:

The Tiger has broken out of his den.
The Monster has been three days at sea.
The Wretch has landed at Fréjus.
The Brigand has arrived at Antibes.
The Invader has reached Grenoble.

The General has entered Lyon.
Napoleon slept last night at Fontainebleau.
The Emperor proceeds to the Tuileries today.
His Imperial Majesty will address his loyal subjects tomorrow.[14]

Although in fact the first days of his advance were cautious, avoiding areas north of Marseille known to be unsympathetic, the progress soon assumed mythic proportions – from the simply dressed Emperor summoning the troops that barred his way to shoot him dead if they wished, via Ney's swiftly broken promise to bring him back in an iron cage, to the fantastical and overnight transformation of Paris into an imperialist city upon his arrival. Scarcely had Louis XVIII vacated his palace to the tears of his loyal servants when Napoleon's retinue returned, their uniforms unpacked and brushed down, to resume their briefly interrupted roles. The *tricoleur* replaced the white Bourbon ensign on every flagpole and steeple. Shop signs were repainted, or merely turned around to reveal their Bonapartist messages, and as the ladies of the imperial court awaited Napoleon's first audience, they busily unpicked royal *fleurs-de-lys* from the carpet under their feet to reveal again the Napoleonic golden bees.[15]

While welcoming, and indeed demanding, this monarchical loyalty, Napoleon also played other political cards. Abolishing the royalist House of Peers (though he was soon to nominate a new one), he banished some prominent returned royalist exiles, played up to a Jacobinical rhetoric against the crowned heads of Europe, and announced a package of liberalising constitutional reforms, the *Acte Additionel*, that were soon approved by plebiscite. Whether they actually meant anything is a moot point, for the Emperor showed no sign of relaxing his firm grip on all the levers of real power, and while making diplomatic noises about peace and contentment, rapidly began rearming France. A regular army of 284,000 was summoned, with 220,000 National Guards in reserve.[16]

Whatever Napoleon might have asserted about hopes for peace, he can have been under little illusion about the allied reaction. The Vienna Congress declared Napoleon an outlaw, who had 'rendered himself subject to public vengeance' by 'again appearing in France with projects of confusion and disorder'.[17] By 12 March, when all that was clearly known was that he had left Elba, Wellington was able to report to London that forces were already mustering to confront him – 150,000 Austrians in Italy, 200,000 Austrian and assorted German troops in the Rhineland, 200,000 Russian troops in reserve, and a mixed British–Dutch–Prussian force in the Netherlands. Wellington's command here had also been agreed.[18] Bickering over exact responsibilities, and the extent to which military commitments might be repaid by diplomatic leverage in the ongoing struggle for a final settlement in Germany, slowed but did not halt the steady accumulation of these forces, as the news from France grew steadily worse. Wellington reached Brussels in early April, to find very few troops and a logistical organisation in disarray. Fortunately, of course, he was just the man to put things right, which he did with weeks of desperate work.

Wellington's army in the 1815 campaign was very far from the well-oiled machine that crossed the Pyrenees. Though he was able to obtain some high-quality units, including battalions of the famous green-jacketed 95th Foot, the Rifles, and a strong detachment of the Guards, few of his troops were real veterans. A significant proportion of the army was made up of those referred to as 'Dutch-Belgians', a product of the takeover of former French territory by the expanded Netherlands state freshly created as a buffer against French expansionism. French-speaking, and in some cases French-uniformed, these troops had been born and raised on soil ruled by France, and their loyalty to a Dutch-speaking dynasty installed over them by Great Power diplomacy was very shaky indeed. A third part of his forces were Hanoverians (including parts of the old King's German Legion), Brunswick and Nassauer Germans – some very good, some entirely raw.

Meanwhile, half the allied strength in the region was composed of Prussian troops who advanced westwards under Marshal Blücher, looting as they came and declaring that all would be paid for by the British. Operating effectively as a separate army, and so chauvinistic that even Saxon troops under their command mutinied in protest (and saw their ringleaders shot), the Prussians had strength in numbers, but little else obviously to recommend them.[19] Their chief of staff, Gneisenau, had been enraged to discover, thanks to Napoleon's mischievous publication of diplomatic correspondence from the previous months, that Britain and the Bourbons had been in agreement to curtail Prussian territorial ambitions. He regarded Wellington as untrustworthy and declined to coordinate plans with him. Fortunately Blücher had no such reservations, being a simple (and indeed illiterate) soldier's soldier with no interest in politics. The Duke thought him a 'very fine fellow', though 'if anything too eager' to hurl his troops into a fight.[20]

Wellington's establishment of his army was further handicapped by the general situation. Outlawing Napoleon was not the same as declaring war, it transpired, which meant that, legally, Militia regiments could not be pressed into overseas service, while some veteran units had to be discharged because their enlistment periods had expired. Various parliamentary manoeuvres were necessary to circumvent such issues, but Wellington only ever received 30,000 of the 40,000 British infantry he sought, and only around 7000 were really experienced. Officers were easier to come by, and indeed so many high-born young men wanted to serve in Napoleon's final drubbing that Wellington had practically to drive them away. Only a last-minute burst of common sense from the Duke of York and the Prince Regent prevented two of their brothers from turning up in Belgium in search of glory.

Fortunately, Wellington was able to secure the services of almost twenty veteran generals, including 'Daddy' Hill and the ferocious Picton – though the latter's lust for battle had given way to premonitions of death, and he is said to have jumped into an open grave to try it for size before departing. As his commander of cavalry – with which he was for once well supplied, none having been shipped to America – Wellington had to accept Lord Uxbridge, promised the post by the Prince Regent. To his credit, Wellington was able to overlook the fact that Uxbridge had eloped with the wife of his brother Henry Wellesley in 1809, the two divorcing their respective spouses to marry the following year. He was more concerned with the fact that Uxbridge, despite performing brilliantly during the retreat to Corunna, had not seen active service for six years.[21]

There seems never to have been any doubt that Napoleon would strike north first. A crushing blow to the United Netherlands could shatter that kingdom, returning the Belgian provinces to their French loyalties, and providing a stark warning to the other powers, who might back off to safeguard central Europe.[22] Pushing Wellington's men into the sea also had great attraction. In emotional terms, was 'England' not, as always, the great enemy? But neither in practical terms could Wellington's forces be allowed to remain in place, so close to the roads to Paris, if France was to have a chance of beating off the huge attacks beginning to roll in from the east.[23]

By the end of May, the imperial cause had already suffered one decisive defeat in that direction. Murat, rediscovering his French loyalties (and perhaps fearing that dethronement would follow further French defeat, Metternich's promises notwithstanding), had risen from his throne as King of Naples as soon as the escape became known, leading 40,000 raw troops north and issuing proclamations of Italian liberation. He got as far north as the Po valley, but with supporters failing to rally, was driven back over a hundred miles south and decisively defeated at Tolentino on 3 May. Always brave, always stupid, Murat had to flee back to Naples, and then by sea to the south of France, where an infuriated Napoleon ordered him to remain, as Italy was secured for the allied advance.[24]

A speedy move in the north was thus essential. Wellington feared that the Emperor would seek to outflank the allied position to the west, cutting them off from seaborne reinforcements and supplies, and possibly capturing Louis XVIII, who sat with his court in exile in Ghent. With little knowledge of French movements – the state of semi-war did not allow for full-scale cavalry reconnaissance across the frontier – the allied armies were strung across a front of over fifty miles, and would take days to concentrate. Prussian reluctance to cooperate meant that initial reports on 13 June of campfires across the border were not passed on speedily, and when the French did breach the frontier near Charleroi on 15 June, Wellington famously proclaimed that he had been 'humbugged'.

News reached the Duke in the legendary setting of the Duchess of Richmond's Ball in Brussels, where the cream of his young officers had assembled to be courted by the miniature version of London society that had gathered there in the previous weeks.[25] Some would march to battle in their dancing pumps, for there was now no time to lose. Rather than operate on a flank, Napoleon was striking at the centre, the other of his two signature campaigning moves. Storming the 'seam' between the allied forces, the French would punch left and right, shifting focus to keep a local superiority until first one, then both wings of the enemy were overwhelmed and broken. That was the plan, and all the action of the next four days was about preventing it coming to pass.

Napoleon's first strike was against the Prussians. After a rearguard action on the 15th, the next day the main Prussian force stood to receive the French attack at Ligny. Wellington visited the Prussian leaders as they stood waiting, their troops arrayed on a forward slope, open to enemy bombardment. The Duke tried tactfully to point this out, but Gneisenau retorted that 'My men like to see their enemy.'[26] Marshal Grouchy's French right-wing corps was reinforced by Napoleon in personal command of the Guard and cavalry reserves. Many of the Prussian forces were poorly trained militias, and did indeed suffer grievously at the hands of the French artillery, but they showed their fighting spirit in a stiff day-long engagement that required the commitment of the Emperor's final reserve, the Old Guard, to break their resistance. Marshal Blücher, personally leading a desperate cavalry counter-attack, fell from his wounded horse and was ridden over by both sides before his aides could carry him, semi-conscious, to safety. Battle raged until eight in the evening before the Prussians began a staged withdrawal, and the rearguard was still in place on the morning of the 17th, with the French reluctant to press them. Theoretically, the first of Napoleon's hammer-blows had fallen according to plan, but his simultaneous left jab had collided awkwardly with a cautiously wielded glove.

Marshal Ney, *le brave des braves*, but like Murat not always the most intelligent of commanders, led the French left-flank corps towards the British-led forces on the morning of 16 June. His job was to push through the strategic crossroads of Quatre Bras and advance a further ten miles or so, which would open a clear gap between the allied armies. With Wellington still concerned about his westward flank, and therefore reluctant to order his troops to concentrate close to the Prussians, this was a distinct possibility. Indeed, it required some prudent disobedience – ironically, from some 'unreliable' Dutch-Belgian officers – to begin to gather forces at Quatre Bras in sufficient numbers to resist the French. In rolling countryside, with head-high cornfields and scattered woodlands, the French could not be sure of how large an enemy they faced, and Ney was reluctant to commit his full strength.

In fact he outnumbered the initial allied forces by at least two, and some sources suggest three, to one, but combat was not joined until around 2 p.m., by which time substantial British reinforcements were on the march. Throughout the afternoon, new contingents continually arrived, and were fed into a developing line of battle. The Duke himself, after his meeting with the Prussians, had arrived by 4 p.m., and took charge of a long evening of seesaw action that eventually involved over 20,000 French and 35,000 allied troops. Fierce French cavalry charges cost one regiment its precious 'colour', but in general looming dusk saw the forces held more or less where the battle had opened, with around 4000 casualties on both sides.

Ney's advance had faltered, but as news of the Prussian misfortunes at Ligny reached Wellington, he had no option but to pull back, or risk being outflanked by the advancing enemy to the east. The day's action overall was therefore almost a success for the French, for Wellington's forces withdrew along the main road to Brussels, which diverged slowly but distinctly from the Prussians' line of retreat to Wavre. Within twenty-four hours, the allied armies were almost twice as far apart as they had been. The 17th was a day of regrouping for them, though not for Napoleon. He marched his main force to join Ney, and sought to launch an attack on the Quatre Bras position, only to find it abandoned. A rearguard skirmish was all that ensued as the French came forward, before a violent summer rainstorm began to sweep across the landscape, stifling action. Napoleon's right wing, under Grouchy, continued in pursuit of the Prussians.

Historians have argued ever since about this march, which was covered by vague orders and executed without particular vigour, but like many aspects of the battle to come, it reflected the difficulties of making war. Regardless of his image as a genius, some of Napoleon's own greatest victories had been achieved almost by accident, and at other occasions, such as Borodino, he had shown himself capable of indolence, inertia and weak judgment. No special explanation is needed for the fact that the Prussians were able to reach Wavre unmolested, and from there could turn west along a major road to join Wellington. If it had been down to Gneisenau, they might not have done so. The determination of Blücher, fortunately recovered from his fall, to send help to his ally was decisive. Wellington was informed by note early on the morning of the 18th that the Prussians would be coming, which confirmed him in his intention to give battle. The only real question was when they would arrive.

The battlefield that would become known as Waterloo had been reconnoitred by the Duke en route to his Paris embassy almost a year before. It was a classic reverse-slope defensive position, like those he had used at Bussaco and Talavera. A low ridge ran across the Brussels road defining the northern edge of a compact battle-field, with woods and settlements fringing it, and the latter providing strongpoints for flanking detachments. Wellington's west-ern wing was further strengthened by the manor house and walled gardens of Hougoumont, which were rapidly turned into a minia-ture fortress, while his centre was marked by a smaller farm at La Haye Sainte and a disused sand quarry, to both of which he posted elite detachments, including the Rifles.

His eastern wing was relatively weak, though screened by ground waterlogged by the overnight rains, and the garrisoned village of Papelotte. It was from this direction that he expected the Prussians, of course, hopefully no later than midday. Gneisenau, however, made this impossible by deciding to send the relatively fresh Prussian IV Corps towards Waterloo first – which meant passing it, and its artillery, through the rest of the army, and through the clogged streets of Wavre itself, where the outbreak of a fire ham-pered movement further. Unknown to Wellington, this delay set the stage for some of the most intense hours of combat that even the most experienced observers present had seen.

The Battle of Waterloo has been recounted innumerable times. As a fount of martial legends, and bitter national historiographical disputes, it has few equals.[27] In literature, Lord Byron, Victor Hugo, Stendhal and Thackeray, Sir Arthur Conan Doyle and Sir Walter Scott each refought it to their different artistic purposes, and it has been reduced to a series of dramatic snapshots, where truth and myth are difficult to disentangle. Napoleon's opening orders for the battle were simple – two corps, d'Erlon's and Reille's, were to advance on the village of Mont Saint-Jean, keeping in parallel, and overwhelm the British line. To facilitate this, the advanced position of Hougoumont was to be stormed by a subsidiary division under the Emperor's brother Jérôme. Napoleon himself spent most of the day back from the actual battlefield, delegating immediate control to Ney – thus he was unaware that Wellington's main line was actually forward from the village, and his personal orders had little impact on the development of the main attacks on this line.

One aspect he could see was the attack on Hougoumont, and he continued to pour resources into it as allied resistance, led by British Guards troops, repulsed the initial attacks before noon. At one point a storming party of Frenchmen was inside the courtyard of the house, before the gates were forced shut by a desperate press of Guardsmen. Despite shellfire setting it ablaze, the house was held through the day as artillery from both sides pounded the struggling troops. Some 14,000 French were engaged there, though it took almost as many allies to support the small initial garrison and hold open the lane north from the house. What began as a small clearing operation became a major part of the battle.

Reille's corps was essentially caught up around Hougoumont, while to its east what should have been half the main attack against the ridge, launched by d'Erlon's corps, went in alone at around 1 p.m. Napoleon's main artillery battery could only engage the ridge at extreme, and thus inaccurate, range, and many cannonballs sank into the wet ground rather than rolling on to hit the allied lines. With much of Wellington's strength concealed on the reverse slope, d'Erlon, who had met this tactic in Spain, avoided over-commitment to column attacks. Instead his battalions advanced in lines, but in ranks one behind another, so that, as they made contact, the rear battalions could be fanned out to open fire. In this way, several Dutch-Belgian formations posted as a first line were driven back, and the farmhouse at La Haye Sainte was nearly surrounded. General Picton's troops were lying down behind the ridge and leapt up to engage the advancing enemy, but even they were hard-pressed. Picton, eccentrically costumed in a top hat, was shot and killed as he led a desperate counter-attack.

Now came another great legendary moment. Lord Uxbridge ordered the two British heavy cavalry brigades, the 'Household brigade' of four regiments of mounted Guards, and the 'Union brigade' of the Royals, Scots Greys and (Irish) Inniskillings, to crest the ridge and charge to the relief of the infantry. Mounted on heavy horses superior to anything remaining on the war-ravaged continent, this attack was devastatingly effective. The Household brigade hammered through a French infantry brigade, and even routed a flanking formation of armoured cuirassier cavalry. The Union brigade did even better, smashing three infantry brigades and capturing two regimental eagles. Charging onwards, the Scots Greys crossed the battlefield and drove away the gunners from Napoleon's main battery of artillery. But they had no equipment to destroy or even damage the guns, and found themselves counter-charged by superior forces of French cuirassiers and lancers. Though not massacred as some accounts depict, and indeed able to reform and perform more defensive charges against French cavalry later, the 'heavies' suffered major casualties. But they had saved the line.

By now it was around 4 p.m., and the first formations of Prussian troops had become visible to the east. At first there was a hope amongst the French that these were Grouchy's troops, but orders for them to join the battle had not yet reached them (a source of much later recrimination). Discovery amongst the ranks that these were Prussians, and not the promised reinforcements, was a factor in claims of betrayal that marked the latter stages of the battle. Meanwhile, Napoleon committed his last reserves of line infantry to hold them off, and Ney opened the next phase of the epic. The hard-pressed British lines were marked, even from a distance, by a fluctuating trickle of casualties to the rear, and in one of its larger eddies Ney thought he saw the beginnings of a retreat.

At once he sent a corps of heavy cavalry forward, later reinforced with two more and the cavalry of the Imperial Guard, in a series of charges that would seem to swirl around the allied troops for hours. The infantry formed squares, and were initially impregnable to the horsemen, who died by the hundred. Immobile, however, the squares were unable to give mutual support beyond their own musket range, and rallied French infantry succeeded at last in storming La Haye Sainte, threatening to open up the allied centre. Moreover, eventually Ney ordered forward his horse artillery, which was able to blast the pinned formations at short range. It was the textbook response to the situation, and it had a textbook effect. The 27th Foot, the Inniskillings, reputedly died to a man, the battalion lying in perfect formation. Two other battalions were pounded so hard they had to merge to keep their defences intact. Across the field, the allies were now definitively hard-pressed. Wellington rode the lines, as he had all day, shuffling reserves into place, adjusting his deployments with finesse, and now above all demanding of officers and men alike that they continue to hold out. A reckless advance now would only deliver them into the guns of the French.

The Prussians were at last arriving in strength. Some 30,000 were already in action by late afternoon, especially around the village of Plancenoit, directly to the east of the French starting positions, and thus ideally positioned as a springboard to envelop them. As well as his infantry reserve, Napoleon had to commit units of the Young Guard, and even several battalions of the Middle Guard, to keep the fight for the village on a knife-edge. Other Prussian forces arrived closer to Wellington's lines, and by around 7 p.m. the French were seriously stretched, still barred from Hougoumont, and with their battlefield positions running from there in a tight curve north-east to La Haye Sainte and Papelotte, then sharply south to Plancenoit.

In Wellington's army, things were equally finely poised. Under continual pressure of artillery fire and menacing cavalry, some of his less reliable units, including a whole brigade of raw Bruns-wickers, made for the rear in disarray. As well as his customary battlefield roving – and he had seemed, as always, to be every-where, and always at the decisive moment – Wellington had to order his light cavalry reserves to stand behind the infantry lines in close order to block further routs. It was time for the last gambler's throw. The remainder of the Middle Guard, with the last few battalions of the Old Guard in reserve, marched stoically towards the centre of Wellington's line, intent on achieving on the battlefield what the larger campaign had signally failed to do: split Wellington's and Blücher's armies apart and send them reeling away from each other.

At first the attacks seemed to succeed. Two grenadier battalions pushed through the allied first line, but then were counter-attacked by an entire division of Dutch troops, and pounded by artillery. Only after this and a bayonet charge with overwhelming numbers did they fall back. Two Guard chasseur battalions, meanwhile, crested the ridge in the face of the British Guards, who rose up, fired their customary volleys and charged with the bayonet. For a moment this seemed decisive, but support from a third chasseur battalion turned the tables and the British Guards themselves fell back, until a flank attack with bullet and bayonet from the 52nd Light Infantry completed the rout.

Wellington had been on the spot for the whole exchange, alerting the Guards' commander with the terse cry 'Now's your time,' before personally ordering the troops to stand and fire.[28] As the nearby battalions followed the retreating enemy, the Duke again took a rapid survey of the battlefield. The retreating Guards had sent a visible shockwave through the remaining French – never before had they failed. This might be the tipping point. To the east there were suddenly signs of intensified fighting – the Prussians had broken through and the French were in retreat. 'Oh, dammit,' he muttered. 'In for a penny, in for a pound!'[29] Standing in his stirrups, he waved his hat three times and signalled a general advance. The battle was not yet over, but it was won.

EPILOGUE

Forty thousand men lay dead and wounded on the field of Waterloo, as scavenging locals and those victorious soldiers neither too exhausted nor too squeamish began to loot them. Amongst the few who tried to give aid to the injured in those awful hours was Sir Sidney Smith, Napoleon's 'English Pirate', who had thwarted him at Acre in 1799 and was now present, as a tourist, to see his final downfall. He had been one of the very first to congratulate Wellington on his victory, before turning his attention to casualties on both sides.[1]

Meanwhile, returned to his Spartan headquarters, Wellington snatched at sleep in the brief summer darkness, having twice escaped injury in the past few hours. The first time is legendary: he was beside Lord Uxbridge when a cannonball shot past him and smashed the latter's leg. Uxbridge cried out 'By God! I've lost my leg.' Wellington's terse response – 'Have you, by God?' – might have owed something to their family history, but he had supported the collapsing general until help arrived. The second time was ironic: his horse, the doughty Copenhagen, had aimed a vicious kick at him in return for a pat on the rump after he finally dismounted, and only narrowly missed.[2]

At 3 a.m. the Duke was awoken by his staff surgeon John Hume

with the news that a favourite aide, Alexander Gordon, had just suc-
cumbed to his wounds. So ferocious had been the action around
Wellington, and so frantic the business of relaying orders, that
almost all his personal staff were killed or wounded. He held the
doctor's hand as he listened to a list of the casualties that had
arrived over the last few hours, and Hume felt tears falling on his
fingers. Brushing them away from his still sweat-grimed face, the
Duke in a broken voice said, 'Well, thank God, I don't know what
it is to lose a battle; but certainly nothing can be more painful
than to gain one with the loss of so many of one's friends.'[3]

No more than twenty miles away, Napoleon also wept as he
contemplated the ruin of his ambitions. Over the next few days,
he attempted to rally his forces, but the will to listen to him had
gone. The arch-survivors Talleyrand and Fouché – 'vice, leaning
on the arm of crime' – joined forces to muster political opposition.[4] His own marshals, including Ney, argued for Napoleon's
downfall in the Paris legislature, and he abdicated on 22 June.[5]
With the allies refusing an armistice, Napoleon became something ever closer to a fugitive, heading first south towards the
capital, then west ahead of the vengeful Prussians who had taken
charge of the pursuit. Paris capitulated on 3 July, allied troops
entered formally on the 7th, and Louis XVIII returned the next
day. The remnants of the Bonapartist army retreated behind the
Loire, the dogged Marshal Davout keeping them together by
main force as he tried to negotiate a political amnesty for himself
and others. Nobody was listening, however, and on 14 July – final
symbolic humiliation – the last remnant of everything that had
followed from the Revolution of 1789 submitted to royal
authority.[6]

By this time Napoleon was in the western port of Rochefort,
negotiating desperately with British naval forces off the coast for a
safe passage, preferably to America. Unsurprisingly, they did not
yield, and on the 15th the former Emperor surrendered to the captain of the seventy-four-gun battleship HMS *Bellerophon*. This was

an entirely fitting vessel for the job, a veteran of the Glorious First of June in 1794, and of both the Nile and Trafalgar. Hard fighting at Aboukir Bay had seen her captain Henry Darby wounded along with 147 of his shipmates, and 49 killed. At Trafalgar she was heavily engaged in Collingwood's division, losing her then captain John Cooke and 26 other men killed, with 123 wounded. Now she was captained by Frederick Maitland, one of the extensive Scots family that also included Thomas, governor of Malta and conqueror of the Luddites. Captain Maitland as a dashing young officer had volunteered to command a boat detachment during the 1801 invasion of Egypt, and saw action at the decisive battle where Sir Ralph Abercromby perished. Ship and captain alike were drawing long histories of service and valour to a close when General Bonaparte stepped aboard.[7]

Audacious to the last, Napoleon sent through Maitland a message to the British government, declaring that he had 'closed his political career' and wished 'to throw myself upon the hospitality of the British people'. Though this met with guffaws in Cabinet, his claim to 'put myself under the protection of their laws' was not without problems for them.[8] As the *Bellerophon* lay at anchor first in Torbay, and then in Plymouth harbour, Sir Francis Burdett was only narrowly dissuaded by political friends from seeking a writ of habeas corpus for Napoleon's release – he was, after all, charged with no crime in law, so why was he held?

The Whig circles around Charles James Fox's nephew Lord Holland were vocal in their continuing sympathy for a man they had always proclaimed as peace-loving and misunderstood. A summons for him to appear as a witness in a London libel trial was actually issued, though strict naval instructions to prevent all visitors to the ship stopped it being served. However, such actions remained those of an isolated fringe. Despite great popular curiosity to see the man so often represented as a demon in human form – reportedly on occasions as many as ten thousand people in small boats swarmed around the ship – there was no widespread movement of sympathy for him, and no great outcry when the decision was quickly taken to ship him off to Saint Helena.[9]

While Napoleon suffered the mild personal indignities of genteel captivity, the country that had rallied to him was ravaged. In the weeks after Waterloo, 1.2 million troops (including a substantial cohort of late-coming and opportunistic Spaniards) poured across its borders, and all demanded to be fed and lodged at French expense. One of the first things the Prussian army did upon reaching Paris was to demand 100 million francs, and 110,000 sets of new clothes and boots for its men.[10] The Musée Royale in the Louvre was pillaged by official order, all the goodwill of 1814 towards its artistic unity long evaporated. Only the personal plea of Louis XVIII, and a guard of British soldiers, stopped the Prussians from blowing up the Pont d'Iéna that celebrated their 1806 humiliation. Russian Cossacks again watered their horses in the Seine, and their angry demands for quick service in the city's bars gave the French a new word, *bistrot!*

Not all the damage was done by foreigners, as the resurgent Jacobin rhetoric of Napoleon's return prompted a sudden outburst of counter-revolutionary revenge upon his fall. Dozens of men were hunted down and slaughtered for their opinions, especially in the south-east, as a royalist 'White Terror' revived memories of the 1790s. A newly elected ultra-royalist legislature, nicknamed the *Chambre introuvable*, as one would never find its like again, had to be dissolved the following year, lest its efforts to bring back the Old Regime bring civil war instead. Napoleon's marshals, whose conduct in 1815 had been variable, to say the least, were whipped into line by the arrest in August of Marshal Ney. Tried for treason on 6 December, he was allowed the next day to give his own firing squad the order to shoot. The equally brave, though undeniably stupid, Joachim Murat had done the same in distant Calabria two months earlier, after a final futile attempt to raise the population.

There would be new haggling at Vienna before the end of the

year. As a result France would shrink a little more on the map, and the institutions created to control Europe – a German Confederation dominated by Metternich's beady-eyed Austria, and a 'Congress System' of international meetings – would be a little more finely tuned against the possibility of liberal subversion than they might have been without the Jacobinism of 1815. Russia was able to pose for a while as the 'Gendarme of Europe', its forces poised in their new Polish outposts to resist any threat to order. In the longer term, however, Russian inability to match the accelerating pace of industrial change would render its claims to hegemony ever more hollow. Despite the oversight of Metternich and the Tsars, Europe entered an age of revolutions and ideological conflict even more turbulent than that provoked by the ambitions of General Bonaparte.

For the nation that clung to that disrespectful form of address, Waterloo was the climax of a great epic. Despite all the setbacks, and occasional disasters, of the past decade, the British Army had never been defeated in open battle by the forces of the Empire. Now, in what Wellington called 'the nearest run thing you ever saw in your life', the triumph was complete.[11] News of the victory had reached London in appropriately dramatic fashion. The officer who brought Wellington's dispatch to the city on 21 June sought out Castlereagh and found him at dinner at his neighbour's house, with Prime Minister Liverpool and the Prince Regent also present. He could thus cast the two French eagle standards he was carrying at royal feet and announce the great triumph, then wave the same captive colours as the Prince was acclaimed by the cheers of a gathering crowd, stepping out on to the balcony to choruses of 'God Save the King!'[12]

Regency England was at its zenith in those moments. The phrase – vastly more common in use than 'Regency Britain' – sums up an age that is mostly known for the images of its culture. The baroque swirls of the Georgian era, in everything from men's hair to chair-legs, are replaced by straight lines and a particularly refined sense of neoclassical order. Women wear light shift dresses that gather under the bust, abandoning (temporarily at least) centuries of corsetry, and put up their hair in styles that recall Roman cameos. Men, under the influence of the Regent's favourite man of fashion, Beau Brummell, opt for close-fitting jackets and long trousers. Such 'dandies' reject the effeminacy of the old century's fops in favour of a more restrained, more modern masculinity. The novels of Jane Austen, meanwhile, portray a society of order and hierarchy, notoriously never allowing the years of war to ruffle their surface.

Like the apparent adulation of the Prince Regent in those moments on the evening of 21 June 1815, all this is a misleading façade. As we have already seen, Jane Austen was nothing if not familiar with the wider conduct of the war, and her novels have profound subtexts of social engagement. The wider Regency culture, too, is full of complexities and contradictions. Supposed neoclassical elegance in ladies' dress – borrowed in the first place from the French 'Empire style' – evolved in pitiable isolation from European norms, and often meant in practice a fashion for the outrageously gaudy and gauzy. Prince Schwarzenberg, on first meeting the eminently respectable Lady Castlereagh, was driven to record in astonishment how someone so 'very fat' could dress 'so *young*, so *tight*, so *naked*'. At least one party of English tourists in liberated Geneva were confined to their hotel by the authorities, for fear that the women's indecent garments would cause a riot. A French observer of British women at the Congress of Vienna was blunt: their 'ridiculous costumes' were of an 'extreme indecency ... so tight that every shape is exactly drawn ... open in front down to the stomach'. Another noted that skirts worn 'a couple of fingers below the knee' made noblewomen look like circus performers or prostitutes.[13]

Brummell's dandies, meanwhile, were aping military dress in their new fashions, and their style of masculinity, when they escaped from ladies' drawing-rooms, was far from refined. Watching, and gambling on, bare-knuckle boxing was one of their favourite pursuits – such pugilism itself was lauded in one best-selling publication as 'the manly art of Boxing, [which] has infused that heroic courage, blended with humanity, into the hearts of Britons, which has made them so renowned, terrific, and triumphant, in all parts of the world'.[14] Humanity was not always obvious in the descriptions of famous fights to be found in the pages of this *Boxiana*, first published in 1810, and frequently updated and reprinted in the following years. Rather it often seemed to glory in the descriptions of men pummelling each other for an hour or more, with sometimes the final ten or dozen 'rounds' being an unresisted assault on an exhausted and defenceless opponent.

When the fashionable young men of 'the Fancy' that followed boxing were not watching someone 'tap the claret' from another's face, they were likely to be betting on horse races, cock fights or cards, or perhaps frolicking with any of the tens of thousands of prostitutes for which London had been notorious for decades. Some of these men might be military officers on leave (the Navy kept a far tighter rein on its young lieutenants), but many were simply running through parental allowances, or building up debts in the expectation of an inheritance – a type, again, well known in the pages of Austen. Beau Brummell himself went bankrupt in 1816, and had to flee to France – now available once more as a refuge – to avoid debtor's prison. He and his ilk were perhaps not hypocrites in their pleasures, but they managed to hold a distinguished place in a society which otherwise practised hypocrisy on a monumental scale. The year before Brummell's flight, Emma Hamilton had died penniless in Calais, shunned by an establishment that had lauded Nelson's memory, but ignored his wishes for the security of the great love of his life.

At the pinnacle of this society was George, the Prince Regent, who had assumed that role in 1811 at the age of forty-eight.[15] Flattered by court painters who gave him a strong chin, a firm profile and curling romantic locks, he was in fact an obese monster, addicted to brandy and laudanum, indifferent to public duties, and tyrannical to his family. Throughout his life he was profligate in expenditure, and while this made him one of the age's great connoisseurs of interior design and art, it also shaped his image as a decadent spendthrift callously unconcerned by the waves of economic suffering that swept across the country. His vanity had much to do with the changes in fashion he helped to lead. High military-style collars hid his double chins, while pantaloons and dark jackets softened the impact of his bulk. His self-regard, and coterie of flatterers, allowed him to shamelessly harass his estranged wife with charges of sexual misconduct, while himself squiring a string of mistresses. His position also permitted him to be somewhat more elevated in his selection than his brother the Duke of York (and far more so than the notorious Richard Wellesley): an overlapping series of companions from the 1790s onwards included the Countess of Jersey, the Marchioness of Hertford and the Marchioness Conyngham.

What, meanwhile, of the king lauded in 1809 as 'Our Geordie'? Almost blind, increasingly deaf, alternating between mere alienation and raving mania, he was secluded at Windsor Castle. Denounced by Luddite pamphlets as 'a Silly Old Man', who with his 'Son more silly and their Rogueish Ministers' put a 'hateful Yoke' upon the country, his ambitions to make the monarchy the moral centre of the country seemed to have died along with his reason. The last few years of his life, as the country wrestled to come to terms with peace, saw Luddism revive at the end of 1816 in the Midlands, at the same time as straggling bands of revolutionaries in London used the cover of mass meetings of the disaffected to attempt an assault on the Tower of London. In 1817, government agents provocateurs produced the conviction of a forlorn group of deluded Derbyshire insurrectionaries for their abortive 'Pentrich Rising' – evidence to establishment eyes that harsh measures, including the suspension once more of habeas corpus, had been justified.

Those laws also produced the 'March of the Blanketeers', in which several hundred distressed Lancashire weavers set out from Manchester to bring a petition to the Prince Regent in London. Attacked by cavalry even as they set off, all had been rounded up as vagrants and potential subversives within days. Discontent festered, and democratic demands rose, until the great demonstration on St Peter's Field in Manchester on 16 August 1819. With over 60,000 people in attendance, gathered from all across the north-west, it was a huge expression of popular, but disciplined (and indeed festive) dissent and demands for change.[16] Charged down by yeomanry and regular cavalry, who killed over a dozen and wounded hundreds, it was dubbed within days the 'Peterloo Massacre', ironic tribute to the great victory four years earlier that seemed to have brought so little good to the common people.

One final grim chain linked old King George to the democrats and radicals that had dogged the crown for decades. His death in January 1820 was seized upon by some of the same revolutionaries who had attempted a London insurrection in 1816. Now, in the uncertain moments of succession, they plotted to murder the Cabinet and execute a *coup d'état*. Betrayed by spies before they had even begun (and with the whole plan being more or less a provocation by the authorities), these 'Cato Street Conspirators' were rounded up, tried, hanged and beheaded. They provided convenient retrospective justification for a swathe of repressive legislation against everything from the expression of dissident opinion to the drilling of potential rebel soldiers, rammed through Parliament at the end of 1819.[17]

Public and political attention swiftly passed to the elaborate and grotesquely public efforts of the new King George IV to divorce his long-suffering wife through a parliamentary bill – effectively a public trial of her morals which also occasioned sharp comment on his own. Narrowly passed, but subsequently withdrawn by government under pressure of public contempt, this led to the extraordinary spectacle the following year of the titular Queen of the United Kingdom of Great Britain and Ireland being physically barred from her husband's coronation.[18] There seemed almost literally no end to the discontents and degradations of the era.

From another perspective, however, all this was a mere passing distraction. By 1820 the political class had long accustomed itself to an indolent ruling figure, and probably felt it was a better situation than to have a king who was either an erratic meddler or an autocrat of Napoleon's or Tsar Alexander's type. The history of popular protest and its brutal suppression is shocking and tragic, and a firm reminder that there was no consensus about national community or social peace in these years, but despite the radicals' best efforts it simply did not move the country at large (things would be different a decade later, when the middle classes finally decided that their wealth merited the franchise). In crude material terms, and despite some violent short-term fluctuations, Britain remained the richest country in the world, and through these years continued to extend both its technological lead in industrialisation and its grip on an expanding global empire.

Moreover, the experience of the wars had been crucial in cementing a new role for the aristocracy in this advancing superpower society. One in ten of the country's 500 leading families had a member at Waterloo, and three-quarters of such families had at least one member who served in the wars.[19] Out of this practical commitment – and remembering that blue blood splashed as red as any other on the battlefield, and officers were killed and wounded in higher proportions than their men – the nobility and gentry of the United Kingdom forged a case for themselves as not merely the historic, but the modern, ruling elite.

The Duke of Wellington stands as a symbol of this, becoming an unshakeable bastion of the developing 'Tory' party, and having throughout his career exerted himself to promote men who were both talented and socially distinguished. When he became Prime Minister in 1828, his Cabinet held three other men who had been Peninsular generals – including his quartermaster-general, Sir

George Murray, as Secretary for War, and the architect of the Portuguese contribution, now Viscount Beresford, as Master-General of Ordnance. The Cabinet also included other marks of institutional and familial continuity – the Earl of Aberdeen who had been a diplomat on campaign in 1813–14, and the son of Henry Dundas, Pitt's great imperialist colleague.

At junior ministerial rank could be found the son of Charles Stewart, the *beau sabreur* of anti-Napoleonic diplomacy, and the younger brother of the Duke of Beaufort, one of Wellington's favourite aides-de-camp, along with the son of former Prime Minister Spencer Perceval. Outside Parliament, 'Daddy' Hill, now Viscount Hill, who had seconded Wellington so often on campaign, took over from him as commander-in-chief of the Army. Ireland, Canada, Cape Colony, New South Wales, Mauritius and of course India were ruled over by veteran generals, men from a class that had distinguished itself by its service, and now took the rewards, and the continuing burdens, of imperial power.[20] At lower levels – resident officers in the Colonial Service, 'emigration officers' dealing with movements to Canada, Australia and New Zealand, even chief constables in the new police forces of mid-century (the first Commissioner of the Metropolitan Police was a Peninsular and Waterloo veteran) – the army and navy built up before 1815 provided a generational leadership cohort of thousands who would shepherd the institutions of state and empire for the next half-century.[21]

That empire had grown dramatically in the years of war. While the French and Dutch got most of their Caribbean colonies back at the peace, the former lost Mauritius and its strategic Indian Ocean ports to Britain, and the latter were definitively deprived of the Cape, and of Ceylon (where Trincomalee offered the best deep-water port for hundreds of miles around). The Dutch did get Java and the Spice Islands back, but not before British commercial interests had been permitted the time and space to decisively penetrate South-east Asian markets (in particular with Indian opium), and to lay the groundwork for eventual dominion over Malaya, and the island fortress city of Singapore.

Britain meanwhile consolidated its position in the Mediterranean, confirming its hold on Malta, and taking control for a further decade of the Ionian Islands, the 'Septinsular Republic' over which France and Russia had contested in the 1790s. This marked the start of a slow process of encroachment on the Ottoman Empire, shortly to go further with support for Greek independence, and ultimately to result a century later in complete regional dominance. Here, and in Africa, all the imperialism of the later nineteenth century was in a very real sense merely filling in the gaps in a global network firmly outlined before 1815.[22]

The work that Wellington and his brother Wellesley had done to begin a new phase of British expansion in India had also continued apace. Here 1815 did not even register a pause in a process of territorial conquest and political aggrandisement that was rapidly becoming self-sustaining.[23] Mere weeks before the Battle of Waterloo, tens of thousands of British troops had driven Gurkha forces from neighbouring princedoms in the foothills of the Himalayas, a 'liberation' that brought those regions' rulers under firm (and expensive) 'protection'. Nine months later, the Gurkha kingdom itself was brought to a peace treaty that yielded up half its territory, as well as its troops as British auxiliaries. Meanwhile, after a decade of uneasy peace, the Marathas were again confronted (indeed provoked), and finally subjugated, in a series of campaigns that lasted through into 1819. Although many territories in central India remained nominally independent after these events, the absolute dominance of British power everywhere east and south of Delhi was now clear.

Such wars were presented by the imperial elite as 'absolutely necessary ... measures of self-defence'. Their view of the native 'Predatory Powers' of the region was that 'We owe our security to the dread of our power alone.'[24] Even ten years after Waterloo, the veteran diplomat and general Sir David Ochterlony – who in his personal life was noted for his love of all things Indian – reported that gaining 'consent' to British rule in India meant in practice establishing 'a belief in the governed that the Wisdom, Resources, but above all, the Military strength of the Rulers, remains unexhausted and invincible'.[25] Such ideas, fostered in the atmosphere of conflict against Napoleon, provided not merely a justification, but an entire ideology of rule.

A revival of an aristocratic sense of imperial mission had begun in the aftermath of the disastrous loss of the American colonies. A new generation of leaders identified the problems of the 'old' imperialism, with its focus on trade and settlement, as an absence of moral leadership. This had led to a series of failings: an excessive focus on self-enrichment from individuals who were supposed to be in command, in the East India Company in particular; a proliferation of quasi-republican governmental arrangements, in North America notably, encouraging fissiparous tendencies; a general attention to short-term mercantile gain at the expense of social order, stability and development.[26] Many of these criticisms could be made from a liberal or radical direction, but in this instance they came from men intent on reviving a conservative sense of hierarchy and duty, while blending this with a pragmatic commitment to economic modernisation.[27]

Some aspects of the reforming drive were self-consciously backward-looking in their adherence to monarchy and hierarchy. Sir Thomas Maitland became in 1818 the first Grand Master of the Order of Saint Michael and Saint George, created in Britain's new Mediterranean dominions to provide a chivalric reward for public service. In the cathedral at Valletta, meanwhile, he kept the throne of the Grand Master of the Knights of Malta vacant for the absent King George.[28] Other aspects were forward-looking – earlier in the century Wellesley had created a college in India to train incoming British administrators how to look after their territories professionally, and rein in the debauchery to which many young Company employees were prone.

Couching such innovations in terms of the 'habitual dissipation and corruption of the people of India' revealed the sharp racial as well as social hierarchies at work, as did Maitland's reluctance to agree the creation of a 'Hellenic University' in the Ionian Islands – though one was founded, in 1823, and flourished until independence.[29] Men whose sense of social identity bound them to a seamless blend of military and civil action found a broad spectrum of ways to apply those efforts to reviving and establishing a stable, monarchical, Anglican, paternalist social order. To the extent that they thus consolidated their own social and political position, they were strikingly effective. The degree to which their ideals addressed the real needs of others, however, is far more questionable.

Many of this new imperial aristocracy's ideas were reasonable in outline – it was undoubtedly better to envisage raising the productivity of agriculture, rather than just squeezing a peasantry in Bengal (or Ireland) for ever higher rents. The quest, which extended worldwide, to create a hardily independent 'yeoman' class of farmers, with plots large enough to be worth investing in, and a stake in sustaining a stable social hierarchy, was a clear step up from mere exploitation. But in the face of an unwillingness to address the realities of many cultures' complex relationships with land-ownership and social rank, what seemed ideal on paper could easily founder in practice.[30] Even closer to home, the realities of the Highland Clearances, and continued rack-renting in Ireland, showed that the distinction between a paternalistic global vision and individuals' decisions about their own income could be stark.[31]

Closest to home of all, within Britain, the years after 1815 were the time of the Corn Laws. Passed explicitly to protect the incomes of landowners, these prohibited the import of food-grains unless the price in the home market reached crisis levels. Effectively, therefore, they condemned the population to paying a high price for home-grown bread, protected against competition, regardless of other economic conditions. In collision with an increasingly industrialised society, this blatant favouring of the aristocratic class caused repeated protests, but it was not until 1846 that the balance of politics shifted far enough to bring about their end. More generally, with a National Debt that had soared from £238 million in 1793 to £902 million in 1816, giving the prosperous investing class an income from interest payments funded by taxation, the imposition on the general population to service the wealthy was significant.[32]

Men such as William Cobbett would build continuing careers on this revived evidence of the ills of 'Old Corruption', but their activism did not conspicuously dent the armour of power. Major John Cartwright continued to campaign until his death in 1824 – having at seventy-nine in 1819 been prosecuted for conspiracy after speaking out in the wake of Peterloo. Sir Francis Burdett's radicalism likewise continued to be a parliamentary fixture until moderated by age and the passing of the 1832 Reform Act. He had served three months in jail after denouncing Peterloo, but in old age grew close to the newly defined Conservative Party. His main contribution to nineteenth-century public life may however have been as the father of Angela Burdett-Coutts, who from 1837 inherited the family's massive fortune, and spent it on a range of philanthropic charities so vast that she was eventually honoured with a peerage in her own right.

The social, economic and political histories of the first half of the nineteenth century are far too complex to go into here; suffice it to say that they would raise up the other classes of Britain, in Political Unions, the Anti-Corn-Law League, and the campaign for the People's Charter amongst others, in ways which made the Wellesleys' and Maitlands' approaches to life seem increasingly anachronistic. Yet if we look further ahead, the massive solidity of influence established by the Napoleonic generation clearly persisted. A century and a half after those wars began, Britain was led through the early and mid 1950s by Sir Winston Churchill, nephew of a duke (and a Duke of Marlborough at that), and Sir Anthony Eden, son of the seventh baronet Eden. The man who took office in 1957, Harold Macmillan, was of rather different stock by birth – son and grandson of publishers, great-grandson of a Scottish crofter – but in his public image, and his private life – Eton, Oxford, the Grenadier Guards (wounded five times in action), married (awkwardly, and ultimately disastrously) to a daughter of the Duke of Devonshire – easily the equivalent of any of the well-connected strivers who came after Pitt, and died, like Macmillan, as belted earls.[33]

So much for the pinnacle of society; what of the common soldiers, and the land they returned to? In some respects it was a militarised society, albeit one in the process of being run down. Over a hundred new bases and barracks had been built in the war years, raising the accommodation for troops in Britain to 155,000 places. There were thirty-four official garrisons in Britain, and a further twelve in Ireland.[34] Massive building works had already begun to expand naval facilities in Portsmouth and Plymouth from the 1770s, but in the early 1800s these were augmented with further fortifications and practical facilities. One royal duke declared the works under way at Portsmouth in 1800 to be 'as lasting a monument of our naval grandeur as any Roman edifice'. The naval dockyard was one of the largest industrial enterprises in the world, directly employing over 4200 craftsmen. Haslar hospital, nearby, had beds for over 2000 naval patients and invalids. Meanwhile in London, the assemblage of military works at Woolwich covered 114 acres: the Grand Store completed in 1813 combined the functions of a warehouse with monumental neoclassical architecture; the Royal Artillery barracks, completed 1802, had a 1000-foot façade – still today the longest in the country, and longer, but less ornamented, than the grand structure of the Royal Military Academy, finished in 1808, a mere 720 feet across.[35]

Most common soldiers and sailors were, of course, locked out of the massive power structure that such buildings represented. While the government did pay modest pensions to a remarkably large number of men with well-attested disabilities or long service – over 75,000 in all – many others received no official help: the crippled

Waterloo veteran, begging on the streets of the capital, soon became a cliché.[36] Some men, of course, remained in service. William Wheeler, whose letters illuminate the Peninsular campaign, was in garrison on Corfu in the early 1820s, guarding the new Mediterranean British Empire, when his correspondence and recollections were first gathered for publication.[37] Rifleman Costello remained in service for several years, but upon discharge in 1819 endured periods of idleness and penury, trying to support a French wife and newborn child on a sixpenny pension (his Vitoria loot having vanished). Rejected in his appeals to senior officers for assistance, he was reduced at one point to contemplating highway robbery before a more sympathetic officer helped him get back on his feet (not before his wife had returned alone to France and died there of unknown causes, alas).[38] Overall, hundreds of thousands were no longer required for military and naval service after 1815, and the slump in demand for labour they contributed to was one reason for the bitterness of radical protest over the rest of the decade. The militant patriotism that the elite had so gingerly invoked during the years of invasion scare, and which had backfired in the disciplined radical displays, and Luddite manoeuvres, of the following decade, was pushed away when those who had taken up its call outlived their use.[39]

William Blake in his poem *Jerusalem*, which he worked and reworked obsessively through these decades, feared for the new generations of veterans and workers, lamenting that all the 'Arts of Life' had been 'chang'd into the Arts of Death in Albion'; all that was of 'simple workmanship' had been struck down, replaced by 'intricate wheels' to 'perplex youth' and 'bind' them:

> *Kept ignorant of its use: that they might spend the days of*
> *   wisdom*
> *In sorrowful drudgery to obtain a scanty pittance of bread,*
> *In ignorance to view a small portion & think it All,*
> *And call it Demonstration, blind to all the simple rules of life.*[40]

A year almost to the day after Waterloo, another artistic vision was born, as its author was carried 'far beyond the usual bounds of reverie' lying abed after an evening's discussion of 'philosophical doctrines', seeing in this state the image of a 'pale student of unhallowed arts' bringing life to a monstrous creation through 'the working of some powerful engine'.[41] Thus Mary Shelley described the birth of *Frankenstein*, a meditation on the dangerous power of modern science to interfere with the natural order, and a work in which the ostracised 'monster' ultimately appears as more sympathetic than his eponymous creator. Both Shelley and Blake offer powerful artistic visions of the consequences of the new industrial social order into which post-war Britain was plunging headlong, but such reflections were not beyond the powers of humbler creators, either.

An anonymous printed ballad from the years after Waterloo – one of hundreds that formed the popular music of the age – records the science-fictional tale of a veteran of the battle, returned home missing an arm, to an unwelcoming wife. Conjuring up the technological spirit of the coming age, the protagonist has himself fitted with a steam-powered mechanical arm, but the device proves uncontrollably powerful. It knocks down his wife, then a posse of policemen and the local mayor, before he is finally confined to a cell – though not for long:

> *Down fell the walls, and out popp'd the arm.*
> *He soon escaped and reached his door,*
> *And knocked by steam raps half a score,*
> *But as the arm in power grew more and more,*
> *Bricks, mortar, and wood soon strew'd the floor.*

His wife seemed now to welcome him, but all did not go well:

> *O come to my arms, she cried! my dear,*
> *When his steamer smashed the crockery-ware.*
> *He left his house, at length out right,*

And wanders about just like a sprite;
For he can't get sleep either day or night
And his arm keeps moving with two horse might.[42]

It might be going too far to see in this ephemeral production a prophetic vision of the fate of the common man, caught between a generation of war and the coming age of steam, but in the image of the forlorn war hero, uprooted and condemned to wander alone by the monstrous power of machinery, there is certainly space to see exactly that.

NOTES

Prologue – Battle in Egypt

1   For an overview of life in the sailing navies, see N.A.M. Rodger, *The Wooden World: an anatomy of the Georgian Navy*, New York: W.W. Norton, 1996. On shipbuilding, see N.A.M. Rodger, *The Command of the Ocean: a naval history of Britain, 1649–1815*, London: Penguin, 2006, ch. 27.

2   The word 'battleship' here, as aficionados will know, is an anachronism, but a convenient one that does convey the essential role of such vessels.

3   For the Battle of the Nile, see Noel Mostert, *The Line Upon a Wind: an intimate history of the last and greatest war fought at sea under sail – 1793–1815*, London: Jonathan Cape, 2007, ch. 19; Roy Adkins and Lesley Adkins, *The War for All the Oceans: from Nelson at the Nile to Napoleon at Waterloo*, London: Penguin, 2008, chs 1–2.

4   Steven Englund, *Napoleon: a political life*, New York: Simon & Schuster, 2004, is a relatively balanced introduction to the subject; for a more in-depth examination of Bonaparte's early career, see Philip Dwyer, *Napoleon: the path to power 1769–1799*, London: Bloomsbury, 2007.

5   Adkins, *War*, p. 7.

6   For a comparative study of the 'heroisation' of Nelson, see Gerald Jordan and Nicholas Rogers, 'Admirals as Heroes: Patriotism and Liberty in Hanoverian England', *Journal of British Studies*, 28 (1989), pp. 201–24.

7   See (amongst a plethora of texts) the recent biography by Roger Knight, *The Pursuit of Victory: the life and achievement of Horatio Nelson*, London: Penguin, 2006.

8   The short-lived republican colony established by Bonaparte's army is a fascinating topic in itself. Two recent wide-ranging studies are Paul Strathern, *Napoleon In Egypt: the greatest glory*, London: Jonathan Cape, 2007, and Juan Cole, *Napoleon's Egypt: invading the Middle East*, Basingstoke: Macmillan, 2007.

9   Adkins, *War*, p. 19.

10 Adkins, *War*, p. 22.

11 Adkins, *War*, p. 13.

12   Adkins, *War*, p. 28.

13   Adkins, *War*, p. 29.

14   Portrait attributed to Guy Head, viewable here: < http://www.nmmprints.com/
      image/328168/guy-head-rear-admiral-horatio-nelson-1st-viscount-nelson-1758-1805>.

1 Revolutionary Terrors

1   William Hague, *William Pitt the Younger*, London: HarperCollins, 2004, p. 415.

2   For a long-term overview of British strategic dilemmas in the wars of this period, see
      Jeremy Black, 'British Strategy and the Struggle with France 1793–1815', *Journal of
      Strategic Studies*, 31 (2008), pp. 553–69.

3   For a brisk summary of Pitt's approach to office, see Jennifer Mori, 'The Political
      Theory of William Pitt the Younger', *History*, 83 (1998), pp. 234–48.

4   Hague, *William Pitt*, p. 306.

5   Gunther E. Rothenberg, 'The Origins, Causes, and Extension of the Wars of the
      French Revolution and Napoleon', *Journal of Interdisciplinary History*, 18 (1988),
      pp. 771–93.

6   For an overview of recent work on this subject, see Emma Vincent Macleod,
      'British Attitudes to the French Revolution', *Historical Journal*, 50 (2007),
      pp. 689–709.

7   See my earlier work, *1789: the threshold of the modern age*, London: Little, Brown,
      2008, for more of this background.

8   See, classically, John Brewer, *The Sinews of Power: war, money and the English
      state, 1688–1783*, London: Unwin Hyman, 1989; and Geoffrey Clark, 'Review:
      Money and the State', *Journal of British Studies*, 37 (1998), pp. 348–55.

9   Douglas Hay et al., *Albion's Fatal Tree: crime and society in eighteenth-century
      England*, London: Allen Lane, 1975; Peter Linebaugh, *The London Hanged:
      crime and civil society in the eighteenth century*, London: Penguin, 1993.

10   Frank O'Gorman, *The Long Eighteenth Century: British political and social history
      1688–1832*, London: Arnold, 1997, p. 322. The Scots population was relatively stable
      at just under 1.5 million; that of Ireland had risen from three million to above four
      in the half-century to 1790.

11   Elizabeth Burton, *The Georgians at Home, 1714–1830*, London: Longman, 1967, ch.
      1.

12   For one, failed, attempt to change this, see Miles Ogborn, 'Designs on the City:
      John Gwynn's plans for Georgian London', *Journal of British Studies*, 43 (2004),
      pp. 15–39.

13   See the articles introduced by Frank Mort and Miles Ogborn, 'Transforming
      Metropolitan London, 1750–1960', *Journal of British Studies*, 43 (2004), pp. 1–14.

14   This is a theme of Ben Wilson, *Decency and Disorder: the age of cant, 1789–1837*,
      London: Faber & Faber, 2007.

15   Jonathan Conlin, 'Vauxhall Revisited: the afterlife of a London pleasure garden,
      1770–1859', *Journal of British Studies*, 45 (2006), pp. 718–43.

16   Burton, *Georgians at Home*, pp. 21–3; O'Gorman, *Long Eighteenth Century*,
      pp. 323–4.

17   Julian Hoppit, 'The Nation, the State, and the First Industrial Revolution', *Journal
      of British Studies*, 50 (2011), pp. 307–31, discusses the intimate connection between

elite-sponsored legislation and economic development in this period.

18 John Rule, *Albion's People: English society, 1714–1815*, London: Longman, 1992, pp. 25–30 and Ch. 8. On economic development generally across the eighteenth century, see John Rule, *The Vital Century: England's developing economy 1714–1815*, London: Longman, 1992.

19 The extent to which Burke's opposition to the French Revolution was seen as a puzzling change of political coloration is discussed by Iain McCalman, 'Mad Lord George and Madame La Motte: riot and sexuality in the genesis of Burke's Reflections on the Revolution in France', *Journal of British Studies*, 35 (1996), pp. 343–67.

20 One collection of such literature runs to eight volumes and over 3500 pages: Gregory Claeys (ed.), *The Political Writings of the 1790s*, London: Pickering & Chatto, 1995. A shorter introduction can be found in Pamela Clemit (ed.), *The Cambridge Companion to British Literature of the French Revolution in the 1790s*, Cambridge: CUP, 2011.

21 E.P. Thompson, *The Making of the English Working Class*, London: Penguin, 1968 [first edition 1963], p. 19.

22 Emma Vincent, '"The Real Grounds of the Present War": John Bowles and the French revolutionary wars, 1792–1802', *History*, 78 (1993), pp. 393–420, examines one loyalist response.

23 Kevin Gilmartin, 'In the Theater of Counterrevolution: loyalist association and conservative opinion in the 1790s', *Journal of British Studies*, 41 (2002), pp. 291–328.

24 Elizabeth Sparrow, 'Secret Service under Pitt's Administrations, 1792–1806', *History*, 83 (1998), pp. 280–94; Michael Durey, 'William Wickham, the Christ Church Connection and the Rise and Fall of the Security Service in Britain, 1793–1801', *English Historical Review*, 121 (2006), pp. 714–45.

25 Alfred Cobban (ed.), *The Debate on the French Revolution, 1789–1800*, London: Adam & Charles Black, 1960, p. 333.

26 Thompson, *Making*, p. 21.

27 Philip Schofield, 'British Politicians and French Arms: the ideological war of 1793–1795', *History*, 77 (1992), pp. 183–201.

28 O'Gorman, *Long Eighteenth Century*, p. 322.

29 For detail on this movement, see Marianne Elliott, *Partners in Revolution: the United Irishmen and France*, New Haven: Yale University Press, 1990.

30 Clarke Garrett, *Respectable Folly: millenarians and the French Revolution in France and England*, Baltimore: Johns Hopkins University Press, 1975, p. 190.

31 Garrett, *Respectable Folly*, pp. 196–7.

32 Garrett, *Respectable Folly*, pp. 203, 205.

33 Garrett, *Respectable Folly*, p. 206.

34 Marilyn Morris, 'Princely Debt, Public Credit, and Commercial Values in Late Georgian Britain', *Journal of British Studies*, 43 (2004), pp. 339–65; see pp. 343–4 for figures.

35 John Barrell, *The Spirit of Despotism: invasions of privacy in the 1790s*, Oxford: Oxford University Press, 2006, p. 44.

36 R.A.E. Wells, *Insurrection: the British experience 1795–1803*, Gloucester: Alan Sutton, 1983, pp. 44–5.

37 Thompson, *Making*, p. 150.

38 Wells, *Insurrection*, pp. 46–7.

39 Amnon Yuval, 'Between Heroism and Acquittal: Henry Redhead Yorke and the inherent instability of political trials in Britain during the 1790s', *Journal of British Studies*, 50 (2011), pp. 612–38.

40 Thompson, *Making*, pp. 180–1.

41 Hague, *William Pitt*, pp. 384–5; Richard Cooper, 'William Pitt, Taxation, and the Needs of War', *Journal of British Studies*, 22 (1982), pp. 94–103.

42 Wells, *Insurrection*, pp. 81–3.

43 Clive Emsley (ed.), *Collection of Nineteenth and Twentieth Century Documents*, *Part 1*, Milton Keynes: Open University Press, 1973, p. 15.

44 See Wells, *Insurrection*, pp. 84–9 for the course of the mutinies in general.

45 Wells, *Insurrection*, p. 104.

46 Albert Goodwin, *The Friends of Liberty: the English democratic movement in the age of the French Revolution*, London: Hutchinson, 1979, pp. 411–13.

47 Wells, *Insurrection*, pp. 105–6.

2 Sedition and Stalemate

1   Hague, *William Pitt*, pp. 412–13.

2   Wells, *Insurrection*, p. 111.

3   David Wilkinson, 'The Pitt-Portland Coalition of 1794 and the Origins of the "Tory" Party', *History*, 83 (1998), pp. 249–64.

4   Barrell, *Spirit of Despotism*, p. 30. For more on the national, and nationalist, culture of prints in this period, see Tamara Hunt, *Defining John Bull: political caricature and national identity in late Georgian England*, Aldershot: Ashgate, 2003.

5   Thompson, *Making*, p. 181.

6   J. Ann Hone, *For the Cause of Truth: radicalism in London, 1796–1821*, Oxford: Clarendon Press, 1982, pp. 32–3.

7   Hone, *For the Cause of Truth*, p. 35.

8   Hone, *For the Cause of Truth*, p. 37.

9   Hone, *For the Cause of Truth*, p. 39.

10 Hone, *For the Cause of Truth*, pp. 43–4.

11 Wells, *Insurrection*, p. 113.

12 Wells, *Insurrection*, p. 118.

13 Thompson, *Making*, p. 188.

14 Wells, *Insurrection*, p. 130.

15 Piers Mackesy, *Statesmen at War: the strategy of overthrow, 1798–1799*, London: Longman, 1974, p. 9.

16 Mackesy, *Statesmen at War*, pp. 10–11.

17 Wells, *Insurrection*, p. 140.

18 Wells, *Insurrection*, p. 139.

19 Wells, *Insurrection*, pp. 134–5.

20 Ian Haywood, *Bloody Romanticism: spectacular violence and the politics of representation, 1776–1832*, Basingstoke: Palgrave, 2006, p. 112.

21 Wells, *Insurrection*, p. 145.

22 Hone, *For the Cause of Truth*, pp. 44–5.

23 Ian Germani, 'Combat and Culture: imagining the Battle of the Nile', *The Northern Mariner/Le Marin du nord*, 10 (2000), pp. 53–72; citation p. 54, and see esp. pp. 64–9 for images.

24 Mackesy, *Statesmen*, pp. 33–5.

25 Mackesy, *Statesmen*, pp. 40–7.

26 Mackesy, *Statesmen*, pp. 47–51.

27 Adkins, *War*, p. 40.

28 Mackesy, *Statesmen*, pp. 55–7.

29 See the brisk summary of operations in P.J. Marshall, William Roger Louis, Roger Louis, Alaine M. Low, *Oxford History of the British Empire: the eighteenth century*, Oxford: Oxford University Press, 1998, pp. 190–1.

30 This whole system is frequently remarked on by historians. See for example C.J. Bartlett, *Castlereagh*, London: Macmillan, 1966, pp. 52–5.

31 Mackesy, *Statesmen*, pp. 93–4.

32 For the centrality of Dundas to the rising imperial influence of Scots in this period, see David J. Brown, 'The Government of Scotland under Henry Dundas and William Pitt', *History*, 83 (1998), pp. 265–79.

33 Bruce Collins, *War and Empire: the expansion of Britain, 1790–1830*, London: Longman, 2010, p. 98.

34 Mackesy, *Statesmen*, p. 4.

35 Mackesy, *Statesmen*, pp. 5–6.

3 Uneasy Yearning for Peace

1 Paul Fregosi, *Dreams of Empire; Napoleon and the first world war, 1792–1815*, London: Cardinal, 1991, pp. 129–33.

2 Fregosi, *Dreams*, p. 173; Collins, *War*, p. 116.

3 Mackesy, *Statesmen*, p. 94. On the general difficulty of securing 'patriotic' disinterestedness from elites and citizens, see J.E. Cookson, 'Service without Politics? Army, Militia and Volunteers in Britain during the American and French Revolutionary Wars', *War in History*, 10 (2003), pp. 381–97.

4 Mackesy, *Statesmen*, pp. 142–3.

5 Mackesy, *Statesmen*, p. 156; Collins, *War*, p. 408.

6 Philip G. Dwyer, '"It Still Makes Me Shudder": memories of massacres and atrocities during the Revolutionary and Napoleonic Wars', *War in History*, 16 (2009), pp. 381–405, at pp. 381–3.

7 Michael Durey, 'The British Secret Service and the Escape of Sir Sidney Smith from Paris in 1798', *History*, 84 (1999), pp. 437–57.

8 Hague, *William Pitt*, pp. 450–1. On the new dangers of revolutionary warfare, see David A. Bell, *The First Total War: Napoleon's Europe and the birth of modern warfare*, London: Bloomsbury, 2007.

9 Andrew Jainchill, *Reimagining Politics after the Terror: the republican origins of French liberalism*, Ithaca, NY: Cornell University Press, 2008, p. 197.

10 *London Packet*, 29 January 1800, reporting the trial at Leeds two days earlier.

11 *True Briton*, 22 February 1800.

12 R.A.E. Wells, *Wretched Faces: famine in wartime England, 1793–1801*, Gloucester:

Sutton, 1988, pp. 1, 35.

13 Wells, *Wretched Faces*, pp. 316–18.

14 Regional variations in such responses in this period are a key topic of John Bohstedt, *Riots and Community Politics in England and Wales, 1790–1810*, London: Harvard University Press, 1983.

15 Douglas Hay, 'The State and the Market in 1800: Lord Kenyon and Mr Waddington', *Past and Present*, 162 (1999), pp. 101–62.

16 Wells, *Wretched Faces*, pp. 147–9.

17 Wells, *Wretched Faces*, p. 150.

18 Thompson, *Making*, p. 516.

19 *Aberdeen Journal*, 22 September 1800.

20 Thompson, *Making*, p. 518.

21 Wells, *Wretched Faces*, p. 334.

22 A. Aspinall and E. Anthony Smith (eds), *English Historical Documents*, vol. xi, London: Eyre & Spottiswoode, 1969, p. 262.

23 *English Historical Documents*, xi, p. 262.

24 David Wilkinson, '"How Did They Pass the Union?": secret service expenditure in Ireland, 1799–1804', *History*, 82 (1997), pp. 223–51.

25 Hague, *William Pitt*, p. 454.

26 *English Historical Documents*, xi, p. 83.

27 Hague, *William Pitt*, p. 464.

28 Hague, *William Pitt*, p. 468.

29 See Charles John Fedorak, 'Catholic Emancipation and the Resignation of William Pitt in 1801', *Albion*, 24 (1992), pp. 49–64.

30 Hague, *William Pitt*, pp. 477–9.

31 See Schroeder, *Transformation*, pp. 217–20, for details of this remarkable volte-face.

32 Hugh Ragsdale, 'A Continental System in 1801: Paul I and Bonaparte', *Journal of Modern History*, 42 (1970), pp. 70–89.

33 John D. Grainger, *The Amiens Truce: Britain and Bonaparte, 1801–1803*, Woodbridge: The Boydell Press, 2004, pp. 20–1.

4 Peace Through War, and War for Peace

1 Charles John Fedorak, 'The Royal Navy and British Amphibious Operations during the Revolutionary and Napoleonic Wars', *Military Affairs*, 52 (1988), pp. 141–6, esp. pp. 144–5.

2 Fregosi, *Dreams*, pp. 258–9.

3 *Encyclopaedia Britannica*, 1911, entry for 'Abercromby, Sir Ralph'.

4 *Caledonian Mercury*, 30 May 1801.

5 Grainger, *Amiens Truce*, pp. 17, 27–8.

6 For the extraordinary life story of Emma Hamilton, from pioneering actress to courtesan, wife, lover, and grieving abandoned mother, see Kate Williams, *England's Mistress: the infamous life of Emma Hamilton*, London: Arrow, 2007.

7 Adkins, *War*, pp. 78–81.

8 Adkins, *War*, pp. 88, 89–90.

9 Frederick W. Kagan, *The End of the Old Order: Napoleon and Europe 1801–1805*, Cambridge, MA: Da Capo Press, 2006, p. 19.

10   Grainger, *Amiens Truce*, pp. 8ff.

11   Grainger, *Amiens Truce*, p. 31.

12   Grainger, *Amiens Truce*, pp. 36–7.

13   Schroeder, *Transformation*, pp. 222–3.

14   *Morning Post and Gazetteer*, 21 May 1801.

15   Thompson, *Making*, p. 524.

16   Thompson, *Making*, pp. 525–8.

17   Simon Burrows, *French Exile Journalism and European Politics, 1792–1814*, Woodbridge: Boydell Press, 2000, p. 112.

18   Burrows, *French Exile Journalism*, pp. 120–4.

19   Jon Newman, '"An Insurrection of Loyalty": the London Volunteer Regiments' response to the invasion threat', in Mark Philp (ed.), *Resisting Napoleon: the British response to the threat of invasion, 1797–1815*, Aldershot: Ashgate, 2006, pp. 75–89, at p. 75.

20   Philip Ziegler, *Addington: a life of Henry Addington, first Viscount Sidmouth*, London: Collins, 1965, p. 81.

21   Hague, *William Pitt*, pp. 502–3.

22   Hague, *William Pitt*, p. 505.

23   See Fregosi, *Dreams*, ch. 11.

24   Kevin B. Linch, '"A Citizen and Not a Soldier": the British Volunteer movement and the war against Napoleon', in Alan Forrest, Karen Hagemann and Jane Rendall (eds), *Soldiers, Citizens and Civilians: experiences and perceptions of the Revolutionary and Napoleonic Wars, 1790–1820*, Basingstoke: Palgrave Macmillan, 2009, pp. 205–21.

25   Cookson, *Armed Nation*, p. 75.

26   Cookson, *Armed Nation*, p. 76.

27   Cookson, *Armed Nation*, p. 78.

28   Cookson, *Armed Nation*, p. 79.

29   Collins, *War*, p. 234.

30   Richard Glover, *Britain at Bay: defence against Bonaparte, 1803–14*, London: Allen & Unwin, 1973.

31   Ziegler, *Addington*, p. 155.

32   Adkins, *War*, p. 103.

33   Adkins, *War*, p. 104.

34   Adkins, *War*, pp. 105, 107.

35   Adkins, *War*, pp. 107–10.

36   On Pitt's relations with, and 'management' of, the Commons in general, see Michael Duffy, 'The Younger Pitt and the House of Commons', *History*, 83 (1998), pp. 217–24.

37   Hague, *William Pitt*, p. 513.

5 Alone against the Emperor

1   Grainger, *Amiens Truce*, pp. 191–2.

2   Grainger, *Amiens Truce*, pp. 194–6.

3   Hague, *William Pitt*, p. 520; Collins, *War*, p. 235, notes this, and that Lord Melville similarly took command of over 2000 volunteers from the East India Company's

workforce in London.
4 Philp (ed.), *Resisting Napoleon*, plate 14, n.p.
5 Hague, *William Pitt*, p. 522.
6 Andress, 1789, p. 357.
7 Hague, *William Pitt*, p. 524.
8 Hague, *William Pitt*, p. 525.
9 Hague, *William Pitt*, p. 529.
10 Schroeder, *Transformation*, pp. 248–51.
11 See Kagan, *End of the Old Order*, chs 3–6, for an exhaustive discussion.
12 Adkins, *War*, pp. 148–9.
13 Schroeder, *Transformation*, pp. 262–3.
14 Schroeder, *Transformation*, pp. 266–7, 271–2.
15 Adkins, *War*, pp. 150–1.
16 For some questions about the precise nature of Nelson's intentions, see Marianne Czisnik, 'Admiral Nelson's Tactics at the Battle of Trafalgar', *History*, 89 (2004), pp. 549–59.
17 Collins, *War*, p. 239.
18 Adam Nicolson, *Men of Honour: Trafalgar and the making of the English hero*, London: HarperCollins, 2005, p. 151.
19 Nicolson, *Men of Honour*, pp. 49–50.
20 Nicolson, *Men of Honour*, pp. 50–1.
21 Nicolson, *Men of Honour*, pp. 205–6.
22 On the Battle of Trafalgar itself, see for example Roy Adkins, *Trafalgar: the biography of a battle*, London: Little Brown, 2004; Andrew Lambert, *War at Sea in the Age of Sail*, London: Cassell, 2000, ch. 8.
23 Nicolson, *Men of Honour*, p. 215, mistakenly gives the name as Harwood.
24 Nicolson, *Men of Honour*, p. 227.
25 Collins, *War*, pp. 241–2.
26 Michael Duffy, '"All Was Hushed Up": the hidden Trafalgar', *Mariner's Mirror*, 91 (2005), pp. 216–40.
27 Hague, *William Pitt*, pp. 562–3.
28 Hague, *William Pitt*, p. 565.
29 David Chandler, *The Campaigns of Napoleon*, London, 1967, p. 439.
30 Hague, *William Pitt*, pp. 571, 577.
31 Laurence Brockliss, John Cardwell and Michael Moss, 'Nelson's Grand National Obsequies', *English Historical Review*, 121 (2006), pp. 162–82. For a view of the various political and social forces striving to assert themselves in the ceremonies, see Timothy Jenks, 'Contesting the Hero: the funeral of Admiral Lord Nelson', *Journal of British Studies*, 39 (2000), pp. 422–53.
32 Hague, *William Pitt*, p. 578.

6 Shifting Sands

1 Loren Reid, *Charles James Fox: a man for the people*, London: Longman, 1969, pp. 328–9, 332–3.
2 Reid, *Charles James Fox*, p. 410.
3 Reid, *Charles James Fox*, p. 411.

4 A.D. Harvey, 'The Ministry of All the Talents: the Whigs in office, February 1806 to March 1807', *Historical Journal*, 15 (1972), pp. 619–48.

5 Reid, *Charles James Fox*, pp. 412–13.

6 Giles Hunt, *The Duel: Castlereagh, Canning and deadly Cabinet rivalry*, London: I.B. Tauris, 2008, p. 30.

7 Bartlett, *Castlereagh*, pp. 7–12.

8 Bartlett, *Castlereagh*, pp. 14–17.

9 P.J.V. Rolo, *George Canning: three biographical studies*, London: Macmillan, 1965, pp. 18–20, 28.

10 Hunt, *The Duel*, pp. 49–56.

11 Rolo, *George Canning*, pp. 68–76.

12 Rolo, *George Canning*, pp. 79–80.

13 Hunt, *The Duel*, p. 90.

14 Reid, *Charles James Fox*, p. 413.

15 Reid, *Charles James Fox*, p. 415.

16 Adkins, *War*, pp. 168–9.

17 Durey, 'British Secret Service', esp. pp. 440–1. The 1798 escape plan cost the British government (p. 453) around £10,000 – Smith and Wright's strategic value was evidently considerable.

18 Schroeder, *Transformation*, pp. 289–92.

19 Reid, *Charles James Fox*, pp. 418–19.

20 Schroeder, *Transformation*, pp. 296–7.

21 Reid, *Charles James Fox*, pp. 424–7.

22 On the life and opinions of John Horne Tooke, see Goodwin, *Friends of Liberty*, pp. 47, 114, 218–19, 353–7.

23 Thompson, *Making*, p. 493; Hone, *Cause of Truth*, pp. 121–2.

24 Hone, *Cause of Truth*, p. 113.

25 Katrina Navickas, '"That sash will hang you": political clothing and adornment in England, 1780–1840', *Journal of British Studies*, 49 (2010), pp. 540–65, at pp. 545, 552.

26 Hone, *Cause of Truth*, pp. 133–5; Thompson, *Making*, p. 494.

27 See Leonard Schwarz, 'Custom, Wages and Workload In England during Industrialization', *Past and Present*, 197 (2007), pp. 143–75; and for a survey, John Rule, *The Labouring Classes in Early Industrial England, 1750–1850*, London: Longman, 1986.

28 Adrian Randall, *Before the Luddites: custom, community and machinery in the English woollen industry, 1776–1809*, Cambridge: Cambridge University Press, 1991, pp. 72–5, citation p. 74.

29 Andress, *1789*, pp. 191–2.

30 Randall, *Before the Luddites*, pp. 51–2.

31 Randall, *Before the Luddites*, pp. 54–5.

32 Randall, *Before the Luddites*, ch. 5, esp. pp. 158–63.

33 Randall, *Before the Luddites*, pp. 224–7.

34 Seymour Drescher, 'Whose Abolition? popular pressure and the ending of the British slave trade', *Past & Present*, 143 (1994), pp. 136–66.

35 Katrina Navickas, *Loyalism and Radicalism in Lancashire, 1798–1815*, Oxford: Oxford University Press, 2009, pp. 131–5.

36 Navickas, *Loyalism and Radicalism*, pp. 212–13.
37 Navickas, *Loyalism and Radicalism*, pp. 214–15.

7 Isolation and Determination

1   Hone, *Cause of Truth*, p. 153.
2   Peter Spence, *The Birth of Romantic Radicalism: war, popular politics and English radical reformism, 1800–1815*, Aldershot: Scolar Press, 1996, p. 36.
3   Hone, *Cause of Truth*, p. 153.
4   Spence, *Romantic Radicalism*, pp. 26–7.
5   Spence, *Romantic Radicalism*, p. 29.
6   Spence, *Romantic Radicalism*, p. 38.
7   Spence, *Romantic Radicalism*, p. 40.
8   Spence, *Romantic Radicalism*, pp. 43–4.
9   H.V. Livermore, 'Captain Gillespie and the 58 Anglophiles of Buenos Aires in 1806', *Hispanic American Historical Review*, 60 (1980), pp. 69–78.
10 Adkins, *War*, pp. 193–6.
11 Bell, *First Total War*, pp. 263–5, 270–4.
12 Collins, *War*, p. 246.
13 *Morning Post*, 1 April 1807.
14 Collins, *War*, p. 233.
15 Rory Muir, *Britain and the Defeat of Napoleon, 1807–1815*, London: Yale University Press, 1996, pp. 6–7.
16 *Morning Post*, 6 March 1807, 'Letter from our correspondent, Portsmouth, Thursday, March 5'.
17 Charles Esdaile, *Napoleon's Wars: an international history 1803–1815*, London: Penguin, 2007, p. 288.
18 Collins, *War*, pp. 247–8.
19 Bell, *First Total War*, p. 239.
20 Schroeder, *Transformation*, pp. 302–6.
21 Karen Hagemann, '"Desperation to the Utmost": the defeat of 1806 and the French occupation in Prussian experience and perception', in Alan Forrest, Karen Hagemann and Jane Rendall (eds), *Soldiers, Citizens and Civilians: experiences and perceptions of the Revolutionary and Napoleonic Wars, 1790–1820*, Basingstoke: Palgrave Macmillan, 2009, pp. 191–213.
22 Bell, *First Total War*, p. 240.
23 Gavin Daly, 'English Smugglers, the Channel, and the Napoleonic Wars, 1800–1814', *Journal of British Studies*, 46 (2007), pp. 30–46.
24 Katherine B. Aaslestad, 'War Without Battles: civilian experiences of economic warfare during the Napoleonic era in Hamburg', in Forrest et al. (eds), *Soldiers, Citizens and Civilians*, pp. 118–36, at pp. 120–3. On the role of the Royal Navy in keeping open trade with northern Europe, see A.N. Ryan, 'The Defence of British Trade with the Baltic, 1808–1813', *English Historical Review*, 74 (1959), pp. 443–66.
25 For a classic overview, see François Crouzet, 'Wars, Blockade, and Economic Change in Europe, 1792–1815', *Journal of Economic History*, 24 (1964), pp. 567–88.
26 Rolo, *George Canning*, p. 82.
27 Hunt, *The Duel*, p. 84.

28 Bartlett, *Castlereagh*, pp. 62–3.
29 Thomas Biskup, 'Napoleon's second sacre? Iéna and the ceremonial translation of Frederick the Great's insignia in 1807', in Alan Forrest and Peter H. Wilson (eds), *The Bee and the Eagle: Napoleonic France and the end of the Holy Roman Empire, 1806*, London: Palgrave, 2009, pp. 172–90.
30 Esdaile, *Napoleon's Wars*, pp. 293–4.
31 Esdaile, *Napoleon's Wars*, p. 297.
32 Hunt, *The Duel*, p. 93.
33 For another view of attitudes to abolition, see Christer Petley, '"Devoted Islands" and "That Madman Wilberforce": British proslavery patriotism during the age of abolition', *Journal of Imperial and Commonwealth History*, 39 (2011), pp. 393–415.
34 Muir, *Britain*, p. 24.
35 Muir, *Britain*, pp. 23–4; Esdaile, *Napoleon's Wars*, pp. 311–12.
36 Collins, *War*, pp. 248–9.
37 Spence, *Romantic Radicalism*, pp. 56–7.
38 Esdaile, *Napoleon's Wars*, p. 313.
39 Bartlett, *Castlereagh*, p. 64; Muir, *Britain*, pp. 25–6.
40 Muir, *Britain*, p. 26.
41 See A. Harvey, 'European Attitudes to Britain during the French Revolutionary and Napoleonic era', *History*, 58 (1978), pp. 356–65.
42 Schroeder, *Transformation*, p. 330.

8 The State of the Nation

1   J.F.C. Harrison, *The Second Coming: popular millenarianism, 1780–1850*, London: Routledge and Kegan Paul, 1979, pp. 86–93.
2   Harrison, *Second Coming*, p. 107.
3   Harrison, *Second Coming*, pp. 110–18.
4   Stuart Semmell, *Napoleon and the British*, Yale University Press, 2004, p. 78; see pp. 72ff. for a general introduction to this milieu.
5   Semmell, *Napoleon and the British*, p. 83.
6   Semmell, *Napoleon and the British*, pp. 104–5. The individuals in question were Spencer Perceval and Samuel Whitbread.
7   Semmell, *Napoleon and the British*, p. 95.
8   Blake's life is widely documented and debated; see e.g. E.P. Thompson, *Witness Against the Beast: William Blake and the moral law*, Cambridge: Cambridge University Press, 1994, and the classic David V. Erdman, *Blake: Prophet Against Empire*, Princeton: Princeton University Press, 1954.
9   G.E. Bentley, Jr, *The Stranger from Paradise:; a biography of William Blake*, London: Yale University Press, 2001, pp. 249–55.
10 Bentley, *Stranger from Paradise*, p. 264.
11 Bentley, *Stranger from Paradise*, p. 329.
12 Bentley, *Stranger from Paradise*, p. 330.
13 Bentley, *Stranger from Paradise*, p. 332.
14 Bentley, *Stranger from Paradise*, p. 317.
15 Tim Fulford, 'Sighing for a Soldier: Jane Austen and military Pride and Prejudice', *Nineteenth-Century Literature*, 57 (2002), pp. 153–78.

16 See for example, Sandra Macpherson, 'Rent to Own: or, what's entailed in *Pride and Prejudice*', *Representations*, 82 (2003), pp. 1–23.

17 Kathleen Jones, *A Passionate Sisterhood: the sisters, wives and daughters of the Lake Poets*, London: Virago, 1998, p. 106.

18 Jones, *Passionate Sisterhood*, pp. 171–8.

19 Brian Goldberg, *The Lake Poets and Professional Identity*, Cambridge: Cambridge University Press, 2007, pp. 215–16.

20 Jones, *Passionate Sisterhood*, p. 126.

21 Leonore Davidoff and Catherine Hall, *Family Fortunes: men and women of the English middle class, 1780–1850*, London: Routledge, 1987, pp. 13–18.

22 *English Historical Documents*, xi, p. 550.

23 *English Historical Documents*, xi, pp. 552, 555.

24 Dudley Miles, *Francis Place, 1771–1854: the life of a remarkable radical*, Brighton: Harvester Press, 1988, pp. 6–17.

25 Miles, *Francis Place*, pp. 18–29.

26 Miles, *Francis Place*, p. 53.

27 Miles, *Francis Place*, p. 53.

28 Miles, *Francis Place*, pp. 43, 71.

29 Miles, *Francis Place*, pp. 105ff.

30 Asa Briggs, *How they Lived*, vol. 3, 1700–1815, Blackwell, 1969, pp. 391–4.

31 Rule, *Albion's People*, pp. 174–6.

32 Andress, *1789*, p. 166.

33 Cookson, *Armed Nation*, p. 95.

34 Cookson, *Armed Nation*, pp. 86–8.

9 New Hopes and New Disasters

1 Esdaile, *Napoleon's Wars*, p. 319.

2 Muir, *Britain*, p. 29.

3 Esdaile, *Napoleon's Wars*, pp. 324–5.

4 Esdaile, *Napoleon's Wars*, pp. 336–45.

5 Collins, *War*, p. 255.

6 See Jean-Claude Lorblanches, *Les soldats de Napoleon en Espagne et au Portugal, 1807–1814*, Paris: L'Harmattan, 2007, ch. 1, for a gruelling account of this advance, and what it foreshadowed.

7 Muir, *Britain*, pp. 32–3.

8 Esdaile, *Napoleon's Wars*, pp. 347–8.

9 Bartlett, *Castlereagh*, pp. 71–2.

10 Collins, *War*, p. 257.

11 Muir, *Britain*, pp. 44–9.

12 Bartlett, *Castlereagh*, p. 74.

13 Collins, *War*, p. 259.

14 Michael Glover, *The Peninsular War 1807–1814: a concise military history*, London: David & Charles, 1974, p. 74.

15 Collins, *War*, p. 260.

16 Muir, *Britain*, pp. 68–75.

17 Mark Urban, *The Man Who Broke Napoleon's Codes: The story of George Scovell*, London: Faber and Faber, 2001, pp. 6–7. Some 3000 horses were slaughtered in and around the town.

18 Rachel Eckersley, 'Of Radical Design: John Cartwright and the redesign of the reform campaign, c.1800–1811', *History*, 89 (2004), pp. 560–80.

19 J. E. Cookson, *Friends of Peace: Anti-war Liberalism in England 1793–1815*, Cambridge University Press, 2008, pp. 206–7.

20 Navickas, *Loyalism and Radicalism*, p. 144.

21 Navickas, *Loyalism and Radicalism*, pp. 184–6.

22 Navickas, *Loyalism and Radicalism*, pp. 186–9.

23 Navickas, *Loyalism and Radicalism*, p. 203.

24 Navickas, *Loyalism and Radicalism*, pp. 220–1.

25 Cookson, *Friends of Peace*, pp. 208–13.

26 Spence, *Romantic Radicalism*, pp. 110–15; Anna Clark, *Scandal: the sexual politics of the British constitution*, Princeton: Princeton University Press, 2004, pp. 151–7.

27 Donna T. Andrew, '"Adultery à-la-Mode": privilege, the law and attitudes to adultery 1770–1809', *History*, 82 (1997), pp. 5–23.

28 Spence, *Romantic Radicalism*, pp. 120–1.

29 Hone, *Cause of Truth*, pp. 172–4.

30 Clark, *Scandal*, pp. 162–9.

31 Philip Harling, 'The Duke of York Affair (1809) and the Complexities of War-Time Patriotism', *Historical Journal*, 39 (1996), pp. 963–84, esp. pp. 979–83.

32 Clark, *Scandal*, pp. 171–2.

33 Clark, *Scandal*, pp. 172–3; Hone, *Cause of Truth*, pp. 177–8.

34 Schroeder, *Transformation*, pp. 351–2, 358–9, 362–6.

35 Collins, *War*, pp. 261–2.

36 Bartlett, *Castlereagh*, pp. 82–4.

37 T.H. McGuffie, 'The Walcheren Expedition and the Walcheren Fever', *English Historical Review*, 62 (1947), pp. 191–202.

38 McGuffie, 'Walcheren Expedition', p. 201; Muir, *Britain*, pp. 102–3.

39 Hunt, *The Duel*, pp. 96ff., discusses these issues in detail.

40 Bartlett, *Castlereagh*, pp. 94–5.

41 Hunt, *The Duel* pp. 114–26.

42 Bartlett, *Castlereagh*, pp. 96–8.

43 Hunt, *The Duel*, p. 143.

44 Linda Colley, 'The Apotheosis of George III: loyalty, royalty and the British nation, 1760–1820', *Past and Present*, 102 (1984), pp. 94–129, at p. 111.

45 Colley, 'Apotheosis', p. 112; 112, n. 59.

46 Colley, 'Apotheosis', p. 116; 116, n. 70.

47 Colley, 'Apotheosis', p. 121.

48 For a recent in-depth biography, see Grayson Ditchfield, *George III: an essay in monarchy*, Basingstoke: Palgrave, 2002.

49 Cookson, *Armed Nation*, pp. 222–3.

50 Colley, 'Apotheosis', pp. 110–11.

51 Colley, 'Apotheosis', pp. 123–4.

52 Hone, *Cause of Truth*, pp. 183–4.

53 Spence, *Romantic Radicalism*, pp. 151–3.

54 Hone, *Cause of Truth*, pp. 184–5.

10 The Sepoy General and the Spanish Ulcer

1 See Elizabeth Longford, *Wellington: the years of the sword*, London: Panther, 1971, chs 1–8; Richard Holmes, *Wellington: the Iron Duke*, London: HarperCollins, 2003, chs 1–2.
2 Fregosi, *Dreams*, pp. 306–9.
3 Hunt, *The Duel*, p. 76.
4 Hunt, *The Duel*, p. 96.
5 Muir, *Britain*, pp. 42–7.
6 Muir, *Britain*, pp. 55, 57.
7 Richard M. Schneer, 'Arthur Wellesley and the Cintra Convention: a new look at an old puzzle', *Journal of British Studies*, 19 (1980), pp. 93–119.
8 Muir, *Britain*, pp. 79–81, 82–3.
9 Muir, *Britain*, p. 86.
10 Muir, *Britain*, p. 94.
11 For an overview, see Charles Esdaile, 'War and Politics in Spain, 1808–1814', *Historical Journal*, 31 (1988), pp. 295–317.
12 Michael Broers, 'The Concept of "Total War" in the Revolutionary-Napoleonic Period', *War in History*, 15 (2008), pp. 247–68, at p. 258.
13 Collins, *War*, p. 261.
14 On all these complexities, Charles Esdaile, *The Peninsular War: a new history*, London: Penguin, 2003, is an excellent guide. See also David Gates, *The Spanish Ulcer: a history of the Peninsular War*, Cambridge, MA: Da Capo Press, 2001 [first published 1986].
15 Muir, *Britain*, p. 98.
16 Longford, *Wellington*, p. 240.
17 The column attack has often been stereotyped as a clumsy mass, but the reality was far more subtle: see James R. Arnold, 'A Reappraisal of Column versus Line in the Peninsular War', *Journal of Military History*, 68 (2004), pp. 535–52.
18 Rory Muir, *Tactics and the Experience of Battle in the Age of Napoleon*, New Haven: Yale University Press, 1998, pp. 95–7.
19 Longford, *Wellington*, p. 247.
20 Longford, *Wellington*, p. 268.
21 Longford, *Wellington*, p. 260.
22 Collins, *War*, p. 264.
23 Muir, *Britain*, p. 117.
24 Collins, *War*, p. 265.
25 Longford, *Wellington*, p. 269.
26 Muir, *Britain*, p. 126.
27 Longford, *Wellington*, p. 279.
28 Longford, *Wellington*, pp. 282–3.
29 Michael J. Durey, '"Black Bob" Craufurd and Ireland, 1798–1804', *War in History*, 16 (2009), pp. 133–56.
30 Longford, *Wellington*, p. 286.
31 Collins, *War*, pp. 266–7.

11 The Sorrows of War

1   Longford, *Wellington*, p. 292.
2   *Caledonian Mercury*, 26 July 1810.
3   Muir, *Britain*, pp. 136–7.
4   *Morning Chronicle*, 25 October 1810.
5   *Aberdeen Journal*, 24 October 1810.
6   See for example the *Aberdeen Journal* of 5 December 1810, and the *Derby Mercury* of 15 November 1810 – which struggles valiantly to print a whole series of rumours without entirely crediting any of them.
7   Longford, *Wellington*, p. 290.
8   Muir, *Britain*, p. 143.
9   Don W. Alexander, 'French Military Problems in Counterinsurgent Warfare in Northeastern Spain, 1808–1813', *Military Affairs*, 40 (1976), pp. 117–22. More generally see Charles J. Esdaile (ed.), *Popular Resistance in the French Wars: patriots, partisans and land pirates*, Basingstoke: Palgrave Macmillan, 2005.
10 For a less successful, almost simultaneous effort near Málaga, see Thomas M. Barker, 'A Debacle of the Peninsular War: the British-led amphibious assault against Fort Fuengirola 14–15 October 1810', *Journal of Military History*, 64 (2000), pp. 9–52.
11 Esdaile, *Peninsular War*, pp. 333–6.
12 Esdaile, *Peninsular War*, p. 338.
13 Muir, *Britain*, p. 145.
14 Esdaile, *Peninsular War*, pp. 330–1.
15 Muir, *Tactics*, p. 227.
16 The astonishing resilience of French peninsular forces is in stark contrast to the structural weakness of their support mechanisms: see Don W. Alexander, 'French Replacement Methods during the Peninsular War, 1808–1814', *Military Affairs*, 44 (1980), pp. 192–7.
17 Esdaile, *Peninsular War*, pp. 353–4.
18 Muir, *Tactics*, p. 196.
19 Muir, *Tactics*, p. 218.
20 Muir, *Tactics*, p. 183.
21 Muir, *Tactics*, p. 190.
22 Longford, *Wellington*, p. 319.
23 Muir, *Britain*, pp. 181–6.
24 Esdaile, *Peninsular War*, pp. 369–70.
25 Esdaile, *Peninsular War*, p. 376.
26 Gunther E. Rothenberg, *The Art of Warfare in the Age of Napoleon*, Stroud: Spellmount, 2007, pp. 236–7.
27 Longford, *Wellington*, p. 329.
28 Longford, *Wellington*, p. 335.
29 Esdaile, *Peninsular War*, p. 386.
30 Esdaile, *Peninsular War*, pp. 386–7.
31 Longford, *Wellington*, pp. 394–5.
32 See Cookson, *Armed Nation*, for a thorough discussion of these issues.

33 John E. Cookson, 'Regimental Worlds: interpreting the experience of British soldiers during the Napoleonic Wars', in Forrest, Hagemann and Rendall, *Soldiers, Citizens and Civilians*, pp. 23–42.

34 Collins, *War*, p. 407.

35 See Joanna Bourke, *An Intimate History of Killing: face-to-face killing in twentieth century warfare*, London: Granta, 1999, for a sensitive discussion of such issues in a supposedly even more 'civilised' age.

36 Longford, *Wellington*, p. 337.

37 Longford, *Wellington*, p. 338.

38 Collins, *War*, pp. 241–2.

39 Adkins, *War*, pp. 327–32.

40 This campaign is fictionalised in Patrick O'Brian, *The Mauritius Command* (1977), but the history is equally extraordinary: see Stephen Taylor, *Storm and Conquest: the battle for the Indian Ocean, 1808–10*, London: Faber, 2007.

41 Adkins, *War*, p. 365.

42 Fregosi, *Dreams*, pp. 386–7.

43 James Davey, 'Supplied by the enemy: the Royal Navy and the British consular service in the Baltic, 1808–12', *Historical Research*, 85 (2012) pp. 265–83.

45 Robert Reid, *Land of Lost Content: the Luddite revolt, 1812*, London: Heinemann, 1986, pp. 49–50.

12 The Uncertain Tide of Victory

1   The only full-length biography remains Denis Gray, *Spencer Perceval: the evangelical prime minister 1762–1812*, Manchester: Manchester University Press, 1963.

2   Iain McCalman, *Radical Underground: prophets, revolutionaries and pornographers in London, 1795–1840*, Cambridge: Cambridge University Press, 1988, pp. 41–2.

3   McCalman, *Radical Underground*, pp. 36–8.

4   McCalman, *Radical Underground*, pp. 39–41.

5   McCalman, *Radical Underground*, p. 42.

6   Hone, *Cause of Truth*, pp. 180–1, 187–8.

7   Hone, *Cause of Truth*, p. 188.

8   Hone, *Cause of Truth*, pp. 192–3.

9   Spence, *Romantic Radicalism*, pp. 163–7. See also Philip Harling, 'The Law of Libel and the Limits of Repression, 1790–1832', *Historical Journal*, 44 (2001), pp. 107–34.

10 Arthur N. Gilbert, 'Sexual Deviance and Disaster during the Napoleonic Wars', *Albion*, 9 (1977), pp. 98–113, esp. pp. 103, 106–8; citation p. 112. For a contrasting study of the intermittent prosecution of 'sodomy' in the regions, see H.G. Cocks, 'Safeguarding Civility: sodomy, class and moral reform in early nineteenth-century England', *Past and Present*, 190 (2006), pp. 121–46.

11 Navickas, *Loyalism*, pp. 241–3; Thompson, *Making*, p. 620.

12 Thompson, *Making*, p. 614.

13 Thompson, *Making*, pp. 577–8.

14 Thompson, *Making*, pp. 579–82.

15 Thompson, *Making*, p. 590.

16 Thompson, *Making*, p. 605.

17 Thompson, *Making*, pp. 606–8.

18 Brian Bailey, *The Luddite Rebellion*, Stroud: Sutton, 1998; pp. 34–8.

19 Bailey, *Luddite Rebellion*, pp. 41–2.

20 Reid, *Land of Lost Content*, p. 60.

21 Bailey, *Luddite Rebellion*, p. 44.

22 Thompson, *Making*, p. 609.

23 Reid, *Land of Lost Content*, pp. 5–9.

24 Katrina Navickas, 'The search for "General Ludd": the mythology of Luddism', *Social History*, 30 (2005), pp. 281–95.

25 Thompson, *Making*, pp. 609–10.

26 Bailey, *Luddite Rebellion*, pp. 45–7.

27 Reid, *Land of Lost Content*, pp. 122–5.

28 Thompson, *Making*, p. 612.

29 Reid, *Land of Lost Content*, pp. 150–2.

30 Bailey, *Luddite Rebellion*, pp. 74, 80–1.

31 Reid, *Land of Lost Content*, p. 157; Bailey, *Luddite Rebellion*, pp. 69–70.

32 Thompson, *Making*, p. 623.

33 Kathleen S. Goddard, 'A Case of Injustice? the trial of John Bellingham', *American Journal of Legal History*, 46 (2004), pp. 1–25.

34 Muir, *Britain*, pp. 194–7; Esdaile, *Peninsular War*, pp. 388–9.

35 Longford, *Wellington*, p. 348.

36 Longford, *Wellington*, p. 352.

37 Esdaile, *Peninsular War*, pp. 394–5.

38 Longford, *Wellington*, p. 352.

39 Muir, *Britain*, p. 204.

40 Longford, *Wellington*, pp. 355–6.

41 Longford, *Wellington*, p. 357.

13 Madrid to Moscow

1 Esdaile, *Napoleon's Wars*, p. 472. For a history in stunning, appalling detail of this tragic campaign, see Adam Zamoyski, *1812: Napoleon's fatal march on Moscow*, London: HarperCollins, 2004.

2 Schroeder, *Transformation*, pp. 424–5.

3 For an intriguing, if speculative, discussion of Napoleon's real motives for this move, see Harold T. Parker, 'Why Did Napoleon Invade Russia? a study in motivation and the interrelations of personality and social structure', *Journal of Military History*, 54 (1990), pp. 131–46.

4 Esdaile, *Napoleon's Wars*, p. 453.

5 Frederick C. Schneid, 'Kings, Clients and Satellites in the Napoleonic Imperium', *Journal of Strategic Studies*, 31 (2008), pp. 571–604.

6 Esdaile, *Napoleon's Wars*, p. 452.

7 Alan Forrest, 'Napoleon as Monarch: a political evolution', in Forrest and Wilson (eds), *Bee and the Eagle*, pp. 112–30 at pp. 124–5.

8 Schroeder, *Transformation*, p. 428.

9 Esdaile, *Napoleon's Wars*, pp. 454–5.

10 Esdaile, *Napoleon's Wars*, p. 442.

11 Esdaile, *Napoleon's Wars*, p. 442.

12 Esdaile, *Napoleon's Wars*, p. 443.

13 For a survey of recent views on the nature of Napoleonic imperialism, see Steven Englund, 'Monstre Sacré: the question of cultural imperialism and the Napoleonic Empire', *Historical Journal*, 51 (2008), pp. 215–50.

14 Edward James Kolla, 'Not So Criminal: new understandings of Napoléon's foreign policy in the East', *French Historical Studies*, 30 (2007), pp. 175–201.

15 Esdaile, *Napoleon's Wars*, pp. 444–7. See also Philip Dwyer, 'Napoleon and the Universal Monarchy', *History*, 95 (2010), pp. 293–307.

16 Zamoyski, *1812*, pp. 96–7.

17 Zamoyski, *1812*, pp. 101–2, 135–8.

18 Zamoyski, *1812*, pp. 142–3.

19 Esdaile, *Napoleon's Wars*, pp. 464–5.

20 Esdaile, *Napoleon's Wars*, p. 469.

21 Zamoyski, *1812*, pp. 216ff.

22 Esdaile, *Napoleon's Wars*, pp. 476–8.

23 Zamoyski, *1812*, pp. 353–6.

24 Zamoyski, *1812*, pp. 388ff., which gives more detail on this process than many readers will comfortably bear.

25 Zamoyski, *1812*, pp. 478–9.

26 Muir, *Britain*, pp. 216–17.

27 Naomi C. Miller, 'Major John Cartwright and the Founding of the Hampden Club', *Historical Journal*, 17 (1974), pp. 615–19.

28 Naomi C. Miller, 'John Cartwright and Radical Parliamentary Reform, 1808–1819', *English Historical Review*, 83 (1968), pp. 705–28, at p. 717.

29 Miller, 'Major John Cartwright', p. 619.

30 Muir, *Britain*, p. 233. For the longer-term relationship of American trade with European wars, see Donald R. Adams, Jr., 'American Neutrality and Prosperity, 1793–1808: a reconsideration', *Journal of Economic History*, 40 (1980), pp. 713–37.

31 Adkins, *War*, pp. 373–4.

32 J.C.A. Stagg, 'James Madison and the Coercion of Great Britain: Canada, the West Indies, and the War of 1812', *William and Mary Quarterly*, Third Series, 38 (1981), pp. 3–34.

33 Muir, *Britain*, pp. 235–6.

34 Lawrence S. Kaplan, 'France and the War of 1812', *Journal of American History*, 57 (1970), pp. 36–47.

35 Adkins, *War*, p. 377.

36 Adkins, *War*, pp. 379–84.

37 Collins, *War*, pp. 322–3, 325.

38 Peter J. Kastor, 'Toward "the Maritime War Only": the question of naval mobilization, 1811–1812', *Journal of Military History*, 61 (1997), pp. 455–80.

39 G.E. Watson, 'The United States and the Peninsular War, 1808–1812', *Historical Journal*, 19 (1976), pp. 859–76.

40 Gavin Daly, 'Napoleon and the "City of Smugglers", 1810–1814', *Historical Journal*, 50 (2007), pp. 333–52. For a longer-term view of the illicit economy, and politics, of the English Channel, see Renaud Morieux, 'Diplomacy from Below and

Belonging: fishermen and cross-Channel relations in the eighteenth century', *Past and Present*, 202 (2009), pp. 83–125.

41 Muir, *Britain*, pp. 235, 237.
42 Collins, *War*, pp. 326–7.
43 Longford, *Wellington*, p. 361.
44 Esdaile, *Peninsular War*, pp. 411–13.
45 Longford, *Wellington*, p. 366.
46 Esdaile, *Peninsular War*, pp. 416–17.
47 Longford, *Wellington*, p. 368.
48 Esdaile, *Peninsular War*, p. 418.
49 Longford, *Wellington*, pp. 369–70.

14 In the Balance

1 Reid, *Land of Lost Content*, p. 179.
2 See Bailey, *Luddite*, ch. 5 generally, and esp. pp. 74–5.
3 Bailey, *Luddite*, p. 73.
4 Bailey, *Luddite*, p. 97.
5 Bailey, *Luddite*, pp. 95–7, 99–101, citation p. 99; Reid, *Land of Lost Content*, pp. 240–7.
6 Reid, *Land of Lost Content*, pp. 267–8.
7 Bailey, *Luddite*, p. 103.
8 Bailey, *Luddite*, p. 106.
9 Bailey, *Luddite*, p. 105.
10 Adam Zamoyski, *The Rites of Peace: the fall of Napoleon and the Congress of Vienna*, London: HarperCollins, 2007, pp. 1–4.
11 For a detailed account, see Guido Artom, *Napoleon is Dead in Russia*, London: Allen & Unwin, 1970.
12 Esdaile, *Napoleon's Wars*, p. 491.
13 Frederick C. Schneid, 'The Dynamics of Defeat: French army leadership, December 1812–March 1813', *Journal of Military History*, 63 (1999), pp. 7–28.
14 Esdaile, *Napoleon's Wars*, p. 488.
15 Isser Woloch, 'Napoleonic Conscription: state power and civil society', *Past & Present*, 111 (1986), pp. 101–29.
16 Esdaile, *Napoleon's Wars*, pp. 492–3.
17 Muir, *Britain*, pp. 212–13, 218–19.
18 Muir, *Britain*, pp. 222–4.
19 Muir, *Britain*, pp. 226–7.
20 Esdaile, *Napoleon's Wars*, p. 496.
21 Esdaile, *Napoleon's Wars*, p. 496.
22 Muir, *Britain*, pp. 247–8.
23 John Rydjord, 'British Mediation between Spain and Her Colonies: 1811–1813', *Hispanic American Historical Review*, 21 (1941), pp. 29–50. A recent survey of the vexed issue of South America in the Napoleonic context is Rafe Blaufarb, 'The Western Question: the geopolitics of Latin American independence', *American Historical Review*, 112 (2007), pp. 742–63.
24 Esdaile, *Peninsular War*, pp. 431–9.

25 Collins, *War*, p. 281.
26 Esdaile, *Peninsular War*, pp. 429, 440.
27 Longford, *Wellington*, pp. 373–4; Esdaile, *Peninsular War*, p. 441.
28 Longford, *Wellington*, p. 377.
29 Crouzet, 'Wars, Blockade, and Economic Change', p. 574.
30 Collins, *War*, p. 269.
31 Muir, *Britain*, p. 275.
32 Esdaile, *Peninsular War*, pp. 429–30.
33 Broers, 'Concept of "Total War"', p. 262; see <http://www.populstat.info/Europe/portugac.htm> for population statistics.
34 Gavin Daly, 'A Dirty, Indolent, Priest-Ridden City: British soldiers in Lisbon during the Peninsular War, 1808–1813', *History* (2009), pp. 461–82.
35 Collins, *War*, p. 270.
36 Huw Davies, 'Wellington's Use of Deception Tactics in the Peninsular War', *Journal of Strategic Studies*, 29 (2006), pp. 723–50, esp. pp. 743–9.
37 Urban, *The Man Who*, pp. 104–10, 136–41.
38 Collins, *War*, pp. 294–5.
39 Longford, *Wellington*, p. 378; Esdaile, *Peninsular War*, pp. 443–4.
40 Collins, *War*, pp. 292–3.
41 Esdaile, *Peninsular War*, p. 447.
42 Muir, *Tactics*, p. 82.
43 Esdaile, *Peninsular War*, pp. 450–1; Longford, *Wellington*, pp. 386–8.
44 Muir, *Tactics*, pp. 250–1.
45 Esdaile, *Peninsular War*, p. 456.
46 Esdaile, *Peninsular War*, pp. 462–3.
47 Esdaile, *Peninsular War*, p. 468.
48 Esdaile, *Peninsular War*, pp. 469–70; Longford, *Wellington*, pp. 405–7.

15 Endgames

1 Schroeder, *Transformation*, pp. 456–7.
2 Muir, *Britain*, pp. 255–6.
3 Esdaile, *Napoleon's Wars*, p. 503.
4 Schroeder, *Transformation*, p. 460.
5 See Schroeder, *Transformation*, pp. 460–6, for a discussion of this complex set of perceptions and counter-perceptions.
6 Woloch, 'Napoleonic Conscription', p. 101.
7 Esdaile, *Napoleon's Wars*, p. 506.
8 Muir, *Britain*, pp. 253–4.
9 H.V. Bowen, *War and British Society 1688–1815*, Cambridge: Cambridge University Press, 1998, pp. 64ff.
10 Bowen, *War and British Society*, p. 73.
11 Muir, *Britain*, pp. 260–1.
12 Michael V. Leggiere, 'From Berlin to Leipzig: Napoleon's gamble in north Germany, 1813', *Journal of Military History*, 67 (2003), pp. 39–84.
13 Esdaile, *Napoleon's Wars*, pp. 512–13.
14 See Esdaile, *Napoleon's Wars*, pp. 513–16, Muir, *Britain*, pp. 288–90, for the Battle

of Leipzig in general.

15 Charles J. Esdaile, 'De-Constructing the French Wars: Napoleon as anti-strategist', *Journal of Strategic Studies*, 31 (2008), pp. 515–52.

16 Zamoyski, *Rites*, pp. 50–1, 60.

17 For a longer-term history of the eventual 'professionalisation' of British diplomacy through this period, see Jennifer Mori, *The Culture of Diplomacy: Britain in Europe, c. 1750–1830*, Manchester: Manchester University Press, 2011.

18 Zamoyski, *Rites*, pp. 48, 75, 93.

19 Zamoyski, *Rites*, pp. 98–101.

20 Muir, *Britain*, pp. 290–1 ; Zamoyski, *Rites*, p. 131.

21 Zamoyski, *Rites*, pp. 38, 64–6, 74, 120.

22 Schroeder, *Transformation*, pp. 489–90.

23 Schroeder, *Transformation*, p. 491; Muir, *Britain*, pp. 295–6.

24 Zamoyski, *Rites*, pp. 137–8, 141–2.

25 Esdaile, *Peninsular War*, pp. 475–82.

26 Collins, *War*, p. 303.

27 Longford, *Wellington*, pp. 412–13.

28 Collins, *War*, p. 302.

29 Longford, *Wellington*, pp. 417–19.

30 Esdaile, *Peninsular War*, pp. 483–4, and ch. 18 more generally.

31 Esdaile, *Napoleon's Wars*, p. 519.

32 Esdaile, *Napoleon's Wars*, pp. 520–1.

33 Collins, *War*, pp. 304–5.

34 Zamoyski, *Rites*, pp. 150–1.

35 Esdaile, *Napoleon's Wars*, pp. 522–3.

36 Muir, *Britain*, pp. 315–17.

37 Zamoyski, *Rites*, pp. 155–6.

38 Zamoyski, *Rites*, pp. 157–60.

39 Full text available at <http://en.wikisource.org/wiki/Treaty_of_Chaumont>. See Zamoyski, *Rites*, pp. 167–8; Schroeder, *Transformation*, pp. 501–2. For a brisk summary of the transformation in coalition warfare that this event marked, see Philip G. Dwyer, 'Self-Interest versus the Common Cause: Austria, Prussia and Russia against Napoleon', *Journal of Strategic Studies*, 31 (2008), pp. 605–32.

40 Longford, *Wellington*, pp. 420–1.

41 Schroeder, *Transformation*, pp. 507–8.

42 Zamoyski, *Rites*, p. 191.

43 Zamoyski, *Rites*, p. 194.

16 Reckoning and Return

1 Zamoyski, *Rites*, pp. 211–14; Muir, *Britain*, p. 330.

2 Zamoyski, *Rites*, p. 203.

3 Adkins, *War*, p. 388.

4 Adkins, *War*, p. 389.

5 Adkins, *War*, p. 390.

6 <http://www.london-gazette.co.uk/issues/16750/pages/1329>, *London Gazette* of 6–10 July 1813.

7 Adkins, *War*, p. 391.
8 Collins, *War*, pp. 334–9.
9 Muir, *Britain*, pp. 332–4.
10 Philip Mansel, *Paris Between Empires, 1814–1852: monarchy and revolution*, London: Phoenix Press, 2001, pp. 55–8.
11 Muir, *Britain*, pp. 331–2.
12 Mansel, *Paris*, pp. 59–60. See Longford, *Wellington*, pp. 423–8, 449–64, for detailed discussion of his lifestyle as ambassador.
13 Mansel, *Paris*, pp. 61–2, 67.
14 Muir, *Britain*, pp. 343–4. Longford, *Wellington*, p. 476 reports 'Ogre' for 'Monster' and 'Buzzard' for 'Brigand'; the lines no doubt existed in different versions.
15 Zamoyski, *Rites*, pp. 455–7; Mansel, *Paris*, pp. 68–75.
16 Collins, *War*, p. 349.
17 Longford, *Wellington*, pp. 475–6.
18 Zamoyski, *Rites*, p. 461.
19 Zamoyski, *Rites*, pp. 470–1.
20 Longford, *Wellington*, p. 490.
21 Longford, *Wellington*, pp. 482–3.
22 Collins, *War*, p. 350.
23 For the Waterloo campaign, the account in Longford is excellent, complemented by the classic Christopher Hibbert, *Waterloo: Napoleon's last campaign*, London, New English Library, 1967, and the recent Alessandro Barbero, *The Battle: a new history of the Battle of Waterloo*, London: Atlantic Books, 2006.
24 Muir, *Britain*, p. 347.
25 See Catriona Kennedy, 'From the Ballroom to the Battlefield: British women and Waterloo', in Forrest et al. (eds), *Soldiers, Citizens and Civilians*, pp. 137–56.
26 Longford, *Wellington*, p. 513.
27 For an example of the level of detail to which disputes can descend, see John Hussey, 'Towards a Better Chronology for the Waterloo Campaign', *War in History*, 7 (2000), pp. 463–80, which hinges on what various vague measures of time in an assortment of primary sources can or cannot tell us about who knew what when about enemy movements.
28 Longford, *Wellington*, p. 574.
29 Longford, *Wellington*, p. 577.

Epilogue

1 Fregosi, *Dreams*, p. 463.
2 Longford, *Wellington*, pp. 577–8, 582.
3 Longford, *Wellington*, p. 584.
4 The epithet is Châteaubriand's: see <http://www.lrb.co.uk/v28/n22/david-a-bell/one-does-it-like-this>.
5 Collins, *War*, pp. 354–5.
6 Muir, *Britain*, p. 366.
7 David Cordingly, *Billy Ruffian: the Bellerophon and the downfall of Napoleon*, London: Bloomsbury, 2003.
8 Muir, *Britain*, pp. 367–8.

9   Semmell, *Napoleon and the British*, pp. 170–4.

10   Zamoyski, *Rites*, p. 490.

11   Longford, *Wellington*, p. 589. This is the source of the common misquotation, 'A damn close-run thing'.

12   Zamoyski, *Rites*, p. 487.

13   Zamoyski, *Rites*, pp. 192, 345.

14   Wilson, *Decency*, p. 290.

15   A detailed account can be found in the two-volume biography by Christopher Hibbert, *George IV: Prince of Wales* and *George IV: Regent and King*, London: Prentice Hall, 1972, 1973, recently reissued as *George IV: The rebel who would be King*, London: Palgrave, 2007.

16   Robert Poole, 'The March to Peterloo: Politics and festivity in late Georgian England', *Past & Present*, 192 (2006), pp. 109–53.

17   McCalman, *Radical*, pp. 128–52.

18   Jonathan Fulcher, 'The Loyalist Response to the Queen Caroline Agitations', *Journal of British Studies*, 34 (1995), pp. 481–502.

19   Collins, *War*, p. 426.

20   Collins, *War*, pp. 475–6.

21   N. Gash, 'After Waterloo: British society and the legacy of the Napoleonic Wars', *Transactions of the Royal Historical Society*, 5th series, 28 (1977), pp. 145–57, at pp. 149–50.

22   C.A. Bayly, *Imperial Meridian: the British Empire and the world, 1780–1830*, London: Longman, 1989, p. 100.

23   D. George Boyce, 'From Assaye to the Assaye: reflections on British government, force, and moral authority in India', *Journal of Military History*, 63 (1999), pp. 643–68.

24   Collins, *War*, p. 372.

25   Collins, *War*, p. 371.

26   See Lauren Benton, 'Abolition and Imperial Law, 1790–1820', *Journal of Imperial and Commonwealth History*, 39 (2011), pp. 355–74, for a discussion of the authoritarian imposition of order on recalcitrant planter colonies through the policing of slave trade abolition.

27   On this see Bayly, *Imperial Meridian*, esp. chs 4 and 5.

28   Bayly, *Imperial Meridian*, p. 112.

29   Bayly, *Imperial Meridian*, pp. 115, 200–1.

30   See Andress, *1789*, pp. 137–40 for the shortcomings of the attempted 'permanent settlement' of taxation and land titles in British Bengal in the 1790s.

31   Bayly, *Imperial Meridian*, pp. 196ff.

32   See Peter J. Jupp, 'The Landed Elite and Political Authority in Britain, ca. 1760–1850', *Journal of British Studies*, 29 (1990), pp. 53–79. On the gradual shift away from the state's focus on funding war, see Philip Harling and Peter Mandler, 'From "Fiscal-Military" State to Laissez-Faire State, 1760–1850', *Journal of British Studies*, 32 (1993), pp. 44–70.

33   See the extended biographical review by Ferdinand Mount: <http://www.lrb.co.uk/v33/n17/ferdinand-mount/too-obviously-cleverer>, accessed 2 September 2011.

34   Collins, *War*, p. 397.

35 Collins, *War*, p. 399.

36 Collins, *War*, p. 431.

37 B.H. Liddell Hart, (ed), *The Letters of Private Wheeler*, Boston: Houghton Mifflin, 1952, pp. v–vi.

38 Edward Costello, *Adventures of a Soldier*, London: Henry Colburn, 1841, pp. 309–19.

39 This is not to say that all returning veterans posed a social problem: see J.E. Cookson, 'Early Nineteenth-Century Scottish Military Pensioners as Homecoming Soldiers', *Historical Journal*, 52 (2009), pp. 319–341, for counter-examples.

40 Cited in Humphrey Jennings, *Pandaemonium: the coming of the machine as seen by contemporary observers*, London: André Deutsch, 1985, p.136.

41 Jennings, *Pandaemonium*, p. 141.

42 'Steam Arm' (The Madden Ballad Collection, microfilm vol. 18, no. 413). I am grateful to my colleague Karl Bell for this item.

INDEX

226–7; campaign of 1810, 228–33, 234–6, 238–9; campaign of 1811, 239–41, 242–7, 248–9; campaign of 1812, 249–53, 264, 276, 277–81, 291–2, 298–300, 307; campaign of 1813, 311–13, 314–19, 320–1, 327; capture of Salamanca (October 1809), 226–7; Convention of Cintra (30 August 1808), 191, 196, 201, 212, 213–14, 225; French atrocities during, 233, 236, 240; French loss of numerical superiority (1811-13), 311; improved British supply/provisions, 312, 315–16; Lines of Torres Vedras, 234–6; logistics of Spain, 228–9; military tactical innovations and, 220–2; Sir John Moore and, 191–3, 213, 214, 215; Napoleon's demands for troops elsewhere and, 248–9, 276; Napoleon's invasion of Russia (1812) and, 286; retreat to Corunna, 192–3, 218; Royal Navy and, 315; sieges of Badajoz and (1811, 1812), 242, 244, 246–7, 250–2, 253, 264; size of British forces, 229, 247; Spanish guerrillas and partisans, 314, 315; Wellington's strategy (1809-10), 227, 229, 230, 232–3, 234–6; Whig suspicions over, 236–7

'Pentrich Rising' (1817), 376

Perceval, Spencer, 202, 208, 214, 225, 238, 257–8, 259; assassination of (11 May 1812), 274–5, 293; suppression of radical groups by, 261–2, 263; 'The Book' and, 259, 261

'Peterloo Massacre' (16 August 1819), 377, 383

Pfuhl, Ernst von, 284

Phaeton, HMS, 254–5

Philippon, Armand, 250

Picton, General, 231, 312, 317, 320, 359–60, 365

Pitt, William: Addington government and, 94–5, 99, 108, 109; army landings in Germany (October 1805), 124, 127, 212; campaign of national defence, 106–8; George Canning and, 95, 132–3, 202; concept of public service and, 57; death of (January 1806), 128, 130, 133, 205; death of Nelson and, 125; diplomacy for grand coalition (1804-5), 111, 112, 127, 325; diplomacy in 1797-8 period, 46, 47, 48, 52; dominance of politics, 129, 134; duel with Tierney, 150, 202; Charles James Fox and, 41, 43, 129, 130, 136, 139; George III's favouring of, 17, 24, 41; ill health, 78, 95, 103, 107, 110, 125–6, 127, 128;

invasion of Holland (1799) and, 62; Ireland and, 19, 51, 75, 77, 78–9, 131; last months of, 125–6, 127–8, 130, 155, 161, 205; parallel administration (1801), 79–80, 84; as patron of Addington, 79, 80, 94; Perceval and, 258; political career (to 1793), 17, 18, 19, 24, 94, 139; resignation of (5 February 1801), 75, 79, 94, 133; return as Prime Minister (18 May 1804), 109–10, 152, 258; riots and demonstrations against, 30–1, 40, 209; seeks peace (1796-7), 32, 39; speech to Parliament (23 May 1803), 103; speech to Parliament (November 1797), 15–16, 43; suppression of radical groups, 26; taxation and borrowing, 17, 32, 43, 109; war aims of (February 1800), 69

Place, Francis, 180–2, 183, 184, 260

Pläswitz, armistice of (June 1813), 324–5

Plymouth, 35, 38, 101, 371, 384

Poland, 164, 248, 282, 285, 287, 333, 343, 349, 353–4

political culture, British: aristocracy as political class, 24, 57, 72, 133–5; Mary Anne Clarke scandal (1809), 196–8, 201, 260; endemic corruption of, 151, 152–3, 172, 196–9, 201, 260, 383; Foxite 'secession' from Parliament, 41–3, 129; franchise reform attempts, 19, 40, 292, 378; 'Glorious Revolution' (1688) and, 19–20, 27; 'Grenville–Fox axis', 108, 109, 129, 130; pamphlet wars, 25; patronage and, 24, 57, 150, 161, 210; Pitt's dominance, 129; unity of ruling elite, xi, 15–16, 40, 42; wartime coalition (from 1794), 41

Political Register, 152

Pomerania, 162, 309

Pompée, HMS, 36

Poniatowski, Marshal, 332

Poor Rate relief system, 71, 182

Popham, Sir Home, 155, 157–8

population growth, 21–2, 24

Portland, Duke of, 41, 43–4, 161, 164, 167, 212, 252, 270; fall of government of (1809), 201–3, 225

Portsmouth, 34, 35, 101, 384

Portugal: army of, 215–16, 229, 230–3, 244, 276, 277, 279, 312, 314, 318, 340; blockade of Almeida (1811), 242, 243–4; British army in 1809 period, 214–17; British subsidies to, 240, 313, 328; British trade with, 72, 81; British troops' arrival in (July 1808), 190–1, 212, 213; British withdrawal into (summer 1809), 224, 226; Bussaco (27 September 1810),